Soviet Dissident Literature
a critical guide

A
Reference
Publication
in
Literature

Soviet Dissident Literature

a critical guide

JOSEPHINE WOLL
in collaboration with
Vladimir G. Treml

G.K.HALL&CO.

70 LINCOLN STREET, BOSTON, MASS.

Copyright © 1983 by Josephine Woll.

Library of Congress Cataloging in Publication Data

Woll, Josephine.
  Soviet dissident literature, a critical guide.

  Rev. ed. of: Soviet unofficial literature—samizdat.
1978.
  Includes index.
  1.   Russian literature—20th century—Bibliography
2.   Russian literature—Foreign countries—Bibliography.
3.   Underground literature—Soviet Union—Bibliography.
4.   United States—Imprints.   5.   Europe—Imprints.
6.   Civil rights—Soviet Union—Bibliography.   I.   Treml,
Vladimir G.   II.   Title.
Z2511.U5W64   1983   016.8917   83-56
[PG3026.U5]
ISBN 0-8161-8626-X

This publication is printed on permanent/durable acid-free paper
MANUFACTURED IN THE UNITED STATES OF AMERICA

Contents

The Author

Josephine Woll received her Ph.D. in Russian language and literature from the University of North Carolina at Chapel Hill, writing her dissertation on Pushkin's "little tragedies." After teaching at Duke University she moved to Washington, D.C., where she has been teaching at Howard University since 1977, at first language and literature courses, and now literature and film.

While maintaining an interest in Pushkin, and publishing some reviews and articles on Pushkin's work, her interest in contemporary Russian literature has grown to include both officially published works and unofficial "samizdat." She has written on such dissident writers as Andrei Siniavski and Vladimir Voinivich, and on such official prosaists as Iuri Trifonov. Her articles and reviews have appeared in scholarly journals such as "Slavic Review" and "Russian Language Journal" and in such general periodicals as the New Republic, Dissent, and the New Leader.

Preface

Before the advent of samizdat, the Soviet Union was largely a closed society, both to foreigners and in a very real sense to its own citizens. Then, about twenty years ago, the phenomenon of samizdat began, at first as a sporadic, barely noticeable trickle of words, but within a few years growing to a phenomenon of flood proportions. Within the Soviet Union it has been a channel for otherwise inaccessible information, and for important belletristic writing, for the expression of alternative political and social theories, for protests and petitions, for intellectual arguments and philosophical debates. Its most important function has always been, and continues to be, that of serving its primary audience—Soviet citizens who want to write and read what is not permissible within the official boundaries that govern the written word in the USSR. Samizdat has exposed hundreds of thousands of Russians to their own literature; it has enabled Soviet writers to by-pass the hurdles of official censorship (though not, to be sure, with impunity, and often at considerable risk indeed) in order to say what they want to say, and be heard.

In the West samizdat has played a rather different role. As dissent has itself become a respectable discipline, so has its literary vehicle, samizdat, which has been accorded the legitimacy of a Library of Congress catalogue number and a definition in Webster's Third New International Dictionary. Samizdat has provided us in the West with invaluable material on various aspects of Soviet life which are unexplored in the range of officially sanctioned writing, as well as information on dissent and the dissidents. Political scientists find in samizdat data on the nature and extent of political protest, and by extension on the nature and range of official oppression. Historians find new facts and differing perspectives on issues long-suppressed or distorted in Soviet scholarship. Students of the Kremlin find in samizdat clues to the shifting winds of official Soviet attitudes toward an array of subjects ranging from psychiatry to national minorities, from trade unions to emigration, from World War II to de-Stalinization. And lovers of Russian literature have, through the medium of samizdat, discovered a great deal of exciting, innovative and moving fiction, poetry and drama, some excavated from Russia's Stalinist past, some brand-new.

The word "samizdat," combining two Russian words "sam" (self) and "izdatelstvo" (publishing house), literally means "self-publishing," and in some cases the word signifies the process quite precisely: an author starts the chain of samizdat circulation himself, "publishing" handwritten, typewritten or mimeographed copies of his work. In other instances the circulation of work originates elsewhere: a reader, a researcher, the recipient of a letter perhaps, copies and passes on a manuscript without the author's knowledge or consent. In the latter process the usual authorial control over the editorial process, approval of the final text and authorization for publication are, of course, absent. And in either case, since samizdat is copied and recopied by readers, inadvertent changes and deletions, as well as occasional purposeful editing, are unavoidable. Soviet authors whose samizdat manuscripts reach the West have sometimes managed to establish channels of communication with their Western publishers (more and more often in the case of better-known writers), and have therefore some control over the final version—although even then they rarely, if ever, have opportunities to check galleys or page proofs. But frequently the copy which finally finds its way to a Western publisher was not seen by its author, and occasionally—though rarely—the author flatly denied his authorship. Thus users of this bibliography should remember that the standard concepts, definitions and responsibilities of authorship are not always applicable to samizdat works published in the West.

As samizdat networks expanded over the years, and as more of it became available to Western readers, certain scholarly needs arose. This bibliography is intended to meet one of those needs, that of access. Until now there has been no easy way to ascertain precisely what samizdat has appeared in Western publications, and where and when it appeared. A few bibliographies of the works of individual authors (such as Solzhenitsyn) exist, but the majority of poems, stories, articles and books have never been catalogued in a single source, and Western readers have been forced to scout around, unsystematically and with not a little difficulty, to find what they want. This bibliography should to some extent redress that gap.

For a number of reasons an initial decision was made to compile a selective, not comprehensive, bibliography, primary among them that Radio Liberty, in Munich, catalogues almost every piece of samizdat which reaches the West, printing some of the texts themselves and an index to the texts for reference purposes. Its "Samizdat Archive" is the obvious and essential source for certain specific types of investigations, and is indispensable as well for anyone working intensively within the Sovietological field. There seemed no point in duplicating the job Radio Liberty does so well.

Moreover, a larger audience exists to whom this selective bibliography is addressed. That audience consists of scholars and students who may or may not read Russian, of researchers in a wide range of disciplines, of readers curious about the "alternative" literature of Russia, of individuals who pose the question, "What works of value has samizdat produced, and where are they?" It is for these readers, as much as for specialists in Soviet studies, that the bibliography should prove most useful. It contains the following categories of work: all belletristic samizdat that could be found in Western periodicals or books (poems, songs, stories, novels, novellas, dramas); all nonfiction books; articles and essays, as well as substantial pieces of documentation, which seem to the editor to contribute information, views, insights or analyses of some significance. It also includes many book-length collections of articles or documents which did not circulate as such within the samizdat network, but are compilations of samizdat material edited by Western scholars or Russian émigrés; they are included because they provide easy access to items which might otherwise have to be tracked down individually, a laborious and unnecessary process. All works included were, to the best of my knowledge and with the qualified exception of the Western collections, written in the Soviet Union, though many of the authors subsequently emigrated, often bringing with them texts which circulated both before and after their departures. Also included are works published officially but in censored form whose uncensored texts circulated in samizdat, and works which were eventually published officially but first circulated "underground," such as some of Akhmatova's poetry.

The original version of this bibliography was completed in 1978 in fulfillment of a contract with the Office of External Research, U.S. Department of State. In it annotation was restricted to the genre and broad subject category of each item. Upon deciding to update and expand the book, I felt its utility could be substantially increased by amplifying the annotations. Thus with the exceptions of poetry and short fiction, every item is accompanied by a content-annotation describing or summarizing the work. In the introductory essay I have attempted to offer an overview of the history and achievements of samizdat literature. Readers unfamiliar with the names of individual samizdat authors will find a subject-index at the end, enabling them to locate nonfiction works pertaining to a wide range of topics, and extensive cross-referencing should provide additional information and increased ease of access.

One caveat: since this bibliography is selective rather than comprehensive, and as such excludes the enormous mass of petitions and appeals which circulated in samizdat over the years, it does not provide a realistic representation of the proportion of samizdat material devoted to various subjects. Thus many more petitions circulated on the repression of Baptists and Lithuanian Catholics than on, for instance, Solzhenitsyn's expulsion from the USSR, but that fact is not reflected either in the index nor in the entries proper. Conversely, there are relatively few samizdat texts on economics and trade unionism, but those texts are substantive or important enough to warrant inclusion in the book and to justify a category in the index.

All works included appeared in the West before roughly January 1982. They are entered alphabetically by author, or by title when anonymous, and under each author alphabetically by title. When a work first appeared serially or was excerpted in a periodical, and later appeared in book form, the book-length volume is given first (in Russian, English, French and German when translations are available), followed by periodic publication in chronological order. Only after each entry is complete—that is, when all its available forms of publication have been given—is the entry annotated, and only one number is assigned to any given work, no matter in what varying forms and under what varying titles it appeared. Thus entry #240, for example, is Lydia Chukovskaia's statement after she was expelled from the Union of Soviet Writers. It was printed, in toto or in part, by three Russian-language periodicals, each time under a different title, and in English under yet another. All are one and the same essay, hence the single number and the single annotation.

The transliteration system used throughout the body of the bibliography is the simplified Library of Congress system; in the Preface and Introduction I have, for the sake of simplicity, omitted the symbols for hard and soft signs and anglicized some of the vowels. Since French and German transliterate Russian differently from English, and indeed since English uses more than one transliteration system, variant spellings of names are included where necessary to facilitate locating items in other catalogues and indices. Also included, in parentheses following the author's name, are pseudonyms when those pseudonymous authors could be properly identified. Abbreviation has been kept to a minimum, and is used only when the full title is clear (for instance, Novoe russkoe slovo is shortened to Nov. rus. slovo).

* * * * * * * * * *

As any bibliographer will agree, the pitfalls of such a project are myriad. Some, such as the publishing time-lag which ensures that the book will be out of date as soon as it appears, are entirely unavoidable. A selective bibliography, when the criterion for selection is essentially the editor's judgment of what is or is not significant, runs the additional risk of pleasing some readers and displeasing others. For the errors of fact and unintentional omissions I apologize in advance; for what will be perceived as errors of judgment I accept full responsibility. I only hope that despite such flaws, the bibliography will serve the purpose with which it was conceived: to provide, as reference source and research tool, accessibility to the extraordinary phenomenon that is samizdat literature.

I owe thanks to many, many people and institutions. First and foremost my collaborator, Dr. Vladimir Treml, whose imagination conceived and inspired this project, whose personal library served as its seedbed, whose knowledge, care and painstaking efforts contributed in a measure which cannot be overstated. Abraham Brumberg, who

A Critical Guide

in his former capacity of Projects Officer in the External Research
Division of the State Department, offered official encouragement and
funding, and who in his "unofficial" capacity as my husband has consistently supported me in this undertaking. The Research and Development Committee of the American Association for the Advancement of
Slavic Studies, for its generous help. Natalia Lusin, Regina Avra-
shova, Lydia Treml, and Jeffrey Jarosz for valuable assistance with
the research. Duke University, where the project began and with
whose aid its initial version was completed. The exceptionally cour-
teous staff at St. Antony's College and the Taylorean Institute at
Oxford, and the staffs of the Radio Free Europe/Radio Liberty libraries in both New York and Munich. A great many individuals took time
and effort to check the original version for errors, and I am particularly indebted to Edward Kline, Dmitry Pospielovsky, Martin Dewhirst
and Peter Dornan; their voluminous and profound knowledge of samizdat is responsible for much that is good about the bibliography. My
colleagues and friends at Howard University have provided practical
and moral support, as have my editors, Janice Meaghar and Meghan
Wander, and my typist, Inge Engel, has accomplished a back-breaking,
eye-straining job with immense skill and grace. To all of them my
sincere gratitude.

Josephine Woll

Introduction

"Yes, the hands itch for action and one cannot fail to act. But—'in the beginning was the Word.' The word, the idea, that is the first point which, in the logic of things, must precede others." So wrote Boris Shragin, under the pseydonym of Lev Ventsov, before he emigrated from the Soviet Union.[1] And insofar as dissent within the Soviet Union has existed as a significant trend—that is, for the past twenty years—its major medium of expression has been unofficial literature, samizdat.

Soviet samizdat consists of two kinds of writing: belles-lettres, which includes poetry and fiction, and the broad category of non-belletristic writing, which in the history of samizdat has included scholarly essays, journalism, sermons, memoirs, open letters, appeals and petitions. Shragin's notion of the word's precedence over the deed applies doubly to samizdat, because not only has any dissident activity (organizing religious seminars or literary discussion groups, applying for emigration, demonstrating against illegal acts, etc.) been preceded by and grounded in the literature of samizdat in its wider sense; additionally, the specifically belletristic literature of samizdat proved to be the midwife for the birth of all later samizdat, as well as of dissent generally. The 1958-59 controversy over the publication of Pasternak's Doctor Zhivago scattered the seeds of dissent; Aleksandr Esenin-Volpin's book of poetry and prose, A Leaf of Spring, nurtured them; the 1966 trial of Andrei Siniavski and Iuli Daniel, both writers of fiction, forced them into bloom. For twenty years this symbiotic process has been manifest: Siniavski and Daniel's fiction caused their arrest; their trial engendered Aleksandr Ginzburg's 1966 White Book; Ginzburg's own trial, in 1968, in conjunction with the International Year of Human Rights, engendered The Chronicle of Current Events; Aleksandr Solzhenitsyn's novels, Cancer Ward and First Circle, had extra-literary consequences including a flood of protests when he was expelled from the Writers Union; the circulation through samizdat of Leon Uris' Exodus spurred Jewish demands for emigration, and so on.

The chain reaction is endless, and characterizes not only the activities of participants in the world of samizdat, whose roles as reader, writer and "activist" constantly overlap, but also the relationship between the two kinds of writing, which often treat the same subjects. Stalinism is a major focus of samizdat, whether fiction or fact, poetry or polemic. The chain of Stalinist labor camps mapped by Solzhenitsyn as the Gulag Archipelago is documented as authentically in the samizdat stories of Varlam Shalamov as in the testimony gathered in Solzhenitsyn's several volumes. Spiritual yearnings felt by some part of Russia's population are articulated in poetry and songs as much as in the essays of Anatoli Levitin-Krasnov, the sermons of Father Dmitri Dudko or the compilation of photographs and texts on desecrated and defiled religious sanctuaries. In other words, the issues dealt with in samizdat, the subjects which preoccupy its authors and its readers, recur in every genre and in every form. The history of samizdat has been an intertwining of both types of literature, and the history of dissent has been, essentially, the history of samizdat, itself a form of dissent as well as dissent's mouthpiece and record.

Dissent and Samizdat

Samizdat did not arise in isolation, nor was its timing fortuitous. During the long years of Stalinism a phenomenon like samizdat could not exist, and for all practical purposes did not exist, if only for the most weighty of reasons, fear—in this case a fear endemic to Russian life for more than twenty years. As Lydia Chukovskaia—novelist, critic, editor and dissident—notes in the introduction to her The Deserted House:

> This story was written twenty-two years ago, in Leningrad in the winter of 1939-1940. . . . I had, of course, no hope at the time of seeing this story in print. I had little hope even that the school exercise book containing the clean copy of it would escape destruction and be preserved. To keep it in the drawer of my desk was dangerous, but to burn it was more than I could bring myself to do. I regarded it not so much as a story as a piece of evidence, which it would be dishonorable to destroy. . . .[2]

Why she "of course" had no hope of publishing her novella need not be elaborated—nor, for that matter, how lucky she was that the friends who kept her manuscript were honorable and themselves lucky people. Until Stalin's death the very idea of circulating literature, even among close friends, was virtually unthinkable. Indeed, as she notes further on, what marked the beginning of the end of fear was Khrushchev's speech at the 20th Party Congress in 1956, in which he denounced Stalin's "excesses" and crimes, and his later speech at the 22nd Congress, in which he encouraged further de-Stalinization.

In between those two speeches came the Pasternak affair, marking on the one hand a return to a species of Stalinism and on the other the genesis, however muted, of dissent. Iuri Maltsev, an émigré who

has written a history of samizdat, notes that Pasternak's Doctor
Zhivago was "more than a book. It was an historic event. After long
decades of silence, when Russian literature in effect ceased to exist
and was reduced to boring official illustrations of party resolutions,
suddenly a bold, strong voice of living Russia emerged."[3] The literary and moral significance of Zhivago reflected Pasternak's sweeping
vision of the causes, events and consequences of the 1917 revolutions,
a vision apolitical if not antipolitical and aghast to the core at
the travesties committed in the name of freedom and equality. The
extra-literary significance of Zhivago's publication abroad derived
from the official campaign of calumny and slander mounted against
Pasternak.[4] When, in 1959, Pasternak was forced to refuse the Nobel
prize, proffer a humiliating apology to Khrushchev and plead to be
allowed to remain in Russia, silence prevailed even among those hor-
rified by the regime's obscene vilifications.[5] Nevertheless, when
Pasternak died a year later, and despite the absence of any public
announcement about his funeral, several thousand people attended;
among his pallbearers were Andrei Siniavski and Iuli Daniel.[6]

Shouldering a coffin or mourning at funeral obsequies may seem
rather slight acts of dissent. But they were the beginning, however
fragile, of a far more profound phenomenon. And for a few years official policy seemed to promote a general liberalization, as exempli-
fied by Khrushchev's speech in 1961, the publication of Ilia Ehrenburg's memoirs, Evgeni Evtushenko's public reading of his poem de-
nouncing anti-Semitism, "Babi Iar," and its publication in the official "literary" newspaper, Literaturnaia gazeta. The time for samizdat was ripe, and its first fruits were underground journals full of
poetry and fiction.

The poets and prosaists of magazines like Sintaksis (Syntax) and
Feniks (Phoenix) were, in those early days, as interested in breaking
away from orthodox literary tradition and the stultifying doctrine of
socialist realism as they were in political heterodoxy. The range of
skill was wide. As critic Sidney Monas says:

> In all these journals the level of competence is 'amateur'—
> very uneven and, on the whole, rather low. . . . Some of
> the overtly political, discursive writing has bounce and
> feeling, but . . . it shows little mastery. . . . The abili-
> ty to see things freshly is not something that 'comes natural';
> it has to be learned. In an environment so thoroughly in-
> fested with Stalinist stereotypes, cliches and conventions,
> the learning does not come easily.[7]

Side by side with the amateurishness of some of the poetry, however,
was some highly sophisticated work—the controlled lyrics of Bella
Akhmadulina, for instance, and the allusive and dense imagery of
Joseph Brodski.

In any event, the interval of "liberalism," of a climate relatively favorable to greater honesty and freedom in official literature and of a semitolerance of unofficial writing, was all too brief.
By 1963, only two years after Khrushchev's de-Stalinization speech,
the walls were closing in again. Solzhenitsyn's novella of camp life,
One Day in the Life of Ivan Denisovich, was published in Novyi mir,
the foremost "liberal" literary journal, in 1962, but within months
it was attacked; so were such writers as Victor Nekrasov and Evgenii
Evtushenko. Khrushchev delivered a peroration in which he reaffirmed
the preeminence of socialist realism in literary matters, and partially rehabilitated Stalin; an array of conservative articles filled
the leading newspapers.[8] Thus the stage was set for two important
literary/political events: the trial of Joseph Brodski, in February
1964, and the trial of Siniavski and Daniel, in February 1966.

Brodski, charged with parasitism, was predictably enough found
guilty; he was sentenced to five years in an Arkhangel forced-labor
camp (though he served only two of those years).[9] Unpredictably—and
unprecedentedly—a number of leading intellectuals both testified in
his behalf and wrote to Khrushchev praising Brodski's talents and
petitioning for a fair trial. While the trial itself was a standard
farce—what novelist Vasili Aksenov, referring to his own later mis-
adventures, calls the "real-life theater of the absurd"—it did not
slide into oblivion. Frida Vigdorova, who was in the courtroom, re-
corded the proceedings and disseminated the transcript within the
Soviet Union; it was smuggled out to the West and was there published.[10]

Brodski's trial was considered by some Western pundits to be a
device by which the regime meant to discredit the liberal intelligentsia.[11] If so, the attempt failed, a failure no less evident in
the coalition of artists, writers and scholars who spoke out in Brodski's defense than in the much greater unity of opposition which
greeted the arrest of two men much better known to the Moscow intelligentsia than Brodski, Andrei Siniavski and Iuli Daniel. Nineteen
months separated Brodski's trial from Siniavski and Daniel's arrest,
a turbulent period in which Khrushchev fell from power and was re-
placed by Brezhnev and Kosygin, in which a much tougher line was
noticeable in Pravda and Izvestia and the most liberal of the literary journals, Novyi mir and Iunost, came under severe criticism, and
in which a wave of repressions swept the Ukraine.[12] The Siniavski-
Daniel trial was a symbol of the new atmosphere and a sign, as well,
of the newly-awakened dissident movement.[13]

The trial was unique. As Siniavski noted in his final plea, it
was the first time that a defendant was held "criminally responsible
for his creative activity." While it was hardly the first time defendants' words were quoted out of context, it was the first time the
words of fictional characters were cited—out of context—as expressions of the author's opinions, and were used to prove "intent to
subvert or weaken the Soviet regime."[14] At the same time, this was
perhaps also the first time that neither defendant, charged among other

things with "slander of the future of human society," admitted his
guilt. The transcript of the trial, at which the defendants refuted,
point by point, the prosecutor's case, circulated extensively in the
Soviet Union. Widespread support for Siniavski and Daniel was expressed not merely by avoidance of attack (as was the case, as trans-
lator and critic Max Hayward points out, for liberal intelligentsia
during the Pasternak campaign),[15] but by the writing and circulating
of protest letters, petitions and appeals, letters sent to (though
not published by) Izvestia by such prominent "establishment" literary
figures as Kornei Chukovski, Ilia Ehrenburg, Victor Shklovski, Veniamin Kaverin and Iuri Nagibin. In fact, of the official Soviet literary elite, only Mikhail Sholokhov lent his name and prestige to the
regime, an act for which he was excoriated by, among others, Lydia
Chukovskaia:

> By reducing complex propositions to simple ones, by bandying
> about the word "treason" in such an unworthy manner, you have
> once again . . . been false to your duty as a writer, your
> duty to explain and convey the complexity and contradictory
> nature of the literary and historical process. . . . Siniav-
> ski and Daniel's committal to trial was itself illegal. Be-
> cause a book, a piece of fiction, a story, a novel—in brief,
> a work of literature . . . cannot be tried in any court. It
> can only be tried in the court of literature.[16]

The Siniavski-Daniel trial also illustrated the confluence of
literary and dissident activity. Aleksandr Esenin-Volpin, who organ-
ized the demonstration protesting Siniavski and Daniel's arrest and
demanding an open and public trial, was himself a poet and essayist;
for two poems he wrote in the 1940s he was incarcerated in the Lu-
byanka Prison, and for his 1961 collection A Leaf of Spring, circulated
in samizdat and published abroad, he was again arrested and sent to a
mental institution. Vladimir Bukovski and Vadim Delone, both of whom
circulated poetry in samizdat, were tried for participating in a protest against the trial, and their own trial was documented by Pavel
Litvinov, who also disseminated the trial transcript of the group of
activists (Aleksandr Ginzburg, Iuri Galanskov, Aleksei Dobrovolski
and Vera Lashkova) who were guilty of recording and distributing the
transcript of the Siniavski-Daniel trial.

The Ginzburg-Galanskov trial took place in 1968, which was a year
of special significance for both dissent and samizdat. Those who
tried, in letters and petitions, to defend Ginzburg and his code-
fendants were subjected to increasing harassment and repressions, as
were Ukrainian activists who circulated impassioned protests against
the Russification policy of the regime. After the Soviet invasion of
Czechoslovakia, a group of protesters demonstrated; the episode was
documented by the poet Natalia Gorbanevskaia in Red Square at Noon.
The year 1968 witnessed the eruption of controversy over Solzhenitsyn's Cancer Ward and the concomitant campaign of slander and
threats mounted against him which resulted in his November 1969

expulsion from the Union of Writers. One Western analyst, Abraham Rothberg, designated 1968 the year of "re-Stalinization."[17]

But 1968 was also the year designated by the United Nations "International Human Rights Year," and it gave birth to what was a cornerstone and has become a symbol of the democratic and dissident movement in the Soviet Union: The Chronicle of Current Events. In a blunt, accurate introductory comment to his English edition of the first 11 issues of Chronicle, Peter Reddaway calls it "one of the most important documents ever to come out of the Soviet Union."[18] The Chronicle of Current Events is the "journal of record" of the dissent movement,[19] appearing fairly regularly for the past 14 years, with the exception of one 18-month period between 1972 and 1974 when the KGB took measures against hundreds of people connected with it and succeeded in temporarily preventing its publication. CCE systematically publishes—and publicizes—carefully documented accounts of human rights violations; arrests, searches and interrogations; repressions against religious believers and ethnic minorities; information from and about prisons and camps; material on the use of psychiatric treatment against dissidents or for political motives; attempts to form free trade unions, and so on. CCE regularly contains summaries of, and sometimes excerpts from, texts circulating in samizdat, as well as information on the authors of samizdat material. Its aim, as Peter Reddaway says, is "openness, non-secretiveness, freedom of information and expression"; it regards itself as legal "because it merely compiles an accurate record of events, and where there is truth there can—legally speaking—be no libel."[20]

While CCE's thrust is legal, not literary, it consistently displays in its pages the connection between the two domains. When Solzhenitsyn was expelled from the Union of Writers, Soviet readers learned of Western reaction from the pages of CCE. When Andrei Siniavski and critic Anatolii Iakobson were forced to emigrate, CCE so informed its readers. CCE summarized the contents of the important samizdat collection of essays, Iz glubiny,[21] and noted the circulation and nature of samizdat journals like Zemlia (Earth) and Evrei v SSSR (Jews in the USSR). The fiftieth issue of CCE was devoted entirely to the trials of summer 1978 (Ginzburg, Shcharanski, Podrabinek et al.); its fifty-second issue reported on the compilation of Metropol', a literary almanac, and the consequent repressions against its authors and editors; its fifty-third i.a. summarized Lithuanian samizdat; its fifty-fourth documented repressions against two samizdat journals. In several issues the editors even report on tamizdat, the literature sent abroad for publication.

The interrelationship between politics and literature manifest in CCE, as well as in the examples noted above, is not, of course, a creation of Soviet dissidents. They are reacting to the interrelationship between the two realms that has always existed in Soviet history, more dramatically perhaps during the Stalin years but no less importantly now. It was the regime which insisted on the

political significance of Zhivago's publication; it was the regime
which tried Siniavski and Daniel's fiction on political charges; it
was the regime which turned Cancer Ward and First Circle into political causes célèbres. Soviet censorship in each case judged literary
works as politically unacceptable and the Soviet regime reacted in a
correspondingly political fashion.

Soviet Censorship and Samizdat

Over the past twenty-odd years thousands of works have circulated
in samizdat, ranging from open letters protesting individual arrests
or group repressions to lyric poetry, from historical or archival
documents to satires on the homosexual underworld, from anti-Semitic
tracts to profound expressions of Christian (or Jewish) faith, from
analyses of alcoholism to analyses of Stalinism, from surrealist
plays to semisocialist realist stories with almost-positive heroes.
All have been prohibited, either tacitly or explicitly, from official
publication. The question then arises: apart from their common tabu,
have such disparate works anything else in common? Or, phrased differently, have they anything in common to cause that tabu? Is there
an identifiable line between what is permissible and what is not?

Émigré historian Aleksandr Nekrich, who himself suffered the
constraints of censorship, cites with some amusement the per-
tinent entry in the Soviet Historical Encyclopedia: "Socialist revolutions put an end to bourgeois censorship. The constitutions of
socialist countries guarantee the workers freedom of the press."[22]
In fact, of course, censorship operates continually, on both external
and internal levels, and most Soviet émigrés agree that the external
form is the less invidious and less onerous. It is, nevertheless,
powerful. The censors are housed in what is commonly called Glavlit,
though its official title is The Main Board for the Protection of
State and Military Secrets in the Press. Journal editors or publishing house staffs submit material to the censor who, usually after
much delay, approves, rejects or requests alterations in the text.
The censors never have direct communication with authors; all suggestions are channeled through editors. If an editor objects to the
censor's "suggestions," he cannot be forced to make the desired
changes; on the other hand, such obduracy results in printing a text
without the censor's approval, often tantamount to resigning from
one's job. After changes have been made, the manuscript is sent to
the press, which prints up to 10 copies, and then the censor again
checks to make sure that no unwarranted emendations have been made
after the first examination. Only then can the manuscript be returned to the printer for production.[23] The censors are guided in
part by an index of forbidden subjects, which includes military information, information on "earthquakes, avalanches, landslides etc.,"
figures on government and party salaries, comparisons between individuals' budgets and the prices of goods, reports on improved living
standards "anywhere outside the socialist camp," food shortages, and

so on. They are also subordinate to what might be called "supercensors"—those who supervise, and sometimes overrule, the censors.

The mechanism of censorship operates much the same way for fiction and poetry as for nonfiction, although a number of censors who work on belletristic literature are editors as well and may allow themselves to be more sensitive to literary criteria. According to several writers now in the West, however, editorial boards take over much of the censorship function from the official censors. Andrei Siniavski, describing Novyi mir's censorship of his own work, writes: "Glavlit wasn't really the main problem; . . . [the editorial board] knew what was allowed and what wasn't."[24] Indeed, so did Siniavski himself. In 1962 Siniavski wrote an article on Pasternak, analyzing his poetry in a very positive vein (Novyi mir, No. 3, 1962). He added a paragraph denigrating Doctor Zhivago, hoping to provide a counterweight to the praise and thus ensure publication. When the censors informed him that Zhivago was not to be mentioned at all, Siniavski was able to substitute a far more general and less derogatory paragraph which, ironically, the censors accepted.[25]

In that particular case self-censorship backfired to Siniavski's advantage. Generally, however, self-censorship is devastating, and it is ubiquitous. Anatoli Kuznetsov, whose novel Babi Iar was published in the Soviet Union only with substantial cuts, comments, "Self-censorship, in one form or another, operates in every writer."[26] Anatoli Gladilin, whose The Making and Unmaking of a Soviet Writer affords a bitterly wry glimpse into the workings of the Soviet literary establishment, describes what he calls the writer's "agonizing dilemma" of finding something he can write about honestly without forfeiting the chance to publish his manuscript: "In each of us sits our own internal censor."[27] And Aleksandr Nekrich, writing about historical research, says that "Soviet censorship begins in the head of the historian."[28]

Nekrich details some of the prohibited topics in historical research: the real history of the Communist Party of the Soviet Union (impossible because of the ban on Trotski and Bukharin, Kamenev and Zinoviev); the history of non-Bolshevik working- and peasant-class parties; the history of genocide in the USSR; Soviet–German relations during the 1939-41 alliance; subjects which are perceived to denigrate Russian prestige, etc.[29] Censorship of science, both physical and social, is similar. Mark Popovski, a science journalist now in America, describes the unavailability of raw data, of experiments, of statistical information, of literature in the field: "Inaccessible in Soviet scientific libraries are the books of scientists who have emigrated or fled from the USSR"—which in the case of the Lenin Library may amount to about 20 percent. And Popovski explains the criteria for permission to publish a scientific article abroad: "It must contain no new elements, . . . no inventions or discoveries, . . . all problems and questions raised in it [must] have already been discussed."[30]

Drawing on these various émigré sources, as well as on samizdat
texts themselves, one can categorize some of the reasons for prohib-
iting publication. Extrinsically, censorship may be applied for nonliterary or scholarly reasons: authors who have involved themselves
in one way or another in behavior unacceptable to the state find
themselves unable to publish their works. Such has been the case
with many individuals, some quite renowned, who signed statements in
defense of one or another "dissident." In those cases neither the
subject nor the style of the "punished" work is important—merely the
author's unacceptable activities. The satirist Vladimir Voinovich,
for instance, protested both the Siniavski-Daniel and the Ginzburg-
Galanskov trials, and defended Solzhenitsyn after his expulsion from
the Writers' Union. As a result two of his plays were withdrawn from
theater repertoires. A number of Soviet writers who might have re-
mained within the fold of official publications, at least for con-
siderably longer, found themselves unpublishable after such demon-
strations of "anti-Soviet" behavior.

As for censorship on intrinsic grounds, censored or banned texts
which find their way into samizdat are generally unacceptable either
because of stylistic experimentation or because of subject, and occasionally because of both. Stylistic transgressions are found primarily, of course, in literary texts: Siniavski's works, for instance, were pronounced criminal partly for stylistic reasons; they
were considered anti-Soviet "in form."[31] Surrealism and grotesquerie
are particularly suspect. In one of Muza Pavlova's samizdat plays,
"Boxes," she mocks the absurdity of bureaucracy by positing the ac-
cumulation of boxes in a library, boxes which no one has ordered and
which serve no function, but which cannot be removed. Eventually the
boxes, which everyone is afraid to touch, turn out to be empty. In
a manner reminiscent of Ionesco, she treats realistically completely
surreal situations, and the impact derives from the clash between the
two. Novelist Vasili Aksenov, in "The Steel Bird," develops a similar blend of fantasy and reality in a kind of fable about a steel
bird/man invading and taking over a Moscow apartment house. And the
late Andrei Amalrik, who is better known for his polemical and journalistic work, wrote a number of absurdist plays; he, like Siniavski,
felt that Soviet reality could not be described in the traditional
realistic mode, requiring instead the language and style of the absurd. All these writers reveal the influence of Mikhail Bulgakov,
the Soviet dramatist and satirist who died in 1940. In early works
like "Heart of a Dog" and in his last great novel The Master and
Margarita (the uncut text was for a time available to Soviet readers
only through samizdat) the "real" encroaches on the "unreal" in fantastic fashion; in Master and Margarita the "real" world of Moscow
in the 1930s is threatened by the "unreal" appearance of the Devil,
and much of the novel's satiric point derives from the inability of
"rational" people to accept supposedly "irrational" events, even when
the "irrational" so often reigns supreme in their own world.

While some experimentation is tolerated in official Soviet literature (one finds stream-of-consciousness, for instance, in the work of
novelists Rasputin, Trifonov and Bitov), a mixture of stylistic experimentation and tabu subjects virtually guarantees official prohibition. Venedikt Erofeev's From Moscow to Petushki, a surrealistic
narrative of the drunken wanderings, both physical and psychic, of
its alcoholic narrator, is completely beyond the pale. Nikolai
Bokov's Nobody. The Disgospel of Maria Dementnaia, which circulated
in samizdat anonymously, is a similarly surreal mixture of drunken
consciousness, failures of memory (indicated by blank spots in the
text) and monologues, about a professional "applauder." In both
cases neither the depictions of Soviet life (the pervasive drunkenness, the plight of an intellectual who refuses to lie and thereby
loses his job) nor the manner in which they are written could be considered tolerable by official standards.

Works relatively—or entirely—traditional in form can still, by
virtue of their subject matter or theme, exclude themselves from official publication, depending on where precisely the party line is
drawn at any given moment. Thus Georgi Vladimov and Vladimir Voinovich, two writers who were published officially for many years, came
up against the impasse of tightened censorship in the late 1960s and
early 1970s. In Vladimov's novel Faithful Ruslan, the dismantling of
a labor camp after Stalin's death is described from the point of view
of the hero, a guard dog, who has loyally served his Soviet masters
and who finds himself homeless and spiritually lost when the prisoners are amnestied and his job is rendered superfluous. Ruslan is, as
the British scholar Geoffrey Hosking points out, "a caricature of the
Socialist Realist hero,"[32] and thanks in large part to his narrative
voice, the very limitations of which enable the reader to understand
far more than is articulated, delicate questions of loyalty and devo-
tion to evil, of the perversion of admirable qualities in the service
of a frightful "good," are delineated with a complexity wholly unacceptable in the current Soviet press. Even in the heyday of Khru-
shchevian "liberalism" this book would probably have been banned.

The earlier fiction of Voinovich, criticized but nonetheless published, satirized aspects of Soviet reality in a fairly limited fashion. In his samizdat works—The Ivankiad, The Life and Extraordinary
Adventures of Private Ivan Chonkin and Pretender to the Throne—Voinovich goes much further. Hosking encapsulates Voinovich's point of
departure from—and sin against—the Soviet norm: "He was posing the
traditional Socialist Realist questions [how principled action is
possible, how the good man is created] in an entirely new form. . . .
It is not a purpose (still less the Purpose) which draws [his heroes]
on, but rather they discover by trial and error, even by accident,
their own authentic forms of existence."[33] In Chonkin Voinovich
satirizes most acutely the ways in which authoritarian systems and
ideology force individuals to forfeit their humanity and their identity. Only a "fool" like Chonkin is impervious, precisely because he
is a "fool." Virtually all the other characters are what Hosking

calls "inauthentic," from the editor who ensures that Stalin's name
appears not more or less than 12 times in every article, to the
"scientist" who devotes his life to developing a cross between a
potato and a tomato, and offers his guests a home-brew distilled from
dung, the source—according to him—of all life. Like Vladimov, Voinovich deliberately chooses as his hero an individual whose understanding of Soviet society is in some way limited; by juxtaposing that
limited understanding with the facts of Soviet life, he exposes the
underlying unreality of that society. In Voinovich's work the result
is comedy, in Vladimov's it is closer to tragedy, but in neither case
does it conform to the vision prescribed by Soviet literary policy in
the Brezhnev years.

Soviet literary policy changes, of course, and many of the works
found in samizdat were originally intended for official publication.
In the early 1960s the Stalinist "cult of personality" was in such
disrepute that memoirists like Evgenia Ginzburg and Marxist historians
like Roi Medvedev had legitimate hopes of publishing their works.
When censorship tightened, in Khrushchev's last years and after his
fall from power, such hopes were shattered; these and other authors
saw the possibilities for publication as so slim that their only way
of reaching readers was through samizdat. After the publication of
One Day in the Life of Ivan Denisovich Khrushchev warned against the
"flood of manuscripts about the life of people in exile, in prison
and in camps";[34] that flood, diverted from magazine offices and publishing houses, poured instead into the underground canals of samizdat. As the camps, prison, exile—Stalinism—became once more tabu
subjects, they were transformed into the obsessive subject of samizdat authors, who produced some of unofficial literature's most significant works: Ekaterina Olitskaia's memoirs, beginning with her
first arrest as a Left Socialist-Revolutionary in 1924 and continuing
through thirty years spent in prison, camps and exile; Varlam Shalamov's devastating story-cycle Kolyma Tales, detailing life and death
in that part of hell in which he lived for nearly 20 years; Petr
Iakir's Childhood in Prison, which he first entered at the ripe age
of 14, son of an "enemy of the people"; Elena Ishutina's Narym, describing the fate of people exiled to Siberia from Soviet-occupied
territory just before World War II; the entire oeuvre of Aleksandr
Solzhenitsyn.

The natural corollary of texts dealing with Soviet life under
Stalin, whether fictional or factual, are those which treat post-
Stalin Soviet life. And such has been the pattern in samizdat. From
accounts of the camps in the 1930s and 1940s we move to accounts of
the camps today, by Anatoli Marchenko, Edward Kuznetsov, and count-
less unnamed prisoners; from reports, relatively few in number, on
psychiatric repressions in the late 1940s and early 1950s we shift to
General Piotr Grigorenko's account of his own psychiatric "treatment," the Medvedev brothers' A Question of Madness and Aleksandr Podrabinek's Punitive Medicine. Samizdat contains documentation of
Stalinist repressions against various ethnic minorities (the Crimean

Tatars, the Meskhi), and comparable documentation of current repressions against those peoples and many others. Corrections of official falsification of Soviet history are paralleled by corrections of official disinformation on current Soviet life, whether the subject is religious repression, poverty in villages and on collective farms, environmental pollution or the black market. It may no longer be true, as it was under Stalin, that socialist realist doctrine decreed not merely what a writer could not say, but also what he must say; still, the list of tabus is inordinately and unhappily long, and the quantity (and quality) of samizdat correspondingly great.

The Achievements of Samizdat

In his analysis of what he calls "free" literature, Iuri Maltsev includes a chapter entitled "Enlivened Shades." In it he describes one of the most important accomplishments of samizdat: the resurrection of suppressed Russian literature:

> Decades passed, their names [Platonov, Pilniak, Babel,
> Zoshchenko, Mandelshtam, Bulgakov] disappeared even from
> literary articles, it was forbidden to mention them, their
> books were burned, a whole generation grew up which had
> never even heard anything about them, and suddenly some-
> thing completely incredible happened: the dead, those
> buried alive came alive, burned books rose up from ashes,
> unpublished manuscripts, miraculously preserved . . .
> began to multiply and spread over the country. A miracle
> of resurrection occurred.[35]

Eventually, it is true, the official press published some of the work of these authors. Generally, however, the size of editions was small, the publications limited in content, and the availability for average Soviet citizens severely circumscribed. Thus it was primarily through samizdat that Russian readers, especially younger Russian readers, rediscovered a heritage which had been lost for 20, 30, sometimes even 40 years. Samizdat became the gateway to lost literature: to Anna Akhmatova's "Requiem" and "Poem Without a Hero," to the bulk of Mandelshtam's poetry, to Platonov's Kotlovan and Chevengur. It opened the door to certain Western literature as well: Orwell's 1984, Koestler's Darkness at Noon. Moreover, it has spawned a secondary literature on that resurrected heritage, critical analyses like Anatoli Belyi or Levitin-Krasnov's articles on Bulgakov's Master and Margarita, personal memoirs like Gladkov's Meetings with Pasternak and Chukovskaia's Notes on Anna Akhmatova, Evgenia Gertsyk's reminiscences of the Silver Age poets.

The "enlivened shades" include as well nonbelletristic literature. Russian readers have, through samizdat, rediscovered (or sometimes discovered for the first time) much of their spiritual heritage: one entire journal, Nadezhda (Hope), a samizdat Christian periodical,

regularly contains texts pertaining to church history—letters by a
19th century priest, letters written by Bishop German from exile in
1923 and 1936-37 (when he disappeared); Levitin-Krasnov has written
extensively on church history of the 1920s and 1930s. Roi Medvedev's
journal, Dvadtsatyi vek (Twentieth Century, published in English as
Samizdat Register), is devoted primarily to Russian political history,
both Bolshevik and non-Bolshevik; issues have included memoirs by
eyewitnesses of the 1917 revolution, articles on the early Bolsheviks
Kamenev and Zinoviev, the text of the last letter written by a Cos-
sack leader who fought with the Bolsheviks during the Civil War and
was shot in 1921. Through samizdat, primary sources long inaccessible to Soviet readers became available: Pamiat (Memory), a journal which examines the history of the USSR, has contained the diaries
of a leading revolutionary from 1917 to 1921, memoirs of the "cata-
comb church" (a splinter church which for nearly twenty years refused to accept as its leader the Patriarch of the Russian Orthodox
Church), and the like. Some of the Ukrainian, Lithuanian and Georgian samizdat journals have included historical materials in an attempt to counter Soviet falsification of their national histories.
And the old question of Westernizing versus Slavophilism has been the
issue of many debates on the pages of such samizdat journals as Veche
(Assembly) and in such samizdat collections as From Under the Rubble,
debates conducted with an openness, passion and—sometimes—ferocity entirely absent from the desiccated historical analyses of its 19th
century manifestation found in the pages of official publications.

Nadezhda Mandelshtam, whose memoirs circulated widely in samizdat,
was at first slow to realize the potential of samizdat. Then she
understood:

> We have seen the new readers come into being before our very
> eyes. . . . It came about against all the odds. The whole
> educational system was geared to preventing the appearance
> of such readers. . . . It had begun to seem unthinkable that
> any of the [suppressed authors] could ever survive such mas-
> sive efforts to obliterate their memory. Then, quite sud-
> denly, everything changed, and we had samizdat . . . it not
> only exists but also caters to its readers' actual wants.[36]

And so the woman who preserved her husband's poetry for nearly 40
years finally had the means to turn it over to an audience who wanted
it: "It is for him [the reader] that I kept M.'s poetry and it is to
him that I have handed it over."[37] And in a testament that was not
included in her memoirs, she adds a request to future generations to
keep Mandelshtam's poetry from the encroachments of the State, to
keep it the "private," not "State," property it has always been.[38]
By means of samizdat the private property of Russian readers—of prose
and of poetry, of philosophy and religion, of politics and history—
has been returned to its rightful owners.

Poetry

Andrei Siniavski has noted that Russia's poetic heritage was
marginally less disrupted by Stalinism than was its prose legacy.
The Silver Age of Russian poetry—the poetry of Acmeism, Futurism,
Constructivism—had time to flower in the years just before and after
the 1917 revolution, was able, "despite the obstacles, . . . to reach
a certain apogee and realize its potential during the first part of
the century and in the twenties. After that, an attempt was made to
destroy it, but it was more or less saved by Pasternak, Akhmatova and
one or two others, and lived to blossom again."[39] In the first epoch
of Stalinism, for instance, between 1932 and 1935, Pasternak, though
personally unable to write new verse, was allowed to publish seven
collections of his previously published poetry.[40] Akhmatova, who was
prevented from publishing (or republishing) any poetry during the
1930s, managed in 1940 to get some lyrics into a few literary journals, and was permitted to publish a volume of verse (though it was
withdrawn almost instantly).[41] Both poets were able, during the war,
to publish volumes in the temporarily-relaxed climate of censorship;
the postwar years, however, were even more oppressive than the late
1930s, and Akhmatova was singled out for vitriolic attack in 1946.[42]
On the rare occasions during the Stalin years when either poet was
allowed to read or recite in public, the audiences were by all accounts frenzied in their appreciation.

So the legacy of poetry was preserved, even if a great many of
Pasternak and Akhmatova's verses could only be memorized, awaiting the
samizdat network for publication, and even though the poetry of Mandelshtam and Tsvetaeva vanished, for all practical purposes, for
over three decades. And when samizdat began, in the early 1960s,
poetry and its sister-art songs were a staple; thus they have re-
mained. From the first underground journals to the most recent alma-
nacs, poetry has been a constant element. This partially reflects
the practical consideration that poems, being short, are easier to
duplicate, partially the fact that amateurish poetry is relatively
easy to write. It may also reflect a common Russian perception, what
Nadezhda Mandelshtam calls "the healing, life-giving" qualities of
poetry, which can arouse human instincts in "numbed and dormant
spirits."[43]

Certainly if the quality of samizdat poetry is uneven, its range
is enormous. More common in early samizdat, less common now, is
"civic" or overtly political verse, such as some of Naum Korzhavin's
and the late Iuri Galanskov's:

> Ministers, leaders, newspapers—don't trust them!
> Get up, you on your knees! . . .
> Go and break up
> The rotten prison of the state!
>
> Galanskov, "Manifesto of Man"[44]

Galanskov puts his hope not in social revolution, but in a spiritual resurrection, a theme echoed in much of the religious verse of samizdat. Conventionally religious or not, some of the best poets are intensely inward-looking: Akhmadulina, for instance, or Boris Chichibabin's death-drenched poems; Natalia Gorbanevskaia and Stanislav Krasovitski, who translate public events into private or personal experience, internalizing external events or environments in a manner reminiscent of Mandelshtam and Akhmatova. The elderly poet Semen Lipkin is traditionalist in form, as is his much younger colleague Sergei Gandlevski, while others experiment with poetic form: Viktor Krivulin manipulates word repetition and grammatical forms to achieve a multilayered meaning in his work; Gennadi Aigi mixes blank space with blank verse, rearranging syntax and incorporating punctuation (parentheses, ellipses) as integral parts of his poetry.

Nadezhda Mandelshtam characterized contemporary Russian literature as being in a "pre-Gutenberg" phase, since its circulation depended on manuscripts and typescripts rather than on print. Modern technology has, however, added a decidedly post-Gutenbergian twist to the accessibility of poems, in the form of cassettes. And the songs of the Russian underground bards, particularly of Bulat Okudzhava, Aleksandr Galich and Vladimir Vysotski, have reached an audience and had an impact far beyond the intellectual elite of urban centers. Semen Telegin, commenting on the importance of "magnitizdat," the electronic counterpart of samizdat (reproducing unofficial songs on tape), remembers:

> The fashion for Okudzhava might end, but there was no returning to the past, . . . no use waiting for favors from the singers in the camp of Russian warriors. . . . The first sign of the new culture that came into being was the guitar-and-singing craze: no matter how condescendingly the professionals regarded it, it had authenticity, spontaneity and human spirit. . . . Contemporary music for the people is not to be found in the plenary sessions of the composers' union or on the radio, but in the long hours of tape recordings played at gatherings of intellectuals, and in the coaches of suburban trains.[45]

Okudzhava, who in the last several years seems to have avoided the samizdat network (though Soviet émigrés report that he still sings, albeit only for close friends at small parties), evoked the tremendous response he did because of the direct, lyrical sincerity of his songs. His songs contradict the official optimism so characteristic of Soviet lyrics; hardly political, except in the most general sense, they concentrate on private emotions and a personal expression which is at variance with—and proscribed by—the official line.

Aleksandr Galich, who died in a tragic accident a few years after immigrating to the West, wrote songs far more pointedly political in tone. One of his most popular, "We're no Worse than Horace," comments acerbically: "Falsehood wanders from zone to zone,/Sharing Falsehood with its neighbor Falsehood."[46] Others describe the fate of those arrested under Stalin, and a great many treat the possibility of a resurgence of Stalinism in contemporary life. Himself a Jew, Galich devoted a number of lyrics to the mostly-forbidden theme of Soviet anti-Semitism, in both its past and current manifestations: one of his most bitter songs, "Ballad of the Eternal Flame," uses the refrain from the Yiddish folk song "Tumbalalaika," which was played by Auschwitz camp commanders when they led prisoners to their death, as a refrain in a death threnody.[47]

Like Galich, Vladimir Vysotskii treated the theme of anti-Semitism, as well as labor camp life, the criminal underworld and psychiatric repression of sane dissidents, in his slangy, sardonic songs. When he died in 1980, at the age of 42, the editors of the émigré journal Ekho (Echo) memorialized him thus:

> Huge crowds at the burial, weekly pilgrimages to the grave
> (to which people come from all corners of the country)—
> Russia hasn't known the like since, if you will, the death
> of the famous tyrant. . . . His songs transcribed from tape
> recorder to tape recorder, spread over the whole country,
> from big cities·to Godforsaken Siberian villages. He wrote
> around a thousand pieces, sang them in a hoarse Russian
> voice which touched every Russian heart. . . . In his art,
> which the authorities refused to allow (permitting no more
> than perhaps twenty to appear) . . . he, like no one else,
> told us about all of Russia today. . . . Every individual
> . . . received from Vysotskii an understanding and a basis
> from which to evaluate what is good and what bad.[48]

Fiction

Though samizdat fiction is generally proscribed because of its subject, violation of stylistic norms can, as described above, also provide grounds for attack. As Andrei Siniavski explains:

> In the Soviet Union, quite apart from the rules about so-
> cialist realism, party spirit, ideological purity and so
> on, there exists a deeply entrenched cult extolling the
> tradition of nineteenth-century classical Russian litera-
> ture . . . [in] the form of realism that depicts life in
> its natural proportions.[49]

Thus works which depict life in its "unnatural" proportions—whether in the disproportions of surrealism, the grotesque, absurdism or what-ever—are frowned upon and move underground. Nevertheless, the main culprits in fiction are subject matter and what can be called the tone of a work. Samizdat is replete with fiction that depicts contemporary Soviet life in what by official criteria is considered too negative a light. Anatoli Gladilin, for instance, wrote a novel entitled Forecast for Tomorrow, which he almost certainly hoped to publish officially. Indeed, why not? The novel portrays a young physicist, Vladimir Martynov, who after a series of disappointments finds both personal and professional success: personal, in that his love affair ends and he returns to his wife; professional, in that he finds work in meteorology, the field most interesting to him and most compatible with his talents. The ending is upbeat; the conflicts are resolved. In the course of reaching his happy ending, however, Gladilin describes the way bureaucratic rules and government plans circumscribe scientific initiative to such an extent that scientists spend a good part of their working time doing absolutely nothing. And even less acceptably, Gladilin blames this situation not on the defects of "individuals" or "exceptions," but on the system itself:

> A man who, after work, stands for half an hour in line to buy tomatoes (and they get sold out before his turn), then half an hour for undershirts (and they too disappear in front of his nose), then ten minutes in line for apples . . . and the salesgirl gives him a receipt which has to be punched in a different department (what should I do with the receipt?—Sign it at the chief's desk—Where's the chief?—She's gone out!—When's she coming back?—Citizen, you are disturbing me!) —I tell you in complete seriousness that such a man is socially dangerous: he may simply hurl himself at passers-by and start biting them.[50]

A similar commentary on contemporary life is Voinovich's Ivankiad in which he describes his struggle for an apartment. In a sense Ivankiad fulfills all the requirements of socialist realism: it shows how an honest socialist foils the schemes of an unscrupulous, corrupt, bourgeois perverter of socialist ideals. However, that perverter happens to be a party big-wig with KGB connections, and the tactics he deploys to acquire the apartment are shown to be the norm rather than an exception to it. What might once have been admitted to the pages of Tvardovski's Novyi mir now finds its home in samizdat, despite—or rather because of—its fundamental ideological purity, its idealism.

Voinovich is still an idealist of a sort; writers like Nikolai Bokov, Vladimir Maramzin and Viktor Erofeev are far more cynical. Their fiction combines satiric or negative portrayals of contemporary life with stylistic experimentation. For Maramzin, one of whose heroes is a homosexual conformist artist, grammatical errors and intentional distortions of words and sounds serve as a mode of expressing a state of mind—or, more accurately, states of half-mind, undeveloped or aborted consciousnesses which have been dulled and corrupted by constant exposure to and absorption of officially-accepted thought expressed in officially-accepted language.[51] Erofeev, in his "alcoholic epic" From Moscow to Petushki, portrays not just his hero but virtually every character his hero meets as being perpetually sozzled; his hero talks to angels and provides recipes for "cocktails" composed of such ingredients as shoe polish and hair tonic. For Erofeev, drunkenness is an escape route from the falseness and hypocrisy of "sober" Soviet life:

> Oh, if the whole world, if everyone in the world were, as I
> am now, quiet and timid and not sure of anything: not sure
> of oneself, nor of the seriousness of one's place under
> heaven—how good it would be! No more enthusiasms, no more
> heroic deeds of any kind, no more obsessions!—general pusil-
> lanimity. I would agree to live on earth a whole eternity
> if they could show me a corner where there's no place for
> heroic deeds.[52]

It is permissible, on the pages of the official press, to expose the evils of alcoholism in individuals, aberrations from the norm. But only in samizdat is it permissible to expose alcoholism as pervasive, as a means of authenticating oneself or one's consciousness, as a language of thought and a mode of perception. The story of a 19th century Dostoevskian victim of the Tsarist system and of Chernyshevskian positivism, a Petersburg Underground Man, may be published; the story of a 20th century victim of the Soviet system and of enshrined and sanctified positivism, permanently drunk and eternally shuttling between Moscow and Petushki, may only circulate, ironically enough, underground.

Though there are of course exceptions, the preponderant tone of samizdat fiction treating contemporary Soviet life is ironic and satiric, as if the reality of life in Russia today is so absurd that realistic description is an inadequate means of conveying its essence. The reality of life during the Stalin years, on the other hand, was far too horrific to be treated humorously and with very few exceptions (such as Voinovich's Chonkin and chapters of First Circle where Solzhenitsyn's contempt for Stalin and his henchmen verges on mordant satire), the tone of fiction treating the Stalin era is far more realistic, flatter, with less authorial comment. Varlam Shalamov, for example, who died in January 1982 at the age of 74, created in his Kolyma Tales an encyclopedia of life in Kolyma, the corner of northeastern Siberia where several million people were killed as the direct or indirect result of Stalin's ukases. The "byt" of Kolyma—everyday life in the lowest circle of the Gulag's hell—is documented in story after story: convicts who mutilate themselves to avoid, if only for a few days, the impossible-to-survive work; the criminal convicts' treatment of the politicals; the 12 to 16-hour workdays in fifty-below-zero frosts. Shalamov's stories are not merely testimony; as critic Mikhail Geller notes in his introduction to the Russian edition:

> Varlam Shalamov knows that a new genre is necessary. . . .
> He creates a prose appropriate to its subject, at the same
> time story, physiological work, ethnographic investigation.
> Shalamov writes unusually simply, very sparingly, avoiding

> pathos and head-on value judgments. The writer strives
> for maximal compression. . . . As a rule the writer
> takes one event, one scene, even one gesture. In the
> center of the story there is always a portrait. Of an
> executioner or a victim. Sometimes both executioner and
> victim. Instead of analyzing psychology the writer pre-
> fers to show action or gesture. As a rule the last sen-
> tence, compressed, lapidary, like a sudden ray of light,
> illuminates what has gone before, blinding us with horror.[53]

The sufferings of families of those purged, interned, imprisoned
or exiled—a theme Solzhenitsyn treats tellingly in his portrait of
Nerzhin's wife in First Circle—is given even more immediacy by Lydia
Chukovskaia in her two novellas The Deserted House and Going Under.
The former, which circulated in samizdat in the mid-1960s, was written in 1939-1940; unlike almost all the literature about the Terror,
it was written not in retrospect but at the time, and Chukovskaia
preferred not to change it:

> I do not doubt that literary works describing the thirties
> will abound, and that other writers, in possession of far
> more facts than I myself at that time possessed, besides
> greater literary gifts and greater powers of analysis, will
> give a more complete and comprehensive picture of this
> period. I have merely tried, to the best of my ability, to
> record what I personally observed.[54]

What she observed, and set down in limpid, lucid prose, was the atmosphere of those years, what Maltsev calls "the optimism and enthu-
siasm of many simple people who still then believed in the not-too-
distant happy future of the country, in the near and inevitable success of socialism"—and what happened to millions of those people.[55]
Chukovskaia's heroine, Olga Petrovna, and her son Kolia, are just
such believing and enthusiastic individuals who avert their eyes when
other people begin to fall victim to the purges. Until, that is,
they fall victim themselves: Kolia is arrested, Olga Petrovna—fired
and unemployable because of his arrest—is bereft of faith and hope.
In the second half of the novella Olga Petrovna waits on endless
lines in front of NKVD buildings, in corridors and prosecutors' wait-
ing rooms, together with thousands of other women whose sons, hus-
bands, fathers, brothers have likewise fallen victim; ultimately she
is forced to face her absolute helplessness, and hopelessness.

In Going Under, set some ten years later, Chukovskaia in effect
resumes her narrative, although her heroine is far more educated, far
more sophisticated and far more autobiographical. Nina Sergeevna, a
woman whose husband was purged in the 1930s, spends some time in a
Writers' Sanatorium outside Moscow where she means to rest and write.
But she is haunted by her husband's fate—the almost certain death
which she can't quite be certain of because she's not heard a word
from or about him for ten years, except for the official sentence:

10 years without right of correspondence. Her neighbor at the sanatorium, Bilibin, a rare camp survivor, tells her bluntly that her
husband was shot. Chukovskaia contrasts the nightmare world of Nina
Sergeevna's thoughts, doubts and anguish with the hypocrisy and pros-
titution of the literary establishment, and hints at the new wave of
arrests which swept the country in 1948-49. In both Deserted House
and Going Under Chukovskaia compresses the experiences of hundreds
of thousands of families, distills the anguish of millions of women
into a pure, corrosive litany of grief.

The process of losing faith, the lessons learned from the bitter
confrontation between ideals and reality, are dealt with in much of
the fiction of samizdat: in Vladimir Maksimov's Seven Days of Creation, in Aleksandr Bek's The New Appointment, in Vasili Grossman's
Forever Flowing. But in a way the fiction is overshadowed by the
fact: for losing faith is the preeminent theme of the samizdat memoirs of the Stalin era.

Memoirs and History

What characterizes the long list of samizdat memoirs are above
all two needs: one, the simpler to state facts, report history, and
bear witness to events which are either ignored or massively distorted in official Soviet publications. The second, more complex, is
the need to explain and understand how those events could have happened and how a whole society, often including the active participa-
tion of the memoirist, could have allowed them to happen. Two of the
most valuable memoirs, both of which circulated in samizdat in extraordinary numbers, are those of Nadezhda Mandelshtam and those of Evgenia Ginzburg (Ginzburg's son, Vasili Aksenov, estimates that over
5,000 copies of her first volume circulated in the Soviet Union).
Both women deal primarily with the worst years of Stalinism, although
Mandelshtam's second volume backtracks to 1919, when she and her husband first met, and describes in great detail her own life in the
post-Stalin years. Ginzburg, who was a dedicated and idealistic
party member, devotes her two books to the years from the Kirov as-
sassination (1934) through her own arrest in 1937 until her release,
in 1955, after 18 years of prison, camp and exile. They are very
different women, and offer correspondingly different kinds of testimony: Mandelshtam, who never had much political faith to lose, far
more acid, her judgments far sharper; Ginzburg overcome with a sort
of shamed humility at the abominations faith such as hers had led to.
In a somewhat similar vein is the trilogy of Lev Kopelev, a special-
ist in German language and literature who was in camp with Aleksandr
Solzhenitsyn and served as a model for Rubin in First Circle.
Kopelev's ideological commitment lasted far longer than Ginzburg's,
and was at constant war with his moral standards, a conflict por-
trayed by Solzhenitsyn in the novel and by Kopelev in his reminiscences. A suggestive complement to these memoirs are the writings of
Ekaterina Olitskaia, the daughter of a member of the People's Will

group and herself a Left Socialist-Revolutionary; hers is one of the few samizdat works which deal with the camps of the 1920s, where members of deviationist socialist parties—SRs, Social Democrats, anarchists and others—were sent.[56]

Whether the genre is fiction, memoir or scholarly essay, the motivation for exploring the past is similar. As historian Robert Slusser points out, "Two of the major tenets of the democratic opposition—the citizen's right to know the truth about his nation's past, and society's need for open publicity concerning the victims of arbitrary oppression—are at the same time basic to historical research."[57] Certainly much of the historical research of samizdat is directed at answering those needs, and perhaps one more: to prevent a repetition of the past by ferreting out and disseminating the facts of that past. A former activist in the human rights movement, Petr Iakir, makes the connection explicitly:

> Under Stalin there was always an iron curtain and no one knew what was going on here. Millions of people were destroyed and nobody knew anything about it. Now we try to publicize every arrest, every dismissal.[58]

The historical writings of samizdat form a body of publicity given to the past. Thus an early samizdat journal, Feniks 1966, included the last letter written by Bukharin before his death, as well as an essay on the historical roots of Stalinism. Boris Evdokimov, writing under the pseudonym of Ivan Ruslanov, explored at length the role of young people, mostly students, in the Russian revolutionary movement. Roi Medvedev, both in his own scholarly works (such as his analysis of Stalinism, Let History Judge) and in the journals he edited, Dvadtsatyi vek (Twentieth Century) and its predecessor Politicheskii dnevnik (Political Diary), has concentrated on Soviet history, often on the relationship between Leninism and Stalinism, and has frequently incorporated into his work excerpts from various unpublished memoirs and historical texts. Aleksandr Nekrich's June 22, 1941, an account of Soviet unpreparedness on the eve of the German invasion, circulated in samizdat when, shortly after its publication in 1965, it was withdrawn from all but special library archives.

The conviction that a return to Stalinism can be averted only through open discussion about historical Stalinism recurs in open letter after open letter, especially in the late 1960s. One, by Petr Iakir, is wryly amusing: he itemizes Stalin's military crimes and judges him, according to the Criminal Code of the RSFSR, to deserve four death sentences and sixty-eight years' deprivation of freedom.[59] The Chronicle of Current Events, in its ninth issue (1969), summarizes the contents of several issues of a samizdat bulletin, Crimes and Punishment, whose purpose is to record the names and actions of "the butchers, the sadists, the informers and those who committed crimes against humanity, where they are now and what they are doing."[60] And in an important sense all of Solzhenitsyn's massive Gulag Archipelago, the apogee of samizdat literature both factual and fictional on the Stalinist system of repression, is as much aimed at guaranteeing the impossibility of its recurrence as it is a testament to and memorialization of those who were victims of that system.

Contemporary Political-Social Observation

As Petr Iakir's words, cited above, suggest, one of samizdat's functions is to publicize current Soviet repression. And the memoirists of the Stalin camps have heirs, most significantly Anatoli Marchenko and Eduard Kuznetsov. Kuznetsov, in his Prison Diaries, and Marchenko in his My Testimony and From Tarusa to Chuna, offer exceptionally vivid and detailed documentary accounts of conditions in today's Soviet prisons and camps. The Chronicle regularly includes letters, reports and bulletins from and about various camps and prisons. Like the memoirists of Stalinism, these individuals want, as Marchenko puts it, to come out of the camps and tell everyone about what they themselves saw and lived through.[61]

But reportage is hardly confined to camps and prisons; samizdat observers describe far more than the penal system. Andrei Amalrik, who died in 1980 only four years after his emigration, combined in his Involuntary Journey to Siberia an account of his 1965 arrest, conviction for "parasitism," and sentence of two-and-a-half years' exile in hard labor camp (where he contracted meningitis) with a fascinating depiction of life en route to and in a tiny village in Siberia, where he worked in a collective farm, the life of whose inhabitants is a treadmill of perpetual work, tedium, and drinking. More directly political are many of the writings of Andrei Sakharov and Roi Medvedev, as well as several of Solzhenitsyn's pre-emigration articles, and for a time one focus of samizdat publicistic writing was the democratic movement itself, its causes, components, weaknesses and strengths. Of those, Dmitri Nelidov's "Ideocratic Consciousness and Personality" is a probing analysis of Soviet ideology and its relation to individual psychology and social adaptation: he explores the doublethink that has resulted from the imposition of ideological norms over a long period of time on a large number of people, and the emergence of the Democratic Movement as a means of expressing "the humane" in an environment which distorts, perverts and suppresses human nature.[62]

A rather different kind of reportage, but one which springs from similar sources, is the samizdat of the ethnic and religious minorities. In an article on the survival of dissent in the Soviet Union, Peter Reddaway includes a list of samizdat periodicals "of substance" which circulated between 1976 and 1980. Among them are 22 journals produced by Jewish, Lithuanian, Estonian, Georgian, Baptist and Orthodox groups—and that does not include the largest ethnic "minority" of the USSR, and one of the most vocal, the Ukrainians, whose 42 million people comprise over 16 percent of the Soviet population.[63]

Indeed, Ukrainian samizdat was disseminated as early as 1964, when a report circulated in the Ukraine: it accused the KGB of setting fire to and destroying the library of the Ukrainian Academy of Sciences in Kiev. (The report contradicted the official legal finding, which blamed an unbalanced librarian for committing arson for personal motives.) The report goes on to accuse the KGB of a continuing plot "to destroy the Ukrainian national heritage in order to Russify the country more easily."[64] Two waves of arrests of Ukrainian nationalists, in 1961 and 1965, served merely to increase Ukrainian national awareness and, concomitantly, the quantity of Ukrainian samizdat. One journalist, Viacheslav Chornovil, compiled a set of documents on the 1965-66 arrests, investigations and trials;[65] another, Ivan Dziuba, blames Ukrainian discontent specifically on Soviet Russification policies, attacking Russian chauvinism as a phenomenon no less characteristic of Soviet Russia than it was of Tsarist Russia. And other works appeared at more or less the same time: Valentyn Moroz's Report from the Beria Reserve, Mikhail Osadchy's Cataract. In 1970 the Ukrainian Herald, a journal modeled largely on The Chronicle of Current Events, began to appear, publishing six issues between January 1970 and March 1972, and resuming publication (after intensive repressions) in 1974.

One Western analyst, Bohdan Nahaylo, observes that because the West is geared to and has disproportionate access to Moscow and Muscovite dissident activities, it often loses sight of the fact that "the overwhelming majority of political prisoners (and probably religious ones, too) are non-Russians." He cites the report of activist Iuri Orlov, which was smuggled out of a Perm labor camp: Over 40 percent of political prisoners in the Soviet Union are Ukrainian, and another 30 percent are Balts. Moreover, as Nahaylo adds, "for non-Russians the notion of human rights is inseparable from the idea of national rights."[66] This is borne out by, among others, the Lithuanian samizdat, which burgeoned throughout the 1970s and reveals a unification of opposition which cannot be matched by Russians either in Moscow or around the country. An astonishing 17,054 signatures, for example, were affixed to a 1972 memorandum addressed to the United Nations: it called on the Soviet authorities to stop persecuting the Lithuanian Catholic Church.[67] The Chronicle of the Lithuanian Catholic Church has published over 50 issues since 1972, and a large number of other journals have circulated in Lithuania (as reported by The Chronicle of Current Events). One sign of the increased cooperation between national minority dissent and Russian dissent is the increased coverage within the pages of CCE of repressions and investigations of non-Russians, as well as reports on the samizdat of the minorities. A few issues of CCE have given extensive coverage to ethnic minorities—the 31st, for instance, was published on the thirtieth anniversary of the deportation of the Crimean Tatars in 1944 and documented the historic (and contemporary) plight of that small but beleaguered nation.

As for the Jews, they—as always in Russian history—pose something of a special problem. The Soviet émigré Mikhail Meerson-Aksenov explains:

> In spite of Russification, each non-Russian nation in the
> USSR still retains a clearly expressed national character,
> language, culture and territory. . . . Soviet Jews, how-
> ever, are deprived of territory and for all practical pur-
> poses, as a result of a planned assimilation, are almost
> deprived of a language and a national culture as well.[68]

From its inception, therefore, Jewish samizdat has focused on two
problems: the right of emigration from the Soviet Union to Israel,
and the nature of Jewish identity within the Soviet Union. According to Vladimir Lazaris, one of the editors of the samizdat journal
Evrei v SSSR (Jews in the USSR), these two concerns have consistently
been reflected in the nature of Jewish samizdat:

> The Jews demanded in numerous letters and declarations that
> their right of emigration to Israel be realized, debated the
> violation of the law by the Soviet authorities, reacted to
> anti-Zionist and anti-Semitic articles in the Soviet press,
> and followed events in general Jewish and Israeli life.[69]

He enumerates some of the material which circulated: as early as
1961, Leon Uris' Exodus (in the English original at first); journals
which included an interview with Golda Meir, an article on the ultra-
nationalist Zionist leader Jabotinsky, a feuilleton by Israeli humor-
ist Ephraim Kishon; other journals which focused on the right to
emigrate as well as offering technical information on the process of
applying for emigration; translations of Western articles and books
such as Cecil Roth's History of the Jewish People; poetry and prose
with Jewish themes.[70]

The magazine which Lazaris edited for a time, Jews in the USSR,
varied in content and tone as its editors changed: when Aleksandr
Voronel and Viktor Iakhot produced the first eight issues, from 1970
to 1972, they had in mind a semischolarly periodical concentrating on
Jewish history, religion and culture with, as the title suggests, an
emphasis on the role of Jews within the Soviet Union. After their
emigration in 1972, the new editors, Ilia Rubin and Rafail Nudelman,
transformed the magazine into a polemical and literary organ, publishing stories by such authors as Boris Khazanov and Feliks Kandel; this
orientation was continued by the third editorial board, in which
Lazaris participated until his own emigration in 1977. Lazaris notes
the scarcity of material in Jewish samizdat on Judaism as a religion:
only one journal, Tarbut, has included much material on the subject,
and even that is frequently as much cultural as religious—articles on
Jewish holidays, for instance. Not surprisingly, as more and more
Jews were allowed to emigrate, the need for and extent of samizdat
pertaining to emigration dwindled; now that emigration has become increasingly constricted, that theme may reassert itself.

The right of emigration from the Soviet Union, for Jews as well as
for other ethnic minorities, has been part of the larger human rights

issue in the USSR. The nature of Jewish identity has generally re-
mained a specifically Jewish concern, parallel to but distinct from
the quest for self-identity of other national minorities. However,
because of the legacy of Russian and Soviet anti-Semitism on the one
hand, and the high proportion of Jews among Bolshevik and Communist
groups historically, the role of Jews in Russian life has been a
major concern of much samizdat not narrowly "Jewish." What Dimitry
Pospielovsky, a Western scholar who has written extensively on samizdat, entitled "The Jewish Question in Russian Samizdat," straddles
the boundary between Jewish self-identity and Jewish identity in the
eyes of Russians.[71] Aleksandr Galich, a Jew who was an integral part
of the Moscow intelligentsia, wrote in Dress Rehearsal about the effects of Russian anti-Semitism on his career and himself personally;
Grigori Svirski, a journalist now in the West, published in samizdat
his documentary novel Hostages, in which he depicts the situation of
Jews in the Soviet Union based on his own experiences and those of
his family, from the war period, the campaign against "cosmopolitans"
(1948-52), the notorious Doctors' Plot which, but for Stalin's death,
would have marked the beginning of a new wave of anti-Semitic repressions, and into the 1960s when his confrontations with the Writers'
Union were directly connected with his Jewishness.[72]

The Russian perception of Jewish identity has also been treated
by Jews who converted to Russian Orthodoxy: Mikhail Agurski, now in
Israel, and Reverend Aleksandr Men have both devoted much of their
work to that issue in both historical and contemporary terms. And
since it is an issue with wide ramifications, it leads in turn into
the question of Russian self-identity. Russian samizdat expresses a
wide range of attitudes toward Jews and anti-Semitism, from those of
an avowed anti-Semitic Russian nationalist like Gennadi Shimanov,
who, in an interview he gave to Jews in the USSR, defends his stance
as being compatible with his Christian faith and with the respect he
has for Jews, "because Jews are an alien, unassimilable element in
the organism of Russian society," and because of that "particular
Jewish hatred for Russia" without which, he feels, the Bolshevik revolution would not have been victorious.[73] Pospielovsky considers
Shimanov a "sincere and practicing Christian," more tolerant than
samizdat authors who, as he says, "seem to treat religion only as an
ideological conveyor belt for mobilizing the populace," and who are
far more vehement in their accusations that Jews brought misery to
Russia through the revolution, that Russian Jews are really inter-
nationalist, not Russian, and that even those who converted to Orthodoxy are ambivalent in their loyalty.[74] Samizdat also encompasses
the view, held by converted Jews like Agurski as well as liberal
dissidents like Bukovski and Medvedev, that Russian anti-Semitism
can be attributed primarily to official policies, which propagate and
foment anti-semitic attitudes "from above" for purposes of regime
policy and politics.

The question is further complicated because nationalism and the
national renaissance are among the most hotly debated subjects of

Russian samizdat, and because anti-Semitism is traditionally an integral part of those subjects. Vladimir Osipov, for four years editor of the journal Veche (Assembly) until his arrest in 1974, is a
man described by one of his ideological opponents as a "liberal—to
the degree that is possible for nationalists."[75] Osipov has rejected
charges that he is anti-Semitic, and most Western observers agree
with him. At the same time, Osipov is most certainly a Russian nationalist. In his article, "Three Attitudes Toward the Homeland"
Osipov distinguishes hatred toward the homeland, voiced by those who
consider Russia a nation of slaves which has brought its fate on itself, from opportunism, which is essentially official Soviet national
patriotism manipulated by the government's ideology, and both from
love, which can embrace other peoples, races and countries only if it
is first directed at one's own nation. While Osipov's brand of nationalism is not to be confused with the rabid anti-Semitic tracts of
some of his own critics, neither is it entirely disconnected from
them: his own journal, Veche, had two faces: a more liberal one,
represented by Osipov, and a more chauvinist one, represented by
Anatoli Skuratov and Igor Ovchinnikov, and the second came, against
Osipov's wishes, to dominate.[76]

The same concerns motivated the authors of From Under the Rubble,
a samizdat collection of articles by Agurski, Solzhenitsyn, Barabanov
and others, which appeared in response to three widely-circulated
pieces by A. Altaev, V. Gorski and M. Chelnov in the early 1970s.
Altaev, Gorskii and Chelnov attacked the tendency to replace communist ideology with a kind of romantic nationalism. Their collocutors
responded with a group of pieces devoted to the question of Russian
national renaissance, positing Marxism and socialism as phenomena
alien to Russia and the Russian legacy and as the chief culprits for
the evils of the Soviet system. With nearly one voice they reject
political and social avenues of change as superficial and inadequate;
Russia's salvation, they feel, lies rather in individual moral rebirth, a return to traditional Russian (peasant) values and to genuine Christian faith.

Thus the nature of religious faith in general, and the Orthodox
church in particular, is an important component of the nationalism
debate. As Meerson-Aksenov, who has written both before and after
his emigration on the role of Christianity in Russian life, notes:
"Russian history as a whole is inseparable from Orthodoxy, and every
Russian writer or thinker is connected to it in some degree: he
either spurns it or is attracted to it."[77] Virtually all the samizdat writers who align themselves, roughly speaking, with Agurski and
Solzhenitsyn regard Orthodoxy as the wellspring of a renewed national
consciousness which has the potential to save Russia from its current
social and moral disintegration. It is in no way surprising to find
so many of these individuals, who were at one time ideologues of
Marxism and Leninism, rejecting that faith for an older one, replacing
positivist materialism with a spiritual morality, and stressing individual responsibility over the kind of collectivism that has been

characteristic of—and, as they see it, destructive to—Soviet life for more than sixty years. Nor is the institution of the church for them synonymous with faith: Solzhenitsyn, in his "Lenten Letter" to Patriarch Pimen, charges the church with betraying its spiritual responsibility by collaborating with the State, calling it "a Church ruled dictatorially by atheists."[78] His letter sparked a discussion of the whole issue of Orthodoxy in a secular state, with contributions by Reverend Sergei Zheludkov, Meerson-Aksenov, Barabanov, and many others.

For most of the writers of religious samizdat, whether Orthodox, Baptist, or Catholic, religion provides spiritual and moral truths entirely absent from or corrupted by Soviet ideology. Anatoli Levitin-Krasnov, whose writings constitute a profound exploration of his own religious faith as well as a history of the church in the Soviet era, describes in a letter to Pope Paul VI the younger generation's pull toward religion as being part of their larger quest for truth.[79] (According to figures cited by Barbara Wolfe Jancar, the Baptist dissent movement is overwhelmingly a young people's movement; she also cites a samizdat memorandum indicating that "the most sought-after books by young people in the Soviet Union after the Bible or the Four Gospels are the writings of the Russian Christian philosophers."[80]) In a society dominated by a bankrupt materialist creed, the attractions and significance of religion are patent; in a society whose history has been washed not in the blood of Christ but in the blood of the Gulag, the notions of individual responsibility and conscience, and of a moral law higher than and separate from the laws of power are enticing. Thus several of the recent samizdat journals are devoted to Christian thought: Nadezhda (Hope) contains essays on the history of the church and the meaning of faith, as well as religious poetry and letters from churchmen; the Leningrad journal 37 often explored the relationship between Christian belief and social responsibility; even the short-lived feminist journal, Zhenshchina i Rossiia (Woman and Russia) was intended to include a regular section called "Women and the Church." As Western scholar Philip Walters comments, "The Orthodox Christian writers come closest to asserting that in all spheres of human activity Christians should serve God rather than Caesar. . . ."

> If people cease to believe in God, they cease to believe in each other, and this leads to the collapse of the family, to immorality and crime, and to the atomisation of society.[81]

Or, in the words of Tatiana Goricheva, a Christian feminist and one of the founders of Zhenshchina i Rossiia, ". . . the dictatorship of reason turned out to be the dictatorship of will, and the dictatorship of will that of arbitrariness. The arbitrariness of one idea became a prison for all the rest."[82]

Those words, Dostoevskian in tone and import, suggest a final area in which samizdat has made a significant contribution to Russian letters: documentation and analysis of the relationship between science and politics. A number of years ago a practicing Soviet psychiatrist published in samizdat an anonymous article entitled "Ignorance in the Service of Arbitrariness." In it he describes what he calls the "liquidation" of the science of psychiatry in Russia, the creation of the Serbski Institute, and the theories of preeminent Soviet psychiatrist A. V. Snezhnevski.[83] Partially in response to increased government use of psychiatry as a means of repressing dissidents, samizdat authors have produced dozens, if not hundreds, of texts dealing with all aspects of psychiatric theory and practice, from a "Manual on Psychiatry for Dissidents" by Vladimir Bukovski and Semen Gluzman, in which the authors provide a summary of the basic tenets of Soviet psychiatric theory, as well as information on the legal rights of those subjected to psychiatric examination and practical recommendations on tactics for dealing with examiners, to personal memoirs of dissidents who have been incarcerated in psychiatric hospitals, to letters and petitions on behalf of such repressed dissidents.[84] Two are of particular interest insofar as they go beyond the specific issues raised by individual cases of repression into the broader area of political manipulation of science: General Piotr Grigorenko's account of his own incarceration and Zhores Medvedev's account of his. Grigorenko explicitly states the problem: admitting that the concept of special psychiatric hospitals is not inherently bad, Grigorenko goes on:

> But the great misfortune is that the whole matter has been completely removed from public supervision and placed in the hands of a specially chosen staff. The doctors are appointed according to a selection process in which no consideration is given to their medical qualifications. Other qualities take precedence, the main one being the ability to submit to authority and to refrain from manifesting any medical initiative. . . . Can psychiatric examinations of political cases be objective if the investigator and the medical experts are subordinate to one and the same superior and are bound by military discipline?[85]

The problem, then, is the subordination of science to a political system or ideology which imposes extra-scientific demands on its scientific practitioners, and the absence of institutional safeguards against the manipulation of those individuals. Again according to Grigorenko: "Although I have never had cause to regret my faith in the honesty of the doctors, I nevertheless insist—as I always have—that a system in which the only hope lies in the honesty of the doctors is worthless."[86]

The case of Zhores Medvedev is instructive because not only was he incarcerated in a psychiatric hospital—although, thanks to publicity, only briefly—the experience of which he recounts in <u>A Question of</u>

Madness; the reason for his incarceration was the circulation in samizdat of his The Rise and Fall of T. D. Lysenko, a history of Soviet genetics and an exploration of the relationship between politics and science. Lysenko, together with I. V. Michurin, attacked Mendelian theories of inheritance, espousing instead a Lamarckian doctrine which held that altering environments could result in altered inherited characteristics. Because Lysenko's theories were a kind of application of Marxist social doctrine to the realm of physical sciences, they were adopted by the state; for thirty years they were the sole acceptable theory in Soviet genetics and agrobiology (the leading Soviet proponent of Mendelianism, Nikolay Vavilov, was arrested in 1940 and died in prison in 1943). Thus for writing a book which probes the political manipulation of one branch of science, Medvedev was subjected to the political manipulation of another branch of science, psychiatry.

Emigration and Samizdat

Zhores Medvedev is now in England. Piotr Grigorenko lives in New York. Tatiana Goricheva works and lives in Paris. Of the authors mentioned in this essay, more than half have emigrated, usually involuntarily, from the Soviet Union and now make their homes in America, Israel and Western Europe. The effects of this emigration on samizdat literature, the relationship between Russian literature abroad and Russian literature at home, both official and unofficial, and the possible future of samizdat are the final points to be considered here. Most of the belletristic authors who once published in samizdat and now publish in Western periodicals regard their countrymen as their primary audience. They publish, in émigré journals like Kontinent, Vremia i my and Grani, fiction, poetry and essays which they hope will reach Russian readers. Some of those Russian readers are, to be sure, members of the growing émigré community around the world. But most of them are still at home, and they seem to be reading what their countrymen in the West write. What emerges from a reading of the émigré periodicals is a confluence of samizdat and émigré literature: parts of every issue of virtually every magazine are given over to current samizdat writing, and parts are given to writers in emigration. Obviously the channel to the West is far wider than the channel to the East; nevertheless, the extent of samizdat works which address themselves to writing published in Western periodicals indicates that there is a two-way flow, if not an equal one.

A similar confluence is visible in the relationship of official and unofficial writing within the Soviet Union. A certain school of thought holds that no honest writer can publish officially in the Soviet Union. Iuri Maltsev, for instance, a highly intelligent and perceptive critic, views with something bordering on contempt official Soviet writers who edge toward the truth but, in the hopes of publication, pervert or distort or limit their explorations. Others

are even harsher, concluding that nothing published officially in
the Soviet Union is even worth considering, given the process of
emasculation, self-censorship and external censorship which a writer
must surmount to publish his work. On the other hand, an author like
Andrei Siniavski disagrees. He not only considers some of what is
officially published valuable literature; he concludes that such
literature is published partially as a result of the existence of
samizdat:

> With the appearance of ventures which the state interprets
> as hostile to itself—samizdat, the activities of the dissi-
> dents and so on—the censorship has tended to be more lenient
> with certain official writers, who are therefore permitted
> to deal quite boldly with subjects which, although not the
> most burning in social and political terms, are nonetheless
> of considerable peripheral interest, like the subject of the
> Soviet past and individual destinies. You thus have writers
> operating completely within the official limits who never-
> theless write interesting works. And the state is obliged
> to tolerate them, because if they banned them completely
> they would all go straight into samizdat or emigrate to the
> West. . . . The influence of dissident literature is very
> real, not because the official writers are starting to imi-
> tate the dissidents—though I would interject and say that
> imitation is not exactly the right word, and that there cer-
> tainly is a confluence between dissident and official
> writers—but because the decision of so many writers to become
> dissidents is forcing the authorities to somewhat loosen the
> screws.[87]

A number of authors who warily tread that wavering line between
official and unofficial literature have been the beneficiaries of
samizdat, in precisely the sense that Siniavskii means: Iuri Trifonov, for one, whose untimely death in 1981 cut off a series of works
increasingly bold, probing and—one would have thought—officially unacceptable, was published in the pages of Druzhba narodov, a magazine
often erroneously labeled "conservative." In nonbelletristic writing
a similar symbiosis exists, though the more directly political the
samizdat, the less its direct impact on official publications. A
book like historian Aleksandr Nekrich's June 22, 1941, which was published in the mid-1960s but was almost immediately withdrawn from
virtually all libraries, went on to circulate in samizdat: it was
certainly read by Soviet historians, and will be used by scholars as
a source, however unacknowledged until the political climate eases,
for their own more cautious and tolerated work. The massive samizdat writings on psychiatric abuses have at least generated discussion
within the profession—and the fact that a number of the samizdat works
on the subject are written by anonymous practicing psychiatrists suggests that while psychiatry may not immediately change in any dramatic fashion, the theoretical groundwork exists for such changes. A
relatively new book, on environmental abuse and destruction in the

Soviet Union, has been written by a pseudonymous Soviet ministry official under the nom de plume of Boris Komarov; the fact that he chose
to write pseudonymously suggests not only that he is afraid of repressive measures had he written under his own name, but also that
there exist in official offices and ministries individuals who are
conscious of the kind of problems he describes, are willing to write
about them, and may—as long as their identity is protected—eventually
be able to influence official policy.

This, then, is perhaps the greatest achievement of Soviet samizdat: that it has raised a generation of readers and writers who don't
care whether a piece of writing is labeled "official" or "unofficial,"
samizdat or tamizdat, émigré or internal. These writers, these
readers care rather about the quality and the integrity of a work.
And in that sense there is only one Russian literature, undivided by
geographical or political boundaries. No policy dictated by the
Soviet regime can turn back or reverse the development of readers'
consciousness or taste—thus the future of Russian literature, in samizdat or elsewhere, seems guaranteed.

NOTES

1   Boris Shragin, "Dumat'!" ["To Think"] Vestnik RSKhD (Paris):
    No. 98, IV-1970; p. 93.

2   Lydia Chukovskaya, The Deserted House (New York: Dutton,
    1967), p. 7.

3   Iurii Mal'tsev, Vol'naia russkaia literatura [Free Russian
    Literature] Frankfurt: Posev, 1976; p. 16. My translation.

4   For details of the Pasternak affair, see for instance Abraham
    Rothberg, The Heirs of Stalin (Ithaca and London: Cornell
    Univ. Press, 1972); Robert Conquest, The Pasternak Affair:
    Courage of Genius (Philadelphia: Lippincott, 1962); Max Hay-
    ward, "Pasternak's Dr. Zhivago," Encounter (London): May
    1958.

5   For the text of Pasternak's apologia, see Conquest.

6   Max Hayward, On Trial: The Case of Sinyavsky (Tertz) and
    Daniel (Arzhak), eds., Leopold Labedz and Max Hayward (London:
    Collins & Harvill, 1967), p. 5.

7   Sidney Monas, "Engineers or Martyrs: Dissent and the Intelli-
    gentsia," in A. Brumberg, ed., In Quest of Justice (New York:
    Praeger, 1970), pp. 32-34.

8   For an account of this period, see Rothberg, pp. 71-84.

9   For a fuller account, see Rothberg, pp. 127-33. In an ironic footnote to the Brodski trial, Mikhail Kheifets, the editor and annotator of a 5-volume samizdat collection of Brodski's poetry, was arrested in 1974 and sentenced to six years.

10   For English text of trial transcript see Encounter (London): Sept. 1964; pp. 84-91.

11   See, for instance, New York Times Book Review, July 21, 1964.

12   The repressions were documented by Viacheslav Chornovil in The Chornovil Papers (Toronto: McGraw Hill, 1968).

13   Perhaps the best overview and analysis of the trial and its significance is provided by Max Hayward, in his introduction to On Trial (see fn. 6).

14   Hayward, p. 26. Hayward also points out that even in Brodski's case the charge of parasitism was based on the defendant's way of life, not on the content of any of his works (p. 24).

15   Hayward, p. 28.

16   Lidiia Chukovskaia, "Otkrytoe pis'mo pisatel'nitsy L. Chukovskoi Mikhailu Sholokhovu." Grani (Frankfurt): No. 62, Nov. 1966. My translation.

17   Rothberg, p. 252.

18   Peter Reddaway, ed. and tr., Uncensored Russia: Protest and Dissent in the Soviet Union (London: Cape and New York: McGraw Hill, 1972), p. 15.

19   Peter Reddaway, "Can the Dissidents Survive?" Index on Censorship (London): Aug. 1980; Vol. 9; No. 4; p. 29.

20   Reddaway, Uncensored Russia, p. 26.

21   The collection was published in the West as Iz-pod glyb (Paris: YMCA, 1974), in English as From Under the Rubble (Boston-Toronto: Little, Brown, 1975).

22   Aleksandr Nekrich, "Rewriting History," Index on Censorship (London): Aug. 1980; Vol. 9; No. 4; p. 6.

23   Leonid Finkelstein, in Martin Dewhirst and Robert Farrell, eds., The Soviet Censorship (Metuchen, N.J.: Scarecrow Press, 1973); pp. 50 ff.

24   Andrei Sinyavsky, "Samizdat and the Rebirth of Literature,"
      Index on Censorship (London): Aug. 1980; Vol. 9; No. 4; p. 8.

25   Recounted by Natalia Belinkova in Dewhirst and Farrell, pp.
      81-82.

26   Anatoli Kuznetsov, in Dewhirst and Farrell, p. 27.

27   Anatoli Gladilin, The Making and Unmaking of a Soviet Writer
      (Ann Arbor, Mich: Ardis, 1979), p. 16.

28   Nekrich, p. 5.

29   Nekrich, p. 5.

30   Mark Popovsky, "Science in Blinkers," Index on Censorship
      (London): Aug. 1980; Vol. 9; No. 4; pp. 15-17.

31   Sinyavsky, p. 10.

32   Geoffrey Hosking, Beyond Socialist Realism (London: Granada,
      1980), p. 156.

33   Hosking, p. 145.

34   Cited by Rothberg, p. 79.

35   Maltsev, p. 145; my translation.

36   Nadezhda Mandelshtam, Hope Abandoned (New York: Atheneum,
      1974), p. 9.

37   Mandelshtam, p. 10.

38   Nadezhda Mandelshtam, "Moe Zaveshchanie" ["My Testament"]
      Vestnik RSKhD (Paris): No. 100, II-1971; pp. 153-60; Eng. in
      Survey (London): Winter 1972.

39   Sinyavsky, p. 11.

40   Ronald Hingley, Nightingale Fever (New York: Knopf, 1981),
      p. 173.

41   Hingley, p. 244.

42   For account, see Hingley, p. 238.

43   Mandelshtam, pp. 10-11.

44   Iuri Galanskov, tr. in Bosley, Russia's Other Poets (London:
      Longman and New York: Praeger, 1968), p. 29.

45   Cited by Gene Sosin, "Magnitizdat," in Rudolf Tokes, ed., Dissent in the USSR (Baltimore and London: Johns Hopkins Univ. Press, 1975), p. 277.

46   Aleksandr Galich, Pokolenie obrechennykh. Frankfurt: Posev, 1972 and 1975; tr. in Sosin, p. 287.

47   Galich, Pokolenie obrechennykh; tr. in Sosin, p. 242.

48   Ěkho (Paris): No. 2, 1980; p. 6. My translation.

49   Sinyavsky, p. 9.

50   Gladilin, Prognoz na zavtra. Frankfurt: Posev, 1972; pp. 150-51. My translation.

51   Vladimir Maramzin, Blondin obeego tsveta (Ann Arbor, Mich.: Ardis, 1975).

52   Venedikt Erofeev, Moskva-Petushki (Paris: YMCA, 1976); p. 144. My translation.

53   Mikhail Geller, in Varlam Shalamov, Kolymskie rasskazy (London: Overseas Publications Ltd., 1978), p. 11. My translation.

54   Chukovskaya, p. 8.

55   Maltsev, p. 208.

56   For a good introduction to Olitskaia's memoirs, see Dmitrii Pospielovskii, "Razvenchennyi Lenin. O vospominaniakh Ekateriny O." ["Lenin Debunked: On Ekaterina O.'s Memoirs"] Posev (Frankfurt): No. 2, Feb. 1972; pp. 40-46.

57   Robert Slusser, "History and the Democratic Opposition," in Tokes, p. 329.

58   Cited by Slusser; p. 330.

59   Petr Iakir, "Stalinu--k ugolovnoi otvetstvennosti," Rus. mysl' (Paris): April 24, 1969; Eng. in Survey (London): Winter-Spring 1969 and Problems of Communism (Washington, D.C.): July-Oct. 1969.

60   Translated in Reddaway, Uncensored Russia, pp. 428-29.

61   Anatolii Marchenko, Moi pokazaniia (Frankfurt: Posev, 1969), p. 5.

62   Dmitrii Nelidov, "Ideokratichskoe soznanie i lichnost',"
      <u>Vestnik</u> <u>RSKhD</u> (Paris): No. 106, I-1974. Eng. tr. in Michael
      Meerson-Aksenov and Boris Shragin, <u>The Political</u>, <u>Social and</u>
      <u>Religious Thought of Russian</u> "<u>Samizdat</u>"—an <u>Anthology</u> (Belmont,
      Mass.: Nordland, 1977).

63   Bohdan Nahaylo, "The Non-Russians: Alive, If Not Well," <u>Index</u>
      <u>on Censorship</u> (London): Aug. 1980; Vol. 9; No. 4; p. 39.

64   George Luckyj, "Turmoil in the Ukraine," in Brumberg, p. 54.
      The report itself was published by Suchasnist (Munich), in
      1965.

65   See fn. 12.

66   Nahaylo, p. 39.

67   Marite Sapiets, "Lithuania's Unofficial Press," <u>Index</u> on <u>Cen-
      sorship</u> (London): Aug. 1980; Vol. 9; No. 4; p. 35.

68   Meerson-Aksenov and Shragin, p. 585.

69   Vladimir Lazaris, "The Saga of Jewish Samizdat," <u>Soviet</u> <u>Jewish</u>
      <u>Affairs</u> (London): I-1979; Vol. 9; No. 1; p. 5.

70   Lazaris, p. 7.

71   Dimitry Pospielovsky, "The Jewish Question in Russian Samiz-
      dat," <u>Soviet</u> <u>Jewish</u> <u>Affairs</u> (London): 2-1978; Vol. 8; No. 2;
      pp. 3-23. See also his "Russian Nationalist Thought," in
      <u>Soviet</u> <u>Jewish</u> <u>Affairs</u>, I-1976; Vol. 6; No. 1; pp. 3-17.

72   Aleksandr Galich, <u>General'naia</u> <u>repetitsia</u>, Frankfurt: Posev,
      1974; Grigorii Svirskii, <u>Zalozhniki</u> (Paris: Reunis, 1974).
      Eng. tr.: <u>Hostages</u> (New York: Knopf, 1976).

73   Cited by Lazaris, p. 15.

74   Pospielovsky, "The Jewish Question in Russian Samizdat," p. 12.

75   Aleksandr Yanov, <u>The</u> <u>Russian</u> <u>New</u> <u>Right</u> (Berkeley: Inst. of
      International Studies, 1978), p. 63.

76   See Yanov, pp. 62 ff. Yanov also devotes a chapter to Gennadi
      Shimanov's thoughts and dogmas.

77   Meerson-Aksenov and Shragin, p. 506.

78   Translation in <u>Solzhenitsyn</u>: <u>Critical</u> <u>Essays</u> <u>and</u> <u>Documentary</u>
      <u>Material</u>, edited by John Dunlop, Richard Haigh and Alex
      Klimoff (London: Collier Macmillan, 1975), 2nd ed., p. 554.

His letter echoes points raised in 1965 by Fathers N. Eshliman and Gleb Iakunin, in their letter to the Patriarch, published in Grani (Frankfurt): No. 61, Oct. 1966, and translated in St. Vladimir's Seminary Quarterly (New York): Vol. X, Nos. 1-2.

79   Anatolii Levitin-Krasnov, "O polozhenii Russkoi Pravoslavnoi Tserkvi," Vestnik RSKhD (Paris): No. 95-96, I-II-1970; pp. 75-92.

80   Barbara Wolfe Jancar, "Religious Dissent in the Soviet Union," in Tokes, p. 205.

81   Philip Walters, "Christian Samizdat," Index on Censorship (London): Aug. 1980; Nov. 9; No. 4; pp. 47-48.

82   Cited by Walters, p. 48.

83   "Nevezhestvo na sluzhbe proizvola," Vestnik RSKhD (Paris): No. 101-102, III-IV-1971; pp. 153-75; No. 103, I-1972; pp. 223-36; No. 104-105, II-III-1972; pp. 172-77. Eng. in Survey (London): August 1973; pp. 45-65; Vol. 19; No. 4.

84   For a comprehensive discussion based largely on samizdat sources, and with a section of documents which includes the Bukovskii-Gluzman manual, see Sidney Bloch and Peter Reddaway, Psychiatric Terror (New York: Basic Books, 1977). British edition: Russia's Political Hospitals (London, 1977).

85   P. G. Grigorenko, The Grigorenko Papers (Boulder, Col.: Westview, 1973), pp. 127-28.

86   Grigorenko, p. 132.

87   Sinyavsky, p. 9.

Soviet Dissident Literature

A

A.B.: See AGURSKII et al. (#11).

1 A.B.V. and G.D.E. "Pamiati Mura"; "Sredniaia Aziia"; "Oblaka"; "Utrennii sonet," NOVYI ZHURNAL (New York): No. 80, Sept. 1965; pp. 41-44. Poems.

2 A.G.U. "Iosifu Brodskomu"; NOV. RUS. SLOVO (New York): Nov. 13, 1966; p. 4. Poems.

ABOVIN-EGIDES: See Poiski No. 2 (#941).

3 ADMONI, VLADIMIR. [b. 1909] "Rekviem." VREMIA I MY (New York/Paris/Jerusalem): No. 45, Sept. 1979; pp. 78-85. Poem.

4 _____. "Tret'ia vstrecha"; "a pereklichka let. . . ." ÈKHO (Paris): No. 3, 1980; pp. 137-40. Poems.

5 _____. "Zimniaia pamiat'." KONTINENT: No. 27, 1981; pp. 71-75. Poem.

6 AFANAS'EVA, ZOIA. "Otechestvo nam--tsarskoe selo." GRANI (Frankfurt): No. 107, Jan.-March 1978; pp. 68-73. Poem.

7 AGURSKII, MIKHAIL (MELIK). [b. 1933, em. 1974] "Mezhdunarod-noe znachenie 'Pis'ma k vozhdiam'." ["The International Significance of 'Letter to Leaders'"] VESTNIK RKhD (Paris): No. 112-113, II-III-1974; pp. 217-25.
    Brief essay comparing Zionism and Russian nationalism in the context of Solzhenitsyn's "Letter to the Soviet Leaders"; thinks Western critics misunderstand Solzhe-nitsyn's desire for a dictatorship which would not be totalitarian and would represent great progress.

8 _____. "Evrei-khristiane v russkoi pravoslavnoi tserkvi." ["Jewish Christians in the Russian Orthodox Church"] VESTNIK RKhD (Paris): No. 114, IV-1974; pp. 52-71; No. 115, I-1975; pp. 117-38; No. 116, II-III-IV-1975; pp. 86-108.

_____. (AGURSKIJ) "Die Judenchristen in der Russisch-Orthodoxen Kirche." OSTKIRCHLICHE STUDIEN (Würzburg): Vol. 23, No. 3, Sept. 1974; pp. 137-76; Vol. 24, No. 4, Dec. 1974; pp. 281-300. Tr., P. Coelestin Patock and Hannelore Tretter.
    Historical analysis of Jews who converted to Russian Orthodoxy, the role of Orthodox missionaries, the failure to organize an all-church mission and the church's in-ability to combat Russian antisemitism toward converted,

AGURSKII

baptized ex-Jews. Discusses several individual cases of conversion, their causes and consequences.

9   AGURSKII, MIKHAIL (MELIK). "Neonatsistskaia opasnost' v Sovetskom Soiuze." ["Neonazi Danger in the Soviet Union"] NOVYI ZHURNAL (New York): No. 118, March 1975; pp. 119-227. (Eng. tr. in MEERSON-AKSENOV and SHRAGIN, #801.)
Essay describes influence of neo-Nazi movement in Soviet Union, to be seen in anti-Semitic propaganda and the exculpation of Nazis for the Holocaust as presented in unofficial lectures which form Soviet public opinion.

10   _____. "V chem pravy i nepravy brat'ia Medvedevy." ["The Medvedev Brothers: Partly Right, Partly Wrong"] RUS. MYSL' (Paris): Dec. 27, 1973; p. 4.
Brief assessment of Medvedevs' views on detente.

AGURSKII, MIKHAIL: See also Al'manakh Samizdata, No. 1 (#49).

11   AGURSKII, M. S., BARABANOV, E. V., BORISOV, N. M., A.B., KORSAKOV, F., SOLZHENITSYN, A. I., SHAFAREVICH, I. R. Iz-pod glyb: sbornik statei. Paris: YMCA Press, 1974; 276 pp.

_____. (SOLZHENITSYN, A. I. et al.) From Under the Rubble. Boston-Toronto: Little, Brown, 1975; 308 pp. Tr., A. M. Brock, Milada Haigh, Martia Sapiets, Hilary Sternberg, Harry Willetts, under dir. of Michael Scammell.

_____. (SOLJÉNITSYNE, ALEXANDRE et collab.) Des Voix sous les décombres: 7 méditations d'écrivains russes restés à l'Est et 3 de Soljénitsyne. Paris: Seuil, 1975; 296 pp. Tr., J. Michaut, G. Nivat, H. Zamoyska.

_____. (SOLSCHENIZYN, ALEXANDER u.a.) Stimmen aus dem Untergrund: Zur geistigen Situation in der UdSSR. Darmstadt: Luchterhand, 1975; 291 pp.
Collection contains the following essays:
SOLZHENITSYN: "As Breathing and Consciousness Return" (response to Sakharov's "Razmyshleniia," disagreeing with Sakharov's tolerance of socialism); "Repentance and Self-Limitation in the Life of Nations" (relationship between individual and societal qualities—nation as mystically united community of guilt, with destiny of common repentance as step toward renewal); "The Smatterers" (analysis of Russian intelligentsia).
SHAFAREVICH: "Socialism in our Past and Future" (ideological significance of socialism in Russian history, socialism today as an ideal, in theory and practice, and

its future); "Separation or Reconciliation? The Nationalities Question in the USSR" (criticism of those who attack Russian colonialism as unfair and misguided); "Does Russia Have a Future?" (yes--through God and a renunciation of present values).
AGURSKII: "Contemporary Socioeconomic Systems and Their Future Prospects" (compares flaws of capitalism and communism, and discusses future system based on spiritual and moral values).
A.B.: "Direction of Change" (toward Christian consciousness).
KORSAKOV: "Russian Destinies" (Russia's need for Orthodoxy).
BARABANOV: "Schism Between the Church and the World" (which should be obliterated; discusses need for Christian initiative to counter "godless humanism").
BORISOV: "Personality and National Awareness" (the inner source necessary for any national transformation); see #144.

12   AIGI, GENNADII. [b. 1934] "Bez nazvaniia"; "Liubimoe v avguste"; "K utru v detstve"; "Vtoroi madrigal"; "Raspredelenie sada"; "K raspredeleniiu sada." GRANI (Frankfurt): No. 74, Jan. 1970; pp. 171-74. Poems.

13   _____. "Stikhi raznykh let: 'Zdes';' 'Konstantin Leont'ev: Utro v Optinoi Pustyni'; 'Pole za Ferapontom'; 'Progulka: Gvozdiki na mogile Vladimira Solov'eva'; 'Ty--likami tsvetov'; 'Dve berezy'; 'Dolgo: solntse'; 'Ty moia tishina'." VESTNIK RKhD (Paris): No. 118, II-1976; pp. 220-27. Poems.

14   AIKHENVAL'D, Iu. "Dialog o vechnom zhide." GRANI (Frankfurt): No. 70, Feb. 1969; p. 117. Poem.

15   _____. "Iz tsikla 'Vorob'inye pesni'." NOVYI ZHURNAL (New York): No. 116, Sept. 1974; pp. 102-103; No. 117, Dec. 1974; pp. 101-102. Poems.

16   _____. Po grani ostroi. [On the Razor's Edge] Munich: Neimanis, 1972; 290 pp. Poems and stories.

17   _____. (ÈIKHENVAL'D [sic]) "Poèma o moei liubvi." GRANI (Frankfurt): No. 65, Sept. 1967; pp. 38-50. Poem.

18   AKHMADULINA, BELLA. [b. 1937] "From 'Rain'." ENCOUNTER (London): XXVIII No. 5, May 1972; pp. 42-43. Tr., Elaine Feinstein. Poem, later published in Tbilisi.

AKHMADULINA

19   AKHMADULINA, BELLA. "Osen'"; "Biograficheskaia spravka";
     "Snegopad." GRANI (Frankfurt): No. 74, Jan. 1970;
     pp. 3-6. Poems.

     AKHMADULINA: See also Sintaksis (#1072); BOSLEY (#147);
     BRUMBERG (#178); Metropol' (#808).

20   AKHMATOVA, ANNA. [b. 1889, d. 1966] "Dva chetverostishiia
     A. Akhmatovoi: 'Chto voiny, chto chuma. . .'; 'Za menia
     ne budete v otvete'." VESTNIK RSKhD (Paris): No. 100,
     I-1971; pp. 224-25. Poems.

21   _____. "Dva [neizdannykh] pis'ma Anny Akhmatovoi k N.
     Ia. Mandel'shtam." VESTNIK RKhD (Paris): No. 117, I-1976;
     p. 162.
     Two brief personal letters from Akhmatova to N. Mandel'-
     shtam from 1945.

22   _____. "Dva [neizdannykh] stikhotvoreniia: 'Vse, kogo i
     ne zhdali v Italii. . .'; 'Mozhet byt', potom nenavi-
     del. . .'" VESTNIK RKhD (Paris): No. 117, I-1976;
     p. 161. Two poems dated 1958 and 1963.

23   _____. "Kak zhivut poèty v SSSR." RUS. MYSL' (Paris):
     March 8, 1966; p. 1. Poem.

24   _____. "Neizdannaia stranitsa iz vospominanii A. A.
     Akhmatovoi ob O. E. Mandel'shtame." ["Unpublished page
     from Akhmatova's memoirs about O. E. Mandel'shtam"]
     VESTNIK RSKhD (Paris): No. 93, III-1969; pp. 66-67.
     Reminiscence.

25   _____. "Neizdannoe pis'mo A. Akhmatovoi O. Mandel'-
     shtamu." ["Unpublished letter from Akhmatova to O.
     Mandel'shtam"] VESTNIK RKhD (Paris): No. 116, II-III-IV-
     1975; p. 186. Letter.

26   _____. "Neizdannoe stikhotvorenie Anny Akhmatovoi: 'Vse
     ushli, i nikto ne vernulsia'." VESTNIK RSKhD (Paris):
     No. 93, III-1969; p. 65. Poem.

27   _____. "Neizdannyi otryvok iz tragedii 'Son vo sne'."
     ["Unpublished excerpt from 'Dream in a Dream'"] VESTNIK
     RSKhD (Paris): No. 80, I-II-1966; pp. 45-46.
     Excerpt of tragedy written during World War II, burned
     in 1944 and reconstructed and rewritten by Akhmatova in
     the 1960s; at that time only a small portion was published
     in the Soviet Union.

28   AKHMATOVA, ANNA. "Piat' neizdannykh stikhotvorenii: 'Mne
     kazhetsia. . .'; 'Ne liroiu vliublennogo. . .'; 'Drugie
     uvodiat liubimykh'; 'Ty naprasno mne pod nogi mechesh';'
     'Vy menia, kak ubitogo zveria. . .'." VESTNIK RSKhD
     (Paris): No. 95-96, I-II-1970; pp. 126-28. Poems.

29   _____. Poèma bez geroia. Ann Arbor, Mich.: Ardis,
     1973; 54 pp. Tr., Carl Proffer with Assya Humesky.

     _____. Le Poème sans héros. Paris: Segtiers, 1970;
     144 pp. Bilingual ed. Paris: Cinq Continents, 1977;
     96 pp. Tr., Jeanne Rude.
        Poem. See also Requiem. . . . (#30); Selected Poems
     (#32); Sochineniia (#33).

30   _____. "Rekviem." GRANI (Frankfurt): No. 56, Oct.
     1964; pp. 11-17.

     _____. (ACHMATOWA) Requiem Frankfurt: Posev, 1964;
     40 pp. Tr., Mary von Holbeck. Bilingual ed.

     _____. Requiem. Paris: Editions de minuit, 1966;
     47 pp.; 1977; 45 pp. Tr., Paul Valet. Bilingual ed.

     _____. Requiem and Poem Without a Hero. London: Elek
     and Athens, Ohio: Ohio Univ. Press, 1976; 78 pp. Tr.,
     D. M. Thomas.
        Poems. See also Selected Poems (#32), Sochineniia (#33).

31   _____. Selected Poems. London: Oxford University
     Press, 1969; 111 pp. Tr., Richard McKane. Poems.

32   _____. Selected Poems. Ann Arbor, Mich.: Ardis, 1976;
     202 pp. Ed. and tr., Walter Arndt. "Requiem" tr., Robin
     Kemball; "Poem Without a Hero" tr., Carl Proffer. Poems.

33   _____. Sochineniia. [Works] Munich: Inter-Language
     Literary Associates, 1965. Vol. I, 464 pp.
        Poems, some published within the Soviet Union, others
     only in samizdat.

34   _____. "Stikhi: 'V kazhdom kolose telo Khristovo. . .';
     'I vovse i ne prorochitsia. . . .'" VESTNIK RSKhD (Paris):
     No. 101-102, III-IV-1971; pp. 230-31. Poems.

35   _____. Stikhi, perepiska, vospominaniia, kinografiia.
     [Poetry, Correspondence, Memoirs, Scenarios] Ann Arbor,
     Mich.: Ardis, 1977. Ed., E. Proffer.
        Collection of assorted writings.

AKHMATOVA

36   AKHMATOVA, ANNA. "Stikhotvorenie A. A. Akhmatovoi, posvia-
      shchennoe O. Mandel'shtamu." VESTNIK RSKhD (Paris): No. 97,
      III-1970; p. 136. Poem.

37   AKSENOV, VASILII. [b. 1932, em. 1980] "Gibel' Pompei."
      ["The Destruction of Pompei"] VREMIA I MY (New York/Paris/
      Jerusalem): No. 56, Sept.-Oct. 1980; pp. 113-37. Story.

38   _____. Ozhog. [The Burn] Ann Arbor, Mich.: Ardis,
      1980; 442 pp.

      _____. "Arest materi. Poluostrov 'Krym'." VREMIA I MY
      (New York/Paris/Jerusalem): No. 57, Nov.-Dec. 1980;
      pp. 5-29.
      Autobiographical novel which goes from Khrushchev thaw
      years back to Stalin's regime, from life in Moscow in the
      1970s back to the revolution.

39   _____. "Stal'naia ptitsa." ["The Steel Bird"] GLAGOL
      (Ann Arbor, Mich.): No. 1, 1977; pp. 25-95.
      Satiric novella.

40   _____. "Tsaplia." ["The Heron"] KONTINENT: No. 22,
      1980; pp. 118-93. Play.

      AKSENOV, VASILII: See also Metropol' (#808).

41   Al'bom razrushennykh i oskvernennykh khramov. [Album of
      Destroyed and Desecrated Temples] Frankfurt: Posev,
      1981; 224 pp.
      Collection of photographs of and texts on churches,
      monasteries and other religious edifices destroyed or
      damaged, accidentally or deliberately.

      AL'BREKHT, V.: See Vol'noe slovo No. 27 (#1248).

42   ALEINIKOV, V.: See Sfinksy No. 1 (#1011), SMOG (#1080),
      Feniks 1966 (#337); 37 (#1162).

43   ALEKSANDROV, G. M. Ia uvozhu k otverzhennym selen'iam. [I
      Lead Toward Abandoned Settlements] Paris: YMCA, 1975;
      vol. 1, 376 pp.; vol. 2, 392 pp.
      Camp novel, folk epic in style (almost oral narrative)
      on the life in the Gulag of simple Russians.

      ALEKSANDROVA, V: See Nadezhda (#827).

44   ALEKSEEV, IURII. "Peterburg"; "Nad Petropavlovskoiu
      angel. . . ." KONTINENT: No. 22, 1980; pp. 46-49. Poems.

45 ALEKSINA, O. "Dom"; "Posleslovie"; "Mol'ba"; "Sobaka." NOVYI
    ZHURNAL (New York): No. 71, March 1963; pp. 55-57. Poems.

46 _____. "Nezabudka"; "Loshad'"; "Korova"; "Los'";
    "Zakat." NOVYI Zhurnal (New York): No. 70, Dec. 1962;
    pp. 135-41. Poems.

47 _____. "Pole"; "Romans"; "Garderobshchitsa." NOVYI
    ZHURNAL (New York): No. 77, Sept. 1964; pp. 71-73. Poems.

ALESHKOVSKII, IUZ: See Metropol' (#808).

48 ALLILUEVA, SVETLANA. [b. 1925 or 26, em. 1967] Dvadtsat'
    pisem k drugu. New York and Evanston: Harper & Row,
    1967, 216 pp.

    _____. Twenty Letters to a Friend. New York and Evans-
    ton: Harper & Row, 1967; 246 pp. Tr., Priscilla Johnson.

    _____. Vingt lettres à un ami. Paris: Seuil, 1967;
    255 pp. Tr., Jean-Jacques and Nadine Marie.

    _____. (ALLILUJEWA) Zwanzig Briefe an einen Freund.
    Vienna: Molden, 1967; 344 pp. Tr., Xaver Schaffgotsch.
        Memoirs by Stalin's daughter, about his death, Beria's
    "misleading" of Stalin, his responsibility, as she sees it,
    for Stalin's growing isolation; her family life; her
    mother's suicide.

49 Al'manakh Samizdata: nepodtsenzurnaia mysl' v SSSR. [Samiz-
    dat Almanac: Uncensored Thought in the USSR] No. 1.
    Amsterdam: Herzen, 1974; 116 pp.
        Contains works by Sakharov, Agurskii, Khodorovich,
    Liubarskii, Maramzin, Voinovich, Naritsa, Ètkind, Nina
    Bukovskaia, Regel'son, Ginzburg. Of particular interest:
    Agurskii's "Èkonomicheskaia sistema Vostoka i Zapada,"
    also in AGURSKII et al. (#11), Khodorovich's "Obrashchenie
    i ocherk 'Nakazanie bezumiem'" (about Pliushch's mental
    health; also in KHODOROVICH (#525); "Otk. pis'mo Pred.
    VAAP" (see Voinovich #1220).

50 _____. No. 2. Amsterdam: Herzen, 1975; 128 pp.
        Contains collection of appeals and statements entitled
    "Opyt blagotvoritel'noi deiatel'nosti ili istoriia aresta
    Andreia Tverdokhlebova" ["A Venture in Charitable Activity
    or the History of Andrei Tverdokhlebov's arrest"]

51 ALTAEV, O. A. "Dvoinoe soznanie intelligentsii i psevdokul'-
    tura." VESTNIK RSKhD (Paris): No. 97, III-1970; pp. 8-32.

ALTAEV

ALTAEV, O. A. "The Dual Consciousness of the Intelligentsia and Pseudo-Culture." SURVEY (London): Vol. 19, No. 1 (86), Winter 1973; pp. 92-113. Eng. tr. also appears in MEERSON-AKSENOV and SHRAGIN (#801).
Attack on contemporary Russian intelligentsia for its loss of "aristocratic asceticism and sense of guilt before the people," its embourgeoisement, its atheism and denial of the religious foundations of morality, its liberal illusions and its readiness to coexist in a symbiotic relationship with the authorities it criticizes.

52 AMAL'RIK, ANDREI. [b. 1938, em. 1976, d. 1980] "Ideologii v Sovetskom obshchestve." RUS. MYSL' (Paris): Sept. 9, 1976; p. 5; Sept. 16, 1976; p. 5.

_____. "Ideologies in Soviet Society." SURVEY (London): Vol. 22, No. 2 (99), Spring 1976; pp. 1-11.
Schematic analysis of liberalism, Marxism and nationalism, with various subcategories and "subideologies"--conservative, egalitarian, middle-class reformism, etc. Questionable samizdat: written with intention of publishing it in Survey, but almost certainly did circulate within Soviet Union before he left. (Written in 1975)

53 _____. "Inostrannye korrespondenty v Moskve." ["Foreign Correspondents in Moscow"] POSEV (Frankfurt): No. 11, Nov. 1970; pp. 42-48.

_____. "News from Moscow." NEW YORK REVIEW OF BOOKS (New York): March 25, 1971; pp. 9-13.
Account of the ways in which foreign correspondents can, and cannot, and should not, gather information: what the KGB does to stop them; his own experiences with them.

54 _____. "Nezhelannoe puteshestvie v Kalugu." ["Involuntary Journey to Kaluga"] RUS. MYSL' (Paris): July 1, 1976; p. 8; July 15, 1976; p. 8.

55 _____. "Arrest on Suspicion of Courage." HARPERS (New York): Vol. 253, No. 1515, August 1976; pp. 37-56. Tr., Thompson Bradley.
Account of his 24-hour arrest in February 1976; Fr. tr. appeared in L'Express (June 14-20, 1976); German translation in Die Zeit (July 2, 1976).

56 _____. Nezhelannoe puteshestvie v Sibir'. New York: Harcourt Brace Jovanovich, 1970; 294 pp.

8

AMAL'RIK, ANDREI. Involuntary Journey to Siberia. New York:
Harcourt Brace Jovanovich, 1970; 297 pp. Tr., Manya
Harari and Max Hayward.

_____. Voyage Involuntaire en Sibérie. Paris: Galli-
mard, 1970; 296 pp.

_____. Unfreiwillige Reise nach Sibirien. Hamburg:
Christian Wegner, 1970; 242 pp. Tr., N. Nielsen-Stokkeby.
Account of his first trial, his trip east and his life
as an exile on a collective farm, 1965-66. Excerpts first
appeared in L'Express (Nov. 1970).

57   _____. "An Open Letter to Kuznetsov"; "I Want to be
Understood Correctly." SURVEY (London): No. 74/75,
Winter-Spring 1970; pp. 95-110. Also appears in MEERSON-
AKSENOV and SHRAGIN (#801).
Occasioned by 1969 defection of Kuznetsov who had, in
order to be allowed to emigrate, written deliberately absurd denunciations of some writers and actors and who
later justified his actions by claiming that all writers
compromise with the secret police. Amal'rik insists on
the possibility of remaining honest and condemns the
"philosophy of helplessness and self-justification."

58   _____. P'esy. [Plays] Amsterdam: Herzen, 1970;
287 pp.

_____. Nose! Nose? No-se! and other plays. New York:
Harcourt Brace Jovanovich, 1973; 228 pp. Tr., Daniel
Weissbort.

_____. Les quatorze amants de l'affreuse Mary-Ann (et
autres pièces). Paris: Gallimard, 1974; 200 pp. Tr.,
N. Krivocheine and M. Gorbov.

_____. Die Nase & Ist Onkel Jack ein Konformist?
Zurich: Diogenes, 1971. Plays.

59   _____. "Poslednee slovo Andreia Amal'rika." NOV. RUS.
SLOVO (New York): Dec. 13, 1970; p. 3.

_____. "Delo A. Amal'rika." RUS. MYSL' (Paris):
Feb. 11, 1971; p. 2.

_____. "Andrei Amalrik's Final Plea." INDEX ON CENSOR-
SHIP (London): Vol. 1, No. 1, Spring 1972; pp. 79-80.

AMAL'RIK

AMAL'RIK, ANDREI. "Amalrik's Trial." RUSSIAN REVIEW (Stanford, Calif.): Vol. 30, No. 4, 1971; pp. 385-87. Tr., J. Critchlaw.
Memorandum presented to the court since Amal'rik refused to participate in court proceedings. (From Khronika tekushchykh sobytii, No. 17 [#533].)

60 _____. Prosushchestvuet li Sovetskii Soiuz do 1984 goda? Amsterdam: Herzen, 1969; 71 pp.

_____. Will the Soviet Union Survive Until 1984? New York and Evanston: Harper & Row, 1970; 93 pp.

_____. L'Union soviétique survivra-t-elle en 1984? Paris: Fayard, 1970; 118 pp.; Paris: L. G. F., 1977; 317 pp. Tr., Michel Tatu.

_____. Kann die Sowjetunion das Jahr 1984 erleben? Zurich: Diogenes, 1970; 87 pp. Tr., B. Nielsen-Stokkeby.

_____. "Will the Soviet Union Survive Until 1984?" SURVEY (London): No. 73, Autumn 1969; pp. 47-79. Tr., Hilary Sternberg.

_____. "Prosushchestvuet li Sovetskii Soiuz do 1984 goda?" NOV. RUS. SLOVO (New York): May 23, 1970; p. 4; May 25, 1970; p. 2; May 27, 1970; p. 2.; May 28, 1970; p. 2; May 29, 1970; p. 2; May 30, 1970; p. 2; June 1, 1970; pp. 2-3; June 2, 1970; p. 2.
Analysis of the development of the democratic movement in the USSR, and discussion of possible Soviet conflict with China.

61 _____. SSSR i zapad v odnoi lodke. [The USSR and the West in the Same Boat] London: Overseas Publications Interchange Ltd., 1979; 242 pp.
Collection containing Prosushchestvuet li. . . . (#60), "Ideologii v sovetskom obshchestve" (#52), title piece (written in 1975, pub. in New York Times, Oct. 22, 1975), "Est' li politzakliuchennye v SSSR?" ["Are There Political Prisoners in the USSR?" written in 1976, published in Menschenrechte No. 6, 1976] and "Nezhelannoe puteshestvie v Kalugu" (#54).

62 _____. Stat'i i pis'ma 1967-70. [Articles and Letters] Amsterdam: Herzen, 1971; 100 pp.
Collection of writings; includes letters to Izvestia, the Journalists' Union, Kuznetsov (#52); "Inostrannye korrospondenty. . . ." (#53), final plea (#59) et al.

63 AMAL'RIK, ANDREI. "Stikhi Andreia Amal'rika." RUS. MYSL'
    (Paris): Aug. 14, 1975; p. 7. Poems.

AMAL'RIK, ANDREI: See also SLAVINSKY (#1075).

64 AMAL'RIK, GIUZEL'. [b. 1942, em. 1976] Vospominaniia o moem
    detstve. [Memories of my Childhood] Amsterdam: Herzen,
    1976, 153 pp.

_____. Souvenirs d'enfance et de misère. Paris:
Calmann-Levy, 1976; 256 pp.

_____. Eine russische Kindheit. Reinbek b. Hamburg:
Rowohlt, 1976.
    Memoirs of author's childhood as part of poor Tatar
family living in very rough Moscow neighborhood; the effects of poverty and prejudice on sensitive child.

ANATOLII, A.: See KUZNETSOV, A.

65 ANDREEV, DANIIL. "Izmenenie." ["The Alteration"] GRANI
    (Frankfurt): No. 110, Oct.-Dec. 1978; pp. 5-35. Story.

66 ANDREEV, D. [b. 1906, d. 1959] "Stikhi: 'Tuman v lozhbinakh
    techet. . . ; 'Chasy, chasy laskat' glazami'; 'Ty osuzh-
    den. . . '; 'O, ne tak velichave. . . '; 'Tkali v Kitezhe--
    grade. . . .'" VESTNIK RSKhD (Paris): No. 103, I-1972;
    pp. 279-86.
    Poems dating from 1950s, taken from manuscript collec-
tion Zelenaia poima.

67 _____. "Khlebnikov." NOVYI ZHURNAL (New York): No.
    101, Dec. 1970; pp. 107-108. Poem.

ANDREEV, GERMAN: See MEDVEDEV (#772).

68 ANDREEV, PAVEL (Pseud.). "Besprosvet'e i prosvet." ["Hope-
    lessness and Hope"] KONTINENT: No. 22, 1980; pp. 349-65.
    Analysis of Bulgakov's Master and Margarita.

69 Antievreiskie protsessy v Sovetskom Soiuze (1969-71). Doku-
    menty i iuridicheskie kommentarii. [Anti-Jewish Trials in
    the Soviet Union] Ed., A. Rozhanskii. Jerusalem: Hebrew
    Univ. Center, 1979; 2 vols.
    Collection of documents (& commentary) on many trials.

70 ANTOKOL'SKII, P. "My vse, lavreaty premii. . . ." GRANI
    (Frankfurt): No. 56, Oct. 1964; pp. 195-96.
    Poem, listed in Table of Contents under "Stikhi Lenin-
gradskikh poètov."

ANTONOV

71   ANTONOV, N. (Pseud.) "Gody bezvremenshchiny: o romane
     'Sem' dnei tvoreniia' V. Maksimova." ["Years of Timeless-
     ness: about V. Maksimov's novel 'Seven Days of Creation'"]
     GRANI (Frankfurt): No. 89/90, July-Dec. 1973; pp. 229-46.
        Analysis of the Dostoevskian dialectical principle in
     Maksimov's novel, amid generally very favorable evaluation
     of it.

72   _____. "Krest i kamen' (o romane V. Maksimova 'Karan-
     tin')." ["The Cross and the Rock: (About V. Maksimov's
     Novel 'Quarantine')"] GRANI (Frankfurt): No. 92/93,
     April-Sept. 1974; pp. 295-310.

     _____. "Krest i kamen'." RUS. MYSL' (Paris): Sept. 5,
     1974; pp. 4-5.
        Analysis of psychological and spiritual development of
     characters in novel.

73   ANTONOV-OVSEENKO, ANTON. Portret tirana. [Portrait of a
     Tyrant] New York: Khronika, 1980.

     _____. The Time of Stalin: Portrait of a Tyranny. New
     York: Harper & Row, 1981; 374 pp. Tr., George Saunders.
        Author, son of a Bolshevik leader who led the storming
     of the Winter Palace and was purged in 1938, and who him-
     self spent years in Stalin's prisons and camps, discusses
     the collectivization, Stalin-Hitler pact, the purges, etc.,
     and adds new information on Stalin himself.

74   ARDOV, V. [b. 1900] "Vstrecha Anny Akhmatovoi s Marinoi
     Tsvetaevoi." ["Akhmatova and Tsvetaeva's Meeting"] GRANI
     (Frankfurt): No. 76, July 1970; pp. 110-14.
        Reminiscence of meeting author arranged between two
     poets in 1940--their first and probably their last.

75   AR'EV, ANDREI. "Dolgota dnia." ["The Duration of a Day"]
     VREMIA I MY (New York/Paris/Jerusalem): No. 23, 1977;
     pp. 91-124.
        Story from the Leningrad samizdat almanac Chasy (1976).

76   [ARGENTOV, ALEKSANDR.] [b. 1951] "Delo A. Argentova."
     ["The Case of A. Argentov"] VESTNIK RKhD (Paris); No.
     119, III-IV-1976; pp. 281-334.
        Documents pertaining to psychiatric treatment of Argen-
     tov, an Orthodox believer; letters re Argentov, article by
     A. Ogorodnikov on Christian circle in Moscow, letters from
     various religious individuals including Father D. Dudko.

     ARKANOV, ARKADII: See Metropol' (#808).

77   ARKHANGEL'SKII, MAKSIM. "O simvolike rannikh khristianskikh
i pravoslavnykh khramov." ["On the Symbolism of Early
Christian and Orthodox Temples"] NOVYI ZHURNAL (New York):
No. 129, Dec. 1977; pp. 140-54.
About certain repeated architectural symbols, like
basilici, and geometric forms (like triangles) in early
church history.

78   "Artemii Mikhailov." (Anon.) RUS. MYSL' (Paris): Oct. 16,
1975; p. 10. Poem.

ARONOV, A.: See Sintaksis (#1072), BOSLEY (#147).

ARTAMONOV, S.: See Russkoe slovo (#972).

79   ARTEMOVA, A., RAR, L., SLAVINSKII, M. Eds. Kaznimye
sumasshestviem: sbornik materialov. [Prisoners of Mad-
ness] Frankfurt: Posev, 1971; 508 pp.

           . Condamnés à la folie. Paris: Stock.
    Collection of samizdat materials pertaining to incar-
ceration in psychiatric hospitals of mentally healthy individuals, usually for political purposes. Thirty-five
"cases," many of them drawn from Khronika tekushchikh sobytii. Also contains first-hand testimony by people who have
been in psychiatric hospitals, and articles about Soviet
psychiatric repression of dissidents—some samizdat, some
not. Includes Grigorenko's "O spetsial'nykh psikhiatriche-
skikh bol'nitsakh" excerpts from his diaries; Esenin-Vol'-
pin's letter (see #316), sometimes verbatim, sometimes in
paraphrase; excerpt from Naritsa's "Prestuplenie i nakazanie" (see #834); Gorbanevskaia's "Besplatnaia meditsin-
skaia pomoshch'"; "O prinuditel'noi gospitalizatsii v psi-
khiatricheskie bol'nitsy" (from samizdat collection Obsh-
chestvennye problemy).

80   "An Attempt to Understand the Meaning of O. Altayev's article
'The Dual Consciousness of the Intelligentsia and Pseudo-
Culture'." (Anon.) SURVEY (London): Vol. 19, No. 1 (86),
Winter 1973; pp. 114-22.
    Response to ALTAEV (#51): accuses Altaev of attribut-
ing disproportionate significance to the intelligentsia;
says that intelligentsia today is part of the people—all
educated people—and works and "plays an important role in
overall production."

81   AVDEEV, IGOR'. "Zerkal'nye strely. . ."; "Apokalipsis."
GRANI (Frankfurt): No. 85, Oct. 1972; pp. 53-57.
    Poems written by camp inmate, dated 1961; listed in
Table of Contents under "Iz kontslagernoi poèzii."

AVERBUKH

82   AVERBUKH, ISAI. "Proshchanie s Rossiei." NOVYI ZHURNAL (New
     York): No. 106, March 1973; pp. 44–48. Poem.

83   Avgust chetyrnadtsatogo chitaiut na rodine: sbornik statei i
     otzyvov. [August '14 is Read in the Homeland: Collected
     Articles and Responses] Paris: YMCA, 1973; 139 pp.

     _____. "Août quatorze" jugé par les lecteurs russes.
     Paris: Seuil, 1973; 187 pp. Tr., L. Nivat and A. Aucouturier.

     _____. "Avgust chetyrnadtsatogo chitaiut na rodine."
     VESTNIK RSKhD (Paris): No. 104–105, II–III–1972; pp. 178–
     96. (First article from collection, by L. O.; author com-
     pares "historicity" of Solzhenitsyn with Pasternak's and
     Tolstoi's.)
        Collection of reactions, both positive and negative, to
     August 1914, by Soviet readers.

AVRUSIN, A.: See Sintaksis (#1072).

AZARIAN, V.: See 37 (#1162).

B

84 BABEL', I. [b. 1894, d. 1939] "Dnevnik konarmii." ["Diary
    of the Red Army"] RUS. MYSL' (Paris): Jan. 22, 1976; p. 8.
    Sketch, perhaps from draft of Red Cavalry.

85 _____. "Evreika"; "Ikh bylo deviat." ["The Jewess";
    "There Were Nine"] NOVYI ZHURNAL (New York): No. 95,
    June 1969; pp. 5-20.
    Stories, never published, the first dating from 1923,
    the second undated but probably from the 1930s; question-
    able samizdat, since source may be personal archive in West.

86 _____. "Potselui." ["The Kiss"] NOV. RUS. SLOVO (New
    York): Oct. 27, 1975; p. 3.
    Sketch; questionable samizdat, since source may be per-
    sonal archive in West.

    BABUSHKIN, A.: see Vol'noe slovo, No. 7 (#1232).

87 BAKUNINA, E. "O poslednikh dniakh patriarkha Tikhona."
    ["About Patriarch Tikhon's Last Days"] VESTNIK RKhD
    (Paris): No. 115, I-1975; pp. 97-107.
    Description of head of Russian Orthodox Church in the
    1920s, written in 1930.

88 "Ballady o neverii: otryvok iz poèmy 'Dekabristy'." (Anon.)
    POSEV (Frankfurt): No. 36 (1111), Sept. 8, 1967; p. 3.
    Poem.

89 BARABANOV, E. [b. 1943] "Iz interv'iu sotrudniku samizdat-
    skogo zhurnala 'Evrei v SSSR'." ["From an Interview Given
    to a Member of the Samizdat Journal 'Jews in the USSR'"]
    VESTNIK RKhD (Paris): No. 121, II-1977; pp. 111-19.
    Discussion of anti-Semitism as a betrayal of Christiani-
    ty, and the inseparable bonds between Judaism and Chris-
    tianity.

90 _____. "Rannekhristianskaia èstetika." VESTNIK RKhD
    (Paris): No. 116, II-III-IV-1975; pp. 53-76; No. 119, III-
    IV-1976; pp. 71-87; No. 120, I-1977; pp. 49-59; No. 121,
    II-1977; pp. 62-76.
    Discussion of aesthetic views of. early Christian fathers
    (like St. Justin); lack of trust in the beautiful; the
    roles of order and harmony; the Biblical tradition of beau-
    ty and the image of sight ("To look and see not").

91 _____. "Sentiabr'skaia vystavka moskovskikh khodozhnik-
    ov." ["September Exhibit of Moscow Artists"] VESTNIK
    RKhD (Paris): No. 116, II-III-IV-1975; pp. 232-45.
    Description of organization of exhibit and some of the
    works presented.

BARABANOV

92　BARABANOV, E. "Nravstvennaia predposylka khristianskogo edinst-
va." ["The Moral Prerequisite of Christian Unity"] RUS.
MYSL' (Paris): Jan. 3, 1974; p. 5. (#2980) Eng. tr. in
MEERSON-AKSENOV and SHRAGIN (#801).
How Soviet foreign policy makers use ecumenical connections of the church for political and non-Christian ends,
and how Western society ignores the falsehood of fictional
ecumenical relations between free churches and the subju-
gated Russian church.

93　_____. "Sud'ba khristianskoi kul'tury." ["The Fate of
Christian Culture"] KONTINENT: No. 6, 1976; pp. 293-328.

_____. (BARABANOW) Das Schicksal der christlichen Kul-
tur. Köln: Benziger, 1977; 56 pp.
Discussion of the historical growth of the separation
between secular and spiritual life and culture, and its effect on contemporary culture.

94　_____. "Zabytyi spor." ["A Forgotten Quarrel"] VESTNIK
RKhD (Paris): No. 118, II-1976; pp. 117-44.
Discussion of Vladimir Soloviev and Christianity, the
latter as an active, creative process; essay followed by
articles of Soloviev's.

BARABANOV, E.: See also AGURSKII et al. (#11); Vol'noe slovo,
No. 13 (#1237); LITVINOV et al. (#702).

95　BARABANOV, E., AGURSKII, M., SHRAGIN, B., KOPELEV, L. et al.
"Svidetel'stva iz SSSR." ["Testimony from the USSR"]
VESTNIK RSKhD (Paris): No. 111, I-1974, pp. 111-35.
Documents pertaining to Gulag, Solzhenitsyn's arrest and
deportation.

96　BARABANOV (DERZHAVIN, P.). "Zametki o natsional'nom vozrozh-
denii." ["Notes on National Rebirth"] VESTNIK RSKhD
(Paris): No. 106, IV-1972; pp. 259-74.
Discussion of nationalism and "nation" as opposed to
"society"; nation as having physical and spiritual roots,
and a self-consciousness; the relationship of nationalism
and government.

97　BARKOVA, ANNA. [b. 1900, d. 1976] "Obyknovennaia zhizn'";
"Zagon dlia chelovecheskoi skotiny"; "Desiat' chasov";
"Nado pomnit', chto ia stara"; "Net davno rodimoi matush-
ki"; "Pesnia pobeditelei"; "Geroi nashego vremeni"; "Skuka
smertniaia. . ."; "Starukha." VESTNIK RKhD (Paris):
No. 121, II-1977; pp. 289-93.
Poems dating from 1949-55, by woman, writing poetry from
1922 on, who spent total of 22 years in prisons and camps.

98   BATSHEV, VLADIMIR. [b. 1946, em. 197?] "Elabuga." GRANI
      (Frankfurt): No. 70, Feb. 1969; p. 114.
          Poem; Eng. tr. in LANGLAND, ACZEL and TIKOS (#656).

99   _____. "Iz venka sonetov." NOV. RUS. SLOVO (New York):
      No. 11, 1973; p. 5. Poem.

100   _____. "Stikhi: 'Sonet L. K.'; 'Sonet drugu'." GRANI
      (Frankfurt): No. 61, Oct. 1966; pp. 5-13.
          Poems from early samizdat anthologies (Feniks, Sintaksis):
      Eng. tr. in LANGLAND, ACZEL and TIKOS (#656).

101   _____. "N."; "Pervaia pesnia pavshikh"; "Prodolzhaetsia
      god neudach"; "Ia-kak graf"; "Pesnia o serdtse"; "Zamalivai
      grekhi!" GRANI (Frankfurt): No. 63, March 1967; pp. 11-15.
          Poems from early samizdat anthologies.

102   _____. "Volkov pereulok"; "Ia edu na tovarnom. . . ."
      GRANI (Frankfurt): No. 71, May 1969; pp. 7-10. Poems.

      BATSHEV, VLADIMIR: See also BOSLEY (#147), BRUMBERG (#178),
      Feniks 1966 (#337), Sfinksy (#1011), SMOG (#1080), LANGLAND
      et al. (#656).

103   BEK, ALEKSANDR. [b. 1903, d. 1974] Novoe naznachenie. [The
      New Appointment] Frankfurt: Posev, 1971; 234 pp.

      _____. Die Ernennung. Frankfurt: S. Fischer, 1972;
      256 pp. Tr., B. and N. Nielsen-Stokkeby.

      _____. "Moia zhestokaia èpokha." POSEV (Frankfurt):
      No. 8, Aug. 1971; pp. 46-51.
          Novel portraying workings of Soviet party/government
      elite during Stalin's regime; manuscript rejected by Novyi
      mir and then offered, by Novosti, to Western publishers in
      1965, who rejected it as "too communist."

104   BELINKOV, ARKADII. [b. 1921, em. 1968, d. 1970] "'Sobiraite
      metallolom!'." ["Gather Scrap-Metal!"] GRANI (Frankfurt):
      No. 100, Apr.-June 1976; pp. 439-57.
          Excerpt from Sdacha i gibel' sovetskogo intelligenta.
      Iurii Olesha. Parts of book were published in Baikal but
      the bulk of it only in samizdat. A quasi-political, quasi-
      literary analysis of Olesha.

      BELOV, IURII: See Vol'noe slovo, No. 37 (#1256).

105   BELYI, ANATOLII. "O 'Mastere i Margarite'." ["About The
      Master and Margarita"] VESTNIK RKhD (Paris): No. 112-13,
      II-III-1974; pp. 178-203.

BELYI

> Analysis of the main characters (Pilate, Woland, the Master, Margarita) of Bulgakov's novel.

106 BERDNIKOV, I. "Portret"; "Iz tsikla dvadtsati nerealisticheskikh stikhotvorenii." GRANI (Frankfurt): No. 54, Nov. 1963; pp. 63-76. Poems.

107 BERG, MIKHAIL. "Iz knigi 'Zapiski na manzhetakh." ["From 'Notes on the Cuffs'"] ĖKHO (Paris): No. 1, 1980; pp. 90-98. Story.

108 BERGGOL'TS, OL'GA. "Iz dnevnikov Ol'gi Berggol'ts." ["From the Diaries of Ol'ga Berggol'ts"] VREMIA I MY (New York/Jerusalem/Paris): No. 57, Nov.-Dec. 1980; pp. 276-302.
Diary entries by poet describing her arrest in 1938 and still-extant faith in Stalin, some poems of 1939-40, the Leningrad blockade.

109 _____. "Tserkov' 'Divnaia' v Ugliche." VESTNIK RSKhD (Paris): No. 74, III-1964; pp. 56-57. Poem.

110 BERMAN, FILIPP. [b. 1936, em. 1981] "Registrator." ["The Registrar"] VREMIA I MY (New York/Jerusalem/Paris): No. 61, July-Aug. 1981; pp. 5-43.
Excerpt from a novel (to be published by Ardis).

111 BETAKI, VASILII. [b. 1930, em. 1973] "Kapitan"; "V bezoblachnosti nad granitnoi krepost'iu. . . ." NOVYI ZHURNAL (New York): No. 112, Sept. 1973; pp. 91-92. Poems dated 1964.

112 _____. "Maslenitsa"; "Uzhe osennikh pesen stol'ko speto. . . ." NOVYI ZHURNAL (New York): No. 113, Dec. 1973; p. 81. Poems.

113 _____. "Pamiati Chekhoslovakii"; "Zelenyi luch." GRANI (Frankfurt): No. 94; Oct.-Dec. 1974; pp. 141-45. Poems.

114 _____. "Pliaski istorii: siuita dlia akterov i figliarov s orkestrom." GRANI (Frankfurt): No. 91, Jan.-March 1974; pp. 3-14. Poems dated Aug. 1966-Nov. 1973.

115 _____. "'Remontniki'." NOVYI ZHURNAL (New York): No. 114, March 1974; pp. 172-78. Poems.

116 BEZHIN. (Pseud.) "O tak nazyvaemom 'Nekapitalisticheskom puti razvitiia'." ["On the So-called 'Noncapitalist path of Development'."] POSEV (Frankfurt): No. 24 (1099), June 16, 1967; pp. 5-6.
On Third World countries whose governments are neither capitalist nor Marxist but nationalist bureaucracies.

BIALOSINSKAIA, N.: See Sintaksis (#1072).

117 BITOV, ANDREI. [b. 1937] Pushkinskii dom. [Pushkin House]
Ann Arbor, Mich.: Ardis, 1979.

_____. "Dezhurnyi." GLAGOL (Ann Arbor, Mich.): No. 2,
1978; pp. 65-88.
Novel, portions of which were published in Soviet Union
but never the whole work; portrays Soviet "superfluous man."

BITOV, ANDREI: See also Metropol' (#808).

118 BLAGOV, D. (Pseud.) "A. Solzhenitsyn i dukhovnaia missiia
pisatelia." ["A. Solzhenitsyn and the Writer's Spiritual
Mission"] GRANI (Frankfurt): No. 64, June 1967; pp. 116-
49; No. 65, Sept. 1967; pp. 100-128.
Discussion of the role of art in the individual's spiritual development; cult of personality and labor camps,
with specific reference to One Day in the Life of Ivan
Denisovich and reactions, both personal and professional,
to it.

119 BOBYSHEV, DMITRII. [b. 1936] "Meditatsii." VESTNIK RKhD
(Paris): No. 127, IV-1978; pp. 80-84. Poem.

120 _____. "Trizhdy-Tiul'panov." ["Three-times Tiul'panov"]
KONTINENT: No. 12, 1977; pp. 345-52.
Discussion of artist and illustrator Tiul'panov.

121 _____. Zianiia. [The Abyss] Paris: YMCA, 1979;
240 pp. Collection of poems.

_____. "Zianiia: 'Spriamlennye puti'; 'Kak topor bez
toporishcha'; 'Dolgoe delo'; 'Tebia, toskuia o tvoei
propazhe'; 'Mgnoveniia'." VREMIA I MY (New York/Paris/
Jerusalem): No. 41, May 1979; pp. 67-75. Poems.

BOBYSHEV, DMITRII: See also Sintaksis No. 3 (#1072); BOSLEY
(#147); LANGLAND et al. (#656).

BOGIN, M.: See MEDVEDEV (#771).

122 BOGORAZ, IOSIF. [b. 1896] "Nasedka." ["The Stoolie"] KON-
TINENT: No. 3, 1975; pp. 5-70; No. 4, 1975.
Novella by man who spent 1936-41 in camps and 1941-57 in
exile, about mass party member arrests of 1937, mistrustful
atmosphere in cells, bewilderment and incredulity of arrested Communists.

BOGORAZ

123   BOGORAZ, IOSIF. Otshchepenets. [The Renegade] Israel:
       1976. Novel about Communist victim of Great Terror.

124   BOGORAZ, LARISA. [b. 1929] "Melkie besy." ["Petty Devils"]
       KONTINENT: No. 12, 1977; pp. 213-22.
          Essay on "Women's fiction," in particular about Anna Gerts's
       K vol'noi vole zapovednye puti (#377), which exploits samiz-
       dat names and phrases in a sensationalist fashion.

125   BOKOV, NIKOLAI. [b. 1945, em. 1975] Bestseller i drugoe
       (proza). [Bestseller and other prose] Paris: Kovcheg,
       1979; 199 pp.

       _____. "Bestseller (Strady Omozolelova)." GNOSIS (New
       York): No. 1, 1978. Collection of stories.

126   _____. "Budni oppozitsii." ["Everyday Opposition"]
       POSEV (Frankfurt): No. 10, Oct. 1975; pp. 28-31..
          From the samizdat text Opyt polnogo analiza; about
       artists' demonstration in 1974, what he calls "the cold
       civil war" between government and dissidents, and brief his-
       tory of relationship between two over previous 20 years.

127   _____. (TSEST, AEKADII) "Chetyre stikhotvoreniia: 'I
       noch svetla, i vozdukh chist i sukh. . .'; 'Sredi chumy
       prekrasen shumnyi pir!"; 'V tot den' dyshalos' sladko i
       legko'; 'O, zoloto volos, ladonei teplota. . .'." RUS.
       MYSL' (Paris): July 29, 1971; 5. 5. Poems.

128   _____. (VASILII) "Chudesa khimii." ["The Miracles of
       Chemistry"] RUS. MYSL' (Paris): April 6, 1972; p. 7.
       Dramatic sketch.

129   _____. (D. L.) "Dver'." ["The Door"] GRANI (Frank-
       furt): No. 84, July 1972; pp. 20-30. Story.

130   _____. "Filosofiia obviniaemogo filosofa." ["The Phi-
       losophy of an Accused Philosopher"] In Cahiers du Samiz-
       dat, (Brussels): No. 30, Sept. 1975.
          Essay analyzing ethical climate of Soviet behavior con-
       ditioned by fear and lack of free expression.

131   _____. "Gorod i vecher." In Kacheli Sud'by (see below,
       #143). Story.

132   _____. (ÈVUS, DMITRII) "Gorod solntsa." ["City of the
       Sun"] GRANI (Frankfurt): No. 81, Nov. 1971; pp. 3-41.
          Story, science-fiction-like, about three people left on
       an earth destroyed by spider-like beings.

20

133   BOKOV, NIKOLAI. (D. L.) "Krest." ["The Cross"] GRANI
       (Frankfurt): No. 83, May 1972; pp. 14-34. Story.

134   _____. (VASILII) "Natasha i Pivovarov." GRANI (Frank-
       furt): No. 102, 1976. Drama.

135   _____. Nikto. Disangelia ot Marii Dementnoi. GRANI
       (Frankfurt): No. 82, Dec. 1971; pp. 3-91. (Published
       anonymously)

       _____. Nobody, or the Disgospel According to Maria
       Dementnaya. London: Calder & Boyars, 1975; 90 pp. Tr.,
       April Fitzlyon.

       _____. Nikto. Le Disangile selon Maria Dementnaia.
       Paris: Denoel, 1973; 173 pp.

       _____. "The Parable of the Chest." INDEX ON CENSORSHIP
       (London): No. 3, Autumn 1975; p. 61. Excerpt.
       Novella about man working as an "applauder," written in
       experimental and surrealistic style.

136   _____. "Obed na poberezh'i." ["Dinner on the Coast"]
       RUS. MYSL' (Paris): Sept. 11, 1975. Sketch dated 1971.

137   _____. (TSEST, ARKADII) "Prozrenie"; "Na polputi. . .";
       "Otdaisia t'me. . . ." GRANI (Frankfurt): No. 82, Dec.
       1971; pp. 92-93. Poems.

138   _____. "Pustyr'." ["The Wasteland"] GRANI (Frankfurt):
       No. 98, Oct.-Dec. 1975; pp. 132-36. Story dated 1972.

139   _____. "Puteshestvie bez ostanovok." ["Journey Without
       Stops"] RUS. MYSL' (Paris): June 16, 1977.
       Story dated 1972.

140   _____. (TSEST, ARKADII) "Rekviem o Violette." GRANI
       (Frankfurt): No. 89-90, July-Dec. 1973; pp. 98-101. Poem.

141   _____. (VASILII) "Smekh posle polunochi." ["Laughter
       after Midnight"] GRANI (Frankfurt): No. 85, Oct. 1972;
       pp. 61-155.
       Series of very brief, sometimes fragmentary, impressions
       and anecdotes; author chats with Death, giving picture of
       contemporary Soviet life and its falseness.

142   _____. (KOCHETOV, VSEVOLOD and IKS) Smuta noveishego
       vremeni ili Udivitel'nye pokhozdeniia Vani Chmotanova.
       Paris: La Presse Libre, 1970; 46 pp.

BOKOV

BOKOV, NIKOLAI. "Troubles of Recent Times or the Amazing Adventures of Vanya Chmotanov." SURVEY (London): Vol. 17, No. 2 (79), Spring 1971; pp. 20-59.

_____. Les Troubles des temps actuels, ou les étonnants aventures de Vania Tchmotanov. Paris: La Quinzaine litteraire, 1972.

_____. "Smuta noveishego vremeni ili Udivitel'nye pokhozdeniia Vani Chmotanova." RUS. MYSL' (Paris): Nov. 26, 1970; pp. 7-10.

_____. "Smuta noveishego vremeni ili Udivitel'nye pokhozdeniia Vani Chmotanova." NOV. RUS. SLOVO (New York): Dec. 2, 1970; pp. 2-3; Dec. 3, 1970; pp. 2-3; Dec. 4, 1970; pp. 2-3; Dec. 5, 1970; pp. 2-3; Dec. 7, 1970; pp. 2-3; Dec. 8, 1970; p. 2; Dec. 9, 1970; p. 2.
Satire depicting the consequences when the hero steals Lenin's head from the mausoleum.

143 _____. Ed. (with Konstantin Bokov). Kacheli sud'by, [Swings of Fate], reprinted in KOVCHEG (Paris): No. 1, 1978.
Collection of samizdat texts, poems and stories. His own works, "Gorod i vecher" and "A tabachok vroz'," (the latter appearing in APOLLON-77 [Paris] are included; individual works appear under authors' names.

144 BORISOV, VADIM. [b. 1945] "Lichnost' i natsional'noe samo-soznanie." ["Personality and National Awareness"] VESTNIK RKhD (Paris): No. 112-13, II-III-1974; pp. 229-60.

_____. "Lichnost' i natsional'noe samosoznanie." RUS. MYSL' (Paris): Dec. 12, 1974; p. 6; Dec. 19, 1974; p. 6; Dec. 26, 1974; p. 6; Jan. 2, 1975; p. 6.
Essay positing need for an inner source for any national transformation. Contained in AGURSKII et al (#11).

145 BORODAEVSKII, N. (Pseud.) "Anne Akhmatovoi"; "Byt' poètom. . . "; "Bez very Rus'. . . . " VESTNIK RSKhD (Paris): No. 99, I-1971; pp. 104-106. (Editors chose pseudonym.) Poems.

146 BORODIN, L. "O russkoi intelligentsii." ["On the Russian Intelligentsia"] GRANI (Frankfurt): No. 96, April-June 1975; pp. 231-64.
From samizdat journal Veche, No. 8 (1973); answer to four samizdat pieces published in VESTNIK RSKhD, No. 97, 1970 (see N. N., O. Altaev, V. Gorskii and M. Chelnov).

Critical of them because author detects in them no love
for Russia, for the Russian nation. Also discusses the
relationship of the 1917 revolution to prior Russian history, and the role of the intelligentsia in it.

147 BOSLEY, KEITH, Ed. Russia's Other Poets. London: Longman
and New York: Praeger, 1968; 92 pp.
Collection of poems, 1961-66, from various samizdat
journals including Feniks 1 and 1966, Sintaksis 1, 2, and
3, and Sfinksy.

148 BOURDEAUX, MICHAEL. Land of Crosses. Devon: Augustine Pub.
Co., 1979; 339 pp.
Contains many documents on the history of the Lithuanian
religious struggle 1939-78.

149 _____. Ed. Patriarchs and Prophets. London: Macmillan
and New York: Praeger, 1969; 359 pp.
Collection of documents pertaining to dissent within and
persecution of Russian Orthodox Church from 1960-68.

150 _____. Religious Ferment in Russia: Protestant Opposition to Soviet Religious Policy. London and New York:
Macmillan, 1968.
Collection of documents pertaining to Baptist Church,
1960-67.

151 BOURDEAUX, M. and ROWE, M., Eds. May One Believe in Russia?
Violations of Religious Liberty in the Soviet Union.
London: Darton, Longman and Todd, 1980; 113 pp.
Documents on Orthodox, Catholic and Evangelical
Churches.

152 BOURDEAUX, MICHAEL and WIENS, GEORGI. Und die Ketten nicht
fürchten. Neuhausen: Hanssler, 1976; 240 pp. See also
VINS (#1204). Baptist documents.

153 BRODSKII, IOSIF. [b. 1940, em. 1972] "A. A. Akhmatovoi";
"Zimnim vecherom v Ialte." NOV. RUS. SLOVO (New York):
June 9, 1972; p. 3. Poems.

154 _____. "Anne Andreevne Akhmatovoi"; "Ostanovka v
pustyne." GRANI (Frankfrut): No. 72, July 1969; pp. 84-
89. Poems.

155 _____. (BRODSKY) Elegy to John Donne, and other poems.
London: Longman, 1967; 77 pp. Tr., Nicholas Bethell.
Poems.

BRODSKII

156 BRODSKII, IOSIF. "Iz starykh stikhov: 'Leti otsiuda. . . ';
     'Pogranichnoi vodoi. . .'." ÈKHO (Paris): No. 1, 1978;
     pp. 7-17. Poems, all dated before 1968.

157 _____. "Konets prekrasnoi èpokhi." KONTINENT: No. 1,
     1974; pp. 14-17. Poem.

158 _____. Konets prekrasnoi èpokhi: stikhotvorenie, 1964-
     1971. [The End of a Beautiful Era: Poetry, 1964-1971]
     Ann Arbor, Mich.: Ardis, 1977; 114 pp. Poems.

159 _____"Na prachechnom mostu"; "Sonet"; "1 ianvaria 1965
     goda." NOVYI ZHURNAL (New York): No. 95, June 1969;
     pp. 51-52. Poems.

160 _____. "Novaia tetrad' stikhov Iosifa Brodskogo." POS-
     EV (Frankfurt): No. 8 (979), Feb. 19, 1965; p. 3; No. 9
     (980), Feb. 26, 1965; p. 6. Poems.

161 _____. "Odinochestvo." NOVYI ZHURNAL (New York): No.
     98, March 1970; p. 104. Poem.

162 _____. Ostanovka v pustyne: stikhotvoreniia i poèmy.
     [Halt in the Wilderness: Poems] New York: Chekhov, 1970;
     228 pp. Poems.

163 _____. "1 sentiabria 1967 goda"; "Otkazom ot skorbnogo
     perechnia. . . ." GRANI (Frankfurt): No. 76, July 1970;
     pp. 84-85. Poems.

164 _____. "Prorochestvo"; "Pesenka." RUS. MYSL' (Paris):
     Dec. 5, 1968; p. 5. Poems.

165 _____. "Kon' voronoi"; "Pamiatnik Pushkinu"; "Rozhdest-
     venskii romans"; "Ryby zimoi." GRANI (Frankfurt): No.
     56, Oct. 1964; pp. 174-78.
     Poems, listed in Table of Contents under "Stikhi molo-
     dykh Leningradskikh poètov."

166 _____. "Rozhdestvenskii romans"; "Kon' voronoi";
     "Ètiud." POSEV (Frankfurt): No. 21 (940), May 22, 1964;
     pp. 2-3. Poems.

167 _____. (BRODSKY) Selected Poems. Harmondsworth:
     Penguin, 1973; 168 pp. and New York and Evanston, Ill.:
     Harper & Row, 1973; 172 pp. Tr., George Kline. Poems.

168   BRODSKII, IOSIF. "Stikhi ob ispantse-mignèle servete, ere-
tike sozhzhennom kal'vinistami." GRANI (Frankfurt): No.
70, Feb. 1969; pp. 111-12. Poem.

169   _____. Stikhotvoreniia i poèmy. [Verses and Longer
Poems] Washington: Interlanguage Literary Associates,
1965; 236 pp. Poems.

170   _____. Collines et autres poèmes. Paris: Seuil, 1966;
112 pp. Tr., J. J. Marie.
Poems drawn from Stikhotvoreniia (#169).

171   _____. (BRODSKIJ) Ausgewählte Gedichte. Esslingen am
Neckar: Bechtle, 1966; 60 pp. Tr., H. Ost and A. Kaempfe.
Poems.

172   _____. "Stuk"; "Iiul'skoe intermetstso." GRANI (Frankfurt): No. 68, July 1968; pp. 5-6. Poems.

173   _____. "Zimnim vecherom v Ialte"; "Stikhi v aprele."
NOVYI ZHURNAL (New York): No. 97, Dec. 1967; pp. 33-34.
Poems.

174   _____. "Otryvok iz zapisei zasedaniia suda nad I.
Brodskim." ["Excerpt from I. Brodskii's trial transcript"]
POSEV (Frankfurt): No. 3 (1130), March 1968; p. 51.

        _____. "Trial of a Young Poet." ENCOUNTER (London):
Vol. XX, No. 9, Sept. 1964; pp. 84-91.

        _____. "The Trial of Iosif Brodsky." NEW LEADER (New
York): Aug. 31, 1964; pp. 6-17.
Protocol of trial in Feb.-March 1964, in which judge
held that being a poet is not considered a job, and writing is not work. Brodskii was sentenced to five years
forced labor.

    BRODSKII, IOSIF: See also BOSLEY (#147), BRUMBERG (#178),
Sintaksis (#1072).

175   BROWNE, M., Ed. Ferment in the Ukraine. London: Macmillan
and New York: Praeger, 1971, 267 pp.
Collection of Ukrainian samizdat documents, 1964-69,
with an extensive bibliography.

176   BRUDERER, G., Ed. Protsess tsepnoi reaktsii: sbornik dokumentov po delu Iu. T. Galanskova, A. I. Ginzburga, A. A.
Dobrovol'skogo, V. I. Lashkovoi. [The Process of a Chain

BRUDERER

Reaction: Collection of Documents on the Case of Galanskov, Ginzburg, Dobrovol'skii and Lashkova] Frankfurt:
Posev, 1971; 488 pp.
Collection of documents (letters, appeals, etc.) pertaining to Jan. 1968 trial of Aleksandr Ginzburg, who compiled samizdat collection of texts on Siniavskii/Daniel'
trial (see #380), Iurii Galanskov, who was involved with
editing and distributing samizdat journal Feniks 66, typist
Vera Lashkova and Alexei Dobrovol'skii for connections with
Russian emigré organization NTS, etc. The last turned
state's evidence, receiving two years; Ginzburg got five
and Galanskov seven. See also LITVINOV (#701).

177 BRUDERER, G. Sowjetische Stimmen zum Russland von morgen.
Programm Dokumente und Entwicklungstendenzen in der Sowjetunion. Bern: Verlag SOI, 1971; 64 pp. Documents.

178 BRUMBERG, ABRAHAM, Ed. In Quest of Justice: Protest and Dissent in the Soviet Union. New York: Praeger, 1970; 477 pp.
Bulk of book consists of samizdat documents pertaining
to trials of various dissidents (Bukovskii, Ginzburg and
Galanskov), nationalities problem, religious dissent,
Czech invasion, as well as poems, short stories and essays
from Feniks (1 and 1966) and Sintaksis.

179 BUGAEVA, KLAVDIIA. "Ob Andree Belom." ["About Andrei Belyi"]
NOVYI ZHURNAL (New York): No. 102, March 1971; pp. 103-109.
Sentimental memoir of poet's act of creating, by widow.

180 _____. "Andrei Belyi na Kavkaze." ["Andrei Belyi in the
Caucasus"] NOVYI ZHURNAL (New York): No. 103, June 1971;
pp. 125-36.
Widow's reminiscence of her trip with husband, his
power of retaining impressions.

181 _____. "Andrei Belyi v zhizni." ["Andrei Belyi as He
Was"] NOVYI ZHURNAL (New York): No. 108, Sept. 1972,
pp. 169-88.
Widow remembers poet's moral stature and personal
qualities.

182 BUKOVSKAIA, NINA. Pis'ma materi. [A Mother's Letters] New
York: Khronika, 1976; 31 pp.
Letters to and about her son Vladimir (see below), his
trial, etc.

183 BUKOVSKAIA, TAMARA. [b. 1947] "Stikhi: 'Sirotstvuia v
otechestve svoem. . .'; 'I gubu zakusiv, ètot vozdukh
muchitel'nyi pei. . .'; 'Nikogda ne vernetsia mladenchestva

legkoe schast'e'; 'Kogda by nam. . .'; 'V aprele myslimy
takie vechera. . .'; 'Esli, Gospodi. . .'; 'Iz tsikla
Shest' tsitat iz Katulla'; 'I tselyi den' ne idet s uma
. . .," "Starykh chashek sukhoi perezvon." VESTNIK RKhD
(Paris): No. 124, I-1978; pp. 148-52. Poems.

184   BUKOVSKII, VLADIMIR. [b. 1941, em. 1976]   "Geroicheskoe
vystuplenie--poslednee slovo podsudimogo Bukovskogo Vladimira Konstantinovicha." RUS. MYSL' (Paris):   Jan. 18,
1968; pp. 3-4.

_____. "Poslednee slovo." NOV. RUS. SLOVO (New York):
Jan. 23, 1968; p. 3.

_____. "Ia absoliutno ne raskaivaius'. . . ." POSEV
(Frankfurt): No. 2 (1129), Feb. 1968; pp. 18-21.
   Bukovskii's final trial statement, Sept. 1, 1967; together with Vadim Delone and Evgenii Kushev he was tried
for demonstrating in support of Galanskov and Dobrovol'skii;
he was sentenced to three years hard labor. In his statement he defends their actions as being in conformity with
Soviet Constitution. Eng. tr. in BRUMBERG (#178).

185   _____. "Odin bestolkovyi vopros doktoru." ["One Point-
less Question for the Doctor"] RUS. MYSL' (Paris):   Jan.
11, 1968; p. 5. Story.

186   _____. "Poslednee slovo Vladimira Bukovskogo." RUS.
MYSL' (Paris): Feb. 24, 1972; p. 5.

_____. "Poslednee slovo Vladimira Bukovskogo." NOV.
RUS. SLOVO (New York): March 26, 1972; p. 3.

_____. "Prestupnik tot, kto v izbe sorit." POSEV
(Frankfurt): No. 3, March 1972; pp. 2-4.

_____. "Poslednee slovo na sude." NOVYI ZHURNAL (New
York): No. 106, March 1972; pp. 249-54.
   Bukovskii's final statement at 1972 trial, where he was
charged under Article 70 of the Soviet Criminal Code for,
among other things, "maintaining that in the USSR sane
people are placed in mental hospitals where they are subjected to inhuman treatment," and for providing foreign
correspondents with information on that subject. In statement he describes abuses of his legal rights and punish-
ments he had observed being administered at Leningrad
Special Psychiatric Hospital. Eng. tr. in "The Case of
Vladimir Bukovsky," SURVEY (#189). Taken from Khronika
tekushchikh sobytii No. 23 (#537).

BUKOVSKII

187   BUKOVSKII, VLADIMIR. "Rasskazy." GRANI (Frankfurt): No. 65,
Sept. 1967; pp. 10–17.
     Stories. Eng. tr. in SCAMMELL (#1005), one in BRUMBERG
(#178).

188   _____. (BOUKOVSKY) Une nouvelle maladie mentale en
URSS: l'opposition. Paris: Seuil, 1971; 238 pp. Tr.,
F. Simon.

    _____. (BUKOWSKIJ) Opposition: Eine neue Geisteskrank-
heit in der Sowjetunion: Eine Dokumentation. Munich:
Hanser, 1971; 198 pp. Tr., Willy Thaler (from French).

    _____. Die "Neue Krankheit" –– Schizoinakomyslie. Bern:
Kuratorium Geistige Freiheit, 1971; 40 pp.
     Collections of documents by and about Bukovskii and
psychiatric repression of dissidents.

189   _____. "Protsess po delu Vladimira Bukovskogo." RUS.
MYSL' (Paris): March 2, 1972; pp. 5–7.

    _____. "The Case of Vladimir Bukovsky." SURVEY (Lon-
don): Vol. 18, No. 2 (823), Spring 1972; pp. 123–60.
     Trial transcript; he received two years prison, five
years camp, five years exile. Taken from Khr. tek. sob.
Nos. 23 and 24 (#537, #538).

190   BUKOVSKII, VLADIMIR and GLUZMAN, SEMEN. "A Manual on Psychiatry for Dissidents." SURVEY (London): Vol. 21, No. 1/2
(94/95), Winter-Spring 1975; pp. 180–200.
     Summarizes basic principles of psychiatric theory needed
to assure behavior least likely to incur charge of non-
responsibility. Discusses laws on psychiatry, the practice
of diagnosing schizophrenia for political purposes, the
psychology of the psychiatrist, tactical advice for behavior both during investigations and in psychiatric hospitals. Also in Khr. Zashch. prav No. 13 (#580).

    BUKOVSKII, VLADIMIR: See also BRUMBERG (#178), various docu-
ments pertaining to 1968 trial, Khr. tek. sob. Nos. 23 and
24 (#537, #538), GERSTENMAIER (#376), LITVINOV (#700),
SCAMMELL (#1005), "Sov. Mental Prisons" (#1130), Vol'noe
slovo Nos. 14/15 (#1238), TUMERMAN (#1170).

191   BULGAKOV, MIKHAIL. [b. 1891, d. 1940] Adam i Eva, Bagrovyi
ostrov, Zoikina kvartira: P'esy. Paris: YMCA, 1971;
255 pp.

BULGAKOV, MIKHAIL. "Bagrovyi ostrov." NOVYI ZHURNAL (New York): No. 93, Dec. 1968; pp. 38-76.
Plays, written in 1930, 1927 and 1926 respectively; the latter two performed in twenties but none published in Soviet Union.

202 _____. "Bagrovyi ostrov." KONTINENT: No. 10, 1976; pp. 343-62.
Story published in 1924 in Berlin, never since and never in Soviet Union.

203 _____. Diaboliad, and other stories. Bloomington, Ind.: Indiana University Press, 1972; 236 pp. Tr., Carl Proffer.

204 _____. Diableries; Les oeufs fatidiques. Lausanne: L'Age D'Homme. Stories, some published in USSR in 1920s.

205 _____. Don Kikhot. Letchworth: Prideaux, 1971; 102 pp. Play, performed but never published.

206 _____. Master i Margarita. Paris: YMCA, 1967; 219 pp.; Frankfurt: Posev, 1969; 498 pp.

_____. The Master and Margarita. New York: Signet, 1967; 384 pp. Tr., Michael Glenny. London: Harvill and New York: Harper & Row, 1967; 402 pp. Tr., Mirra Ginsburg.

_____. (BOULGAKOV) Le maître et Marguerite. Paris: Laffont, 1968; 528 pp. Tr., Claude Ligny.

_____. (BULGAKOW) Der Meister und Margarita. Darmstadt: Luchterhand, 1973; 654 pp.
In part satire on Stalinist Russia of 1930s, when the devil comes to Moscow; in part satire on Soviet literary establishment; in part investigation of courage and cowardice both in Soviet Union and in the Jerusalem of Pontius Pilate and Jesus, all built around the Master's novel about Pilate and how Margarita, making a pact with the devil, saves her lover. Censored version of novel was published in MOSKVA, No. 11, 1966 and No. 1, 1967; uncensored version circulated in samizdat, later printed in USSR.

207 _____. Neizdannyi Bulgakov: teksty i materialy. [The Unpublished Bulgakov] Ann Arbor, Mich.: Ardis, 1977; 212 pp. Ed., E. Proffer.
Collection includes assorted letters by (and about) Bulgakov, the play "Batum," excerpts from the play "Belaia gvardiia." Some are certainly archival; some may have circulated in samizdat.

BULGAKOV

208   BULGAKOV, MIKHAIL. "Pis'ma I. V. Stalinu, A. M. Gor'komu,
V. V. Veresaevu, P. S. Popovu i drugim." NOVYI ZHURNAL
(New York): No. 111, June 1973; pp. 151-74.
Letters from 1929-39, generally about his deteriorating
professional position. One requests permission to leave
Russia for a while (from 1929) and again in 1934; one asks
Stalin to help Erdman, who was in exile, etc.

209   _____. "Pis'mo sovetskomu pravitel'stvu." ["Letter to
the Soviet Government"] POSEV (Frankfurt): No. 39 (1114),
Sept. 29, 1967; pp. 3-4.

_____. "Pis'mo Mikhaila Bulgakova pravitel'stvu SSSR."
VESTNIK RSKhD (Paris): No. 85, III-1967; pp. 59-63.

_____. "Pis'mo M. Bulgakova sovetskomu pravitel'stvu."
GRANI (Frankfurt): No. 66, Dec. 1967; pp. 155-61.

_____. "Letter to the Soviet Government" (under "Docu-
ments"). SURVEY (London): No. 67, Winter 1968; pp. 122-27.
Letter, dated May 28, 1930, defending freedom of press,
characterizing his own work and asking permission to go
abroad because of the impossibility of his continuing writing within the Soviet Union.

210   _____. Sobach'e serdtse. Series Student: Flegon Press,
9/10 1968; 93 pp. and Paris: YMCA, 1969; 159 pp.

_____. The Heart of a Dog. New York: Harcourt, Brace
& World, 1968; 146 pp. Tr., Michael Glenny. New York:
Grove Press, 1968; 123 pp. Tr., Mirra Ginsburg.

_____. (BOULGAKOV) Coeur de chien. Paris: Champ
Libre, 1971; 160 pp. Tr., M. Petris; Paris: YMCA, 1977;
159 pp.

_____. (BULGAKOW) Hundeherz. Darmstadt: Luchterhand,
1974; 159 pp.; 1979. Tr., Gisela Drohla.

_____. "Sobach'e serdtse." GRANI (Frankfurt): No. 69,
Nov. 1968; pp. 3-85.
Novella, satire on "new Soviet man," involving trans-
planting of human organs into dog.

211   _____. "Zoikina kvartira." NOVYI ZHURNAL (New York):
No. 97, Dec. 1969; pp. 57-95; No. 98, March 1970; pp. 55-88.
Drama, performed in 1926 and '27, never thereafter staged
or published.

212 BURIAKOVSKAIA, GELENA. "Rasskazy." ÈKHO (Paris): No. 4,
1980.
Stories from Leningrad samizdat journal 37.

BURICH, VLADIMIR. See Sintaksis 1 (#1072), BOSLEY (#147).

213 BURIKHIN, IGOR'. [b. 1943] "Edem i Gomorra." VREMIA I MY
(New York/Paris/Jerusalem): No. 42, June 1979; pp. 95-99.
Poem.

214 _____. Moi dom--slovo. [My House is the Word] Paris:
Tret'ia volna, 1978.
Poems by Leningrad poet published not at all officially,
only in samizdat.

_____. "Tri stikhotvoreniia iz tsikla Moi dom--slovo."
KONTINENT: No. 8, 1976; pp. 155-59. Poems.

215 _____. "V surovuiu zimu ia proboval zhit'. . . : iz
tsikla adonis-brom (1964-72)." VREMIA I MY (New York/
Paris/Jerusalem): No. 26, 1978; pp. 101-108. Poem.

BURIKHIN, IGOR': See also 37 (#1162).

216 [BURMISTROVICH, IL'IA.] [b. 1938] "Sokrashchennaia zapis'
sudebnogo protsessa Il'i Burmistrovicha." ["Abridged
trial protocol of Il'ia Burmistrovich"] POSEV (Frankfurt):
special issue No. 4, June 1970; pp. 43-61.
Transcript of trial; Burmistrovich was arrested for disseminating the works of Siniavskii and Daniel'.

217 BURZHUADEMOV, D. "Dissidenty na rubezhe 80-kh." ["Dissidents
on the Brink of the '80s"] POSEV (Frankfurt): No. 11,
Nov. 1980; pp. 50-53. Pseud. of V. SOKIRKO.
Rather pessimistic analysis of current dissident movement: pessimistic because of increasing dependence on
West (and corresponding shrinking of movement in size within Soviet Union), what he calls "parasitism"; because of
preponderance within movement of potential émigrés; because
of distancing between movement and "real life," and growing indifference on the part of dissidents toward human
rights in broadest sense, as they affect the majority of
citizens.

218 _____. Ocherki rastushchei ideologii. [Works of a
Growing Ideology] Munich: Neimanis, 1974; 271 pp.
Socio-political analysis of Soviet Union containing
pieces on political and economic aspects of Marxism, of
science and capitalism and science and socialism; describes
such everyday matters as the black market, inflation, etc.

C

219 CHAI, IVAN. "Iazykovye trudnosti admirala." ["The Admiral's Language Difficulties"] GRANI (Frankfurt): No. 79, April 1971; pp. 10-22. Story.

220 _____. "Rukopozhat'e nachal'nika." ["The Boss's Handshake"] GRANI (Frankfurt): No. 69, Nov. 1968; pp. 89-106. Story.

221 CHALIDZE, VALERII. [b. 1938, em. 1972] Ed. Andrei Tverdokhlebov: V zashchitu prav cheloveka. New York: Khronika, 1975; 160 pp.
      Collection of documents pertaining to dissident and human rights activist A. Tverdokhlebov.

222 _____. Ed. Prava cheloveka i Sovetskii soiuz. New York: Khronika, 1974; 304 pp.

      _____. To Defend These Rights: Human Rights and the Soviet Union. New York: Random House, 1975; 340 pp.
      Collection of documents on abuses of human rights.

223 _____. Ed. SSSR--Rabochee dvizhenie? [USSR--Workers' Movement?] New York: Khronika, 1978.
      Collection of documents and materials connected with organizing of first free trade union. See also Vol'noe slovo, No. 30 (#1251).

      CHALIDZE, VALERII: See also Dokumenty Komiteta Prav Cheloveka (#275), Khr. tek. sob. No. 22 (#536).

224 CHALIDZE, V. and LIPSON, L., Eds. Documents on Soviet Criminal Procedure Vol. 2. New York: Khronika, 1979, 494 pp.
      Various documents pertaining to Soviet law.

      Chasy: See AR'EV (#75); ROKHLIN (#964).

225 "Chego zhe ty khochesh'?" ["So What Do You Want?"] (Anon.) NOV. RUS. SLOVO (New York): May 24, 1970; p. 3.
      Satiric sketch.

226 CHELNOV, M. "Kak byt'?" ["How to Be?"] VESTNIK RSKhD (Paris): No. 97, III-1970; pp. 69-80. The religion of Communism.

227 CHEREPOV, GENNADII. "Sovet k vykhodiashchim." GRANI (Frankfurt): No. 85, Oct. 1972; p. 60.
      Poem, listed under "Iz kontslagernoi poèzii."

228 Chernaia kniga. Eds., I. Èrenburg and V. Grossman. Jerusa-
     lem: Tarbut, 1980; 547 pp. Annotated and indexed, Mark
     Kipnis and Hayah Lifshits.

     _____. Black Book: The Ruthless Murder of Jews by
     German-Fascist Invaders Throughout the Temporarily Occupied
     Regions of the Soviet Union and in the Death Camps of Po-
     land During the War of 1941-45. New York: Holocaust
     Library, 1981; 595 pp. Tr., John Glad and James Levine.
     Collection of testimony, letters, diaries and essays on
     the fate of Jews in Ukraine, Belorussia, RSFSR and Latvia
     and in camps. MS. was originally compiled by editors in
     1944-46, was prepared for publication but never came out,
     and in 1948 the printing plates were destroyed. Copies of
     MS. were sent abroad--to the U.S., England, Romania and
     Palestine--and this edition is based on one of those. Not
     strictly speaking samizdat.

229 Chernaia kniga: Moskovskaia legenda. (Anon.) Frankfurt:
     Posev, 1978.

     _____. (Anon.) GRANI (Frankfurt): No. 95, Jan.-March
     1975; pp. 55-75; No. 99, Jan.-March 1976; pp. 48-136.
     Series of "tales," part fantasy, part satire, about
     Muscovites, the book of the Prince of Darkness, etc.

230 CHERNOVA, OL'GA. "Kholodnaia zima." ["Cold Winter"] NOVYI
     ZHURNAL (New York): No. 121, Dec. 1975; pp. 144-62; No.
     122, March 1976; pp. 167-82.
     Essay by stepdaughter of leading SR about the years
     1917-20, when Chernov had to hide from the Cheka.

231 CHERNYI, OSIP. Kniga sudeb. [Book of Fate] Amsterdam:
     Herzen, 1974; 342 pp. Novel based on Lysenko affair.

232 _____. "Pokhorony Borisa Pasternaka." POSEV (Frank-
     furt): No. 12, Dec. 1975; pp. 53-54.
     Personal reminiscence of Pasternak's funeral.

233 CHICHIBABIN, BORIS. [b. 191?] "Ia slishkom dolgo nachinalsia";
     "Bitva"; "Trepeshchu pered chudom gospodnim"; "V ianvare
     na ulitsakh voda"; "Est' poselok v Krymu"; "Vesennii dom";
     "Postel'"; "Vecherom s poluchki"; "Makhorka"; "Verbliud";
     "Bol'naia cherepakha"; "Snimi s menia ustalost', mater'
     Smert'." GLAGOL (Ann Arbor, Mich.): No. 1977; pp. 116-32.
     Poems.

CHICHIBABIN, BORIS: See Poiski No. 1 (#940).

CHORNOVIL

234   CHORNOVIL, VIACHESLAV. [b. 1938] The Chornovil Papers.
       Toronto: McGraw-Hill, 1968; 246 pp.
       His 1965 petition and other documents re Ukrainian na-
       tional identity and dissent. Pub. in original Ukrainian
       as Lykho z rozumu, Baltimore: Smoloskyp, 1967. Eng. tr.
       of opening essay in BRUMBERG (#178).

235   _____. (TCHORNOVIL) Le Malheur d'avoir trop d'esprit.
       Paris, PIUF, 1974; 170 pp. Tr., H. Zamoyska.
       Collection of documents pertaining to Ukrainian
       dissent.

236   CHORNOVIL, V. and MOROZ, V. Voices of Human Courage. New
       York: 1968; 57 pp.

       _____. (TCHORNOVIL) Répression et procès arbitraires
       en Ukraine (1965-67). Paris: EstEuropeen, 1968; 36 pp.
       Information on various trials of Ukrainian dissidents.

237   CHORNOVIL, V. and PENSON, B. "Dialog za koliuchei provolo-
       koi." ["Dialogue from Behind the Barbed Wire"] KONTINENT:
       No. 6, 1976; pp. 173-227.
       Alternating voices give detailed information about camp
       events, such as list of 24-hour food ration, daily menu;
       comparisons between different camps; trials. Fr. tr. in
       Recherches, No. 34, Oct. 1978.

       CHUDAKOV, S.: See Sintaksis (#1072).

238   CHUKOVSKAIA, LIDIIA. [b. 1907] "The Face of Inhumanity."
       SURVEY (London): Vol. 22, No. 2, Spring 1976; pp. 12-15.
       Tr., M. Sternberg. Defense of Dzhemilev.

239   _____. "Gnev naroda." ["the People's Anger"] VESTNIK
       RSKhD (Paris): No. 108-109-110, II-I_I-IV-1973; pp. 251-61.

       _____. "Gnev naroda." NOV. RUS. SLOVO (New York):
       Oct. 7, 1973; p. 2.

       _____. "Gnev naroda." RUS. MYSL' (Paris): No. 1,
       1973; p. 5.

       _____. Under "Documents," in SURVEY (London): Vol. 20,
       No. 2/3 (91/92), Spring-Summer 1974; pp. 228-40.
       Reviews official campaigns of lies against Pasternak,
       Sakharov and Solzhenitsyn.

240   _____. "Moe slovo." ["My Word"] NOV. RUS. SLOVO (New
       York): Feb. 26, 1974; p. 3.

CHUKOVSKAIA, LIDIIA. "K iskliucheniiu L. K. Chukovskoi iz
SSP." NOVYI ZHURNAL (New York): No. 114, March 1974;
pp. 227-31.

_____. "Proryv"; "Slovo L. Chukovskoi na sobranii
Soiuza sovetskikh pisatelei." RUS. MYSL' (Paris): Feb.
28, 1974; p. 3.

_____. "Proryv." POSEV (Frankfurt): No. 3, March 1974;
p. 10.

_____. "Vy nikogda ne zastupaetes' za slovo." POSEV
(Frankfurt): No. 4, April 1974; pp. 7-9.

_____. "To the Secretariat of the Moscow Section of the
Union of Soviet Writers." INDEX ON CENSORSHIP (London):
No. 2, Summer 1974; pp. 7-9.
Statement on the publication of Solzhenitsyn's Gulag
and on her expulsion from the Writers' Union.

241　　_____. "Ne kazn', no mysl', no slovo." ["Not Execution,
but the Thought, but the Word"] POSEV (Frankfurt): No. 8
(1135), Aug. 1968; pp. 47-49.

_____. "Ne kazn', no mysl', no slovo." NOV. RUS. SLOVO
(New York): Aug. 31, 1968; p. 4.

_____. "A Letter. . . ." SURVEY (London): No. 69,
Oct. 1968; pp. 107-112.
Letter to Izvestia on the fifteenth anniversary of
Stalin's death, demanding an investigation and condemna-
tion of the Stalinist "machine" and declaring the "com-
plicity of silence" over. Eng. tr. also in BRUMBERG (#178).

242　　_____. Opustelyi dom. Paris: Five Continents, 1965;
136 pp.

_____. The Deserted House. New York: Dutton, 1967;
144 pp. Tr., Aline B. Werth.

_____. (CHUKOWSKAJA) Ein Leeres Haus. Zurich: Dio-
genes, 1967; 231 pp. Tr., Eva Mathay.

_____. (TSCHUKOWSKAJA) La maison déserte. Paris:
Callman-Levy, 1975; 192 pp. Tr., Serge Duchesse.

_____. "Sof'ia Petrovna." NOVYI ZHURNAL (New York):
No. 83, June 1966; pp. 5-45; No. 84, Sept. 1966; pp. 5-46.
Novella written 1939-40, about the Terror of the 30s,

CHUKOVSKAIA

> written from point of view of a simple woman who believes
> in a rapidly approaching happy future for her country,
> caught in the nightmare of the terror when her son is ar-
> rested, she is fired and can't get another job, and how
> she waits in line at NKVD headquarters, at the prison, at
> the prosecutor's office to find out something about her
> son, such as why he has been arrested.

243   CHUKOVSKAIA, LIDIIA. Otkrytoe slovo. [The Open Word] New
      York: Khronika, 1976; 111 pp.
          Collection of her letters, appeals, articles.

244   _____. "Otvetstvennost' pisatelia i bezotvetstvennost'
      'Literaturnoi gazety'." ["The Writer's Responsibility and
      'Literaturnaia gazeta's' Irresponsibility"] NOV. RUS.
      SLOVO (New York): Nov. 16, 1968; p. 4.

      _____. "Otvetstvennost' pisatelia i bezotvetstvennost'
      'Literaturnoi gazety'." POSEV (Frankfurt): No. 11 (1138),
      Nov. 1968; pp. 39-43.

      _____. "Otvetstvennost' pisatelia i bezotvetstvennost'
      'Literaturnoi gazety'." RUS. MYSL' (Paris): Dec. 12,
      1968; pp. 114-24.

      _____. "Otvetstvennost' pisatelia." NOVYI ZHURNAL (New
      York): No. 93, Dec. 1968; pp. 114-24.

      _____. "Otvetstvennost' pisatelia i bezotvetstvennost'
      'Literaturnoi gazety'." VESTNIK RSKhD (Paris): No. 89-
      90, III-IV-1968; pp. 95-104.
          Response to Literaturnaia gazeta's attack on Solzheni-
      tsyn, in which she corrects factual errors and refutes
      false implications of article.

245   _____. Pamiati detstva. [Memories of Childhood] Paris:
      YMCA, 1978.

      _____. "Pamiati detstva." NOVYI ZHURNAL (New York):
      No. 128, Sept. 1977; pp. 7-22.
          Autobiography of her childhood as daughter of famous
      writer Kornei Chukovskii.

246   _____. "Pis'mo L. Chukovskoi Mikhailu Sholokhovu."
      NOV. RUS. SLOVO (New York): Nov. 22, 1966; p. 3.

      _____. "Otkrytoe pis'mo pisatel'nitsy L. Chukovskoi M.
      Sholokhovu." GRANI (Frankfurt): No. 62, Nov. 1966.
          Criticizes Sholokhov's attack on Siniavskii and Daniel'

and his approval of their sentences. Also contained in
GINZBURG (#380).

247   CHUKOVSKAIA, LIDIIA. <u>Po</u> <u>tu</u> <u>storonu</u> <u>smerti</u>. [<u>On</u> <u>the</u> <u>Far</u>
<u>Side</u> <u>of</u> <u>Death</u>] Paris: YMCA, 1977; 136 pp. Poems.

248   _____. <u>Protsess iskliucheniia</u>: <u>Ocherk literaturnykh</u>
<u>nravov</u>. [<u>The</u> <u>Process</u> <u>of</u> <u>Expulsion</u>: <u>A</u> <u>Work</u> <u>of</u> <u>Literary</u>
<u>Mores</u>] Paris: YMCA, 1979; 230 pp.
      Her account of 20 years of Soviet literary history,
post-Khrushchev: how the regime decimated and destroyed
Russian literature.

249   _____. "Sovest' chelovech'ia." ["Human Conscience"]
RUS. MYSL' (Paris): June 10, 1976; p. 5.
      Defense of Dzhemilev. Eng. tr. #238.

250   _____. Spusk pod vodu. New York: Chekhov, 1972;
131 pp.

           _____. <u>Going</u> <u>Under</u>. London: Barrie & Jenkins, 1972;
New York: Quadrangle/New York Times, 1976; 144 pp. Tr.,
Peter M. Weston.

           _____. (TCHOUKOVSKAIA) <u>La</u> <u>Plongée</u>. Paris: Calmann-
Levy, 1974; 209 pp. Tr., Adele Bloch; Paris: Rombaldi,
1976; 251 pp.

           _____. (TSCHUKOWSKAJA) <u>Untertauchen</u>. Zurich: Dioge-
nes, 1975; 188 pp. Sec. ed., 1978. Tr., Swetlana Geier.
      Novella set in late 1940s; heroine is tormented by the
unknown fate of her husband, who was arrested during 1930s
purges; the new wave of terror and the anti-Semitism of
those years is also touched on.

251   _____. "Stikhi: 'Nevedomo kogda i gde. . .'; 'A
schast'e. . .'; 'Pereputannye tsitaty'; 'Stikhi brat'iam';
'Peredelkino'; 'Moi neozhidannyi blagovestitel'. . .';
'Konets'; 'Cherez 12 let'." NOV. RUS. SLOVO (New York):
Jan. 13, 1974; p. 5. Poems.

252   _____. <u>Zapiski ob</u> <u>Anne</u> <u>Akhmatovoi</u>. [<u>Notes about</u> <u>Anna</u>
<u>Akhmatova</u>] Paris: YMCA, 1976; 2 vols.
      Description of Akhmatova's treatment by the govern-
ment--both direct repression via blackmail, and holding
the poet's son's fate over her head, and indirect via
pressure from neighbors, etc. She describes Akhmatova's
attitude toward art, the relationship between the two of
them, and analyzes some of the poetry.

CHUKOVSKAIA

CHUKOVSKAIA, LIDIIA. "Polumertvaia i nemaia." ["Half-dead and Mute"] KONTINENT: No. 7, 1976; pp. 430-36.
Analysis of Akhmatova's "Poèma bez geroia." (Excerpt from Zapiski ob Anne Akhmatovoi.)

253 The Church Suffering: Chronicle of the Catholic Church in Lithuania. New York: Lithuanian-Roman Catholic Priests' League of America, 1975.
Several volumes of samizdat documents pertaining to repression of Catholic Church in Lithuania (a Lithuanian version of Khronika which printed 53 samizdat issues as of mid-1982). They have also been published in Lithuanian, and parts of them in Russian by Khronika Press. (Address: 351 Highland Blvd., Brooklyn, New York 11207.)

254 COHEN, RICHARD, Ed. Let My People Go. New York: Popular Library, 1971; 286 pp.
Compilation of records of the Leningrad and Riga trials of would-be Jewish emigrés, 1970-71.

D

255 D. Stremia "Tikhogo Dona": Zagadki romana. [The Stirrup of
     "Quiet Don": Riddles of a Novel] Paris: YMCA, 1974;
     195 pp.
        Unfinished work which heatedly attempts to prove, via
     lexical and phraseological analysis, that Sholokhov plagia-
     rized much of Quiet Flows the Don or was at best a "co-
     author."

256 D. D. "Liturgiia vernykh." VESTNIK RSKhD (Paris): No. 81,
     III-1966; pp. 23-28. Poems.

     D. L.: See BOKOV, NIKOLAI.

     D. S.: See 37 (#1162).

257 DANDARON: See SEMEKA, ELENA (#1008).

258 DANIEL', IULII (ARZHAK, NIKOLAI). [b. 1925] Govorit Moskva:
     povesti i rasskazy. New York: Interlanguage Literary
     Associates, 1966; 166 pp.

     _____. This is Moscow Speaking and other stories.
     London: Harvill, 1968 and New York: Dutton, 1969; 160 pp.
     Tr., Stuart Hood, Harold Shukman, John Richardson.

     _____. (ARJAK) Ici Moscou. Nouvelles. Paris: Sedimo,
     1966; 277 pp. Tr., J. Bonnet, A. M. Felkers, M. Michel.

     _____. (ARSCHAK) Hier spricht Moskau und andere Er-
     zählungen. Vienna, Hamburg: Zsolnay,]967; 206 pp. Tr.,
     Hendrik Berinson and Lotte Stuart.

     _____. (ARZHAK) Iskuplenie. [Atonement] New York:
     Interlanguage Literary Associates, 1964; 71 pp.

     _____. (ARZHAK) Ruki; Chelovek iz MINAPa. [Hands; The
     Man from MINAP] Washington: 1963; 38 pp.

     _____. "Ruki." RUS. MYSL' (Paris): Feb. 12, 1966;
     p. 6.

     _____. "This is Moscow Speaking," in Dissonant Voices in
     Soviet Literature, ed., Patricia Blake and Max Hayward. New
     York: Harper & Row, 1964. Tr., John Richardson.

     _____. "Hands." DISSENT (New York): July-August,
     1966; pp. 391-95.
        Bitterly satiric stories mainly dealing with the terror-
     filled atmosphere of Stalinist society and its aftermath.

DANIEL'

"This is Moscow Speaking," passages from which were singled out for attack at Daniel's trial, focuses on an official decree announcing "Public Murder Day," when all Soviet citizens over 16 can kill any other Soviet citizen (with a few exceptions, such as policemen and soldiers), and what happens when the day arrives.

259   DANIEL', IULII. "Pis'mo Iuriia [sic] Danielia k drugu." NOV. RUS. SLOVO (New York): June 29, 1969; p. 2.

260   _____. "Poslednee slovo Iu. Danielia." ["Daniel's Final Plea"] NOV. RUS. SLOVO (New York): May 14, 1965; p. 4. Life in Camp.
       Defends his works, primarily on literary grounds, though he stresses the nonviolent, nonterroristic political message of his work. Contained in GINZBURG (#380).

261   _____. Sbornik proizvedenii. New York: Interlanguage Literary Associates, 1972.
       Collection containing most of his fiction.

262   _____. (ARZHAK) Stikhi iz nevoli. Amsterdam: Herzen, 1971; 94 pp.

       _____. (DANIEL) Prison Poems. London: Calder & Boyars, 1971. Tr., David Burg and Arthur Boyars.

       _____. Poèmes de prison. Paris: Gallimard, 1973; 80 pp. Bilingual ed. Tr., Edith Scherer.

       _____. (ARSCHAK) Berichte aus dem sozialistischen Lager. Hamburg: Hoffmann & Campe, 1972; 71 pp. Tr., Wolf Biermann.

       _____. "Poèma Iuliia Danielia: 'A v èto vremia. . .'." NOV. RUS. SLOVO (New York): June 7, 1970; p. 2.

       _____. (ARZHAK) "A v èto vremia. . . ." GRANI (Frankfurt): No. 77, Oct. 1970; pp. 4-14.

       _____. "from: And at that Time." ENCOUNTER (London): Vol. XXXVIII, No. 4, April 1972; p. 43. Tr., Vera Dunham and Deming Brown.

       _____. "Tiuremnye stikhi." NOV. RUS. SLOVO (New York): Feb. 13, 1972; p. 5. Poems.

263   DANIEL', IULII. "Zaiavlenie Iu. Danielia." RUS. MYSL'
         (Paris): Feb. 13, 1975; p. 4. Re unity of Russian culture.

       DANIEL', IULII: see also GINZBURG (#380), <u>Samizdat</u> <u>I</u>
         (#989), <u>Vol'noe</u> <u>slovo</u>, No. 14-15 (#1238).

264   DANIL'TSEV, LEONARD. "Liubov' idiota." ["The Love of an
         Idiot"] KOVCHEG (Paris): No. 2, 1978; pp. 55-61. Story.

       DAVYDOV, M.: See MEDVEDEV (#773).

265   DECTER, M., Ed. <u>A</u> <u>Hero</u> <u>of</u> <u>Our</u> <u>Times</u>: <u>The</u> <u>Trial</u> <u>and</u> <u>Fate</u> <u>of</u>
         <u>Boris</u> <u>Kochubiyevsky</u>. New York: Academic Committee on
         Soviet Jewry, 1970.
           Documents pertaining to arrest, trial and sentencing of
         Kiev Zionist.

266   _____. <u>Redemption!</u> New York: American Jewish Confer-
         ence on Soviet Jewry, 1970.
           Letters and petitions by and about Jewish emigration
         movement, "refuseniks," etc.

267   "'Delo' krymskikh tatar." ["The 'Case' of the Crimean Tatars]
         NOVYI ZHURNAL (New York): No. 97, Dec. 1969; pp. 169-217.
           Collection of statements, letters, petitions etc. re
         repression, both historic and contemporary, of Crimean
         Tatars.

268   "Delo Slutskogo, Furmana, Gurevicha i drugikh." ["The Case
         of Slutskii, Furman, Gurevich and others"] VESTNIK RSKhD
         (Paris): No. 107, I-1973; pp. 212-40.
           Author was one of a group of students who in 1950-51
         formed a "Union for revolutionary struggle," an anti-
         Stalinist group seeking a return to the ideals of 1917,
         Marxism and Leninism. They were arrested early in 1951
         and author describes her time in solitary in Lefortovo
         (more than a year), her interrogations, one of her investi-
         gators (who was the same as Vadim Delone's in 1968). Nine-
         teen of them were finally charged as being members of a
         "Jewish anti-Soviet terrorist youth organization"; the
         trial lasted two weeks, in Jan. 1952, its "judges" members
         of the War College of the Supreme Court. Three were shot
         (Slutskii, Furman and Gurevich), ten got 25 years camp,
         5 years exile, three got 10 years camp, 5 years exile. In
         1956 all the sentences were curtailed, including those of
         the dead young men.

DELONE

269   DELONE, VADIM. [b. 1947, em. 1975] "Borets za svobodu."
RUS. MYSL' (Paris): Oct. 24, 1968; p. 4. ("Iz tsikla
'Bumerang'"; "Pis'mo Bukovskomu")
Two poems by man tried together with Bukovskii, in 1967.

270   _____. "Slova stuchat po dnu dushi: 'Ne proidet proshchan'e karnavalom. . .'; 'Vse koncheno, sud'ba slepa, kak
chert. . .'; 'Tikho Bogu tverzhu. . .'; 'Zametki k avto-
biografii'; 'Osennii tsikl'." VREMIA I MY (New York/Jeru-
salem/Paris): No. 21, Sept. 1977; pp. 92-99.
Poems dated Moscow 1965-75 (before his emigration).

DELONE, VADIM: See BRUMBERG (#178), Sintaksis (#1072),
LITVINOV (#700).

271   Den' politzakliuchennogo 30 oktiabria 1975 goda. [Political
Prisoner's Day, Oct. 30, 1975] New York: Khronika, 1975,
32 pp.

DERZHAVIN, P.: See BARABANOV

DMITRIEV, V.: See Moskovskoe vremia (#817).

272   DOBROVOL'SKAIA, OL'GA. "Imperator Nikolai II i A. Kerenskii." ["Nicholas II and Kerenskii"] NOVYI ZHURNAL (New
York): No. 114, March 1974; pp. 164-71.
    Memoir, written in Taganrog in 1919, by widow of Count
Nikolai Dobrovol'skii, Imperial Minister of Justice; describes Kerenskii's stay in their apartment just after the
revolution, and his meeting with Tsar Nicholas in Tsarskoe
selo.

273   DOBROVOL'SKII, ALEKSEI [b. 1938] "Vzaimootnoshenie znaniia i
very: apologeticheskii opyt Alekseia Dobrovol'skogo."
["The Interrelationship Between Knowledge and Faith"]
GRANI (Frankfurt): No. 64, June 1967; pp. 194-201.

    _____. "Iz stat'i 'Vzaimootnoshenie znaniia i very'."
RUS. MYSL' (Paris): Oct. 5, 1967; p. 5.

    _____. "Obratit' vzory k miru inomu. . . ." POSEV
(Frankfurt): No. 40 (1115), Oct. 6, 1967; pp. 3-4.
    Essay on the roles of emotion and information in the
development of religious faith. From Feniks 1966 (#337).
(Author was tried together with Ginzburg, Galanskov and
Lashkova.)

274   _____. "Prigovor (A. A. Dobrovol'skii)." RUS. MYSL'
(Paris): March 7, 1968; p. 3.

Text of Dobrovol'skii's 1958 sentence of three years' deprivation of freedom.

DOBROVOL'SKII, ALEKSEI: See BRUDERER (#176), LITVINOV (#700).

275 Dokumenty Komiteta Prav Cheloveka. New York: International League for the Rights of Man (now called International League for Human Rights), 1972; 252 pp.
Documents pertaining to trials, legal and psychiatric repressions, etc.

276 DOMBROVSKII, IURII. [b. 1909, d. 1978] "Dazhe v pekle nadezhda zavoditsia." GRANI (Frankfurt): No. 85, Oct. 1972; pp. 57-58.
Poem, listed under "Iz kontslagernoi poèzii."

277 _____. Fakul'tet nenuzhnzykh veshchei. Paris: YMCA, 1978; 480 pp.

_____. La faculté de l'inutile. Paris: Michel, 1979; 445 pp. Tr., D. Sesemann and J. Cathola.
Novel set in Alma Ata in 1937; hero, thanks to faith in "unnecessary" values, refuses to admit to false accusations and conquers his interrogators. In part an inquiry into terror and the system of informing from a religious and philosophical point of view.

DOMBROVSKII, IURII: See also Poiski No. 1 (#940).

278 "Don Kikhot." (Anon.) VESTNIK RKhD (Paris): No. III, I-1974; p. 109.
Poem, listed under "Golos arkhipelaga."

279 DOVLATOV, SERGEI. [b. 1941, em. 1978] "Nevidimaia kniga." ["The Invisible Book"] VREMIA I MY (New York/Paris/Jerusalem): No. 24, 1977; pp. 56-105 and No. 25, 1978; pp. 55-92.

_____. The Invisible Book. Ann Arbor, Mich.: Ardis, 1979; 134 pp. Tr., D. Burgin and K. O'Connor.
Novel on the inner workings of the world of Soviet literary journals.

280 _____. "Po priamoi." ["On a Straight Line"] KONTINENT: No. 11, 1976; pp. 129-40. Story.

281 DRABKINA, ALLA. "Semenovna." NOV. RUS. SLOVO (New York): March 25, 1966; p. 2; March 26, 1966; p. 2; March 28, 1966; pp. 2-3; March 29, 1966; p. 2; March 30, 1966; p. 2.
Story.

DRUZHNIKOV

282 DRUZHNIKOV, IURII. [b. 1933] "Smert' Fedora Ioannovicha."
["The Death of Fedor Ioannovich"] VREMIA I MY (New York/
Paris/Jerusalem): No. 45, Sept. 1979; pp. 59-77. Story.

DUBIN, B.: See Sfinksy (#1011).

283 DUBNOV, Z. "Belaia polnoch'"; "Skazka." RUS. MYSL' (Paris):
Jan. 6, 1975; p. 8. Poems.

284 _____. "Kak chasto. . .'; "Kak drevnii bog. . .'; "Ia na
osennem kladbishche prirody. . . ." RUS. MYSL' (Paris):
June 7, 1973; p. 9. Poems.

285 _____. "Rekviem." RUS. MYSL' (Paris): Aug. 3, 1972;
p. 6. Poem.

286 _____. "Stikhi o molchanii." GRANI (Frankfurt): No.
81, Nov. 1971; pp. 43-44. Poem.

287 _____. "Stikhi: 'Svoboda'." NOV. RUS. SLOVO (New York):
June 25, 1972; p. 5. Poem.

288 _____. "Svet na tsvetakh"; ". . . I barany revut. . . ."
RUS. MYSL' (Paris): Sept. 28, 1972; p. 6. Poems.

289 _____. "Teni velikikh." RUS. MYSL' (Paris): July 19,
1973; p. 9. Poem.

290 _____. ". . . V tot chas. . . ." RUS. MYSL' (Paris):
Feb. 1, 1973; p. 5. Poem.

291 _____. "Zimniaia noch'." RUS. MYSL' (Paris): Feb. 15,
1973; p. 8. Poem.

292 DUBROV, ANDREI. [b. 1949] "Kak my uchimsia. . . ." ["How
we Learn. . . ."] RUS. MYSL' (Paris): Oct. 12, 1972; p. 4.
Essay on political control of Soviet students. Extracts
in Cahiers du Samizdat No. 3, Nov. 1972.

293 DUDKO, DMITRII (also DIMITRII). "Iz neopublikovannykh besed";
"Iz Kabanovskikh propovedei." VESTNIK RKhD (Paris): No.
118, II-1976; pp. 5-22.
"Chats" and sermons held after he was expelled from
Moscow to a village in the countryside.

294 _____. "Iz 'Slov o tsarstve nebesnom'." ["From 'Words
on the Heavenly Kingdom'."] VESTNIK RKhD (Paris): No.
125, II-1978; pp. 13-34; No. 126, III-1978; pp. 9-21.
Five sermons from 1977 on faith, salvation, and hell on
earth.

295   DUDKO, DMITRII. "Kreshchenie na Rusi." ["Russia's Baptism"; "Russia's Penitence"] VESTNIK RKhD (Paris): No. 117, I-1976; pp. 188-208; 119, III-IV-1976; pp. 254-80 (listed under "Pokaianie na Rusi").
Diary entries concerning baptisms, of adults as well as children, "miracles" (healings following baptisms), anecdotes.

296   _____. O nashem upovanii. [About Our Hope] Paris: Reunis, 1975; 272 pp.

        _____. (DOUDKO) L'Esperance qui est en nous. Paris: Seuil, 1976; 272 pp.

        _____. "O nashem upovanii." VESTNIK RKhD (Paris): No. 112-113, II-III-1974; pp. 7-36.

        _____. "Poslednee slovo." RUS. MYSL; (Paris): July 18, 1974; p. 5.

        _____. "V poiskakh zhemchuga." RUS. MYSL' (Paris): Oct. 14, 1976; p. 5.
Nine sermons and "final plea" plus various materials connected with his case such as the prohibition forbidding him to preach. Sermons, set in question-answer format, deal with faith in God, Orthodoxy, various church matters and the everyday life of Christians in Russia today.

297   _____. "Stikhi sviashchennika D. Dudko: 'Ia k tebe na otdykh ne priedu. . .'; 'Ran'she blizkie, nyne dalekie. . .'; 'Golodnye oborvannye liudi. . .'; 'Ty teper', naverno,vse sedaia. . .'; 'Ty ne budesh' bol'she zhdat' menia. . .'; 'Neizvestnoi materi'; 'Po dorogam poteriannym. . .'; 'Rebenok raskinul ruki'." In #116: "Ia znaiu ty ne zhdesh' . . ."; "Ot liubvi v grudi ostalsia pepel. . ."; "Geroi"; "Za chto pogibli milliony èti?" "Chto èto za narod?" "Chto ty laesh', glupyi pes?" NOVYI ZHURNAL (New York): No. 115, June 1974; pp. 177-81; No. 116, Sept. 1974; pp. 185-89. Poems.

298   _____. Ein ungeschriebenes Buch: Aufzeichnungen eines russischen Priesters. Styria, 1978; 175 pp. Tr., Erwin Lohneisen.

299   _____. "V svete preobrazheniia." ["In the Light of the Transfiguration"] VESTNIK RKhD (Paris): No. 129, III-1979; pp. 269-80; No. 130, IV-1979; pp. 355-60.
Four issues of weekly Orthodox newspaper/sermon (April, May and June 1979, Jan. 1980). Also contained in Vol'noe

DUDKO

slovo, No. 33 (#1253), together with "Vrag vnutri" ["The Enemy Within"].

300 DUDKO, DMITRII. Das Wort ist nicht gefesselt. Styria, 1976; 174 pp.

DUDKO, DMITRII: See also Vol'noe slovo, No. 33 (#1253).

301 DUDKO DMITRII et al. "Delo sviashchennika Dmitriia Dudko." VESTNIK RKhD (Paris): No. 112-113, II-III-1974; pp. 261-81.
Documents pertaining to his case, his "final plea," and various statements and letters by him and by supporters.

302 _____. "Delo sviashch. Dmitriia Dudko." VESTNIK RKhD (Paris): No. 117, I-1976; pp. 240-62.
About the renewed attacks on and repressive measures taken against him in 1975; his own statement and letters by Shafarevich, Regel'son and Iakunin and others.

"Dukhovnye pereput'ia 'Kontinenta'." (Anon.) ["Spiritual Crossroads of Kontinent"] VESTNIK RKhD (Paris): No. 115, I-1975; pp. 204-16.
Discussion of first issue of Kontinent.

DUNLOP, JOHN: See VSKhSON (#1273).

304 DZIUBA, IVAN. [1931] Internatsionalizm ili Rusifikatsiia? Amsterdam: Herzen, 1973.

_____. Internationalism or Russification? A Study in the Soviet Nationalities Problem. London: Weidenfeld & Nicolson, 1970; 263 pp.; New York: Humanities Press, 1968.
Historical analysis of Soviet policy toward the Ukraine, and the relationship between national rights and general human rights. Pub. in original Ukrainian by Suchasnist' (Munich): 1968; 262 pp. Newest Eng. ed.: New York: Monad, 1974; 262 pp.

DZIUBA, IVAN: See BRUMBERG (#178).

E

305   EF. EM. "O massovykh rasstrelakh zakliuchennykh na Vorkuta
       v 1938." ["On the Mass Shootings of Prisoners in Vorkut
       in 1938"] NOVYI ZHURNAL (New York): No. 119, June 1975;
       pp. 110–18.
          Account, by former prisoner, of the killing of over
       1000 prisoners, with names of 184 of them and names as well
       of chief organizers of massacre.

306   EFIMOV (Pseud.). Il faut stopper les Japonais. Paris:
       Hachette, 1974; 153 pp. Tr., Michel Barba.

307   EFIMOV, IGOR' (MOSKOVIT, A.). [b. 1937, em. 1977] "Prak-
       ticheskaia metafizika." ["Practical Metaphysics"] GRANI
       (Frankfurt): No. 87–88, Jan.-April 1973; pp. 333–70.
          Philosophical exploration of the nature of freedom, the
       individual's relationship to the group, the definition of
       will; influenced by Kant and Schopenhauer. Included in
       Metapolitika (Strathcona, 1978).

       ÈIDEL'MAN, NATAN: See Russkoe slovo (#972), BRUMBERG (#178).

308   "Èkspluatatsiia dvoinika." (Anon.) ["Exploitation of the
       Double"] ÈKHO (Paris): No. 2, 1980; pp. 117–25.
          Analysis of poetry of Leningrad writer Elena Shvarts.

309   EKSZEKA. "Operatsiia BANIA." ["Operation BANIA"] VESTNIK
       RSKhD (Paris): No. 101–102, III-IV-1971; pp. 201–21.
          About prisoners in women's camp persecuted for reli-
       gious faith.

310   'ELENA' et al. "Ostanovis'"; "Rozhdestvenskii psalom";
       "Razreshenie"; "Credo"; "Èmigrant." NOVYI ZHURNAL (New
       York): No. 69, Sept. 1962; pp. 131–37. Poems.

311   ÈRDMAN, NIKOLAI. [b. 1902, d. 1970] Mandat. [The Mandate]
       Cologne: Kazak, 1976.
          Play written in 1924, produced but never published.

312   _____. "Samoubiitsa." ["The Suicide"] NOVYI ZHURNAL
       (New York): No. 112, Sept. 1973; pp. 5–24; No. 113, Dec.
       1973; pp. 5–36; No. 114, March 1974; pp. 5–33.
          Play written in 1928, never published in Soviet Union;
       book edition published in U.S. in 1979.

313   EREMIN, MIKHAIL. "Stikhi." ÈKHO (Paris): No. 4, 1980. Poems.

       EREMIN, MIKHAIL: See also Sintaksis (#1072).

314   EROFEEV, VENEDIKT. [b. 1947] Moskva-Petushki. Paris: YMCA,
       1976; 165 pp.

EROFEEV

EROFEEV, VENEDIKT. <u>Moscow to the End of the Line</u>. New York: Taplinger, 1980; 164 pp. Tr., H. Tjalsma.

_____. (EROFEIEV) <u>Moscou-sur-vodka</u> (<u>Moscou-Petouchki</u>). Paris: Michel, 1976; 205 pp. Tr., Anne Abatier and Antoine Pingaud.

_____. (JEROFEJEW) <u>Die Reise nach Petuschki</u>. Munich: Piper, 1978; 168 pp. Tr., Natascha Spitz.

_____. "Moskva-Petushki." AMI (Jerusalem): No. 3, 1973. (Journal no longer exists.)
   Grotesque surreal tale of a drunkard's adventures, his conversations with other drunks (he meets no sober people); horror at Soviet official hypocrisy and pity for its victims, the people.

EROFEEV, VIKTOR: See <u>Metropol'</u> (#808).

315 ESENIN-VOL'PIN, ALEKSANDR. [b. 1925, em. 1972] "Nikogda ia ne bral sokhi." RUS. MYSL' (Paris): April 11, 1968; p. 3. Poem.

316 _____. "Vechnuiu ruchku Petru Grigor'evichu Grigorenko!" ["A Fountain Pen for Grigorenko"] POSEV (Frankfurt): No. 9, Sept. 1970; pp. 24-30.

_____. "Vechnuiu ruchku Petru Grigor'evichu Grigorenko!" RUS. MYSL' (Paris): Sept. 24, 1970; p. 4.

_____. (VOL'PIN, S.) "Pis'mo." NOV. RUS. SLOVO (New York): Oct. 6, 1970; p. 3; Oct. 7, 1970; p. 3; Oct. 9, 1970; p. 3.
   Open letter to Solzhenitsyn describing psychiatric repression of Grigorenko, and on behalf of all political prisoners treated in psychiatric hospitals, describing usual pattern of treatment and violation of rights. Also appears in ARTEMOVA et al. (#79); Eng. Tr. in MEERSON-AKSENOV and SHRAGIN (#801). (Author was himself incarcerated in psych. hospital twice.)

317 _____. (YESENIN-VOLPIN) "A Poet in Jail." ENCOUNTER (London): Vol. XVI, No. 5 (92), April 1961; pp. 92-94. Poems (included in <u>Vesennii list</u>, #318).

318 _____. <u>Vesennii list/A Leaf of Spring</u>. New York: Praeger and London: Thames & Hudson, 1961; 173 pp. Bilingual ed. Tr., George Reavey.

Collection of poems plus "A Free Philosophical Treatise," in which he represents dialectical materialism as a false concept; militantly secularistic and anticlerical.

ESENIN-VOL'PIN, A.: See also ARTEMOVA et al. (#79); BRUMBERG (#178).

320 ÈSHLIMAN, N. and IAKUNIN, G. "Otkrytoe pis'mo sviashchenni-kov Nikolaia Èshlimana i Gleba Iakunina Patriarkhu Alek-siiu"; "Pis'mo. . . Èpiskopam Russkoi Tserkvi"; "Zaiav-lenie predsedateliu Prezidiuma VS SSSR N.V. Podgornomu ot grazhdan SSSR Èshlimana N.I. i Iakunina G.P." ["Open Let-ter to Patriarch Aleksii"; "Letter to the Episcopate of the Russian Church"; "Statement to N.V. Podgornyi, Chair-man of the Supreme Soviet of the USSR, from citizens Èshliman and Iakunin"] GRANI (Frankfurt): No. 61, Oct. 1966; pp. 123-67.

Letters re "sickness" of the Russian church, its com-promises with the government, the latter's unlawful re-gistration of Christians, with which church collaborated, which enabled the regime easily to keep track of religious individuals; the closing of churches, monasteries and church schools, plus brief history of Orthodox church and its relation to Russian culture; a plea that church not be a "weapon" in hands of secular forces. Eng. tr. in St. Vladimir's Seminary Quarterly (New York): Vol. X, Nos. 1-2.

ÈSHLIMAN and IAKUNIN: See also BOURDEAUX (#148).

321 EVDOKIMOV, BORIS. [b. 1923] (RAZUMNYI, SERGEI) "Chto narod zhdal ot 'prazdnikov,' i kak oni proshli." ["What the People Expected from the 'Holidays,' and How They Passed"] POSEV (Frankfurt): No. 11, Nov. 1971; pp. 25-29.

Holiday of title is 50th anniversary of revolution, for which the essay was written in 1967; deals with the fail-ures of Soviet power--inadequate pensions and consumer goods--based on first-hand everyday observations, and people's hopes for an amnesty: "the people demand free-dom."

322 _____. (VOLNY) "The Intelligentsia and the Democratic Movement." SURVEY (London): Vol. 17, No. 3 (80), Summer 1971; pp. 181-91.

Messianic appeal for democratization and for support for democratic movement; what intelligentsia can do to help itself (by cleansing and educating itself), prepare itself for sacrifice, regenerate its spirit.

EVDOKIMOV

323 EVDOKIMOV, BORIS. (RUSLANOV, IVAN) <u>Molodezh' v russkoi</u>
     <u>istorii</u>. [<u>Youth in Russian History</u>] Frankfurt: Posev,
     1972; 142 pp.

_____. (RUSLANOV, IVAN) "Molodezh v russkoi istorii."
GRANI (Frankfurt): No. 68, July 1968; pp. 157-78; No. 80,
Sept. 1971; pp. 191-216; No. 81, Nov. 1971, pp. 180-221.
     Blames Peter the Great's "Europeanization" of Russian
youth for its instability and vacillation, for the development of an upper class alienated from the masses. The 1860
reforms, he feels, created another new class, the intelli-
gentsia/raznochintsy, and he gives an overview of 19th c.
literature in these terms. Also deals with Bolshevik re-
volutionaries as alien outgrowths of this past, foreign to
Russian self-consciousness; compares pre-revolutionary
situations in England, France and Russia; sees Russia as
unable to create its own cultural tradition, neither entirely national nor entirely international.

324 _____. (RAZUMNYI, SERGEI) "Rasstanovka politicheskikh
     sil v KPSS." POSEV (Frankfurt): No. 5, May 1971;
     pp. 41-46.

_____. "Rasstanovka politicheskikh sil v KPSS." RUS.
MYSL' (Paris): April 29, 1971; p. 5.

_____. "Rasstanovka politicheskikh sil kommunistiche-
skoi partii SSSR." NOV. RUS. SLOVO (New York): May 9,
1971; p. 8.

_____. (RAZUMNY) "Political Forces in the CPSU."
SURVEY (London): Vol. 17, No. 2 (79), Spring 1971;
pp. 66-73.
     Sketchy overview of political succession in Soviet
history and the role of the Party.

325 _____. (RAZUMNYI) "Variant gazovoi kamery." ["Variant
     of a Gas Chamber"] POSEV (Frankfurt): No. 2, Feb. 1971;
     pp. 29-35.
     Description of use of psychiatric treatment against
political dissidents, with some specific examples.

326 _____. (RUSLANOV, IVAN) "Zhizn' v tiur'me." ["Life in
     Prison"] POSEV (Frankfurt): No. 4 (1131), April 1968;
     pp. 48-53; No. 4, April 1971; pp. 49-55.
     Reminiscence of prison life: of the richness of eat-
ing bread spread with margarine and sprinkled with sugar
(i.e., the relativity of happiness). Compares it with his
camp experience during the war, and muses on the meaning

Russia has for him, not merely as land or cities, but "Russian heart," "Russian soul," as opposed to "Soviet." To be Soviet is to lose one's soul.

EVDO IMOV, BORIS: See also Vol'noe Slovo No. 40 (#1259).

327   EVREI V SSSR: See GINDIS (#379), FREIMAN (#341). Numbers 1-15 of this samizdat journal which began in 1972 and of which 22 issues have appeared, have been reprinted in the series Jewish Samizdat (Jerusalem: Hebrew University).

328   "Evrei-sviashchennik."   (Anon.)   NOV. RUS. SLOVO (New York): Jan. 1, 1967; p. 8.

"Evrei-sviashchennik."   (Anon.)   RUS. MYSL' (Paris):   Feb. 2, 1967; p. 3.   Poem.

329   "Evreiskii vopros v SSSR."   (Anon.)   ["The Jewish Question in the USSR"]   POSEV (Frankfurt):   No. 12, Dec. 1970; pp. 57-60.
      Formulation of basic problems and demands of Jewish Movement in Soviet Union (discrimination and assimilation). Eng. tr. in MEERSON-AKSENOV and SHRAGIN (#801).

330   EVTUSHENKO, EVGENII.   "Pis'mo Eseninu."   RUS. MYSL' (Paris): Nov. 13, 1965; p. 3.

_____.   "Pis'mo Eseninu."   NOV. RUS. SLOVO (New York): Nov. 16, 1965; p. 3.

_____.   "Pis'mo Eseninu."   POSEV (Frankfurt):   No. 48 (1019), Nov. 26, 1965; p. 4.
      Poem (From Tetradi Sotsialisticheskoi demokratii, samizdat journal, only two issues of which reached the West).

_____.   "Stikhotvorenie Evtushenko Eseninu."   RUS. MYSL' (Paris):   Dec. 18, 1965; p. 7.
      Additional verses to "Pis'mo Eseninu" above.

331   _____.   "Pis'mo Evtushenko o Solzhenitsyne."   ["Evtushenko's Letter About Solzhenitsyn"]   RUS. MYSL' (Paris): March 14, 1974; p. 5.
      Criticizes regime for expelling Solzhenitsyn from country.

332   _____.   (YEVTUSHENKO)   A Precocious Autobiography.   New York: Dutton, 1964; 124 pp.   Tr., Andrew MacAndrew.
      Discusses not only his own life but also the phenomenon of Stalinism; sent it abroad for publication without

ÈVUS

asking Party permission, for which he was threatened with
expulsion from the Writers' Union, and while he recanted,
the attacks continued (largely because he was such a hero
to and of younger generation). Questionable whether it
ever circulated in samizdat. Portions appeared first in
L'Express (Paris), in 1963.

ÈVUS, DMITRII: See BOKOV, NIKOLAI

333 EXODUS, No. 2 and No. 4. London: Institute for Jewish Af-
fairs, 1971.
Zionist samizdat journal, mostly documents pertaining
to emigration. Issues 1 to 4 included in the series
Evreiskii samizdat (Jerusalem: Hebrew University).

F

334   FAIBUSOVICH, GENNADII. [KHAZANOV, BORIS] [b. 1928] "Ia vos-
       kresenie i zhizn'." ["I Am the Resurrection and the Life"]
       VREMIA I MY (New York/Paris/Jerusalem): No. 60, May-June
       1981; pp. 5-100.
       Novella of boy's maturation during Stalin era.

335   FEDIA. "Pis'ma Fedi." ["Fedia's Letters"] POSEV (Frank-
       furt): No. 10, Oct. 1972; pp. 51-57.
       Author, who calls himself a "former citizen of the
       Soviet Union," writes about kolkhozes, his arrest, and
       everyday experiences.

FEDOROV, T.: See 37 (#1162).

336   FENIKS 1961 (No. 1). GRANI (Frankfurt): No. 52, Dec. 1962;
       pp. 86-190.

                    . Phoenix. Junge Lyrik aus dem anderen Russland.
       Munich: Hanser, 1964; 68 pp. Tr., Elimar Schubbe.
       Samizdat literary journal reprinted in its entirety by
       GRANI. Contains poems, stories and essays by Stefan Zweig,
       Boris Pasternak, Iurii Stefanov, V. Kovshin, S. Krasovit-
       skii, V. Khromov, L. Chertkov, A. Petrov, N. Mertsalov, N.
       Nor, A. Shchukin, A. Shug, V. Kalugin, A. Onezhskaia, Iurii
       Galanskov, A. Ivanov, M. Verbin, N. Gorbanevskaia, I. Khara-
       barov, E. Ef., V. Nil'skii, A. Gorchakov, A. Vladimirov, I.
       Peresvetov, A. Karanin and A. Iakovlev. Eng. tr. of poems
       by Galanskov and Stefanov in BRUMBERG (#178). Eng. tr. of
       poems by Pasternak, Galanskov, Gorbanevskaia, Ivanov, Kalu-
       gin, Kharabarov, Kovshin, Mertsalov, Nor, Onezhskaia, Shchu-
       kin in BOSLEY (#147), some items also in GERSTENMAIER (#375),
       and LANGLAND et al. (#656).

337   FENIKS 1966. GRANI (Frankfurt): No. 63, March 1967; pp. 7-8,
       11-15, 29-42, 114-39, 192-203 and No. 64, June 1967;
       pp. 112-174.
       Issue edited by Iurii Galanskov. Includes an editorial
       statement, poems by Batshev, Stefanov, Iaskolka, Gorbanev-
       skaia, stories by Karaguzhin; letters by Mandel'shtam to
       Chukovskii pleading for help; Siniavskii's "V zashchitu
       piramidy!" about Evtushenko (see #1068), letter from Ernst
       Genri to Ilia Erenburg about the latter's quasi-glorifica-
       tion of Stalin. Eng. tr. of Karaguzhin's stories, Siniav-
       skii's essay and Batshev's poetry in BRUMBERG (#178). Eng.
       tr. of poems by Batshev, Gorbanevskaia, Stefanov and Iakol-
       ka in BOSLEY (#147); some items also in GERSTENMAIER (#375),
       LANGLAND et al. (#656).

FENIKS 1967

338 FENIKS 1967. GRANI (Frankfurt): No. 64, June 1967; pp. 112–
     74, 194–201; No. 67, March 1968; pp. 40, 115–43; No. 68,
     July 1968; pp. 101–106, 137–89; No. 70, Feb. 1969; pp. 116,
     118, 119–20; No. 75, April 1970; pp. 3–114.
         GRANI No. 64 contains G. Pomerants' "Kvadril'on" (see
     (#947), A. Dobrovol'skii's "Vzaimootnoshenie znaniia i very"
     and Galanskov's "Organizatsionnye problemy dvizheniia za
     polnoe i vseobshchee razoruzhenie i mir vo vsem mire" (see
     #273); GRANI No. 67 contains poetry by N. Gorbanevskaia,
     Iurii Galanskov's "Otkrytoe pis'mo Mikhailu Sholokhovu"
     (see #349), Pomerants's "O roli nravstvennogo oblika lich-
     nosti v zhizni istoricheskogo kollektiva" (see #950);
     GRANI No. 68 contains poetry by Galanskov, essay misattrib-
     uted to E. Varga entitled "Rossisskii put' perekhoda k
     sotsializmu i ego rezul'taty" (see #1192); GRANI No. 70
     contains poetry by S. Morozov, V. Khromov, N. Ustinova;
     GRANI No. 75 contains V. Vel'skii's "Otkroveniia" (see
     #1202).

     FENIKS: See also BOSLEY (#147), BRUMBERG (#178), GORBANEV-
     SKAIA (#402, #410, #412, #416), LANGLAND et al. (#656),
     GERSTENMAIER (#375).

339 FILANDROV, VLADIMIR. "Iskusstvennoe serdtse." ["Artificial
     Heart"] VREMIA I MY (New York/Paris/Jerusalem): No. 17,
     May 1977; pp. 113–32. Story.

340 For Human Rights (Anon. ed.) Frankfurt: Posev, 1969.
         Texts (in Russian and English) of the First Action
     Group on Human Rights; appeal to the UN; letters by Iakir
     and Petrovskii.

341 FREIMAN, GRIGORII. It Seems I am a Jew. Carbondale, Ill.:
     Southern Ill. Univ. Press, 1980; 97 pp. Tr., Melvyn
     Nathanson.
         From samizdat journal Evrei v SSSR; on anti-Semitism in
     Soviet mathematics--rejection of Jewish applicants, refusal
     to grant degrees to Jews, etc. Russian-language edition
     in Evrei v SSSR (#327).

G

342   GABAI, IL'IA. [b. 1935, d. 1973] "Sud Iova"; "Iudif";
       "Melodiia." NOVYI ZHURNAL (New York): No. 97, Dec. 1969;
       pp. 145-49. Poems.

343   _____. "U zakrytykh dverei otkrytogo suda." ["At the
       Closed Doors of the Open Court"] POSEV (Frankfurt): No. 2,
       Feb. 1970; pp. 31-37.
          Atmosphere in streets around courthouse where those ar-
       rested Aug. 1968, for demonstrating against Czech invasion,
       were being tried; from GORBANEVSKAIA (#411).

344   _____. "V poslednii raz v imen'e rodovom"; "Pozdnee
       kredo Iova." GRANI (Frankfurt): No. 77, Oct. 1970;
       pp. 49-53. Poems.

345   _____. "Volkhvy"; "Popytka ob"iasnit' zamysel"; "Moia
       ispoved'." GRANI (Frankfurt): No. 76, July 1970; pp.
       3-15. Poems.

       GABAI, IL'IA: See also GORBANEVSKAIA (#411 ff).

346   GALANSKOV, IURII. [b. 1939, d. 1972] "Chelovecheskii mani-
       fest." POSEV (Frankfurt): No. 12, Dec. 1972; pp. 5-6.
          Poem. Eng. tr. in BOSLEY (#147); GERSTENMAIER (#375);
       LANGLAND et al. (#656); German tr. in Vorkaempfer der Frei-
       heit, Frankfurt 1967; tr., M. von Holbeck. From Feniks
       No. 1.

347   _____. "O peresmotre karatel'noi politiki." ["On Re-
       consideration of Punitive Policy"] POSEV (Frankfurt):
       No. 7, July 1970; pp. 28-35.

       _____. "Pokazaniia Iu. Galanskova." RUS. MYSL' (Paris):
       July 16, 1970; p. 5; July 23, 1970; p. 5.
          Written from camp (where he was sent in 1968 after dis-
       tributing samizdat journal Feniks 1966 and receiving seven
       years' hard labor sentence); his thoughts on detente, on
       the invasion of Czechoslovakia, on Iulii Daniel' and West-
       ern Communists. Originally pub. in Sunday Telegraph
       (London).

348   _____. "Organizatsionnye problemy dvizheniia za polnoe
       i vseobshchee razoruzhenie i mir vo vsem mire." ["Organi-
       zational Problems of the Movement for Complete Disarma-
       ment and Peace in the World"] GRANI (Frankfurt): No. 64,
       June 1967; pp. 166-74.
          From Feniks 1966; very general discussion of possi-
       bility of disarmament.

GALANSKOV

349   GALANSKOV, IURII. "Otkrytoe pis'mo delegatu XXIII s"ezda
      KPSS M. Sholokhovu." ["Open Letter to Sholokhov"] GRANI
      (Frankfurt): No. 67, March 1968; pp. 115-33.

      _____. "Vyderzhka iz 'Otkrytogo pis'ma M. Sholokhovu'
      Iu. Galanskogo [sic]." POSEV (Frankfurt): No. 4 (1079),
      Jan. 27, 1967; p. 2.
         From Feniks 1966; re Sholokhov's winning of Nobel Prize.
      Letter attacks him (and criticizes Nobel Committee) for
      his behavior in Siniavskii/Daniel' affair as well as com-
      promises with the regime generally. Eng. tr. in GERSTEN-
      MAIER (#375), BRUMBERG (#178).

350   _____. "Pis'ma rodnym i druz'iam." ["Letters to Rela-
      tives and Friends"] GRANI (Frankfurt): No. 94, Oct.-Dec.
      1974; pp. 167-207.
         Posthumous pub. of letters about his time in the camp
      hospital (where he died), an angry letter to Iu. Karelin
      explaining his thoughts and motivation.

351   _____. "Poèt i borets." RUS. MYSL' (Paris): Nov. 2,
      1967; p. 5. Poem.

352   _____. "Spravedlivosti okrovavlennye usta." GRANI
      (Frankfurt): No. 68, July 1968; pp. 101-105. Poem.

353   _____. "On ne iskal ni bogatstva, ni slavy." ["He
      Sought Neither Wealth nor Glory"] POSEV (Frankfurt): No.
      12, Dec. 1972; pp. 2-4.
         Printed as a memorial to Galanskov after his death; a
      mixture of quotes from various texts--the trial transcript,
      his letter to Sholokhov (see above #349), final plea, etc.

354   _____. "Protokol obyska"; "Primechaniia k obysku Galan-
      skova 17. 1. 67"; "Protokol." POSEV (Frankfurt): No. 4
      (1131), April 1968; pp. 9-11.
         Protocol of the search of Galanskov's apartment.

355   _____. "Iu. T. Galanskov--chelovek, poèt i chelovek."
      GRANI (Frankfurt): No. 89-90, July-Dec. 1973; pp. 143-203.
         Collection of poems by and samizdat documents by and
      about Galanskov, who died in camp Nov. 4, 1972, plus his
      letters from camp.

      GALANSKOV, IURII: See also BOSLEY (#147), BRUMBERG (#178),
      Feniks 1, 1966, 1967 (#366-#338), LITVINOV (#701),
      BRUDERER (#176), Vol'noe slovo No. 14/15 (#1238).

356 GALICH, ALEKSANDR. [b. 1919, em. 1974, d. 1977] "Anne Akhmatovoi." RUS. MYSL' (Paris): March 16, 1972; p. 6.
Poem.

357 _____. General'naia repetitsiia. [Dress Rehearsal]
Frankfurt: Posev, 1974; 243 pp.

_____. "General'naia repetitsiia." (Paris): Aug. 22,
1974; p. 5; Aug. 29, 1974; p. 5.
Describes the atmosphere in artistic circles in connection with the production of his play, "Matrosskaia tishina," in 1958, banned after viewing of dress rehearsal.
Also describes how this incident gave birth to his rethink-
ing his views; recalls his last meetings with Mikhoels,
Markish et al.

358 _____. Pesni. [Songs] Frankfurt: Posev, 1969; 132 pp.
Collection of poem/songs.

359 _____. Poèma Rossii: stikhi i pesni sovetskogo pod-
pol'ia. [Poem of Russia: Poems and Songs of the Soviet
Underground] Paris: Société d'impr. périodiques et d'édi-
tions, 1971; 53 pp.

_____. "Poèma Rossii"; "Pesni o dukhovne svobode";
"Ironicheskie pesni." RUS. MYSL' (Paris): March 25,
1971; pp. 7-8. Poems and songs.

360 _____. Pokolenie obrechennykh. [Generation of the
Doomed] Frankfurt: Posev, 1972; 304 pp.; 1975.

_____. "Pesnia o sinei ptitse." GRANI (Frankfurt):
No. 70, Feb. 1969; pp. 113-14. Eng. tr. in LANGLAND et al.
(#656); Carlisle, Poets on Street Corners (New York, 1968).
Collection of magnitizdat poem/songs.

361 _____. "Rus'"; "Zaklinanie dobra i zla." GRANI (Frankfurt): No. 92/93, April-Sept. 1974; pp. 3-7. Poem/songs.

362 _____. "Six Songs." INDEX ON CENSORSHIP (London): No.
3, Autumn 1974; pp. 21-28. Tr., Gerry Smith. Poem/songs.

363 _____. "Staratel'skii vostok"; "Nochnoi dozor." RUS.
MYSL' (Paris): March 21, 1968; p. 5. Poems.

364 _____. "Staryi prints"; "Kogda-nibud' doshly istorik";
"Ia v put' sobiralsia vsegda nalegke"; "Ot bedy moei pust-
iakovoi";"Pesnia." GRANI (Frankfurt): No. 83, May 1972;
pp. 5-13. Poem/songs.

GALICH

365 GALICH, ALEKSANDR. "Stikhi: 'My ne khuzhe Goratsiia'; 'Noch-noi dozor'; 'Poezd'." POSEV (Frankfurt): No. 1 (1128), Jan. 1968; pp. 60-61. Poem/songs.

366 _____. "Stikhi Aleksandra Galicha: 'Pamiati B. L. Pasternaka'; 'Vozvrashchenie na itaku'; 'Pesnia iskhoda'." NOV. RUS. SLOVO (New York): Oct. 22, 1972; p. 5.

367 _____. "Zaklinanie." GRANI (Frankfurt): No. 68, July 1968; pp. 7-8.
　　　Poem. Eng. tr. in LANGLAND et al. (#656).

368 _____. "Ukhodiat druz'ia." RUS. MYSL' (Paris): Aug. 15, 1968; p. 7. Poem.

　　GALICH, ALEKSANDR: See also BOSLEY (#147), Sfinksy (#1011).

369 GANDLEVSKII, SERGEI [b. 1952] "Kogda volnuetsia. . . ." ÈKHO (Paris): No. 2, 1980; pp. 66-69. Poem.

　　GANDLEVSKII, S.: See also Moskovskoe vremia (#817).

　　GARBOVSKII, G.: See Sintaksis No. 3 (#1072), BOSLEY (#147).

370 GARIK, I. "Rodivshis' v sumrachnoe vremia." VREMIA I MY (New York/Paris/Jerusalem): No. 29, 1978; pp. 79-84.
　　　Satiric verse.

371 GAVRILOV, V. "Zaveshchanie." ["Testament"] GRANI (Frankfurt): No. 107, Jan.-March 1978; pp. 77-96. Story.

　　GEFTER, M.: See Poiski No. 1 (#940).

372 "Generatoru meshaiushchego deistviia." ["To the Jammer"] POSEV (Frankfurt): No. 12, Dec. 1975; pp. 24-27.
　　　About Soviet jamming of Western broadcasts.

373 GENRI, ÈRNST. "Otkrytoe pis'mo pisateliu I. Èrenburgu." ["Open Letter to Ehrenburg"] GRANI (Frankfurt): No. 63, March 1967; pp. 192-203.
　　　From Feniks 1966; letter, dated 1965; arguing with some statements Ehrenburg made about Stalin; he discusses Stalin's personal responsibility for the unprepared state of the Soviet Army when the Nazis attacked in June 1941.

374 GERASIMCHUK, VIKENTII. "Prostota khuzhe vorovstva." ["Simplicity Worse than Theft"] RUS. MYSL' (Paris): May 14, 1970; p. 2.

GERASIMCHUK, VIKENTII. "Prostota khuzhe vorovstva." POSEV (Frankfurt): No. 7, July 1970; pp. 49-53.
Re the black market in stolen cars, car parts, gas; also the pervasiveness of theft generally, its causes and consequences.

375 GERSTENMAIER, C. The Voices of the Silent. New York: Hart, 1972; 587 pp. Tr., Susan Hecker. Originally published as Die Stimme des Stummen.
The second half of the book consists of documents: poems from Feniks 1961, Sfinksy, Russkoe Slovo; report of SMOG demonstration, several documents from GINZBURG (#380), Galanskov's letter to Sholokhov from Feniks 1966 (#337), excerpts from LITVINOV (#701), various petitions and letters, essays by Pomerants and Siniavskii, responses to Sakharov's Razmyshleniia (#984), articles by Smirnov, Galanskov et al.

376 _____. Ed. Wladimir Bukowskij: Der unbequeme Zeuge. Stuttgart: Seewald, 1972.
Documents by and about Bukovskii, including samizdat account of Jan. 1972 trial.

377 GERTS, ANNA. (Pseud.) "K vol'noi vole zapovednye puti." ["Forbidden Paths Toward Free Will"] NOVYI ZHURNAL (New York): No. 120, Sept. 1975; pp. 31-77; No. 121, Dec. 1975; pp. 25-70; No. 122, March 1976; pp. 27-77.
About the life of Moscow dissidents of the 1960s. Novel.

378 GERTSYK, EVGENIIA. Vospominaniia. [Memoirs] Paris: YMCA, 1973; 192 pp.

_____. "N. A. Berdiaev." VESTNIK RSKhD (Paris): No. 106, IV-1972; pp. 146-62.
Memoirs not only about Berdiaev, but also about various poets and writers of the Silver Age (i.e., 1900-1930).

_____. "Nenapechatannoe predislovie k 'Vospominaniiam'." ["Unpublished Preface to 'Memoirs'"] VESTNIK RKhD (Paris): No. 115, I-1975; pp. 202-204.

379 GINDIS, ISAAK. "Khronika mestechka Chernopol'." ["The Chronicle of Chernopol"] DVADTSAT' DVA/22 (Jerusalem): No. 2, June 1978; pp. 3-97.
From Evrei v SSSR; Novella involving narrator's return to his home town of Chernopol, in the Ukraine, and a kind of history of the Jewish population of the town, its

GINZBURG

> destruction during the war (at the hands of Ukrainian
> locals, after the Nazis created the Jewish ghetto) and the
> few survivors who were evacuated and then returned.

380   GINZBURG, ALEKSANDR. [b. 1936] Ed. Belaia kniga po delu A.
> Siniavskogo i Iu. Danièl'ia. [The White Book on the Case
> of A. Siniavskii and Iu. Daniel'] Frankfurt: Posev,
> 1967; 430 pp.

> _____. On Trial: The Case of Sinyavsky (Tertz) and
> Daniel (Arzhak). Eds., Leopold Labedz and Max Hayward.
> London: Collins & Harvill, 1967; 384 pp. Tr., Manya
> Harari and Max Hayward; tr. from French, Marjorie Villiers.
> New York: Harper & Row, 1966, 310 pp.

> _____. (GUINZBOURG) Le Livre blanc de l'affaire
> Siniavsky-Daniel. Paris: Table Ronde, 1967; 336 pp. Tr.,
> M. Slavinsky.

> _____. (GINSBURG) Weissbuch in Sachen A. Sinjawskij-
> J. Daniel. Frankfurt: Posev, 1967; 416 pp. Tr., Elena
> Guttenberger.

> _____. "Sud nad A. D. Siniavskim i Iu. M. Danièlem."
> GRANI (Frankfurt): No. 60, June 1966; pp. 94-176; No. 62,
> Nov. 1966; pp. 7-136. (Ginzburg not mentioned in this is-
> sue, but later identified as editor.)

> _____. "Delo A. Siniavskogo i Iu. Danièlia: grazhdan-
> skoe obrashchenie"; "Prizyv gruppy 'Soprotivlenie'." RUS.
> MYSL' (Paris): Nov. 8, 1966; p. 2.

> _____. "Sud nad A. D. Siniavskim i Iu. M. Danièlem."
> RUS. MYSL' (Paris): April 28, 1966; pp. 4-5; April 30,
> 1966; pp. 4-5; May 3, 1966; pp. 4-6; May 5, 1966; pp. 4-5.
> Includes Ginzburg's (unsigned) analysis of trial, stress-
> ing the extraordinary courage and fortitude displayed by the
> accused: neither Siniavskii nor Daniel' would admit his
> guilt. Documents encompass trial transcript, account of
> demonstration in support of defendants, letters by defend-
> ants' wives to prosecutors and Brezhnev, various supporting
> letters, speeches by both prosecuting lawyers and Siniav-
> skii and Daniel's attorneys, and several additional letters
> written after the trial (one by L. Chukovskaia to M. Sholo-
> khov, see #246). Several items also in GERSTENMAIER (#375).

381   _____. "Zapis' poslednego slova A. I. Ginzburga."
> ["Text of Ginzburg's Final Plea"] NOV. RUS. SLOVO (New
> York): June 6, 1968; p. 2.

Brief statement defending his compilation of the White Book and other actions.

GINZBURG, ALEKSANDR: See also BRUMBERG (#178), BRUDERER (#176), LITVINOV (#701), Sintaksis (#1072).

382   GINZBURG, EVGENIIA. [b. 1907 or 1906, d. 1977] Krutoi marshrut. Milan: Mondadori, 1967; 474 pp.

_____. Journey into the Whirlwind. New York: Harcourt, Brace & World, 1967; 418 pp. Tr., Paul Stevenson and Max Hayward.

_____. (GUINZBOURG) Le vertige. Paris: Seuil, 1967; 424 pp. Tr., B. Abbots and J. J. Marie.

_____. (GINSBURG) Marschroute eines Lebens. Reinbek b. Hamburg: Rowohlt, 1967; 380 pp. Tr., Swetlana Geier.

_____. Krutoi marshrut. GRANI (Frankfurt): No. 64, June 1967; pp. 81-111; No. 65, Sept. 1967; pp. 51-99; No. 66, Dec. 1967; pp. 45-151; No. 67, March 1968; pp. 71-88; No. 68, July 1968; pp. 9-100.

_____. "Krutoi marshrut." POSEV (Frankfurt): No. 7 (1082), Feb. 17, 1967; pp. 5-6; No. 8 (1083), Feb. 24, 1967; pp. 3-4; No. 9 (1084), March 3, 1967; pp. 3-4; No. 10 (1085), March 10, 1967; pp. 3-5.

_____. (GINSBURG [sic]) "Paskha na Kolyme, 1940 g." VESTNIK RSKhD (Paris): No. 83, I-1967; pp. 66-67.
    Portions contained in Feniks 1967. Memoir, by formerly staunch Leninist, of her arrest in 1937; her account begins with Kirov's murder and the reactions of party members like herself, and goes on to describe her expulsion from the party, her separation from her family (including son Vasilii Aksenov), the army officers' purge, the transport convoys, prison.

383   _____. Krutoi marshrut. Kn. 2. Milan: Mondadori, 1979.

_____. Within the Whirlwind. New York and London: Harcourt Brace Jovanovich, 1979. Tr., Ian Boland; 423 pp.

_____. "Mea Culpa." VREMIA I MY (New York/Paris/Jerusalem): No. 49, Jan. 1980; pp. 52-61. Excerpt.
    Continuation of her memoirs, describing her years in camp and in exile in Siberia (she spent 18 years, altogether, in prison, camp and exile, and was rehabilitated

GLADILIN

in 1956), her efforts to bring her surviving son out of
Siberia, her marriage to a German Catholic physician.

384   GLADILIN, ANATOLII. [b. 1935, em. 1976] "Kontsert dlia
truby s orkestrom." ["Concert for Trumpet and Orchestra"]
GRANI (Frankfurt): No. 99, Jan.-March 1976; pp. 12-39.
Story.

385   _____. Prognoz na zavtra. [Forecast for Tomorrow]
Frankfurt: Posev, 1972; 190 pp.

_____. Und morgen wechselnd wolkig. Graz: Styria,
1978; 200 pp. Tr., T. Frickhinger-Garanin.
Novel about the tribulations and eventual success of a
young physicist; portrays the negative effects on scientific creativity of Soviet bureaucracy.

386   _____. Repetitsia v piatnitsu. [Rehearsal on Friday]
Paris: Tret'ia volna, 1978; 159 pp.
Contains four works: title piece; "Tigr perekhodit
ulitsu"; "Kontsert dlia truby s orkestrom"; and "Zaporo-
zhets na mokrom shosse." (The last was written after
emigration.)

_____. "Repetitsiia v piatnitsu." KONTINENT: No. 12,
1977; pp. 47-84 and No. 13, 1977; pp. 91-131.
Science fiction/fantasy novella in which Stalin doesn't
die, he merely becomes anabiotic and wakes up in 1974.

_____. "Tigr perekhodit ulitsu." ["The Tiger Crosses
the Street"] KONTINENT: No. 7, 1976; pp. 5-23. Story.

387   GLADKOV, ALEKSANDR. Vstrechi s Pasternakom. [Meetings with
Pasternak] Paris: YMCA, 1973; 159 pp.

_____. Meetings with Pasternak. London: Collins
and Harvill and New York: Harcourt, Brace, Jovanovich:
1977; 223 pp. Tr., Max Hayward.
Memoir by close personal friend of Pasternak's.

388   "Glaz i zub." (Anon.) RUS. MYSL' (Paris): Aug. 28, 1975;
p. 11.
Poem from samizdat collection Kacheli sud'by, edited by
Nikolai Bokov, under whose name it is listed.

GLAZKOV, N.: See Sintaksis (#1072).

389   GLEZER, ALEKSANDR. [b. 1934, em. 1975] "Okruzhaiut menia. . .";
"Eifeleva bashnia." RUS. MYSL' (Paris): March 13, 1975;
p. 8. Poems.

GLUKHOV, K.: See Vol'noe slovo No. 7 (#1232).

390   GLUSHKOVA, TAT'IANA. "Obryv." GRANI (Frankfurt): No. 81,
Nov. 1971; p. 43. Poem.

391   GLUZMAN, SEMEN. "Angel na karnize." ["Angel on the Cornice"]
KONTINENT: No. 24, 1980; pp. 15–27. Story.

392   _____. "Psalmy i skorbi: 'Plach Iova'; 'Piatistishiia';
'Chernomu moriu'; 'V snegu'; 'Potom. Kogda-nibud''; 'Tebe';
'Novorozhdennye kashtany. . .'." VREMIA I MY (New York/
Paris/Jerusalem): No. 60, May–June 1981; pp. 143–49.
Poems.

393   _____. "Russhirennaia sudebnopsikhiatricheskaia za-
ochnaia a èkspertiza trekh sovetskikh anonimnykh psikhiatrov
po delu Grigorenko Petra Grigor'evicha 1907 g.r., ukraintsa,
zhitel'ia g. Moskvy." ["Expanded Legal-Psychiatric Examination by Three Anonymous Soviet Psychiatrists of the Case
of Petr Grigorenko"] RUS. MYSL' (Paris): April 12, 1973;
pp. 6–7.
Young dissident Soviet psychiatrist circulated text of
Grigorenko's psychiatric examination.

GLUZMAN, SEMEN: See BUKOVSKII and GLUZMAN (#190).

GOLIAVKIN, V.: See Sintaksis 3 (#1072), BOSLEY (#147).

394   "Golova i nogi." (Anon.) RUS. MYSL' (Paris): Sept. 25,
1975; p. 5.
Poem from samizdat collection Kacheli sud'by, edited by
Nikolai Bokov, under whose name it is listed.

GOLOVIN, E: See Sfinksy (#1011).

395   GOL'TSOV, ALEKSANDR and OZEROV, SERGEI. "Raspredelenie
natsional'nogo dokhoda SSSR." RUS. MYSL' (Paris): May 24,
1973; p. 4; May 31, 1973; p. 4; June 7, 1973; p. 4; June
14, 1973; p. 4.

_____. "Distribution of the National Income of the
USSR." ASSOC. FOR COMPARATIVE ECONOMIC STUDIES BULLETIN:
Vol. XV, No. 2–3, Summer–Fall 1973; pp. 79–102.
Examination of real size and distribution of national
income, especially the portion expended on defense. Concludes the Soviet national income is 17–20% of American,
that military expenditures account for 41–51% of that income and consumer goods 21–31%. Also in Washington Post,
April 13, 1971; abstract in Khr. tek. sob. No. 24 (#538).

GOLUBEVA

GOLUBEVA, V: See <u>Vol'noe slovo</u> No. 38 (#1257).

GOLUBOV, I: See <u>Russkoe slovo</u> (#972).

396   GOLUMBIEVSKAIA, A. "Za chto iskliuchaiut iz partii." ["Why One is Expelled from the Party"] VESTNIK RKhD (Paris): No. 116, II-III-IV-1975; pp. 259-67.

397   GORBANEVSKAIA, NATAL'IA. [b. 1936, em. 1975] "Dvenadtsat' stikhotvorenii: 'A ne voda polnym-polnyi. . .'; 'Mechtatel'nye nedonoski. . .'; 'Kakuiu muzyku igraiut. . .'; 'O drug moi'; 'Gribnoi dozhd';' 'A!. Mnogolikii--'; 'V krae. . .'; 'Opiat' v viskakh bessonitsa gudit. . .'; 'Mne gore svodit guby. . .'; 'V nekrologe napisano--poèt'; 'Iznemozhenie liubvi'; 'Perelistai menia do korochki. . .'." GRANI (Frankfurt): No. 52, Dec. 1962.
        Poems, from <u>Feniks</u> 1 (#336); Eng. tr. of some in BOSLEY (#147).

398   _____. (GORBANEVSKAYA) "Fourteen poems." INDEX ON CENSORSHIP (London): Vol. 1, No. 1, Spring 1972; pp. 107-15. Tr., Daniel Weissbort. Poems.

399   _____. "Iz knigi 'Dol'goe proshchanie'." DVADTSAT'/DVA 22 (Tel Aviv): No. 1, 1978; pp. 185-87.
        Poems, dated pre-emigration.

400   _____. "Iz poslednei knigi stikhov: 'Ten' moi, ston moi, tikhii ston. . .'; 'Ostat'sia odnoiu'; 'Kak khochetsia mne. . .'; 'Zhuzhzhanie zhuka. . .'; 'Moe liubimoe shosse'; 'O, kak na sklone'; 'Tak ty letish', smeshnaia?'; 'Gospodi Isuse, Presviataia-Bogoroditsa. . .'; 'Ne do zhiru. . .'." KONTINENT: No. 8, 1976; pp. 49-53.
        Poems dated May-Sept. 1975.

401   _____. "Iz stikhov poslednikh let." VESTNIK RSKhD Paris): No. 94, Iv-1969; pp. 112-17. Poems.

402   _____. "Kak andersovskoi armii soldat. . ."; "Liubov', liubov'!"; "Strelok iz luka. . ."; "Narevesh'sia. . ."; "V moem rodnom dvadtsatom veke. . . ." GRANI (Frankfurt): No. 69; pp. 86-88. Poems.

403   _____. "Kak vol'no dyshit Vil'no po kholmam. . ."; "Sukhaia struika dyma. . ."; "Stradan'ia, strasti, radosti i strakh. . ."; "Zasypaiut ch'i-to sny. . . ." RUS. MYSL' (Paris): Sept. 7, 1972; p. 5.

404   GORBANEVSKAIA, NATAL'IA. "Kak vol'no dyshit Vil'no po khol-
       mam. . ."; "Sukhaia struika dyma. . ."; "Stradan'ia,
       strasti, radosti i strakh. . ."; "Zasypaiut ch'i-to
       sny. . . ." NOV. RUS. SLOVO (New York): Sept. 17, 1972;
       p. 5. Poems.

405   _____. "Ne spi na zakate." GRANI (Frankfurt): No. 99,
       Jan.-March 1976; pp. 3-11.
           Poem, also contained in Pereletaia snezhnuiu granitsu,
       Paris: YMCA, 1979, which includes mostly post-emigration
       poetry.

406   _____. "Dolgoe proshchan'e: 'Ne vstretila by nas Moskva
       dozhdem. . .'; 'Obryvki'." VREMIA I MY (New York/Paris/
       Jerusalem): No. 23, 1977; pp. 125-27. Poems.

407   _____. "Nine Unpublished Poems: 'How resonant are the
       echoes. . .'; 'My love, in what region. . .'; 'This world
       is amazingly flat'." RUSSIAN LITERATURE TRIQUARTERLY (Ann
       Arbor, Mich.): No. 9, Spring 1974; pp. 536-40. Poems.

408   _____. "Pamiati Iu. Galanskova." VESTNIK RSKhD (Paris):
       No. 106, IV-1972; pp. 354. Poem.

409   _____. "Pis'mo v redaktsiiu." VESTNIK RKhD (Paris):
       No. 114, IV-1974; pp. 255-57. Letter about samizdat.

410   _____. Poberezh'e. [The Coast] Ann Arbor, Mich.:
       Ardis, 1973; 151 pp. Collection of poems.

411   _____. Polden': Delo o demonstratsii 25 avgusta 1968
       goda na Krasnoi ploshchadi. Frankfurt: Posev, 1970;
       504 pp.

       _____. Red Square at Noon. New York, Chicago, San
       Francisco: Holt, Rinehart & Winston, 1970; 288 pp. Lon-
       don: Andrei Deutsch, 1972. Tr., Alexander Lieven.

       _____. Midi, Place Rouge. Paris: Laffont, 1970; 320
       pp. Tr., Jacques Trivouss and Mariette Aventin.
           Documents and her personal account of demonstration on
       Aug. 25, 1968, in Red Square in protest at Soviet invasion
       of Czechoslovakia and the ensuing trial of P. Litvinov and
       L. Bogoraz.

412   _____. Selected Poems. Oxford: Carcanet, 1972; 156 pp.
       Tr., Daniel Weissbort. Poems.

GORBANEVSKAIA

413   GORBANEVSKAIA, NATAL'IA. "Sharmanka, poi. . ."; "Povernite
       nebo vspiat'." GRANI (Frankfurt): No. 70, Feb. 1969;
       pp. 112-13. Poems.

414   _____. "Stikhi, napisannye v Butyrskoi tiur'me." VESTNIK
       RSKhD (Paris): No. 98, IV-1970; pp. 148-50. Poems.

415   _____. " tikhi, ne sobrannye v knigi: 'Proshchai, pro-
       shchai, proshchai'; 'Ia s toboiu tikho-tikho. . .'; 'Khot' na
       den', khot' na chas. . .'; 'Glukhogo dereva listva. . .';
       'Eshche ne znavshie znachen'ia. . .'; 'Svet moi iasnyi. . .';
       'A na moikh chasakh. . .'; 'Uzhalennyi skhodstvom. . .'."
       GRANI (Frankfurt): No. 76, July 1970; pp. 87-91. Poems.

416   _____. Stikhi: 1956-61. Frankfurt: Posev, 1969;
       180 pp.
           Poems. Also contains "Besplatnaia meditsinskaia
       pomoshch'," which also appears in ARTEMOVA et al. (#79).

417   _____. Tri tetradi: Stikhotvorenie. [Three Notebooks:
       Poetry] Bremen: K-Presse, 1975. Poems.

418   _____. "Twelve Poems." INDEX ON CENSORSHIP (London):
       Vol. 6, No. 1, Jan.-Feb. 1977; pp. 37-41. Tr., D. Weiss-
       bort. Poems.

419   _____. "V sumasshedshem dome. . . ." GRANI (Frankfurt):
       No. 67, March 1968; p. 40.
           Poem, from Feniks 1966 (#337). Eng. tr. in BOSLEY (#147).

420   _____. "Verse." ZET (Heidelberg): No. 11, Oct. 1975;
       pp. 16-17. Tr., Kay Borowsky. Poem.

       GORBANEVSKAIA, NATAL'IA: See also ARTEMOVA et al. (#79),
       BOSLEY (#147), Feniks 1 (#336), Feniks 1966 (#337).

421   GORBUNOVA, ANNA. "Kto plachet, . ."; "Dekabr'. Moskva. . .";
       "Psalom"; "Neuzheli èto navsegda? . ."; "Kanatokhodets";
       "Tak dolgo pet'. . . ." KONTINENT: No. 12, 1977; pp. 85-
       89. Poems.

422   GORENSHTEIN, FRIDRIKH. [b. 1932, em. 1980] "Berdichev."
       VREMIA I MY (New York/Paris/Jerusalem): No. 50, Feb. 1980;
       pp. 41-101 and No. 51, March 1980; pp. 27-87.
           Fictional reminiscence of Jewish town of Berdichev, with
       flashbacks and descriptions of current Jewish population.

423   _____. Iskuplenie. [Redemption] VREMIA I MY (New York/
       Paris/Jerusalem): No. 42, June 1979; pp. 11-94.
           Excerpt from novel.

424   GORENSHTEIN, FRIDRIKH. "Moi Chekhov oseni i zimy 1968 goda."
       ["My Chekhov in the Fall and Winter of 1968"] VREMIA I MY
       (New York/Paris/Jerusalem): No. 55, July-Aug. 1980; pp.
       209-222. Whimsical view of Chekhov.

425   _____. (FELIKS [sic]) "Razgovor." ["Conversation"]
       VREMIA I MY (New York/Paris/Jerusalem): No. 59, March-
       April 1981; pp. 75-80. Story.

426   _____. "Zima 53-ogo goda." ["The Winter of '53"]
       KONTINENT: No. 17, 1978; pp. 11-106; No. 18, 1978; pp.
       133-76. Novella.

       GORENSHTEIN, FRIDRIKH: See also Metropol' (#808).

       GORICHEVA, T.: See 37 (#1162); Vol'noe slovo No. 38 (#1257).

427   GORIUSHKIN, V. "Petrusha"; "Do voskhoda solntsa." ["Petru-
       sha"; "Before Sunrise"] GRANI (Frankfurt): No. 63, March
       1967; pp. 43-57.
       Stories; Eng. tr. of second in SCAMMELL (#1005).

428   GORNYI, VLADIMIR. (Pseud.) "Palach i ego master." ["The
       Hangman and his Master"] NOVYI ZHURNAL (New York): No.
       114, March 1974; pp. 37-57.
       Excerpt from novel, re death of Yagoda.

429   GORSKII, V. "Russkii messianizm i novoe natsional'noe soz-
       nanie." ["Russian Messianism and the New National Con-
       sciousness"] VESTNIK RSKhD (Paris): No. 97, III-1970;
       pp. 33-68.
       Critique of nationalist-patriotic tendency in the con-
       text of a broader analysis of that political and cultural
       tragedy into which Russia was continually dragged by roman-
       tic nationalism. Eng. tr. in MEERSON-AKSENOV and SHRAGIN (#801).

430   "Gorod Vladimir." ["The City of Vladimir"] (Anon.) VESTNIK
       RSKhD (Paris): No. 99, I-1971; pp. 122-34.
       About the prison of Vladimir, unseen by tourists who
       come to admire the ancient city; reproduces administrative
       orders re prison.

431   "Gospod' govorit cheloveku." ["The Lord Speaks to Man"]
       (Anon.) VESTNIK RSKhD (Paris): No. 94, IV-1969; pp. 38-
       40. Religious essay, written in 1937.

432   GR. N. Z. "Ob otnoshenii khristian k iudaizmu." ["On Chris-
       tians' Attitudes toward Judaism"] VESTNIK RKhD (Paris):
       No. 112-113, II-III-1974; pp. 63-90.

GRACHEV

A response to the French Episcopate's statement on the
relationship of Christianity and Judaism. Author considers
the French statement an overstatement of the Christian debt
to Judaism, as well as an exaggeration of the importance
of Jewish history, and attacks it for not stressing Jewish
conversion to Christianity.

433   GRACHEV, RID. [b. 1935?] "Adamchik." ["Little Adam"] ÈKHO
(Paris): No. 2, 1980; pp. 87-110. Story.

434   GREBENSHCHIKOV, NIKOLAI. "Razdumiia." ["Meditations"] GRANI
(Frankfurt): No. 82, Dec. 1971; pp. 94-96.
Fragmentary essays.

435   GREBS, TAT'IANA. "Zhizn'--vsiudu zhizn'." VESTNIK RKhD
(Paris): No. 111, I-1974; p. 110.
Poem, listed under "Golos Arkhipelaga," dated 1950-52.

436   GRIGORENKO, PETR. [b. 1907, em. 1977] Communism vs. Stalinism. London: International Marxist Group, 1974; 15 pp.
Brief essay on Stalinism as divergent from Marxism.

437   _____. Mysli sumasshedshego: Izbrannye pis'ma i vystupleniia. Amsterdam: Herzen, 1973; 335 pp.

_____. The Grigorenko Papers. Boulder, Col.: West-
view, 1976; 187 pp.

_____. Aufzeichnungen aus Gefängnis und Irrenhaus.
Bern: Kuratorium Geistige Freiheit, 1970; 24 pp.

_____. "Dnevnik Generala P. G. Grigorenko." NOV. RUS.
SLOVO (New York): April 12, 1970; p. 7; April 13, 1970;
pp. 2-3; April 14, 1970; p. 2; April 15, 1970; p. 2.

_____. "Zapiski P. Grigorenko." POSEV (Frankfurt):
No. 3, March 1970; pp. 3-11.
Grigorenko's notes, letters, diary entries, statements,
etc., describing various methods of the physical and mental
destruction of political dissidents practiced in psychiatric clinics, including the dispensing of psychedelic drugs.
Rus. ed. contains a bibliography of Grigorenko's samizdat
writings (pp. 326-28) as well as a few other items absent
from the English edition.

438   _____. Sokrytie istoricheskoi pravdy--prestuplenie
pered narodom; pis'mo v redaktsiiu zhurnala "Voprosy
istorii KPSS." [The Concealment of an Historical Truth
is a Crime Before the People] London, Ontario: Izd.
Soiuza bor'by za osvobozhdenie nar. Rossii, 1970; 41 pp.

GRIGORENKO, PETR. "Sokrytie istoricheskoi pravdy--prestuplenie pered narodom!" NOVYI ZHURNAL (New York): No. 96, Sept. 1969; pp. 223-63. (Incorrect page given in Table of Contents.)

_____. "Sokrytie istoricheskoi pravdy--prestuplenie pered narodom!" NOV. RUS. SLOVO (New York): Nov. 12, 1969; p. 2.
Letter sent to "Voprosy istorii KPSS" ("Problems of the History of the CPSU") and never published, in response to negative review of A. Nekrich's 1941. 22 iiunia (pub. 1965), and general analysis of Soviet lack of preparedness for war in 1941, for which he blames primarily Stalin.

439   _____. Staline et la deuxième guerre mondiale. Paris: Herne, 1969; 148 pp. Tr., Olivier Simon.

_____. Der sowjetische Zusammenbruch 1941. Frankfurt: Posev, 1969; 190 pp. Tr., George Bruderer.
Analysis of Stalin's responsibility for the 1941 Soviet collapse.

GRIGORENKO, PETR: See also ARTEMOVA et al. (#79), BRUMBERG (#178), GLUZMAN (#393). MEERSON-AKSENOV and SHRAGIN (#801), Samizdat I (#989), SAUNDERS (#1001).

440   GRIGOR'EV, OLEG. [b. 1943?] "Letnii den'." ["A Summer Day"] ÈKHO (Paris): No. 2, 1980; pp. 71-80.
Story (partial manuscript).

441   GRIGOR'EV, V. "Obrashchenie k mirovoi obshchestvennosti." ["Appeal to World Public Opinion"] NOVYI ZHURNAL (New York): No. 118, March 1975; pp. 261-69.
Statement by political prisoner (religious) asking for help, with account of life in camp.

442   GROBMAN, MIKHAIL. "Stikhi: 'Tiazheleiut snega. . .'; 'V vysokikh snakh. . .'; 'Pod zimnim nebom. . .'; 'V bol'shikh grobakh tela rastenii. . .'." NOVYI ZHURNAL (New York): No. 108, Sept. 1972; pp. 124-25. Poems.

GROIS, B.: See 37 (#1162).

443   GROSSMAN, VASILII. [b. 1905, d. 1964] Vse techet. Frankfurt: Posev, 1970; 207 pp.

_____. Forever Flowing. New York: Harper & Row, 1972; 247 pp. Tr., Jacqueline Lafond.

GROSSMAN

GROSSMAN, VASILII. (GROSSMANN) <u>Tout passe</u>. . . . Paris:
Stock, 1972; 313 pp. Tr., N. Artemoff.

_____. <u>Alles fliesst</u>. Frankfurt: Posev, 1972; 248 pp.
Tr. N. Artemoff.

_____. "Vse techet. . . : "otryvki iz romana." GRANI
(Frankfurt): No. 78, Dec. 1970; pp. 3-33.

_____. "Tikhaia Mashen'ka." POSEV (Frankfurt): No. 11,
Nov. 1970; pp. 51-56.
   Novel whose hero, having spent 22 years in camps, returns to Moscow; he meets a cousin whose life has gone in
a completely different direction, the teacher who informed
on him, and others. Tries to build a new life, but cor-
ruption and embezzlement reign supreme. Contains section
on the forced collectivization. Grossman blames Lenin for
the stifling of freedom, the liquidation of all revolutionary parties, and sees Stalinism as an outgrowth of
Leninist policies.

444   _____. "Za pravoe delo: glavy iz vtoroi knigi romana."
["For a Just Cause: Chapters from the Second Book of the
Novel"] KONTINENT: No. 4, 1974; pp. 179-216; No. 5, 1974;
pp. 7-40; continued under title "Zhizn' i sud'ba" in No. 6,
1976; pp. 151-71; No. 7, 1976; pp. 95-112; Nov. 8, 1976;
pp. 111-33.

_____. "Za pravo delo: otryvok iz vtorogo toma romana."
GRANI (Frankfurt): No. 97, July-Sept. 1975; pp. 3-31.

_____. "Prirodnoe stremlenie cheloveka k svobode neistre-
bimo." POSEV (Frankfurt): No. 7, July 1975; pp. 53-55.

_____. "Dobro vam." AMI (Jerusalem): No. 2, pp. 36-40.
Page number incorrectly listed in Table of Contents; journal no longer exists.
   Book one of the novel was published in 1952, unfinished.
After the author's death in 1964 his manuscripts were confiscated by the KGB; friends managed to save one copy of
the manuscript.

445   _____. <u>Zhizn' i sud'ba</u>. [<u>Life and Fate</u>] Lausanne:
L'Age d'Homme, 1980.

_____. "Sud'ba komissara Krymova." VREMIA I MY (New
York/Paris/Jerusalem): No. 45, Sept. 1979; pp. 13-56.
   Novel, first third of which (<u>Za pravoe delo</u>) was pub-
lished, the rest confiscated (see annotation to #444).

Action set in Stalingrad during the war, author decries
all dogmas and holds that any good, if it is based on dogma, leads man into slavery.

446 GUBANOV, VLADIMIR (LEONID [sic]). "Pobeditelei ne sudiat:
'Otrezvlenie'; 'Ėkho'; 'Natiurmort nastroeniia'; 'Skupo
ogliadyvaias';' 'Mechty velikoi perekrestok'; 'Shutochnoe'."
VREMIA I MY (New York/Paris/Jerusalem): No. 26, 1978;
pp. 93-100. Poems.

447 _____. "Prekloniv koleni: 'Popytka k begstvu'; 'Grust-
naia freska'; 'Zaklinanie'." VREMIA I MY (New York/Paris/
Jerusalem): No. 21, Sept. 1977; pp. 86-91. Poems.

GUBANOV, VLADIMIR: See also SMOG (#1080), Sfinksy (#1011).

448 GUBERMAN, IGOR'. Bumerang. Ann Arbor: Hermitage, 1982;
180 pp. Collection of poems.

449 GUBIN, VLADIMIR. "Bezdozhd'e do sentiabria." ["Drought till
September"] ĖKHO (Paris): No. 1, 1978; pp. 18-51. Story.

450 GUMILEV, NIKOLAI. [b. 1886, d. 1921] "Predsmertnoe stikhotvorenie N. Gumileva." VESTNIK RSKhD (Paris): No. 98, IV-
1970; pp. 64-65.
Poem, written in 1921, by Acmeist poet who was shot that
same year.

451 GUSAROV, VLADIMIR. [b. 1925] "Bestiarii." NOV. RUS. SLOVO
(New York). Fable.

452 _____. "I primknuvshii k nim Shepilov. . . ." ["And
Shepilov who joined them. . . ."] RUS. MYSL' (Paris):
March 18, 1971; p. 5; March 25, 1971; p. 5; April 1, 1971;
p. 5.
Gusarov got acquainted with Shepilov, former politburo
member and foreign minister, in exile; Shepilov joined the
anti-Khrushchev coalition in 1957. Title derives from
Central Committee condemnation of Malenkov, Kaganovich,
Molotov, and Shepilov "who joined them."

453 _____. Moi papa ubil Mikhoèlsa. [My Father Killed
Mikhoels] Frankfurt: Posev; 435 pp.
Son of high Stalin apparatchik describes the atmosphere
of the party elite--the hypocrisy, slavish worship of
Stalin, etc. Gusarov also describes the psychological conflict in the relation between himself, the freethinking
son, and his orthodox-minded father.

GUSAROV

454 GUSAROV, VLADIMIR. "V zashchitu Faddeia Bulgarina." ["In
       Defense of Faddei Bulgarin"] VREMIA I MY (New York/Paris/
       Jerusalem): No. 29, 1978; pp. 134-46.
         Sardonic piece on contemporary literature.

GUSEV, V.: See Sfinksy (#1011).

H

455 HARRIS, ROSEMARY and HOWARD-JOHNSTON, XENIA, Eds. Christian
     Appeals from Russia. London: Hodder, 1969.
          Collection of Baptist appeals and statements,1966-68.

456 The Human Rights Movement in the Ukraine. Baltimore: Smolo-
     skyp, 1980; 277 pp.
          Documents of the Ukrainian Helsinki Group 1976-80.

I

IAKHIMOVICH, IVAN: See BRUMBERG (#178), SAUNDERS (#1001).

457 IAKIR, PETR. [b. 1923] <u>Detstvo v tiur'me</u>. London and Basing-
stoke: Macmillan London Ltd., 1972; 151 pp.

_____. (YAKIR) <u>A Childhood in Prison</u>. New York:
Coward, McCann & Geoghegan, 1973; 155 pp.

_____. (YAKIR) <u>Une enfance russe</u>. Paris: Grasset,
1972; 192 pp. Tr., Marina Gorbov and Nikita Krivochéine.

_____. (JAKIR) <u>Kindheit in Gefangenschaft</u>. Frankfurt:
Insel, 1972; 187 pp. and Frankfurt: Suhrkamp, 1974; 188
pp. Tr., Heddy Pross-Weerth.

_____. "Memuary P. Iakira--l chast': detstvo v tiur'me."
RUS. MYSL' (Paris): Oct. 28, 1971; pp. 2-3; Nov. 4, 1971;
pp. 2-3; Nov. 11, 1971; pp. 2-3; Nov. 18, 1971; pp. 2-3;
Nov. 25, 1971; pp. 2-3; Dec. 2, 1971; pp. 2-3.
Memoir by son of army commander shot in 1937, who spent
from 1937-54 in prisons and camps. The second part of the
memoirs was confiscated by KGB during search of his apartment.
He describes other children he met, some guilty of being
"enemies of the people" because of their parentage, some
themselves accused of terrorist acts, and many "bezpri-
zornye" (homeless), and how they developed, through
the years in prison and camp, norms of behavior and morals
under the influence of the thieves, hooligans, etc.

458 _____. (PAVEL [sic]) "Stalinu--k ugolovnoi otvetstvennosti." RUS. MYSL' (Paris): April 24, 1969; p. 4.

_____. "Stalinu-k ugolovnoi otvetstvennosti." POSEV
(Frankfurt): Vol. 25, no. 7 (July 1969); pp. 57-60.

_____. (YAKIR) "A Plea for a Criminal Investigation."
SURVEY (London): No. 70/71, Winter-Spring 1969; pp. 261-
69. Eng. also in <u>Problems of Communism</u> (Washington): 18,
no. 4-5, July-Oct., 1969; pp. 102-104.
Letter sent to <u>Kommunist</u> after that journal praised
Stalin's military talents. Iakir details some of Stalin's
military crimes and judges him, according to the RFSFR
Criminal Code, to deserve four death sentences and 68
years' deprivation of freedom.

459 IAKOBSON, ANATOLII. [b. 1935, em. 1973, d. 1978] <u>Konets
tragedii</u>. [<u>The End of the Tragedy</u>] New York: Chekhov,
1973. Critical analysis of the poetry of Aleksandr Blok.

IAKUBOVICH, M.: See MEDVEDEV (#772, #773).

IAKUNIN, GLEB: See Vol'noe slovo, Nos. 24, 35-36 (#1246, #1255), ÈSHLIMAN and IAKUNIN (#320), BOURDEAUX (#148), MEERSON-AKSENOV and SHRAGIN (#801).

IAMPOL'SKII, BORIS: See MEDVEDEV and LERT (#770).

460   IANKOV, VADIM. [b. 1935] "O vozmozhnom smysle russkogo demokraticheskogo dvizhenia." ["On the Possible Meaning of the Russian Democratic Movement"] KONTINENT: No. 18, 1978; pp. 183-201.
Analysis of composition and role of current opposition movement in the Soviet Union and its relation to the West.

461   _____. "Serdtsevina sviazi." ["Essential Bonds"] KONTINENT: No. 22, 1980; pp. 317-23.
Inquiry into the nature of religious thought.

IASKOLKA, AIDA: See Feniks 1966 (#337) and BOSLEY (#147).

IBRAGIMOV, T.: See "'Delo' krymskikh tatar" (#267).

462   IGNATOVA, ELENA. [b. 1946] "Stikhi: 'Khlebnyi angel. . .'; 'Vot i ty. . .'; 'Rannii sneg. . .'; 'Vek mozhno provesti . . .'; 'Slepoi pastukh. . .'; 'Tam, gde Vladimir-gorod zhil. . .'; 'Mne v ètom gorode ne vypast' iz pleiady. . .'; 'Vse protiazhen'e broshennoi stolitsy. . .'; 'Mednogubaia muzyka oseni. . .'; 'Nas bylo shestero. . .'; 'O, èto sumasshestvie--ne sad. . .'; 'Ètot grustnyi i prekrasnyi mir. . .'." GRANI (Frankfurt): No. 98, Oct.-Dec. 1975; pp. 120-31. Poems.

463   _____. "My zasypaem bez slez. . ."; "Pamiati druga." KONTINENT: No. 29, 1981; pp. 91-94. Poems.

464   _____. "Stikhi: 'I russkogo stikha prokhladnyi vlazh-nyi srub. . .'; 'Ty--uvidish' mongola. . .'; 'Sidiat bol'-shie muzhiki. . .'; 'Dlia rossiiskoi zheny na chuzh-bine. . .'; 'Sily proshu ia. . .'; 'Marsii'; 'Teper' skazhu. . .'; 'Smutnoe vremia. . .'." GRANI (Frankfurt): No. 103, Jan.-March 1977; pp. 100-105. Poems.

465   _____. "Stikhi: 'Edva li ne snachala sentiabria. . .'; 'Okostenelyi svet. . .'; 'Podval'; 'Vechernei vlagoiu polna listva. . .'." KONTINENT: No. 6, 1976; pp. 105-108. Poems.

IGNATOVA

466   IGNATOVA, ELENA. Stikhi o prichastnostii. [Poems on Communion] Paris: Ritm, 1976; 80 pp. Poems.

467   IKS. "Poslanie iz SSSR na Zapad." ["Message from the USSR to the West"] NOVYI ZHURNAL (New York): No. 78, March 1965; pp. 159-91; No. 79, June 1965; pp. 175-210.

_____. "Poslanie iz SSSR na Zapad." NOV. RUS. SLOVO (New York): Aug. 26, 1965; p. 2; Sept. 10, 1965; p. 2.
Impassioned first-person account of Soviet violations of its own constitution, contrasting official claims with reality in both political areas (e.g., freedoms of religion, word, press, strike) and economic (e.g., shortages of consumer goods, plight of workers and peasants).

468   IL'ICHEV, A. "Mitrofan-arkhiepiskop Astrakhanskii." VESTNIK RSKhD (Paris): No. 116, II-III-IV-1975; pp. 200-224.
Personal reminiscence of Archbishop Mitrofan.

469   IOFE, IURII. [b. 1921, em. 1972] "Domovaia kniga." GRANI (Frankfurt): No. 100, April-June 1976; pp. 22-23. Poem.

470   _____. "Dvadtsatyi vek." VREMIA I MY (New York/Paris/Jerusalem): No. 45, Sept. 1979.
Contains the following samizdat poems: "Aleksandro-Nevskaia lavra"; "Belyi svet zasypan belym snegom"; "Vstrecha v Sukhumi"; "Na Mtatsminde"; "Taininka. Taina detstva. . . ."

471   _____. "Dym." RUS. MYSL' (Paris): May 23, 1974; p. 8. Poem.

472   _____. "Iz knig 'Itak, itog' i 'Vne Rossii'." GRANI (Frankfurt): No. 86, Dec. 1972; pp. 73-75; No. 87-88, Jan.-April 1973; pp. 192-95.
Poems, all but last of which were written before emigration.

473   _____. "Pamiatnik Marksu." RUS. MYSL' (Paris): Oct. 4, 1973; p. 9. Poem.

474   _____. "Sem' raz Kazan': Poètoocherk No. 5, dokumental'nyi, v 4-kh chastiakh, s prilozheniem." GRANI (Frankfurt): No. 92-93, April-Sept. 1974; pp. 245-69.
Mixture of poetry, letters to daughter and petitions on her behalf, diary-like entries about his experiences visiting her in psychiatric hospital.

475   _____. "Stikhi iz SSSR: 'Pravitel'iam zemli'; 'Shikel'-gruber pytal v Berline. . .'; 'To vremia menia v pionerakh

zastalo. . .'." POSEV (Frankfurt): No. 7, July 1972;
pp. 62-63. Poems.

476 IOFE, IURII. "V muzee"; "Vedomost'"; "Taet, tuskneet Solntse."
RUS. MYSL' (Paris): March 14, 1974; p. 8. Poems.

477 _____. "Zapakh detstva. . . ." NOVYI ZHURNAL (New
York): No. 121, Dec. 1975; p. 120. Poem.

478 ISHUTINA, ELENA. [b. 1903, d. 1962] "Narym." NOVYI ZHURNAL
(New York): No. 76, June 1964; pp. 5-54; No. 77, Sept.
1964; pp. 5-37; No. 78, March 1965; pp. 96-119.
Diary with nearly daily entries by a woman who, as a
former Polish citizen who found herself in territory (in
Western Belorussia) taken by Soviet troops, was arrested
and spent several years in Siberian exile during the war.

479 ISKANDER, FAZIL. [b. 1929] Sandro iz Chegema. Ann Arbor,
Mich.: Ardis, 1979. Also Novye glavy [New Chapters]
Ardus: 1981; 235 pp.

_____. "Kroliki i udavy." KONTINENT: No. 22, 1980;
pp. 51-107.

_____. "Pastukh Makhaz." GLAGOL (Ann Arbor, Mich.):
No. 2, 1978; pp. 7-38.
Novel, portions of which were published in Soviet Union;
epic covering several decades in life of Abkhazian family
from end of 19th c. to present.

ISKANDER, FAZIL: See also Metropol' (#808).

480 ISKHOD, Nos. 1 and 2. POSEV (Frankfurt): Special Issue
No. 7, March 1971; pp. 3-45.
Samizdat journal dealing with Jewish emigration, mostly
letters and petitions. See Exodus (#333).

481 "Itog." (Anon.) POSEV (Frankfurt): No. 46 (1069), Nov. 11,
1966; p. 2. Poem.

IVANOV, A.: See NOVOGUDNII

IVANOV, I.: See REMEZOV

482 IVANOV, I. (Pseud.) "Letter from a Russian Writer." EN-
COUNTER (London): Vol. 24, No. 6, June 1964; pp. 88-98.
Discussion of intellectual hypocrisy and fear of Soviet
literati like Simonov and Ehrenburg. Questionable samizdat;
pseudonymous author sent it to a French editor.

IVANOV

483   IVANOV, Iu. [b. 1927] "Posle 16 let lagerei--psikhbol'-
       nitsa." POSEV (Frankfurt): No. 5, May 1974; pp. 2-4.
       Written by a man who has spent many years in prison and
       camps in post-Stalin Russia, about psychiatric abuse of
       political dissidents.

484   IVERNI, VIOLETTA. "Apokalipsis"; "Iz domu uskol'znut'. . . ."
       NOVYI ZHURNAL (New York): No. 112, Sept. 1973; pp. 118-19.
       Poems.

485   _____. "Tak ne speshit oblaskannyi sud'boiu. . .";
       "Peterburg." NOVYI ZHURNAL (New York): No. 113, Dec.
       1973; p. 71. Poems.

486   "Iz perepiski dvukh sviashchennikov." ["From the Correspond-
       ence of Two Priests"] GRANI (Frankfurt): No. 108, April-
       June 1978; pp. 124-50.
       Letter, dated Oct. 1, 1971, pertaining to priest's
       visits to various individuals in Samarkand area, his bap-
       tisms of them, etc. From <u>Nadezhda</u> (#827).

487   "Iz kontslagernoi poèzii." GRANI (Frankfurt): No. 85, Oct.
       1972; pp. 53-60.
       Poems by I. Avdeev, Iu. Dombrovskii, I. Pashkov and
       G. Cherepov (see individual listings by author).

488   "Iz poèzii Samizdata." VREMIA I MY (Tel Aviv): No. 2, Dec.
       1975; pp. 139-40. Poems.

K

489   K.K. "Blatnye lagernye pesni: 'V shalmanakh pil. . .';
       'Techet rechechka. . .'; 'Ves' gorod spit. . .'; 'Mat'
       synochka obnimet. . .'; 'Ètap na sever. . .'; 'Den' i
       noch'. . .'; 'Proshchai moi drug. . .'; 'Obsudili vy nas ni
       za chto. . .'; 'Poberegam Obi. . .'." NOVYI ZHURNAL (New
       York): No. 116, Sept. 1974; pp. 190-96. Camp songs.

490   K.L. "Osen' Rossii." RUS. MYSL' (Paris): Dec. 12, 1974;
       p. 5. Poem.

491   "Kachka." (Anon.) POSEV (Frankfurt): No. 10 (1033), March
       4, 1966; p. 3. Poem. Evtushenko later identified as author.

492   KAGANOVSKII, G. "Na smert' Galanskova." RUS. MYSL' (Paris):
       Dec. 14, 1972; p. 5.

       _____. "V glukhoi Mordovii. . . ." GRANI (Frankfurt):
       No. 86, Dec. 1972; p. 5.

       _____. "V glukhoi Mordovii. . . ." POSEV (Frankfurt):
       No. 1, Jan. 1973; pp. 4-5. Poem.

KALASHNIKOV, S.: See Sintaksis (#1072).

KALOMIROV, A.: See 37 (#1162).

KALUGIN, V.: See Feniks No. 1 (#336), BOSLEY (#147).

493   KANDEL', FELIKS. [b. 1933, em. 1977] "Koridor: chast' per-
       vaia." ["The Corridor: Part One"] GRANI (Frankfurt):
       No. 102, Oct.-Dec. 1976; pp. 3-55. Novel.

494   _____. "Starik Semenych." ["Old Man Semenych"] KONTI-
       NENT: No. 11, 1976; pp. 141-49. Story.

495   KAPITANCHUK, V. "V Optine." ["In Optina"] GRANI (Frank-
       furt): No. 102, Oct.-Dec. 1976; pp. 104-12.
              From Veche, No. 10 (1974); about visit to the site of a
       former Russian Orthodox monastic sanctuary.

496   KARABCHIEVSKII, IURII. [b. 1938] "Tovarishch Nadezhda: Pesni
       Bulata Okudzhavy." ["Comrade Nadezhda: The Songs of
       Bulat Okudzhava"] GRANI (Frankfurt): No. 98, Oct.-Dec.
       1975; pp. 137-58.
              Essay on Okudzhava's songs and their role in author's
       personal life.

497   _____. "Tramvainaia Moskva: 'Chto ia mogu'; 'Dom ot-
       dykha'." VREMIA I MY (New York/Paris/Jerusalem): No. 24,
       1977; pp. 105-11. Poems.

KARABCHIEVSKII

498   KARABCHIEVSKII, IURII. "Ulitsa Mandel'shtama." ["Mandel'-
      shtam Street"] VESTNIK RSKhD (Paris): No. 111, I-1974;
      pp. 136-71.
      Analysis of Mandel'shtam's poetry on occasion o̓f Soviet
      publication of collection of his verse.

499   _____. "Vchera   Segodnia. Zavtra." ["Yesterday.
      Today. Tomorrow"] VREMIA I MY (New York/Paris/Jerusalem):
      No. 57, Nov.-Dec. 1980; pp. 30-125. Novella.

500   _____. "Zhizn' Aleksandra Zil'bera." ["The Life of
      Aleksandr Zil'ber"] VREMIA I MY (New York/Paris/Jerusa-
      lem): No. 55, July-Aug. 1980; pp. 5-103 and No. 56, Sept.-
      Oct. 1980; pp. 5-112.

      _____. "Zhizn' Aleksandra Zil'bera." GRANI (Frankfurt):
      No. 108, 1979; pp. 39-119.
      Novel of boy in Jewish milieu in 1940s who grows up to
      be a writer.

      KARABCHIEVSKII, IURII: See also Metropol' (#808).

      KARAGUZHIN, H.: See Feniks 1966 (#337), BRUMBERG (#178).

501   KARAMOV, IGNATII. "Kirpichnoe"; "Poluotkryli. . ."; "Sosedi";
      "Gora"; "Podushki. . ."; "Noch'iu"; "Utro." GRANI (Frank-
      furt): No. 87-88, Jan.-April 1973; pp. 117-21. Poems.

502   _____. "Stikhi: 'Prometei'; 'Vozvrashchenie bludnogo
      syna'; 'Siiaet bol'; 'Sapog'; 'Obida'; 'Ia'; 'Poèt na li-
      govke'; 'Ptitsy peli na podushke'." GRANI (Frankfurt):
      No. 79, April 1971; pp. 3-9. Poems.

503   KARELIN, FELIKS. "Po povodu pis'ma O. Sergiia Zheludkova A.
      Solzhenitsynu." ["On Father Zheludkov's Letter to Solzhe-
      nitsyn"] VESTNIK RSKhD (Paris): No. 103, I-1972; pp. 160-
      72.
      Criticizes Zheludkov, supports Solzhenitsyn; avers that
      Solzhenitsyn defends the human spirit as stronger than ex-
      ternal circumstances, whereas the Zheludkov letter claims
      the opposite; attacks Zheludkov for lack of faith and
      materialism. Also in Cahiers du samizdat No. 3 (1972).

      KARELIN, FELIKS: See SOLSCHENIZYN et al. (#1124); Vol'noe
      slovo No. 9-10 (#1234).

504   KARSAVIN, LEV. [b. 1882, d. 1952] "Mysli ob iskusstve."
      ["Thoughts on Art"] VESTNIK RSKhD (Paris): No. 68-69,
      I-II-1963; pp. 6-15. Essay.

505   KARSAVIN, LEV. "O molitve Gospodnei"; "Ob apogee chelove-
chestva." ["On the Lord's Prayer"; "On the Apogee of
Humanity"] VESTNIK RSKhD (Paris): No. 104-105, II-III-
1972; pp. 275-97.
Both pieces written in camp between 1949 and 1952 (he
was arrested in 1949); the first deals with the Father/Son
relationship of God and Christ, and both to man; the second
(an excerpt) investigates the philosophical and theological
meanings of the unity among man, nature and God.

506   _____. "Venok sonetov"; "Tertsiny." VESTNIK RSKhD
(Paris): No. 104-105, II-III-1972; pp. 298-318. Poems.

507   KATERLI, NINA. "Treugol'nik Barsukova." ["Barsukov's Tri-
angle"] GLAGOL (Ann Arbor, Mich.): No. 3, 1981; pp. 7-
70. Novella.

508   KAVERIN, VENIAMIN. [b. 1902] "Nasushchnye voprosy
literatury." ["Vital Questions of Literature"] POSEV
(Frankfurt): No. 10, Oct. 1971; pp. 59-63.
Defense of Solzhenitsyn and angry commentary on current
state of Soviet literature. Listed in Table of Contents
as "Rech', ne proiznesennaia na IV s"ezde pisatelei"; from
a samizdat collection about Solzhenitsyn, edited by A.
Samarin in 1970, which includes documents from 1962-69
(Slovo probivaet sebe dorogu).

509   _____. "Pis'mo Kaverina." RUS. MYSL' (Paris): May 23,
1968; p. 4.

_____. "Otkrytoe pis'mo Konstantinu Fedinu." NOV. RUS.
SLOVO (New York): May 29, 1968; p. 2.

_____. "Promolchat' ia ne imeiu prava." POSEV (Frank-
furt): No. 6 (1133), June 1968; pp. 11-12.

_____. "An Open Letter to Konstantin Fedin." SURVEY
(London): No. 68, July 1968; pp. 187-88. Eng. tr. also
in BRUMBERG (#178).
Attacks Fedin's role in literary politics, and especially Fedin's role in insisting on the prohibition of
Cancer Ward's publication; pleads for freeing of Russian
literature.

510   _____. "Pis'mo V. Kaverina k N. Ia. Mandel'shtam."
["Kaverin's Letter to N. Mandel'shtam"] VESTNIK RSKhD
(Paris): No. 108-109-110, II-III-IV-1973; pp. 189-92.
His response to Volume 2 of her memoirs (#731); he ac-
cuses her of slandering honest people, and defends espe-
cially Tynianov.

KAZAKOV

KAZAKOV, A.: See <u>Vol'noe</u> <u>Slovo</u> No. 7 (#1232).

511 KAZAKOV, VLADIMIR. (Pseud.) <u>Moi</u> <u>vstrechi</u> <u>s</u> <u>Vladimirom</u> Kaza-
kovym. [<u>My</u> <u>Meetings</u> <u>with</u> <u>Vladimir</u> <u>Kazakov</u>] Munich: Han-
ser, 1972. Prose pieces and short dramatic sketches.

512 _____. "Odno stikhotvorenie." KONTINENT: No. 23, 1980;
pp. 140-41. Poem.

513 _____. <u>Oshibka</u> <u>zhivykh</u>. [<u>Mistake</u> <u>of</u> <u>the</u> <u>Living</u>] Munich:
Otto Sagner, 1976.

_____. <u>Der</u> <u>Fehler</u> <u>der</u> <u>Lebenden</u>. Munich: Hanser, 1973.
Novel which takes <u>The</u> <u>Idiot</u> as its prototype and re-
fracts it through modern and modernist sensibility.

514 _____. "Poezdka na Kavkaz"; "Arest." RUS. MYSL' (Paris):
May 13, 1971; p. 7. Sketch and Poem.

515 _____. "Zudesnik." KOVCHEG (Paris): No. 1, 1978;
pp. 4-43.
Personal reminiscence of Aleksei Kruchenykh, futurist
poet of the 1920s.

516 KENZHEEV, BAKHYT. [b. 1950] "Stikhi: 'Za vodostochnoiu
truboi. . .'; 'Ne uderzhat' dozhdia pod konets vesny. . .':
'Leta k surovoi proze kloniat'; 'Zatrubili okhotniki v
snezhnyi rog'; 'Vot chelovek v svoei kamorke'; 'Noch'iu
zimnei, noch'iu dlinnoi. . .'." GLAGOL (Ann Arbor, Mich.):
No. 3, 1981; pp. 99-106. Poems.

517 Kh. "Sozertsanie." RUS. MYSL' (Paris): April 30, 1970;
p. 4. Poem.

Kh. U.: See SHRAGIN, BORIS

KHARABAROV, IVAN: See <u>Feniks</u> 1 (#336), <u>Sintaksis</u> 1 (#1072),
BOSLEY (#147).

518 KHARMS, DANIIL. [b. 1905, d. 1942] <u>Izbrannoe</u>. [<u>Selected</u>
<u>Works</u>] Würzburg: Journalfranz, 1974; 380 pp.

519 _____. (IuVACHEV, A. I.) "Padenie vod." NOVYI ZHURNAL
(New York): No. 103, June 1971; pp. 74-75.
Poem written in 1930.

520 _____. "Proza: 'Rytsar';' 'Kar'era Ivana Iakobevicha
Antonova'; NOVYI ZHURNAL (New York): No. 103, June 1971;
pp. 276-95. Stories written between 1937 and 1940.

521   KHARMS, DANIIL. "Rasskazy: 'Siuita'; 'Nado li vykhodit' iz
      rovnovesiia?'; 'Golubaia tetrad' No. 10'; 'Vyvalivshaiasia
      starukha'; 'Proisshestvie na ulitse'; 'Sonet'; 'Sunduk';
      'Son'; 'Poteri'; 'Makarov i Peterson'; 'Fedia Davydovich';
      'Istoriia'; 'Kassirsha'; 'Opticheskii obman'; 'Stoliar
      Kushakov'; 'Sluchai s Petrakovym'; 'Chetyre illiustratsii';
      'Sud lincha'; 'Vstrecha'; 'Neudachnyi spektakl'; 'Chto
      teper' prodaiut v magazinakh'; 'Son draznit Cheloveka'."
      GRANI (Frankfurt): No. 81, Nov. 1971; pp. 65-83.
      Very short fables, stories and sketches dating from the
      1930s.

522   _____. "Starukha." ["The Old Woman"] NOVYI ZHURNAL
      (New York): No. 106, March 1972; pp. 51-74.
      Story written in 1939.

523   KHEIFETS, MIKHAIL. Mesto i vremia. [A Time and A Place]
      Paris: Tret'ia volna, 1978.
      About camps, with particular attention to Jewish point
      of view, by editor of five-volume samizdat collection of
      Brodskii's works, with his commentary (he was arrested for
      it in Sept. 1974).

      _____. "A Time and a Place." INDEX ON CENSORSHIP (Lon-
      don): Vol. 8, No. 5, Sept.-Oct. 1979; pp. 43-51. Tr.,
      R. Chandler. Excerpt from above.

524   _____. "Russkii patriot Vladimir Osipov." ["Vladimir
      Osipov, Russian Patriot"] KONTINENT: No. 27, 1981 and
      No. 28, 1981; pp. 134-79.
      Written in Mordovian camp in 1977, where the author got
      to know Osipov; describes and evaluates him.

525   KHODOROVICH, TAT'IANA, ed. Istoriia bolezni Leonida Pliush-
      cha. Amsterdam: Herzen, 1974; 208 pp.

      _____. The Case of Leonid Plyushch. Boulder, Col.:
      Westview, 1976; 152 pp. Tr., M. Sapiets, P. Reddaway,
      C. Emerson.

      _____. L'Affaire Pliouchtch. Paris: Seuil, 1976; 175
      pp. Tr., Tania Mathon and Jean Jacques Marie.

      _____. "Chto delaiut s L. I. Pliushchem v psikhbol'-
      nitse." NOVYI ZHURNAL (New York): No. 118, March 1975;
      pp. 129-36.
      Collection of documents, letters, petitions, etc.,
      pertaining to incarceration in psychiatric hospital of
      mathematician Pliushch.

KHODOROVICH

KHODOROVICH, TAT'IANA: See also BARABANOV et al. (#95).

526 KHOLIN, A. "Nasha istoriia"; "Prazdnik edy." GRANI (Frankfurt): No. 70, Feb. 1969; pp. 110-11. Poems.

KHOMIN, I.: See Sintaksis (#1072).

KHROMOV, V.: See Feniks 1966 (#337).

527 Khronika tekushchikh sobytii. Nos. 1-6. POSEV (Frankfurt):
Special Issue No. 1, Aug. 1969; 64 pp.

528 _____. Nos. 7-9. POSEV (Frankfurt): Sp. Iss. No. 2, Dec.
1969.

529 _____. Nos. 10-11. POSEV (Frankfurt): Sp. Iss. No. 3,
April 1970; pp. 4-54.

REDDAWAY, PETER, ed. and tr. Uncensored Russia: Protest
and Dissent in the Soviet Union. London: Cape and
New York: McGraw Hill, 1972; 499 pp. Includes Nos. 1-
11, not in order but selections arranged by content.

TARNOW, ALEXANDER VON, ed. Demokratie in der Illegalität:
die "Chronik der laufenden Ereignisse." Stuttgart:
Seewald, 1971; 191 pp. Includes selections from first
10 issues.

_____. No. 2. NOV. RUS. SLOVO (New York): Nov. 24,
1968; p. 3.

_____. No. 3. NOV. RUS. SLOVO (New York): Nov. 3,
1968; p. 2.

_____. No. 3. POSEV (Frankfurt): No. 12 (1139),
Dec. 1968; pp. 11-14.

_____. No. 5. SURVEY (london): No. 74/75, Winter-
Spring 1970; pp. 185-207.

_____. No. 10. NOV. RUS. SLOVO (New York): Jan. 12,
1970; p. 2; Jan. 13, 1970; p. 2; Jan. 14, 1970; p. 2;
Jan. 15, 1970; p. 2; Jan. 16, 1970; p. 2; Jan. 17, 1970;
p. 2; Jan. 19, 1970; p. 2; Jan. 20, 1970; p. 2; Jan. 21,
1970; pp. 2-3; Jan. 22, 1970; p. 2.

_____. No. 11. NOV. RUS. SLOVO (New York): June 3,
1970; p. 2; June 4, 1970; p. 2; June 5, 1970; p. 2; June 6,
1970; p. 2; June 8, 1970; p. 2; June 9, 1970; p. 2; June
10, 1970; p. 2; June 11, 1970; p. 2; June 12, 1970; pp. 2-
3; June 13, 1970; p. 2.

Khronika tekushchikh sobytii.
    All issues contain brief news sections and samizdat
news. The first eleven issues all date from 1968 and
1969. The following summaries indicate main contents of
indiv. issues:

No. 1: (Apr. 30, 1968) Almost exclusively devoted to
Ginzburg-Galanskov trial (see LITVINOV, #701).

No. 2: (June 30, 1968) Summary of history of Crimean
Tatars and their appeals; notes on Solzhenitsyn's work.

No. 3: (Aug. 30, 1968) News of invasion of Czechoslovakia
and report on Red Square Demonstration (see GORBANEVSKAIA,
#411); Marchenko's arrest and trial.

No. 4: (Oct. 31, 1968) More on trial of Red Square de-
monstrators, including sentences of accused and commentary;
search of Iakhimovich's apartment and his arrest; additional information on Siniavskii/Daniel' case.

No. 5: (Dec. 25, 1968) Information on Red Square demon-
strators; on Il'ia Gabai; persecution and harassment of
Ukrainians; summaries of some of Levitin-Krasnov's articles; news of church persecution; information on Leningrad
trials of Dec. 1968.

No. 6: (Feb. 28, 1969) On Palach (Prague student who im-
molated himself) and responses to Czech invasion, including letter by Grigorenko and Iakhimovich; trial of Belo-
gorodskaia; case of Kochubievskii (see DECTER, #265).

No. 7: (April 30, 1969) On Iakhimovich, Viktor Kuznetsov's arrest; resettlement of Crimean Tatars and trials;
history of Meskhis; information on Chornovil, Osadchy and
Moroz; on Baptist dissent; short biography of Sverdlov.

No. 8: (June 30, 1969) Trial of Burmistrovich; news of
Bogoraz, Litvinov and Babytskii; biographical sketch of
Grigorenko's life and activities up to 1969 and text of
his speech at Kosterin's funeral, his May 1969 arrest and
that of Gabai; information on Kharkov branch of Action
Group; reinvestigation of Marchenko; Ginzburg's hunger
strike; Crimean Tatar demonstration on Maiakovskii Square;
more on special psychiatric hospitals; on Kochubievskii.

No. 9: (Aug. 31, 1969) One year after Czech invasion,
more information on protests; Grigorenko and Gabai's investigations; Iakhimovich's trial; Altunian's arrest; V.
Kuznetsov's trial; trials of Crimean Tatars; repression of
Meskhi.

Khronika tek. sob.

Khronika tekushchikh sobytii

No. 10: (Oct. 31, 1969) Persecution of Action Group for Defense of Civil Rights in the USSR; information on Dzhemilev; arrest of Baltic Fleet Officers, accused of founding Union to Struggle for Political Rights; Marchenko's sentence; on Kazan' special psychiatric hospital; trials of V. Borisov, Crimean Tatars; Levitin-Krasnov.

No. 11: (Dec. 31, 1969) More on Grigorenko and Gabai; arrest and trial of Krasin and of Gorbanevskaia; Dzhemilev; trial of Altunian and Kharkov Action Group members; more on Baltic Fleet Officers and transcripts of interrogations; hunger strikes in Mordovian camps; list of political prisoners in Vladimir prison; Grigorenko piece on special psychiatric hospitals; V. Borisov's trial; Dziuba's expulsion from Ukrainian Writers' Union; Solzhenitsyn's expulsion from Writers' Union and reactions; Stalin's 90th anniversary.

530 _____. Nos. 12, 13. POSEV (Frankfurt): Sp. Iss. No. 4, June 1970; pp. 3-42.

_____. No. 12. NOV. RUS. SLOVO (New York): June 22, 1970; p. 2; June 23, 1970; p. 2; June 24, 1970; p. 2; June 25, 1970; p. 2; June 26, 1970; p. 2; June 27, 1970; p. 2; June 29, 1970; p. 2; June 30, 1970; p. 2.

_____. No. 13. NOV. RUS. SLOVO (New York): July 21, 1970; p. 2; July 22, 1970; p. 2; July 23, 1970; p. 2; July 24, 1970; p. 2; July 25, 1970; p. 2; July 27, 1970; pp. 2-3; July 28, 1970; p. 2; July 29, 1970; p. 2.
No. 12 includes Grigorenko's prison notes and more on Solzhenitsyn's exclusion from Writers' Union, as well as information on various trials.
No. 13 contains information on trials in Moscow, Gor'kii and Khar'kov.

531 _____. No. 14. POSEV (Frankfurt): Sp. Iss. No. 5, Nov. 1970; pp. 3-22.

_____. No. 14. NOV. RUS. SLOVO (New York): Oct. 19, 1970; p. 2; Oct. 20, 1970; p. 2; Oct. 21, 1970; p. 2; Oct. 22, 1970; p. 2; Oct. 23, 1970; p. 2; Oct. 24, 1970; p. 2; Oct. 26, 1970; p. 2; Oct. 27, 1970; p. 2; Oct. 28, 1970; p. 2.
Contains information on Amal'rik's arrest and Zhores Medvedev's incarceration in mental hospital; on Grigorenko and Bukovskii; on history of Soviet censorship.

A Critical Guide

532   Khronika tekushchikh sobytii. No. 15, 16. POSEV (Frankfurt):
       Spec. Issue No. 6, Feb. 1971;

_____. No. 15. NOV. RUS. SLOVO (New York): Nov. 14,
1970; p. 2; Nov. 16, 1970; p. 2; Nov. 17, 1970; p. 2; Nov.
18, 1970; p. 2; Nov. 19, 1970; p. 2; Nov. 20, 1970; p. 2;
Nov. 21, 1970; p. 2; Nov. 23, 1970; p. 2; Nov. 24, 1970;
p. 2; Nov. 25, 1970; p. 2; Nov. 26, 1970; p. 2.

_____. No. 15. VESTNIK RSKhD (Paris): No. 98, IV-1970;
pp. 107-47.

_____. A Chronicle of Current Events. Issue No. 16.
London: Amnesty International Publications, Feb. 1971;
36 pp.
       No. 15: on Gorbanevskaia's trial and that of Ol'ga
Iofe; Pimenov's arrest.
       No. 16: on Solzhenitsyn's Nobel Prize, religious per-
secution, various trials.

533   _____. Nos. 17, 18. POSEV (Frankfurt): Spec. Issue
No. 8, June 1971; pp. 3-58.

_____. No. 17. VESTNIK RSKhD (Paris): No. 99, I-1971;
pp. 167-69. Excerpt.

_____. CCE. Issue No. 17. London: Amnesty, April
1971; 66 pp.

_____. No. 18. VESTNIK RSKhD (Paris): No. 99, I-1971;
pp. 169-71. Excerpt.

_____. CCE. Issue No. 18. London: Amnesty, June 1971;
63 pp.
       No. 17: Trials of Amal'rik, Moroz, hijackers; list of
people sentenced and repressed for political crimes, 1969-
70; list of those who died in imprisonment.
       No. 18: On psychiatric hospitals; news of hunger
strikes and camps and ethnic movements.

534   _____. Nos. 19, 20. POSEV (Frankfurt): Special Issue
No. 9, Oct. 1971.

_____. No. 19. VESTNIK RSKhD (Paris): No. 100, II-
1971; pp. 204-205.

_____. No. 20. RUS. MYSL' (Paris): Sept. 30, 1971;
p. 5; Oct. 14, 1971; p. 5; Oct. 21, 1971; p. 5.

Khronika tek. sob.

> Khronika tekushchikh sobytii. CCE. Issues No. 19 and 20.
> London: Amnesty, Sept. 1971; 99 pp. (paginated 268–266).
>   No. 20: On Bukovskii's arrest; the Orel special psy-
> chiatric hospital; appeals by ethnic minorities; list of
> banned films; list of dissidents sentenced in 1960s.
>   No. 21: Information on political trials of May–June
> 1971, including the hijacking trial, in Leningrad, Riga,
> Kishinev, etc.

535   _____. No. 21. Frankfurt: Posev, 1972; 125 pp. First
issue of Vol'noe slovo. Samizdat, Izbrannoe. Dokumental'-
naia seriia.

    _____. CCE. Issue No. 21. London: Amnesty, Dec. 1971.
  No. 21: Information on Dnepropetrovsk psychiatric
hospital; Bukovskii's arrest; Jewish emigration; Solzhenitsyn's letter to Kosygin; memorandum from "Democrats" re
anticonstitutional activities of Communist Party leaders,
with index of names.

536   _____. No. 22. Frankfurt: Posev, 1972; 125 pp. Vol'-
noe slovo No. 2.

    _____. No. 22. NOV. RUS. SLOVO (New York): Nov. 10,
1971; p. 2; Feb. 12, 1972; p. 2; Feb. 14, 1972; p. 2;
Feb. 16, 1972; p. 2; Feb. 17, 1972; p. 2; Feb. 18, 1972;
p. 2; Feb. 19, 1972; p. 2; Feb. 21, 1972; p. 2; Feb. 22,
1972; p. 2.

537   _____. No. 23. Frankfurt: Posev, 1972; 142 pp. Vol'noe
slovo No. 3.

    _____. No. 23. NOV. RUS. SLOVO (New York): March 27,
1972; p. 2; March 28, 1972; p. 2; March 29, 1972; p. 2;
March 30, 1972; p. 2; April 1, 1972; p. 2; April 3, 1972;
pp. 2-3.

    _____. No. 23. RUS. MYSL' (Paris): April 6, 1972; p. 8.

    _____. CCE. Issues No. 22 and 23. London: Amnesty,
March 1972; 112 pp.
  No. 22: Information on Bukovskii; on prisoners in
Mordovian camps and Vladimir prison; on Jewish emigration.
V. Chalidze's "Ko mne prishel inostranets," account of his
arrest, apartment search, questioning etc.

  No. 23: More on Bukovskii; on Emel'kina; hunger strikes
of political prisoners; investigations of believers; documents pertaining to Bukovskii's trial (his petition,

Khronika tek. sob.

interrogations of him and witnesses, lawyers' speeches,
his final plea; cf. BUKOVSKII, #

538 Khronika tekushchikh sobytii. Nos. 24 and 25. Frankfurt:
Posev, 1972. Vol'noe slovo No. 4; 123 pp.

_____. CCE. Issue No. 24. London: Amnesty, 1972;
55 pp. (paginated 113-68).
No. 24: On Bukovskii; various arrests and searches;
hunger strikes; emigration. No. 25: see below.

539 _____. No. 26. Frankfurt: Posev, 1972; 128 pp. Vol'noe
slovo No. 5.

_____. No. 26. NOV. RUS. SLOVO (New York): Sept. 12,
1972; p. 2; Sept. 13, 1972; p. 2; Sept. 14, 1972; p. 2;
Sept. 15, 1972; p. 2; Sept. 16, 1972; p. 2; Sept. 18, 1972;
p. 2; Sept. 19, 1972; p. 2; Sept. 20, 1972; p. 2.

_____. CCE. Issues No. 25 and 26. London: Amnesty,
Oct. 1972; 107 pp.
No. 25: Includes interview with Solzhenitsyn and text
of his letter to Patriarch Pimen.
No. 26: On arrests of Petr Iakir et al.; various
searches, interrogations and trials; political prisoners
in psychiatric hospitals. Includes issues 1 and 2 of
Seiatel', the first dated Sept. 1971, the second undated
but probably late 1971. No. 1 contains goals, platform
and tactics of this social-democratic party; the second
explains the philosophical foundations of the party.

540 _____. No. 27. Frankfurt: Posev, 1972; 127 pp.
Vol'noe slovo No. 6.

_____. No. 27. NOV. RUS. SLOVO (New York): Dec. 16,
1972; p. 2; Dec. 18, 1972; p. 2; Dec. 19, 1972; p. 2; Dec.
20, 1972; p. 2; Dec. 21, 1972; p. 2; Dec. 22, 1972; p. 2;
Dec. 23, 1972; p. 2; Dec. 25, 1972; p. 2; Dec. 26, 1972;
p. 2; Dec. 27, 1972; p. 2; Dec. 28, 1972; p. 2.

_____. CCE. Issue No. 27. London: Amnesty, 1972.
No. 27: Information on investigation of Crimean Tatars;
news from prisons, camps, psychiatric hospitals. Two un-
signed pieces, "Rossia i tserkov' segodnia" and "Tserkov'
i vlast'"; the first is dated April/May 1971, the second
probably a few months earlier. Both deal with relationship between church and regime. Also contains two bulletins of advice to relatives of persecuted Baptists.

Khronika tek. sob.

541 <u>Khronika tekushchikh sobytii</u>. Nos. 28–31. New York: Khronika, 1974.

_____. <u>CCE</u>. Issues No. 28–31. London: Amnesty, April
1975; 167 pp.
No. 28: (Dec. 31, 1972) On Galanskov's death; Dandaron's trial; repressions in Ukraine.
No. 29: (July 31, 1973) Various trials, in Leningrad,
Ukraine; information on Pliushch's case; Amal'rik's trial;
repressions in Orel and Lithuania.
No. 30: (Dec. 31, 1973) Trial of Iakir and Krasin;
trials of Shikhanovich, Bolonkin and Balakirev, Feldman
et al.; investigation of Superfin; news from prisons and
camps.
No. 31: (May 17, 1974) Trials of Akimov and Dzhemilev
and various information and documents on Crimean Tatars.
Whole issue dedicated to Crimean Tatars; in recognition of
30th anniversary of May 1944 deportation.

542 _____. No. 32. New York: Khronika, 1975; 104 pp.

543 _____. No. 33. New York: Khronika, 1975; 72 pp.

_____. <u>CCE</u>. Nos. 32 and 33. London: Amnesty, 1976;
192 pp.
No. 32: (July 17, 1974) On Solzhenitsyn's deportation,
trials of Khaustov, Superfin, Nekipelov and Pirogov;
repressions of Crimean Tatars and Lithuanians; on <u>Veche</u>;
on expulsion from Writers' Union of Chukovskaia and Voinovich and Etkind's dismissal.
No. 33: (Dec. 10, 1974) Report on Political Prisoners'
Day, on Mordovian camps and conditions, and list of political prisoners in Perm camps.

544 _____. No. 34. New York: Khronika, 1975; 96 pp.

545 _____. No. 35. New York: Khronika, 1975; 64 pp.

546 _____. No. 36. New York: Khronika, 1975.

_____. <u>CCE</u>. Nos. 34, 35 and 36. London: Amnesty,
1978; 231 pp.
No. 34: (Dec. 31, 1974) Trials of Kheifets, Ladyzhen-
skii and Korovin and Shtern; arrest of Kovalev (et al.);
news on Georgian samizdat; summary of Solzhenitsyn's <u>Let-
ter to Soviet Leaders</u>.
No. 35: (March 31, 1975) On Pliushch, Marchenko, Vins,
Maramzin; Gabai's final plea.

Khronika tek. sob.

No. 36: (May 31, 1975) Tverdokhlebov's arrest; list of political prisoners in Vladimir prison; repression in Lithuania.

547   Khronika tekushchikh sobytii. No. 37. New York: Khronika, 1976.

548   _____. No. 38. New York: Khronika, 1976.

549   _____. No. 39. New York: Khronika, 1976.

_____. CCE. Nos. 37, 38 and 39. London: Amnesty, 1978; 238 pp.
No. 37: (Sept. 30, 1975) Osipov's trial; trials of those who refused to perform their military service.
No. 38: (Dec. 31, 1975) Reactions to Sakharov's Nobel prize; on Dzhemilev's hunger strike; various trials.
No. 39: (March 12, 1976) Obituary for Grigorii Podiapol'skii; diary of Perm Camp No. 35; information on several psychiatric hospitals.

550   _____. No. 40. New York: Khronika, 1977.

551   _____. No. 41. New York: Khronika, 1977.

552   _____. No. 42. New York: Khronika, 1977.

_____. CCE. Nos. 40, 41 and 42. London: Amnesty, 1979; 288 pp.
No. 40: (May 20, 1976) On Tverdokhlebov's trial and Dzhemilev's.
No. 41: (Aug. 3, 1976) Several pieces on religion and religious persecution; reports on a number of psychiatric hospitals.
No. 42: (Oct. 8, 1976) Information on assorted arrests and searches and news from camps.

553   _____. No. 43. New York: Khronika, 1977.

554   _____. No. 44. New York: Khronika, 1977; 132 pp.

555   _____. No. 45. New York: Khronika, May 1977; 115 pp.

_____. CCE. Nos. 43, 44 and 45. London: Amnesty; 1979; 339 pp.
No. 43: (Dec. 31, 1976) Bukovskii's release; trials of Bashkirov and Voznesenskaia; persecution of participants in religious seminar.
No. 44: (March 16, 1977) Reprisals against various Helsinki Group members; account of explosion in Moscow

Khronika tek. sob.

> Metro; excerpts from <u>Chronicle</u> <u>of</u> <u>Lithuanian</u> <u>Catholic</u>
> <u>Church</u>; statements in defense of Ginzburg, Orlov, Rudenko
> and Tikhii.
>   No. 45: (May 25, 1977) On Shcharanskii's trial and
> various others; news from camps and prisons.

556   <u>Khronika</u> <u>tekushchikh</u> <u>sobytii</u>. No. 46. New York: Khronika,
>   1978; 134 pp.

> _____. <u>CCE</u>. No. 46. London: Amnesty, 1978; 130 pp.
>   No. 46: (Aug. 15, 1977) Investigations of Helsinki
> Groups; information on relief fund for political prisoners;
> various trials.

557   _____. No. 47. New York: Khronika, 1978; 177 pp.

> _____. <u>CCE</u>. No. 47. London: Amnesty, 1978; 192 pp.
>   No. 47: (Nov. 30, 1977) More on Helsinki Groups' in-
> vestigations; Lithuanian repression and repression of
> Catholics, Adventists, Baptists, Pentecostalists.

558   _____. No. 48. New York: Khronika, 1978; 184 pp.

> _____. <u>CCE</u>. No. 48. London: Amnesty, 1978; 190 pp.
>   No. 48: (March 14, 1978) Repressions against Helsinki
> Groups; on the Podrabineks; report on "free trade union"
> meeting and measures taken against some participants.

559   _____. No. 49. New York: Khronika, 1978; 108 pp.

> _____. <u>CCE</u>. No. 49. London: Amnesty, 1978; 114 pp.
>   No. 49: (May 14, 1978) On various trials and prisons;
> Crimean Tatars; right of emigration.

560   _____. No. 50. New York: Khronika, 1978.

> _____. <u>CCE</u>. No. 50. London: Amnesty, 1978; 116 pp.
>   No. 50: (Nov. 1978) Dedicated to the political trials
> of the summer: Orlov, Gamsakhurdia and Kostova, Ginzburg,
> Shcharanskii, Petkus, Lukianenko, Podrabinek and several
> Jewish activists.

561   _____. No. 51. New York: Khronika, 1978.

> _____. <u>CCE</u>. No. 51. London: Amnesty, 1979; 238 pp.
>   No. 51: (Dec. 1, 1978) Information on trials, prisons
> and camps; various kinds of repression, the free trade
> union.

562   Khronika tekushchikh sobytii. No. 52. New York: Khronika,
       1979.

           _____. CCE. No. 52. London: Amnesty, 1979; 164 pp.
       No. 52: More information on the Metro explosion; death
       of Snegirev; defense of the rights of the disabled; on
       Metropol' and consequent repressions; report on the depor-
       tation of Khamshels (or Khemshens), an Armenian Moslem
       sect, in 1944.

563   _____. No. 53. New York: Khronika, 1979.

           _____. CCE. No. 53. London: Amnesty, 1980; 204 pp.
       No. 53: (Aug. 1, 1979) On various trials; Ukrainian
       repressions; report on Lithuanian samizdat.

564   _____. No. 54. New York: Khronika, 1980.

           _____. CCE. No. 54. London: Amnesty, 1980; 171 pp.
       No. 54: (Nov. 15, 1979) On the arrest of Velikanova
       and Iakunin; on repression of samizdat journals Poiski
       (see #940) and Obshchestvo.

565   _____. No. 55. New York: Khronika, 1980.

566   _____. No. 56. New York: Khronika, 1980.

           _____. CCE. Nos. 55 and 56. London: Amnesty, 1981;
       241 pp.
       No. 55: (Dec. 31, 1979) On various trials, arrests,
       searches, prisons.
       No. 56: (March 30, 1980) On Sakharov's exile to
       Gor'kii; persecution of Moscow Helsinki Group and Working
       Committee on Psychiatric Abuses.

567   _____. No. 57. New York: Khronika, 1981.

           _____. CCE. No. 57. London: Amnesty, 1981; 129 pp.
       No. 57: (Aug. 3, 1980) On various investigations,
       trials, arrests.

568   _____. No. 58. New York: Khronika, 1981.

           _____. CCE. No. 58. London: Amnesty, 1981; 102 pp.
       No. 58: (Nov. 1980) Entirely on trials: of Velika-
       nova, Bakhmin, Iakunin, Regel'son, etc.

Khronika zashch. prav

569 Khronika zashchity prav v SSSR. A Chronicle of Human Rights
     in the USSR. No. 1. New York: Khronika, 1973; 80 pp.

     NB: These pamphlets are edited by V. Chalidze, P. Red-
     daway and E. Klein (and, from No. 8 on, P. Litvinov).
     They sometimes contain samizdat texts or portions of such
     texts, sometimes consist of summaries drawn from informa-
     tion derived from samizdat sources. Unlike the Khronika
     tekushchikh sobytii, they are not themselves samizdat
     texts. Annotations indicate extent of samizdat material
     included in each and brief content summaries. Eng. title
     abbreviated to CHR. Eng. and Rus. texts not identical.

     No. 1: Almost no texts, except for statement on Chalid-
     ze's deprivation of citizenship and some open letters.

570 _____. No. 2. New York: Khronika, 1973; 79 pp.

     _____. CHR. No. 2. New York: Khronika, 1973; 79 pp.
     Almost no texts, except Maksimov's letter to Writers'
     Union, appeal by Bonner and Sakharov.

571 _____. No. 3. New York: Khronika, 1973; 80 pp.

     _____. CHR. No. 3. New York: Khronika, 1973; 78 pp.
     Almost no texts.

572 _____. No. 4. New York: Khronika, 1973; 62 pp.

     _____. CHR. No. 4. New York: Khronika, 1973; 64 pp.
     About Il'ia Gabai's suicide; program of group created
     to help prisoners of conscience; transcript of Levitin-
     Krasnov's testimony at Iakir and Krasin's trial.

573 _____. Nos. 5-6. New York: Khronika, 1974; 98 pp.

     _____. CHR. Nos. 5-6. New York: Khronika, 1974;
     104 pp.
     On Medvedev brothers' attitude toward detente; informa-
     tion on searches, arrests and trials; texts of search re-
     cords and trial verdicts.

574 _____. No. 7. New York: Khronika, 1974; 63 pp.

     _____. CHR. No. 7. New York: Khronika, 1974; 63 pp.
     On Soviet reactions to Gulag Archipelago, L. Chukov-
     skaia's expulsion from Writers' Union, including text of her
     statement and statements in her defense; texts in defense
     of Nekipelov, Bukovskii et al.; portions of samizdat

summaries of <u>Chronicle</u> of <u>Lithuanian Catholic Church</u>; texts
dealing with Lefortovo and Vladimir prisons.

575 <u>Khronika zashchity prav v SSSR</u>. No. 8. New York: Khronika,
1974; 63 pp.

_____. CHR. No. 8. New York: Khronika, 1974; 63 pp.
Texts in defense of Superfin, Pliushch, statement by
Marchenko.

576 _____. No. 9. New York: Khronika, 1974; 64 pp.

_____. CHR. No. 9. New York: Khronika, 1974; 62 pp.
Text of trial transcript of Superfin, various statements
in defense of prisoners, documents pertaining to Etkind's
case. (See also <u>Washington Post</u>, May 19, 1974.) Full text
(re Etkind) in Russian, partial in Eng.

577 _____. No. 10. New York: Khronika, 1974.

_____. CHR. No. 10. New York: Khronika, 1974; 63 pp.
Texts re Ogurtsov's confinement in Vladimir, journal
from Perm Camp on hunger strike.

578 _____. No. 11. New York: Khronika, 1974; 64 pp.

579 _____. No. 12. New York: Khronika, 1975; 64 pp.

_____. CHR. No. 11-12. New York: Khronika, 1975; 65 pp.
Sakharov's statement in defense of Kovalev, Kheifets et
al.; transcript of interrogation of Maramzin; statements re
searches; text of talk between a scientist and a psychiatrist.

580 _____. No. 13. New York: Khronika, 1975; 63 pp.

_____. CHR. No. 13. New York: Khronika, 1975; 64 pp.
Texts in defense of Osipov, letter from Gluzman from
camp; text of Bukovskii and Gluzman's "Dissident's Guide
to Psychiatry" (see #190).

581 _____. No. 14. New York: Khronika, 1975.

_____. CHR. No. 14. New York: Khronika, 1975; 64 pp.
Trans. from <u>Khr. tek. sob</u>. on Marchenko, defense of Kovalev, search and interrogation record of Tverdokhlebov.

582 _____. No. 15. New York: Khronika, 1975; 65 pp.

Soviet Dissident Literature

Khronika zashch. prav

> Khronika zashchity prav v SSSR. CHR. No. 15. New York: Khronika, 1975; 40 pp.
> Documents on Novikov and Vashchenko.

583   _____. No. 16. New York: Khronika, 1975.

> _____. CHR. No. 16. New York: Khronika, 1975; 53 pp.
> Appeal for political amnesty; defense of Dzhemilev; report on beatings in Vladimir prison.

584   _____. No. 17. New York: Khronika, 1975; 54 pp.

585   _____. No. 18. New York: Khronika, 1975; 53 pp.

> _____. CHR. No. 17-18. New York: Khronika, 1976; 56 pp.
> Few texts; some statements in defense of Kovalev, Dzhemilev and Osipov.

586   _____. No. 19. New York: Khronika, 1976; 64 pp.

> _____. CHR. No. 19. New York: Khronika, 1976.
> Statements on Dudko, Jewish movement.

587   _____. No. 20. New York: Khronika, 1976.

588   _____. No. 21. New York: Khronika, 1976.

> _____. CHR. No. 20-21. New York: Khronika, 1976; 60 pp.
> Statements in defense of Dzhemilev by Sakharov, Nekrich and Chukovskaia.

589   _____. No. 22. New York: Khronika, 1976; 80 pp.

> _____. CHR. No. 22. New York: Khronika, 1976; 60 pp.
> Texts of letter by Liubarskii and one by Sakharov et al. on situation of scientists.

590   _____. No. 23-24. New York: Khronika, 1976; 100 pp.

> _____. CHR. No. 23-24. New York: Khronika, 1976; 78 pp.
> Summaries of Helsinki Watch Group documents; statements by Romaniuk, Yui-Shi-Lin (Chinese political emigré in prison from 1974).

591   _____. No. 25-26. New York: Khronika, 1977.

> _____. CHR. No. 25-26. New York: Khronika, 1977.

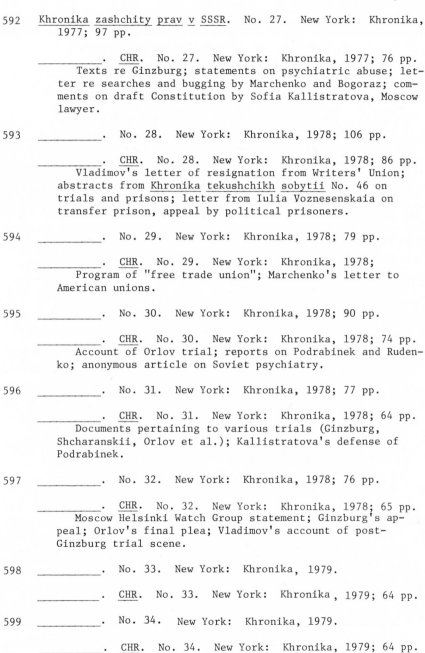

Khronika zashch. prav

592   Khronika zashchity prav v SSSR. No. 27. New York: Khronika,
      1977; 97 pp.

      _____. CHR. No. 27. New York: Khronika, 1977; 76 pp.
      Texts re Ginzburg; statements on psychiatric abuse; let-
      ter re searches and bugging by Marchenko and Bogoraz; com-
      ments on draft Constitution by Sofia Kallistratova, Moscow
      lawyer.

593   _____. No. 28. New York: Khronika, 1978; 106 pp.

      _____. CHR. No. 28. New York: Khronika, 1978; 86 pp.
      Vladimov's letter of resignation from Writers' Union;
      abstracts from Khronika tekushchikh sobytii No. 46 on
      trials and prisons; letter from Iulia Voznesenskaia on
      transfer prison, appeal by political prisoners.

594   _____. No. 29. New York: Khronika, 1978; 79 pp.

      _____. CHR. No. 29. New York: Khronika, 1978;
      Program of "free trade union"; Marchenko's letter to
      American unions.

595   _____. No. 30. New York: Khronika, 1978; 90 pp.

      _____. CHR. No. 30. New York: Khronika, 1978; 74 pp.
      Account of Orlov trial; reports on Podrabinek and Ruden-
      ko; anonymous article on Soviet psychiatry.

596   _____. No. 31. New York: Khronika, 1978; 77 pp.

      _____. CHR. No. 31. New York: Khronika, 1978; 64 pp.
      Documents pertaining to various trials (Ginzburg,
      Shcharanskii, Orlov et al.); Kallistratova's defense of
      Podrabinek.

597   _____. No. 32. New York: Khronika, 1978; 76 pp.

      _____. CHR. No. 32. New York: Khronika, 1978; 65 pp.
      Moscow Helsinki Watch Group statement; Ginzburg's ap-
      peal; Orlov's final plea; Vladimov's account of post-
      Ginzburg trial scene.

598   _____. No. 33. New York: Khronika, 1979.

      _____. CHR. No. 33. New York: Khronika, 1979; 64 pp.

599   _____. No. 34. New York: Khronika, 1979.

      _____. CHR. No. 34. New York: Khronika, 1979; 64 pp.

Khronika zashch. prav

600   <u>Khronika</u> <u>zashchity</u> <u>prav</u> <u>v</u> <u>SSSR</u>.   No. 35.   New York: Khronika, 1979.

            .   <u>CHR</u>.   No. 35.   New York: Khronika, 1979; 73 pp. Note by Nikolaev on origin of Free Trade Union.

601   .   No. 36.   New York: Khronika, 1979.

            .   <u>CHR</u>.   No. 36.   New York: Khronika, 1979; 65 pp. Short text by "Right to Emigrate" group, excerpt of Iakunin's report on situation of Russian Orthodox church.

602   .   No. 37.   New York: Khronika, 1980.

            .   <u>CHR</u>.   No. 37.   New York: Khronika, 1980; 64 pp. Appeals on behalf of Kopelev, Velikanova et al.

603   .   No. 38.   New York: Khronika, 1980.

            .   <u>CHR</u>.   No. 38.   New York: Khronika, 1980; 64 pp. Sakharov's letter from Gor'kii on world situation, Soviet domestic problems, human rights movement; also in <u>New</u> <u>York</u> <u>Times</u> June 8.

604   .   No. 39.   New York: Khronika, 1980.

            .   <u>CHR</u>.   No. 39.   New York: Khronika, 1980; 72 pp. Appeals for Sakharov et al.; texts on independent trade unions.

605   .   No. 40.   New York: Khronika, 1981.

            .   <u>CHR</u>.   No. 40.   New York: Khronika, 1981; 64 pp. Appeal for Rudenko; Moscow Helsinki Watch Group document on political prisoners; Ternovskii's final plea.

606   .   No. 41.   New York: Khronika, 1981.

            .   <u>CHR</u>.   No. 41.   New York: Khronika, 1981; 75 pp. Sakharov's "The Responsibility of Scientists" on his own banishment to Gor'kii, KGB theft of his mss. and notebooks; hope for international outcry against Soviet repression; excerpt from Badzyo's open letter on Ukrainian repression.

607   .   <u>CHR</u>.   No. 42.   New York: Khronika, 1981; 64 pp. Article by Ivan Kovalev, Moscow Helsinki Watch Group member, on current human rights situation. NB: Rus. ed. no longer published.

"Kolkhoznyi

608 Khronika zashchity prav v SSSR. CHR. No. 43. New York:
Khronika, 1981; 64 pp.
Excerpt from Marchenko's "Live As Others Live," on his
initial distaste for intellectuals and subsequent respect
and gratitude.

609 KHVOSTENKO, ALEKSEI. [b. 1940] "Iz 'Venka sonetov'." KON-
TINENT: No. 11, 1976; pp. 164-65. Poem.

610 _____. "Zimnii sonet." VREMIA I MY (Tel Aviv): No. 7,
May 1976; pp. 107-110. Poem.

611 KIM, IULII. [b. 1937] "O sude nad Ginzburgom i Galanskovym";
"Posviashchaetsia Pete Iakiru"; "Sovremennyi dialog." AMI
(Jerusalem): No. 2, May 1971; pp. 75-76. Journ. no longer exists.

_____. "O sude nad Ginzburgom i Galanskovym"; "Posvia-
shchaetsia Pete Iakiru." POSEV (Frankfurt): No. 10, Oct.
1971; pp. 51-52. Poems.

KIM, IULII: See BRUMBERG (#178).

612 "Kladbishche v Rige." (ANON.) GRANI (Frankfurt): No. 71,
May 1969; pp. 11-12. Poem.

KOCHETOV, VSEVOLOD: See BOKOV, NIKOLAI.

KOCHUBIEVSII, BORIS: See DECTER, M. (#265).

613 KOLKER, IURII. [b. 1940] "Zhizn' moego priiatelia." KONTI-
NENT. No. 29, 1981; pp. 87-90. Poem.

KOLOKOL: See SHEL'GA (#1053); V.S. (#1185); VOLGIN (#1225).

614 KOLOSOV, A. (Pseud.) "Dar i otvetstvennost'." ["Talent and
Responsibility"] VESTNIK RSKhD (Paris): No. 108-109-110,
II-III-IV-1973; pp. 129-42.
Witnesses to rebirth of Russian Christian existentialism,
with roots in prerevolutionary intellectual faith of men
like Dostoevskii and Berdiaev. Eng. tr. in MEERSON-AKSENOV
and SHRAGIN (#801).

615 _____. (KOLESOV [sic]). "Neiubileinye razmyshleniia."
["Non-anniversary Reflections"] VESTNIK RKhD (Paris):
No. 112-113, II-III-1974; pp. 122-41.
On the 100th anniversary of Berdiaev's birth; discusses
some fundamental ideas of Berdiaev's philosophy.

616 "Kolkhoznyi trubadur"; "Pervaia vstrecha"; "Skotnik i povarikha";
"Razmolvka." (Anon.) RUS. MYSL' (Paris): Oct. 2, 1975; p. 5.
Satiric and humorous sketches from samizdat collection
Kacheli sud'by, edited by Nikolai Bokov, under whose name
they are listed.

KOMAROV

617 KOMAROV, BORIS. (Pseud.) Unichtozhenie prirody v Sovetskom Soiuze. Frankfurt: Posev, 1978; 208 pp.

_____. The Destruction of Nature in the Soviet Union. White Plains, N.Y.: M. E. Sharpe, 1980; 150 pp.

_____. (KOMAROW) Das grosse Sterben am Baikalsee: Der Bericht eines hohen Funktionärs über die Umweltkrise der Sowjetunion. Hamburg: Rowohlt, 1979; 200 pp. Tr., Anne Herbst-Ottmanns.

_____. "Unichtozhenie prirody." GRANI (Frankfurt): No. 109, 1978; pp. 267-82.
Ministry official describes environmental abuse and destruction--water and air pollution, animal destruction, toxic chemical disposal, etc.

618 KOPELEV, LEV. [b. 1912, em. 1980] Khranit' vechno. Ann Arbor, Mich.: Ardis, 1975; 731 pp.

_____. To be Preserved Forever. Philadelphia, New York: Lippincott, 1977; 266 pp. Tr., Anthony Hustin. British ed.: No Jail For Thought. London.

_____. (KOPELEW) Aufbewahren für alle Zeit! Hamburg: Hoffmann and Campe, 1976; Munich: Taschenbuch, 1979; 618 pp. Tr., H. Pross-Weerth and H. Mandel.
First volume of his memoirs, describing his life from Red Army during the war through imprisonment for--officially--anti-Soviet activities, unofficially for showing concern for treatment of German prisoners of war by Soviets. Moral analysis of relationship between ways and means.

619 _____. I sotvoril sebe kumira. Ann Arbor, Mich.: Ardis, 1978.

_____. The Education of a True Believer. New York: Harper and Row, 1980; 328 pp. Tr., Gary Kern.

_____. (KOPELEW) Und schuf mir einen Götzen. Lehrjahre eines Kommunisten. Hamburg: Hoffmann and Campe, 1978; 424 pp.
Second volume of memoirs, dealing with his early life and ideological development. His youth in Ukraine in 1920s and 1930s.

620 _____. "Pamiati Aleksandra Galicha." ["In Memory of Aleksandr Galich"] KONTINENT: No. 16, 1978; pp. 334-43.
Personal reminiscence of the actor/singer/poet Galich.

621   KOPELEV, LEV. "Pushkin." RUS. LIT. TRIQUARTERLY (Ann Arbor):
No. 10, Fall 1974; pp. 185-98. Tr., David Lapeza.
Remembering his first readings of Pushkin and how Push-
kin was presented in school.

622   _____. "Solzhenitsyn na sharashke." VREMIA I MY (New
York/Paris/Jerusalem): No. 40, April 1979; pp. 178-205.
Excerpt from Utoli moi pechali (Ardis); description of
Solzhenitsyn when he first knew him, in 1947-48, and also
Dmitrii Panin (model for Sologdin in First Circle) as well
as reunion of the three in 1956. Ardis: 1981; 320 pp.

623   _____. "U groba Anny Akhmatovoi." ["At Anna Akhmatova's
Grave"] GRANI (Frankfurt): No. 63, March 1967; pp. 111-13.
Speech he gave at Akhmatova's funeral March 6, 1966,
assessing her as a symbol of Russia.

624   _____. (KOPELEW) Verbietet die Verbote! Dokumente
eines Abtrünnigen. Hamburg: Hoffmann and Campe, 1977;
124 pp. Tr., M. Pross-Weerth.

KOPELEV, LEV: See also BARABANOV et al. (#95), BRUMBERG
(#178), LITVINOV et al. (#702), MEDVEDEV (#772), MEERSON-
AKSENOV and SHRAGIN (#801).

625   KORIN, ALEKSANDR. [b. 1912] "1918 god"; "1919 god." NOVYI
ZHURNAL (New York): No. 137, Dec. 1979; p. 107. Poems.

626   KORIN, GRIGORII. "Esli vse zhivut v obmane: 'Sor ne vynosiat
iz izby. . .'; 'Pamiati kosmonavta'; 'Na kol'tsevoi do-
roge'; 'Khorosho eli letchiki v ètu voinu. . .'; 'Ia
perezhil uzhe tu poru. . .'; 'Vse chashche ia na trizne
pokhoronnoi'; 'Ne ostavliai menia, rabota. . .'." VREMIA
I MY (New York/Paris/Jerusalem): No. 18, June 1977; pp.
89-95. Poems.

627   KORNILOV, VLADIMIR. [b. 1928] "Bez ruk, bez nog." ["Without Arms, Without Legs"] KONTINENT: No. 1, 1974; pp. 12-
122; No. 2, 1974; pp. 95-196.

_____. Ni bras, ni jambes. Paris: Gallimard, 1979.

_____. (KORNILOW) Ohne Arme, ohne Beine. Berlin,
Frankfurt, Vienna: Ullstein, 1975; 198 pp. Tr., Lisa
Meir.
Novel, dated 1965, describing the atmosphere and mood
of Moscow in 1945 through the eyes of a young man.

KORNILOV

628   KORNILOV, VLADIMIR. <u>Demobilizatsiia</u>. [<u>Demobilization</u>]
       Frankfurt: Posev, 1976; 572 pp.
          Novel portraying Soviet life of the 1950s--the Moscow
       intelligentsia, the Soviet army.

629   _____. <u>Devochki i damochki</u>. [<u>Girls and Ladies</u>] Frank-
       furt: Posev, 1975.

       _____. "Devochki i damochki." GRANI (Frankfurt):
       No. 94, Oct.-Dec. 1974; pp. 3-140.

       _____. (KORNILOW) <u>Mädchen und Dämchen, Erzählung</u>.
       Munich: Piper, 1975; 147 pp. Tr., Marianne Weibe.
          Novella, first accepted by <u>Novyi mir</u> and then rejected
       for its "incorrect" depiction of the war. Describes the
       German attack on Moscow in the winter of 1941 through the
       story of one women's brigade sent to the front to dig
       trenches which finds itself undefended, face to face with
       German tanks.

630   _____. "Ryzhikan: povest'." GRANI (Frankfurt):   No.
       100, April-June 1976; pp. 35-166. Novella.

631   _____. "Stikhi: 'Gumilev'; 'Govoriat, vodku goniat iz
       nefti. . .'; 'Kholst'; 'Pamiati Smeliakova'; 'Ekaterinin-
       skii kanal'." KONTINENT: No. 5, 1975; pp. 99-105. Poems.

KORSAKOV, F.: See AGURSKII et al. (#11).

KORZHAVIN, NAUM: See MANDEL', NAUM.

KOSTERIN, ALEKSEI: See SAUNDERS (#1001), <u>Samizdat I</u> (#989).

KOTLIAR, E.: See <u>Sintaksis</u> (#1072).

KOVSHIN, V.: See <u>Feniks</u> 1 (#336), <u>Sfinksy</u> 1 (#1011), <u>Feniks</u>
       1966 (#337), BOSLEY (#147); LANGLAND et al. (#656).

KOZHEVNIKOV, PETR: See <u>Metropol'</u> (#808).

632   KOZLOVSKII, EVGENII. "Dissident i chinovnitsa." ["The Dis-
       sident and the Lady Bureaucrat"] KONTINENT: No. 27,
       1981; pp. 15-53. Story.

633   "Kramol'nye stikhi." (Anon.) NOV. RUS. SLOVO (New York):
       Jan. 8, 1971; p. 2. Poem.

KRASIKOV, A.: See MEDVEDEV (#771).

KRASNOV, A., KRASNOV-LEVITIN, A.: See LEVITIN-KRASNOV, A.

634   KRASOVITSKII, STANISLAV. "Svetloe voskresen'e"; "Legenda";
      "Lukretsiia--Landsknekht. . ."; "Prolog k libretto opery";
      "Nachinaia s uchitel'nitsy"; "Kto ne khochet blesnut';"
      "Otrazhaias' v sobstvennom botinke. . ."; "Ego povstrechal
      ia. . ."; "Vy umerli"; "Ia speshu"; "Avtoportret"; "Muza";
      "Sokol-sviden'e"; "Madrigal Kruchenykh"; "Variatsii na temu
      F. Sologuba"; "Velosiped"; "Astry"; "Shvedskii tupik";
      "Forel'." ÈKHO (Paris): No. 1, 1980; pp. 31-47.
      Poems. Also in KOVCHEG (Paris): No. 2, 1978.

635   KREIDENKOV, VADIM. "Stikhi: 'I v zavikhren'ia. . .'; 'Pov-
      siudu vizhu slavu Bozh'iu'; 'Gospod' mne ulybnulsia radu-
      goi. . .'; 'Sumerki'; 'Besslovesnost' molitvy'." NOVYI
      ZHURNAL (New York): No. 114, March 1974; pp. 60-61.
      Poems dated Leningrad-Rome.

636   "Krestnyi put' preosviashch. Afanasiia." VESTNIK RSKhD
      (Paris): No. 107, I-1973; pp. 170-211.
      Reminiscence on church elder. Questionable samizdat.

637   KRIVULIN, VIKTOR. [b. 1945] "Dvukhchastnaia kompozitsiia
      1980 goda." ÈKHO (Paris): No. 3, 1980; pp. 118-22.
      Poems.

638   _____. "Iz tsikla 'V poliakh Èdema'." KONTINENT: No.
      10, 1976; pp. 143-47. Poems.

639   _____. "Stikhi anonimnogo poèta: 'Forma'; 'Nakryshe';
      'P'iu vino arkhaizmov. . .'. GRANI (Frankfurt): No. 97,
      July-Sept. 1975; pp. 137-42.
      Poems published anonymously.

640   _____. "Vishni"; "Chernika"; "Pomimo. . . ." GRANI
      (Frankfurt): No. 103, 1977; pp. 106-108. Poems.

KRIVULIN, V.: See also 37 (#1162).

641   KUBLANOVSKII, IURII. [b. 1947] "Iz sbornika 'Zemnoe vremia';
      'Peredelkino'; 'Vecher'; 'Iz tsikla 'Deviat' stikho-
      tvorenii'." VESTNIK RKhD (Paris): No. 129, III-1979;
      pp. 91-96. Poems.

642   _____. "Stikhotvoreniia: 'Dushnyi veter. . .'; 'Moloch-
      ko osinoe'; 'Nikolai'; '. . .s nochei, gde komary i
      gnidy. . .'; 'Elegiia'; 'V kreniaishcheisia bashnia. . .';
      'Pamiati Batiushkova'." KONTINENT: No. 22, 1980; pp. 108-
      117. Poems.

KUBLANOVSKII

643   KUBLANOVSKII, IURII. "Veligozh"; "Martem'ianovo"; "Molochko
       osinoe"; "Na otshibe za krasnym labazom. . . ." VESTNIK
       RKhD (Paris): No. 128, I-II-1979; pp. 140-44. Poems.

644   _____. "Vera, Nadezhda, liubov'. . ."; "Pokrov den'";
       "Vecher." VESTNIK RKhD (Paris): No. 130, IV-1979;
       pp. 181-87. Poems.

       KUBLANOVSKII: See also Metropol' (#808); SMOG (#1080).

       KULLE, S.: See Sintaksis (#1072).

645   KUPRIIANOV, BORIS. "Prigovor"; "Stansy"; "Portret"; "Vetrennye
       stikhi o ptich'ikh tainstvakh"; "Uprazhnenie v smekhe."
       VREMIA I MY (New York/Paris/Jerusalem): No. 28, 1978;
       pp. 80-85. Poems.

646   KUSHEV, EVGENII. [b. 1947, em. 1974] Ogryzkom karandasha.
       Stikhi i proza. [With a Pencil Stub] Frankfurt: Posev,
       1971; 111 pp.
       Poems and novella, "Feodal," about the love of a simple
       working-class boy for the daughter of a Raikom secretary,
       and the hero's conflicts with local elite of provincial
       town.

647   _____. "Otryvki iz teksta." ["Excerpts from the Text"]
       GRANI (Frankfurt): No. 91, Jan.-March 1974; pp. 15-130.
       Novella (dated 1971-72) which portrays Moscow Bohemian
       life of writers, artists, etc., restless and disappointed
       angry young men. All three heroes (one student, one
       worker and one son of the elite) kill themselves.

       KUSHEV, EVGENII: See also Feniks 1966 (#337), BRUMBERG (#178),
       Russkoe slovo (#972), LANGLAND et al. (#656).

       KUSHNER, ALEKSANDR: See Sintaksis 3 (#1072), BOSLEY (#147).

648   KUZ'MINSKII, KONSTANTIN. [em. 1975?] "Stikhi iz Zingzi-
       barrrrra." GRANI (Frankfurt): No. 95, Jan.-March 1975;
       pp. 51-52. Poem.

649   KUZNETSOV, ANATOLII. (ANATOLII, A.) [b. 1929, em. 1969, d. 1979]
       "Artist mimansa." NOVYI ZHURNAL (New York): No. 100,
       Sept. 1970; pp. 10-36.
       Story, censored version of which was published in Novyi
       mir in 1968; this is first pub. of uncensored version.

650   _____. (ANATOLII, A.) Babii Iar. Frankfurt: Posev,
       1970; 488 pp.; 2nd ed. 1973.

KUZNETSOV, ANATOLII. Baby Yar. New York: Dial, 1967; 399
pp. Tr., Jacob Guralsky; New York: Farrar, Straus &
Giroux, 1970; 477 pp. Tr., David Floyd.

_____. (KOUZNETSOV) Babi Iar. Paris; Julliard, 1970;
608 pp. Tr., M. Minoustchine-Merant.

_____. "Babii Iar." NOV. RUS. SLOVO (New York): Nov.
24, 1966; p. 4; Nov. 25, 1966; p. 4; Nov. 26, 1966; p. 4;
Nov. 28, 1966; p. 4; Nov. 29, 1966; p. 4; Nov. 30, 1966;
p. 4; Dec. 1, 1966; p. 4; Dec. 2, 1966; p. 4; Dec. 3, 1966;
p. 4; Dec. 5, 1966; p. 4; Dec. 6, 1966; p. 4; Dec. 7, 1966;
p. 4; Dec. 8, 1966; p. 4; Dec. 9, 1966; p. 4; Dec. 10,
1966; p. 4; Dec. 12, 1966; p. 4.

_____. "Babii Iar." NOVYI ZHURNAL (New York): No. 97,
Dec. 1969; pp. 5-32.
Novel, censored version of which was published in Soviet
Union (in Iunost', #8, 9, 10, 1966). Censored chapters
deal with NKVD-provoked outburst in the Kreshchatik neigh-
borhood of Kiev, with the intent of provoking a German
response. The shooting of the Jewish population--at Babii
Iar--was the response.

651　KUZNETSOV, EDUARD. [b. 1941] Dnevniki. Paris: Editions
Reunis, 1973; 374 pp.

_____. Prison Diaries. New York: Stein & Day, 1975;
254 pp. Tr., Howard Spier.

_____. (KOUSNETSOV) Journal d'un condamné à mort.
Témoignage. Paris: Gallimard, 1974; 264 pp. Tr., Jean
Cathala.

_____. (KUZNECOW) Lagertagebuch: Aufzeich. aus d.
Archipel d. Grauens. Munich: List, 1974; 313 pp. Tr.,
Britta Reif-Willenthal.
Diary account of imprisonment, thoughts and musings,
by dissident who was first sentenced to death for his role
in "hijacking" attempt (Leningrad 1970) and then commuted
to fifteen years in special-regime labor camps.

L

652   L.G.   "Sochel'nik";   "Razve odinoko moe serdtse. . . ."   RUS.
      MYSL' (Paris):   Jan. 7, 1971; p. 4.   Poems.

653   LADOV, L.   (Pseud.)   "Kratkie zametki o sovremennom krizise."
      ["Notes on the Current Crisis"]   POSEV (Frankfurt):   No. 1,
      Jan. 1974; pp. 28-30.
        Brief analysis of relationship between political and
      socioeconomic crimes, and attempts at predicting future
      events.

654   LAKSHIN, VLADIMIR.   Solzhenitsyn, Tvardovskii and Novyi mir.
      Cambridge, Mass.:   MIT, 1980; 182 pp.   Tr., M. Glenny.

      _____.   (LAKCHINE)   Réponse à Soljénitsyne.   Paris:
      Michel, 1977; 181 pp.   Tr., A. Sabatier.
        Tvardovskii's former assistant and friend defends the
      editor personally, morally and professionally against
      Solzhenitsyn's characterization in Bodalsia telenok s
      dubom.

      LAKSHIN: See also MEDVEDEV (#771).

655   LANDA, MAL'VA.   V zashchitu prav cheloveka.   [In Defense of
      Human Rights]   New York: Khronika, 1976; 70 pp.
        Documents and information on abuses.

656   LANGLAND, JOSEPH, ACZEL, TAMAS and TIKOS, LASZLO, trs. and
      eds.   Poetry from the Russian Underground.   New York:
      Harper & Row, 1973; 249 pp.
        Bilingual edition containing poems from various samiz-
      dat journals like Feniks, Sfinksy, Sintaksis.

      LASHKOVA, VERA: See BRUDERER (#176), BRUMBERG (#178)
      LITVINOV (#770).

      LEBEDENKO, ALEKSANDR: See MEDVEDEV (#771).

657   LEN, VLADISLAV.   "Byvaet. . .";   "Panikhida."   GRANI (Frank-
      furt):   No. 95, Jan.-March 1975; pp. 48-49.   Poems.

      LERT, RAISSA: See MEDVEDEV (#771).

658   LEVIATOV, VALERII.   "Brat'ia i sestry";   "Nochleg";   "Medovyi
      mesiats."   ["Brothers and Sisters";   "A Night's Lodging";
      "Honeymoon"]   GRANI (Frankfurt):   No. 95, Jan.-March 1975;
      pp. 3-16.   Stories.

659   _____.   "P'ianitsy."   ["Drunks"]   GRANI (Frankfurt):
      No. 94, Oct.-Dec. 1974; pp. 149-66.   Story.

660   LEVITIN, LEV. "Sosedi." ["Neighbors"] VREMIA I MY (New
       York/Paris/Jerusalem): No. 20, Aug. 1977; pp. 97-108.
       Story.

661   LEVITIN-KRASNOV, ANATOLII. [b. 1915, em. 1974] "Analiz anti-
       religioznosti; bibliograficheskie zametki." ["Analysis of
       Antireligiosity; Bibliographic Notes"] GRANI (Frankfurt):
       No. 65, Sept. 1967; pp. 159-88; No. 66, Dec. 1967; pp.
       206-37.
          Polemic with atheists: analyzes and challenges E. Dulu-
       man's Pochemu ia perestal verit' v Bogu, which he derides
       as entirely false and insincere; broadens his argument to
       a general description of faith.

662   _____. Dialog s tserkovnoi Rossiei. [Dialogue with
       Church Russia] Paris: Ikthus, 1967; 113 pp. (Ed.,
       Arkhiepiskop Ioann San-Frantsisskii.)
          Contains various pieces, including response to Nauka i
       religiia (#669).

663   _____. "Drama v Viatke." ["Drama in Viatka"] POSEV
       (Frankfurt): No. 10, Oct. 1969.
          Defense of Talantov.

664   _____. (KRASNOV) "Gospod'--moia nesokrushimaia kre-
       post'." ["God is my Unconquerable Fortress"] POSEV
       (Frankfurt): No. 1 (1976), Jan. 7, 1967; pp. 5-7.
          Autobiographical sketch of both facts of his life and
       his spiritual development.

665   _____. (KRASNOV) "Kaplia v mikroskope." ["Drop Under
       a Microscope"] VESTNIK RSKhD (Paris): No. 83, I-1967;
       pp. 7-28.

       _____. (KRASNOV-LEVITIN) "Novaia ugroza pravoslavnoi
       tserkvi v SSSR: Tsirkuliar Soveta po delam russkoi pravo-
       slavnoi tserkvi predsedateliam ispolkomov." ["New Threat
       to the Orthodox Church in the USSR: Circular from the
       Council on Church Affairs to the Chairmen of Executive
       Committees"] RUS. MYSL; (Paris): June 13, 1967; pp. 3, 6;
       June 15, 1967; p. 3; June 17, 1967; p. 3; June 20, 1967;
       p. 3.
          Describes individual churches as drops of a bottomless
       sea, the Church, but also as drops of a sick church; the
       Russian church as an institution and individual members
       who align themselves with the state instead of with be-
       lievers. Eng. tr. in BOURDEAUX (#149).

LEVITIN-KRASNOV

666   LEVITIN-KRASNOV, ANATOLII. (KRASNOV) "Khristos i master: O
       posmertnom romane M. Bulgakova 'Master i Margarita'."
       ["Christ and the Master: on Bulgakov's Posthumous Novel
       'The Master and Margarita'"] GRANI (Frankfurt): No. 71,
       May 1969; pp. 162-95; No. 72, July 1969; pp. 150-92; No.
       73, Oct. 1969; pp. 175-94.
           Overview of Bulgakov's earlier works, including personal
       reminiscence of the importance and types of theater in the
       1920s, and analysis of the role of Satan and Satanism in
       Master and Margarita.

667   _____. (KRASNOV) "Liubov'iu i gnevom." ["With Love
       and Anger"] RUS. MYSL' (Paris): July 7, 1966; pp. 4-5.
           Support of Ëshliman and Iakunin after they were sus-
       pended by the Patriarch. Eng. tr. in BOURDEAUX (#149).

668   _____. (KRASNOV) "Moe vozvrashchenie." ["My Return"]
       POSEV (Frankfurt): No. 12, Dec. 1970; pp. 47-50.

       _____. (KRASNOV) "Moe vozvrashchenie." GRANI (Frank-
       furt): No. 79, April 1971; pp. 23-100.
           Account of his arrest in 1969, of the practice and ef-
       fects of sentencing political prisoners together with
       ordinary criminals; his stay in Butyrki and in a prison
       in the Caucasus; the roles faith and prayer play for him
       and for fellow prisoners.

669   _____. (KRASNOV-LEVITIN) "Moi otvet zhurnalu 'Nauka i
       religiia'." RUS. MYSL' (Paris): March 4, 1967; p. 3;
       March 7, 1967; pp. 3, 6; March 9, 1967; pp. 3, 6; March
       16, 1967; p. 3.
           Response to Soviet journal's attack on him and its cre-
       do that man creates the meaning of life, and only through
       struggling to build Communism can this meaning be realized.
       Levitin-Krasnov offers, instead, a mixture of Christianity
       and socialism, a theocracy which is at the same time a
       more humane and just community. Included in Stromaty (#676),
       Dialog s tserkovnoi Rossiei (#662).

670   _____. (KRASNOV) "'Ne mechom i kop'em'." ["Not with
       Sword or Spear"] VESTNIK RSKhD (Paris): No. 99, I-1971;
       pp. 136-42.
           Defense of Bukovskii after his 1971 arrest.

670   _____. (KRASNOV-LEVITIN) "O polozhenii Russkoi Pravo-
       slavnoi Tserkvi." ["On the Situation of the Russian Ortho-
       dox Church"] VESTNIK RSKhD (Paris): No. 95-96, I-II-1970;
       pp. 75-92.

108

Letter to Pope Paul VI, describing the attitude of
younger generation to church: unlike first generation
under Communism, which opposed church for its ties with
tsarism; unlike second generation, which was indifferent;
third generation searches for truth, of which religion
plays important part. Eng. tr. in Religion in Communist-
Dominated Areas (New York): IX, 19-20 (Oct. 1970),
pp. 151-7.

672   LEVITIN-KRASNOV, ANATOLII. (KRASNOV) "O tsarstve Bozh'em,
vozrastaiushchem na zemle." ["On the Kingdom of God,
Flourishing on Earth"] POSEV (Frankfurt): No. 2, Feb.
1970; pp. 38-39.
    Statement of faith--the will of God acting through men
to perform miracles. Contained in Stromaty (#676); from
Slovo khristianina.

673   _____. (KRASNOV) "O zapovediakh blazhenstva." ["On
the Commandments of Bliss"] POSEV (Frankfurt): No. 1,
Jan. 1970; pp. 50-54.
    Defines Christian love, poverty, the ability to turn the
other cheek; develops various statements from the Gospels.
From Slovo khristianina; contained in Stromaty (#676).

674   _____. "Pis'ma iz kontslageria." ["Letters from Camp"]
VESTNIK RSKhD (Paris): No. 106, IV-1972; pp. 73-91.
    Moral advice and religious teachings: how best to serve
Orthodoxy, and on Slavophilism.

675   _____. (KRASNOV) "Slushaia radio. . . ." ["Listening
to the Radio"] RUS. MYSL' (Paris): Oct. 27, 1966; p. 3;
Oct. 29, 1966; p. 3. See #667.

    _____. "Slushaia radio. . . ." POSEV (Frankfurt): No.
39, Sept. 23, 1966; No. 40, Oct. 1, 1966. See #667.
    Defense of Eshliman and Iakunin after they were sus-
pended by the Patriarch. Eng. tr. in BOURDEAUX (#149).

676   _____. (KRASNOV) Stromaty. [Miscellany] Frankfurt:
Posev, 1972; 155 pp.
    Collection of various pieces (#669, #672 and #673)
plus "Orlinaia pesnia," also in POSEV (Frankfurt): No. 7,
1969, and "O podlinnoi sushchnosti khristianstva," POSEV
(Frankfurt): No. 12, 1969.

677   _____. (KRASNOV-LEVITIN) "Svet v okontse." ["Light in
the Window"] VESTNIK RSKhD (Paris): No. 93, III-1969;
pp. 97-106.

LEVITIN-KRASNOV

LEVITIN-KRASNOV, ANATOLII. "Svet v okontse." POSEV (Frankfurt): No. 11, Nov. 1969.
Passionate defense of Grigorenko, comparing him to the Good Samaritan.

678 _____. (KRASNOV-LEVITIN). "'Sviataia Rus' v èti dni." ["Holy Russia Today"] RUS. MYSL' (Paris): July 20, 1972; p. 3; July 27, 1972; p. 4; Aug. 3, 1972; p. 4; Aug. 10, 1972; p. 4.
Holy Russia not a geographical or political entity, but a cultural organism--the spirit and life that live in the soul of the Russian people, these days exclusively in the souls of believers. Also thoughts on Khrushchev's death, and his primitive attitude in religious matters.

679 _____. (KRASNOV) "V chas rassveta." ["At the Hour of Dawn"] POSEV (Frankfurt): No. 5 (1132), May 1968; pp. 48-55; No. 6 (1133), June 1968; pp. 47-51.
From samizdat journal Tetradi sotsialisticheskoi demokratii, only two issues of which reached the West. On morality in society and the establishment of spiritual values in a secular world. Eng. tr. in GERSTENMAIER (#375).

680 _____. (KRASNOV-LEVITIN) "Vyrozhdenie antireligioznoi mysli." ["The Degeneration of Antireligious Thought"] RUS. MYSL' (Paris): April 11, 1967; p. 3; April 13, 1967; p. 3; April 18, 1967; pp. 3, 6; April 20, 1967; p. 3; April 22, 1967; p. 3.
Describes typical anti-religious brochures; singles out A. A. Osipov's "Answer to Believers" and discusses harassment of teachers who are believers and the illegal "registration" of priests.

681 _____. (KRASNOV) "Zakat obnovlenchestva: Iz vospominanii." ["The Decline of the Living Church: From Memoirs"] GRANI (Frankfurt): No. 86, Dec. 1972; pp. 93-116; No. 87-88, Jan.-April 1973; pp. 235-74.
Description of an Orthodox group that existed from c. 1920 till the mid-1940s and cooperated closely with the regime from its inception. He was a member from about 1942-44, and focuses on those years and on Aleksandr Vvedenskii (d., 1946).

682 _____. Kampf des Glaubens. Dokumente aus der Sowjetunion. Bern: Schweizerisches Ostinstitut, 1967. See Zashchita very v SSSR (#1287).

LEVITIN-KRASNOV, ANATOLII: See also BRUMBERG (#178), BOURDEAUX (#149), Zashchity very v SSSR (#1287).

683 LEVITIN, ANATOLII and SHAVROV, VADIM. <u>Ocherki</u> <u>po</u> <u>istorii</u>
     <u>russkoi</u> <u>tserkovnoi</u> <u>smuty</u>. [<u>Works</u> <u>on</u> <u>the</u> <u>History</u> <u>of</u> <u>the</u>
     <u>Russian</u> <u>Church</u> <u>Schism</u>] Zurich: Glaube in der 2^e Welt
     Institut, 1978; 3 vols.

     _____. "Ocherki po istorii russkoi tserkovnoi smuty."
     NOVYI ZHURNAL (New York): No. 85, Dec. 1966; pp. 141-78;
     No. 86, March 1967; pp. 159-220; No. 87, June 1967; pp.
     198-244; No. 88, Sept. 1967; pp. 138-69.
     History of the Living Church (see above, #681); analysis
     of the church from 1905 through the revolution and civil
     war, including descriptions of Aleksandr Vvedenskii, Patri-
     arch Tikhon and a huge number of minor church figures. The
     <u>Novyi</u> <u>zhurnal</u> version was censored to delete passages con-
     sidered by the editors too sympathetic to the Living Church
     or too critical of Patriarch.

684 LEWYTZKYJ, BORYS. <u>Die</u> <u>linke</u> <u>Opposition</u> <u>in</u> <u>der</u> <u>Sowjetunion</u>:
     <u>Systemkritik</u>, <u>Programme</u>, <u>Dokumente</u>. Hamburg: Hoffmann
     und Campe, 1974; 191 pp.
     Contains some leftist samizdat texts.

685 _____. <u>Politische</u> <u>Opposition</u> <u>in</u> <u>der</u> <u>Sowjetunion</u>, <u>1960-</u>
     <u>1972</u>. <u>Analyse</u> <u>und</u> <u>Dokumentation</u>. Munich: Deutscher
     Taschenbuch Verlag, 1972; 342 pp.
     Documents include assorted letters, appeals, texts.

686 LIAPIN, VIKTOR. "Vstrecha"; "Mrachnyi bereg"; "Golyi gost'";
     "Chaiki"; "Vecherniaia zvezda." NOVYI ZHURNAL (New York):
     No. 56, March 1959; pp. 141-45. Poems.

687 _____. "Poezdka na mototsikle"; "Arion"; "More." NOVYI
     ZHURNAL (New York): No. 62, Dec. 1960; pp. 47-49. Poems.

     LIIATOV, M.: See <u>Poiski</u> No. 1 (#940).

688 "Limeriki." (Anon.) GRANI (Frankfurt): No. 95, Jan.-March
     1975, pp. 53-54. Poems.

689 LIMONOV, EDUARD. "Ia byl veselaia figura. . ."; "Kropotkin";
     "Kto lezhit. . . ." GRANI (Frankfurt): No. 95, Jan.-
     March 1975; pp. 49-50. Poems.

690 "Liricheskaia"; "Pesnia zastol'naia, pesnia paskhal'naia";
     "Pesnia iz mest ne stol' otdalennykh"; "Anna Karenina."
     (Anon.) NOVYI ZHURNAL (New York): No. 84, Sept. 1966;
     pp. 143-47. Poems.

"Literatura

691   "Literatura o voine v sovremennoi kritike." (Anon.) ["Lit-
      erature about the War in Contemporary Criticism"] NOVYI
      KOLOKOL (London): No. 1, 1972; pp. 131-67.
      Discusses war-lit. of mid-1950s to mid-1960s and its
      treatment by critics.

692   LIPKIN, SEMEN. [b. 1911] "Iz liricheskoi tetradi: 'Na tian'-
      shane'; 'Vorobyshek'; 'Akulina Ivanovna'; 'Telefonnaia
      budka'; 'Dve nochi'; 'Moldavskii iazyk'; 'Zola'; 'Kogda
      boleznennoi dushoi ustanu. . . '; 'Ia sizhu na stupen'-
      kakh. . .'." VREMIA I MY (New York/Paris/Jerusalem):
      No. 46, Sept.-Oct. 1980; pp. 139-47. Poems.

693   _____. "Tuman v gorakh." VREMIA I MY (New York/Paris/
      Jerusalem): No. 54, June 1980; pp. 56-68. Poem, 1952-53.

694   _____. "Literaturnoe vospominanie." VREMIA I MY (New
      York/Paris/Jerusalem): No. 52, April 1980; pp. 76-89.
      Poem.

695   _____. "Poezdka v Iasnuiu Polianu." VREMIA I MY (New
      York/Paris/Jerusalem): No. 50, Feb. 1980; pp. 102-107.
      Poem dated 1952.

696   _____. "Tbilisi v aprele 1956 goda." VREMIA I MY (New
      York/Paris/Jerusalem): No. 48, Dec. 1979; pp. 79-87.
      Poem, from Vozhd' i plemia.

      LIPKIN, SEMEN: See also Metropol' (#808).

697   LISNIANSKAIA, INNA. "Iz poèticheskoi tetradi: 'Ne srazu ona
      s nagotoiu svykalas';' 'Byvalo, vzdokhnu. . .'; 'V moem
      domu--fiasko. . .'; 'Vse okna smotriat na vostok'; 'Net
      bezliudnykh domov. . .'; 'I dlia tupitsy net sekreta';
      'Mysl' neponiatna i rifma slaba'; 'Vdol' chastogo kustar-
      nika'; 'Letalo i pelo. . .'; 'Kakoe blazhenstvo ulech'sia
      i dumat' o proshlom. . .'; 'Gudit, kak shmel', . .'; 'Ot
      uma do serdtsa dal'she'; 'Prebyvaia v piatom izmerenii'."
      VREMIA I MY (New York/Paris/Jerusalem): No. 55, July-Aug.
      1980; pp. 142-52.
      Poems, listed under "Dar v odinochestve zhit'."

698   _____. "Zareshchennye poezda: 'Uzhe ne dumaiu o
      Prave. . .'; 'Rastsveli vdol' moria oleandry'; 'Tugo pere-
      kruchena. . .'; 'Vseobshchie volny katilis'. . .'; 'Sire-
      ny'; 'I vriad li smogu nakhodit'sia v sisteme. . .'; 'Na
      nezhnoi grudi kheruvima'; 'K chemu uprochivat' nam sluchai?';
      'Magdalena pela'; 'Moia palata golubaia'; 'Zdes' mne eshche
      neprivychno'; 'Nishchaet dukh ne ottogo li'; 'Kakie

dlinnye. . .'; 'Pylesos'." VREMIA I MY (New York/Paris/
Jerusalem): No. 52, April 1980; pp. 90-99. Poems.

699   LISNIANSKAIA, INNA. "Opredelennost': 'Predvideno, predska-
zano. . .'; 'Proshchal'naia pesnia'; 'Uzhe ni v kakuiu
palatu. . .'; 'Naprasno vybili. . .'; 'Sred' mertvoi
tishiny. . .'; 'Kak dolzhno Bozh'im sirotam. . .'; 'Shumi,
shumi, moia dubrava!' 'Peredelkinskoe kladbishche'; 'Moi
otets--voennyi vrach. . .'; 'Ni krasi bozhestvennoi'; 'Sud'--
ba pytala, brila nagolo. . .'; 'Ètot gorod--arestantskaia
odevka. . .'; 'Samoubiitsa'; 'Toptun'; 'Voziat na rynok kar-
toshku i salo. . .'; 'Ruf';' 'Nad orekhovoiu ramoi. . .'."
VREMIA I MY (New York/Paris/Jerusalem): No. 49, Jan. 1980;
pp. 66-78. Poems.

LISNIANSKAIA, INNA: See also Metropol' (#808).

700   LITVINOV, PAVEL. [b. 1940, em. 1974] Ed., Delo o demonstratsii na Pushkinskoi ploshchadi 22 ianvaria 1967 goda. London: Overseas Publications Interchange Ltd., 1968; 130 pp.

_____. The Demonstration in Pushkin Square. London:
Harvill, 1969; 129 pp.; Boston: Gambit, 1969; 176 pp.
Tr., Manya Harari.
Record of trials of Khaustov, Bukovskii, Delone and
Kushev.

701   _____. Ed., Protsess chetyrekh: sbornik materialov po
delu Galanskova, Ginzburga, Dobrovol'skogo i Lashkovoi.
Amsterdam: Herzen 1971; 634 pp.

_____. The Trial of the Four. New York: Viking, 1972;
432 pp. Tr., Janis Sapiets, Hilary Sternberg, Daniel
Weissbort.

_____. L'Affaire Guinsbourg-Galanskov. Eds., J.-J.
Marie and C. Head. Paris: Seuil, 1973.
Documents on the Ginzburg-Galanskov trial. For German
version see BRUDERER (#146).

LITVINOV, PAVEL: See also BRUMBERG (#178).

702   LITVINOV, PAVEL, MEERSON-AKSENOV, MIKHAIL and SHRAGIN, BORIS.
Eds., Samosoznanie. [Self-Awareness] New York: Khronika,
1976; 320 pp.
Collection of articles all but two of which were written
for and circulated in samizdat, though most of the authors
are now in the West. The samizdat articles are as follows:

LITVINOV

BARABANOV, EVGENII: "Pravda gumanizma" ["The Truth of
Humanism"], a brief history of humanism and a defense of
it, the Christian component of and compatibility with it.

KOPELEV, LEV: "O novoi russkoi emigratsii" ["On the New
Russian Emigration"], an overview of past waves of emigration from Russia (from Moscovy through Peter the Great to
the post-revolutionary and post-World War II groups), and
an analysis of the motives and characteristics of today's
emigration.

MEERSON-AKSENOV, MIKHAIL: "Rozhdenie novoi intelligentsii"
["The Birth of a New Intelligentsia"], analyzing relationship of past intelligentsia and church, intell. and Bol-
shevism, and the people. (Dated Moscow-Paris, 1972-73)

NELIDOV, DMITRII: "Ideokraticheskoe soznanie i lichnost'"
["Idiocratic Consciousness and Personality"]: See NELIDOV
(#844).   Eng. tr. in MEERSON-AKSENOV and SHRAGIN (#801).

POMERANTS, G.: "Modernizatsiia nezapadnykh stran" ["The
Modernization of Non-Western Countries"], on features of
modernization (its "enclave-ness," its reaction against
the Enlightenment) the role of alienation and "foreigners"
in development, etc.

SHRAGIN, BORIS: "Toska po istorii" ["Anguish for History"]
on the plight of the intelligent and his attitude toward
history, his inability to understand the consequences of
historical movements, a black-and-white approach. (Dated
Moscow-Amherst, 1974-75)

ORLOV, IURII: "Vozmozhen li sotsializm ne totalitarnogo
tipa?" ["Is Socialism of a Non-Totalitarian Type Possible?"], the problem of personal responsibility, from the
point of view of faith in the multiplicity of societal de-
velopments and a faith in historic alternatives; the myth
of "scientific socialism" and a search for an ethical anti-
totalitarian movement.

TURCHIN, VALENTIN: "Chto takoe bespristrastnost'?" ["What
is Impartiality?"], response to Amnesty International's
defense of its own impartiality, supporting the ideals of
Amnesty. Author was chairman of the Soviet Amnesty group.

703   [_____.] Letters and Telegrams to Pavel Litvinov, Dec.
1967-May 1968. Netherlands: D. Reidel, 1969; 199 pp.
Tr., Brian Pearce. Ed., Karel van het Reve.

LITVINOV, PAVEL. Dear Comrade: Pavel Litvinov and the Voices of Soviet Citizens in Dissent. New York, London, Toronto, Tel Aviv: Pittman, 1969; 199 pp. Ed., Karel von het Reve.

_____. Nicht geladene Zeugen: Briefe und Telegramme an Pawel M. Litwinow. Hamburg: Hoffmann and Campe, 1969; 91 pp. Tr., Nonna Nielsen-Stokkeby. Ed., Karel van het Reve.

Collection of both friendly and hostile letters provoked by Litvinov's appeal to public opinion. Some items also included in GERSTENMAIER (#375).

704 LOBAS, E. Raz v zhizni: iz tsikla "Sonet-66". [Once in a Lifetime] GRANI (Frankfurt): No. 97, July-Sept. 1975; pp. 33-136; No. 98, Oct.-Dec. 1975; pp. 5-119.

Novel presenting village life as corrupt, drunken, primitive, etc.

M

705   M., SERGEI. "Stikhi iz SSSR: 'Cherez rizy lits ne vidno
      vovse." RUS. MYSL' (Paris): March 11, 1976; p. 5. Poem.

706   M.K. "Pamiati Evgenii Ginzburg." ["In Memory of Evgeniia
      Ginzburg"] GRANI (Frankfurt): No. 110, Oct.-Dec. 1978;
      pp. 172-81. Reminiscence.

707   "M.A. Sholokhov popadaet v opalu?" (Anon.) ["Is M.A. Sholo-
      khov Falling Out of Favor?"] VESTNIK RSKhD (Paris): No.
      91-92, I-II-1969; pp. 77-80.

708   MAGEN (Pseud.) "Otryvok iz poèmy"; "Postup' predkov"; "Toska";
      "Naum Korzhavin." AMI (Jerusalem): No. 2, May 1975;
      pp. 41-42. Journal no longer exists. Poem.

      MAKARENKO, M.: See Vol'noe slovo No. 12 (#1236).

709   MAKSIMOV, VLADIMIR. [b. 1932, em. 1974] Karantin. [Quaran-
      tine] Frankfurt: Posev, 1973; 362 pp.

      _____. (MAXIMOV) En quarantaine. Paris: Grasset Fas-
      quelle, 1974; 304 pp. Tr., Nina Nidermiller.

      _____. (MAXIMOV) Die Quarantäne. Bern, Munich: Scherz,
      1974; 342 pp. Tr., Axel Jollas.
      Novel portraying heroes' gradual ascent from primitive,
      thoughtless, animal-like existence toward one more aware,
      including an awareness of one's own sins and the overcoming
      of them. Sense of one's own individuality as first step on
      the path of atonement, through which the world of chaos can
      be countered with world of meaning and order.

710   _____. Proshchanie iz niotkuda. [Farewell from Nowhere]
      Frankfurt: Posev, 1974; 428 pp.

      _____. (MAXIMOV) Adieu de nulle part. Paris: Galli-
      mard, 1977; 422 pp.

      _____. (MAXIMOW) Abschied von Nirgendwo. Bern, Munich:
      Scherz, 1976; 400 pp. Tr., Frickinger-Garanin.

      _____. "Proshchanie iz niotkuda." GRANI (Frankfurt):
      No. 87-88, Jan.-April 1973; pp. 3-116; No. 89-90, July-
      Dec. 1973; pp. 3-95.
      Autobiographical novel dealing with childhood in Sokol'-
      niki, the war, his father's death, his running away from
      home and wandering around, spending some time in children's
      colonies, time spent in insane asylum and working in a
      brick factory and as an editor of provincial newspaper, etc.

711   MAKSIMOV, VLADIMIR. Saga o Savve. Frankfurt: Posev, 1975;
       507 pp. Novel.

712   _____. Sem' dnei tvoreniia. Frankfurt: Posev, 1971;
       507 pp.

       _____. (MAXIMOV) Seven Days of Creation. New York:
       Knopf, 1975; 417 pp.

       _____. (MAXIMOV) Les sept jours. Paris: Grasset,
       1973; 432 pp. Tr., Nina Nidermiller.

       _____. (MAXIMOW) Die sieben Tage der Schöpfung. Bern,
       Munich: Scherz, 1972; 454 pp. Tr., Nina and Johannes
       Koch; Munich: Droemer, 1979; 464 pp.

       _____. "Chetverg: pozdnii svet." GRANI (Frankfurt):
       No. 80, Sept. 1971; pp. 15-102.

       _____. "Dvornik Lashkov." GRANI (Frankfurt): No. 64,
       June 1967; pp. 3-78. (Retitling of "Sreda. Dvor posredi
       neba"; published anonymously, with Maksimov identified in
       Grani No. 80. Eng. tr. in SCAMMELL (#1005), as "House in
       the Clouds.")

       _____. "Kakaia sila brosaet liudei iz storony v storo-
       nu?' 'S chego nachinat' sledovalo." RUS. MYSL' (Paris):
       Dec. 23, 1971; p. 9.
          Novel about three generations of a family of workers,
       the Lashkovs, which encompasses the entire post-1905
       society of Russia: How they help make the revolution,
       help fight the revolution's innumerable enemies, and final-
       ly disappointed in the revolution, conclude that it was a
       mistake, and that the struggle was unnecessary and wrong,
       and that other ideals and genuine truth must be pursued:
       a sense of oneself as part of a harmonious whole, an under-
       standing that it is not external circumstances but inter-
       nal consciousness which must change.

713   _____. "Stan' za chertu." ["Turning Point"] NOVYI
       ZHURNAL (New York): No. 116, Sept. 1974; pp. 5-25; No.
       117, Dec. 1974; pp. 19-44. Drama.

       MAKSUDOV: See MEDVEDEV (#773).

714   MAL'TSEV, IURII. [b. 1932, em. 1974] Reportazh iz sumasshed-
       shego doma. [Reporting from the Madhouse] New York:
       Izdanie Novogo Zhurnala, 1974; 71 pp.

MAL'TSEV

MAL'TSEV, IURII. "Reportazh iz sumasshedshego doma. NOVYI
ZHURNAL (New York): No. 116, Sept. 1974; pp. 3-71.
Firsthand account of author's questioning by psychia-
trists and his experiences in psychiatric hospital.

715 "Malye voiny." (Anon.) RUS. MYSL' (Paris): Aug. 8, 1968;
p. 6. Poem.

716 MAMLEEV, IURII. [b. 1931, em. 1974] "Polet"; "Nabeg sil'-
fid"; "Ne te otnosheniia." ["Flight"; "The Sylph's Raid";
"Not Those Relationships"] NOVYI ZHURNAL (New York):
No. 120, Sept. 1975; pp. 5-18. Stories.

717 MANDEL', NAUM. [b. 1925, em. 1974] (KORZHAVIN) "Kladbishche
v Tige"; "On byl v takoi glubokoi t'me." GRANI (Frankfurt):
No. 71, May 1969; pp. 11-14.
Poems, published anonymously; Korzhavin identified in
Grani No. 80. See #877.

718 _____. (KORZHAVIN) "Naivnost'." POSEV (Frankfurt):
No. 2, Feb. 1969; pp. 52-53.
Poem, published anonymously; reprinted, with corrections
and author identified, in Posev No. 4, April 1975; pp. 53-
54.

719 _____. (KORZHAVIN) "Poèma grekha." NOVYI ZHURNAL (New
York): No. 116, Sept. 1974; pp. 72-77. Poem.

720 _____. (KORZHAVIN) "Russkoi intelligentsii"; "Pamiati
Tsvetaevoi"; "Mozhno strochki nanizyvat';" "Vstuplen'e k
poème 1952 goda." GRANI (Frankfurt): No. 80, Sept. 1971;
pp. 10-14. Poems.

721 _____. (KORZHAVIN) "Stikhi: 'Credo'; 'Dvadtsatye gody';
'V zashchitu progressa'; 'Liudi mogut dyshat'. . .'; 'Ot
sozidatel'nykh idei, . .'" KONTINENT: No. 3, 1975, pp.
71-78. Poems, all dated before emigration.

722 _____. (KORZHAVIN) "Stikhi raznykh let: 'Stikhi o
sobstvennoi gibeli'; 'Apokalipsis'." RUS. MYSL' (Paris):
May 2, 1974; p. 6. Poems.

723 _____. (KORZHAVIN) "Sud'ba Iaroslava Smeliakova."
GRANI (Frankfurt): No. 91, Jan.-March 1974; pp. 131-79.
Essay about the fate of one poet during the years of
Stalin and Khrushchev, and of poetry generally in those
eras, including a description of Tvardovskii's career.

724 MANDEL', NAUM. (KORZHAVIN) "A Thousand-Year-Old Song" (tr., S. Kunitz); "The Trumpeters" (tr., G. Orr); "You Fly Along. . ." (tr., C. Proffer); "Free woman from all torments. . . ." RUS. LIT. TRIQUARTERLY (Ann Arbor, Mich.): No. 5, Winter 1973; pp. 25-29.
Poems. Russian texts, pp. 629-32.

725 _____. (KORZHAVIN) "Tserkov' Spasa na krovi." NOVYI ZHURNAL (New York): No. 113, Dec. 1973; pp. 106-107.
Poem.

726 _____. (KORZHAVIN) Vremena: Izbrannoe. [Times: Selected Works] Frankfurt: Posev, 1976, 386 pp.
Collection of poems.

727 MANDEL'SHTAM, NADEZHDA. [b. 1899, d. 1980] Chapter 42. London: Menard, 1973; 39 pp. Tr., D. Rayfield.
Expanded text of last chapter of Vtoraia kniga, including poems by Osip Mandel'shtam.

728 _____. "Moe zaveshchanie." VESTNIK RSKhD (Paris): No. 100, II-1971; pp. 153-60.

     _____. "Moe zaveshchanie." NOV. RUS. SLOVO (New York): Feb. 27, 1972; p. 2; Nov. 5, 1972; p. 2.

     _____. "My Testament." SURVEY (London): Vol. 18, No. 1 (82), Winter 1972; pp. 1-7.
     Statement, not included in her memoirs, requesting future generations to keep Mandel'shtam's poetry from the encroachments of the State--to keep it "private," not "state," property.

729 _____. "Motsart i Sal'eri." VESTNIK RSKhD (Paris): No. 103, I-1972; pp. 237-78.

     _____. Mozart and Salieri. Ann Arbor, Mich.: Ardis, 1973; 119 pp. Tr., R. A. McLean.
     Her version of Mandel'shtam and Akhmatova's interpretation of the Pushkin play and of the two types incarnated in the characters.

730 _____. Vospominaniia. New York: Chekhov, 1970; 429 pp.

     _____. Hope Against Hope. New York: Atheneum, 1970; 431 pp. Tr., Max Hayward.

     _____. Souvenirs; t. 1: Contre tout espoire. Paris: Gallimard, 1972; 437 pp. Tr., Maya Minoustchine.

MANDEL'SHTAM

MANDEL'SHTAM, NADEZHDA. Das Jahrhundert der Wölfe: Eine
Autobiographie. Frankfurt: Fischer, 1968; 401 pp. Tr.,
Elisabeth Mahler.

_____. "Iz vospominanii o Mandel'shtame." VESTNIK
RSKhD (Paris): No. 97, III-1970; pp. 125-36.

_____. "Iz 'Vospominanii' N. Ia. Mandel'shtam." RUS.
MYSL' (Paris): Dec. 31, 1970; p. 4.
Memoirs by widow of arguably Russia's greatest 20th
century poet. She gives, in great detail, an account of
the demoralization of the intelligentsia under Stalin, her
husband's work, life and destruction and death at Stalin's
hands, much information about Akhmatova, Pasternak, Khlebnikov, Babel' and others. Of particularly controversial
significance is her evaluation of the 1920s, frequently
considered a sort of golden age of culture which Stalin
killed in the early 1930s: she, rather, sees it as a
period of capitulation, when humanist and humane values
were betrayed and inhuman ideology already ruled, and words
like honor and conscience lost their meaning. The body of
the book deals with 1934, when Mandel'shtam was first arrested, to 1938, when he was reported to have died in a
camp near Vladivostok, and the years between when they
lived in Voronezh.

731   _____. Vtoraia kniga. Paris: YMCA, 1972; 712 pp.

_____. Hope Abandoned. New York: Atheneum, 1974; 687
pp. Tr., Max Hayward.

_____. Souvenirs; t. 2: Contre tout espoire. Paris:
Gallimard, 1974; 320 pp. T. 3: Contre tout espoire.
Paris: Gallimard, 1975; 336 pp. Tr., Maya Minoustchine.

_____. Generation ohne Tränen: Erinnerungen. Frank-
furt: Fischer, 1975; 381 pp. Tr., Godehard Schramm.

_____. "Vtoraia kniga." RUS. MYSL' (Paris): April 27,
1972; p. 5; May 4, 1972; p. 3; May 11, 1972; p. 3; May 18,
1972; p. 5; May 25, 1972; p. 5; June 1, 1972; p. 3; June 8,
1972; p. 3; June 15, 1972; p. 3.

_____. "Vtoraia kniga." NOV. RUS. SLOVO (New York):
June 3, 1972; p. 5; June 5, 1972; p. 3; June 6, 1972; p. 3;
June 7, 1972; pp. 3-4; June 8, 1972; p. 3; June 9, 1972;
p. 4; June 10, 1972; p. 6; June 12, 1972; pp. 2, 4; June
13, 1972; p. 4; June 14, 1972; p. 4; June 15, 1972; p. 4.

MANDEL'SHTAM, NADEZHDA. "T. S. Èliot. K opredeleniiu ponia-
tiia kul'tury." NOVYI ZHURNAL (New York): No. 111, June
1973; pp. 279-83.
Continuation of memoirs. Author gives background on
her and Mandel'shtam's life together from their first meeting in 1919 up to his 1934 arrest, and much information on
her own life after his death--30 years which she effective-
ly dedicated to preserving his poetry. Also contains her
interpretation of events and people which illumine Mandel'-
shtam's work.

MANDEL'SHTAM, OSIP [b. 1891, d. 1931].

NB: With Osip Mandel'shtam, as with Solzhenitsyn, comprehensive editions of works are listed first, followed by
publications of individual works. Wherever possible, editor
has indicated after individual work which, if any, comprehensive edition contains it.

732 _____. Sobranie sochinenii v chetyrekh tomakh. [Collected
Works in Four Volumes] Ed., G. Struve and B. A. Fillipov.
Washington: Interlanguage Literary Associates.
Includes much, but not all, of his poetry, letters,
prose writings both fictional and nonfictional. Some circulated in samizdat for the first time, never having been
published in the Soviet Union; others (indicated below)
were published, generally in the 1920s, quickly went out
of print and came to the attention of Soviet readers only
via manuscript copies circulated in samizdat.

733 _____. Sochineniia. [Works] New York: Chekhov, 1955;
414 pp.

734 _____. The Complete Poetry of Osip Emilyevich Mandelshtam. Ed., Sidney Monas. Albany: SUNY Press, 1973;
353 pp. Tr., Burton Raffel and Alla Burago.

735 _____. The Complete Critical Prose and Letters. Eds.,
Jane Gary Harris and Constance Link. Ann Arbor, Mich.:
Ardis, 1979; 725 pp.

736 _____. The Prose of Osip Mandelstam. Princeton, N.J.:
Princeton Univ. Press, 1965; 209 pp. Tr., Clarence Brown.
(Contains "The Noise of Time," pub. orig. in 1925, "Theo-
dosia," written c. 1925 and "Egyptian Stamp," pub. orig.
in 1928.)

737 _____. Selected Essays. Austin: Univ. of Texas Press,
1977; 245 pp. Tr., Sidney Monas.

MANDEL'SHTAM

738   MANDEL'SHTAM, OSIP. Selected Poems. London: Oxford Univ.
      Press, 1974 and New York: Atheneum, 1974; 100 pp. Tr.,
      Clarence Brown and W. S. Merwin.

739   _____. Selected Poems. Cambridge: River Press and New
      York: Farrar, Straus and Giroux, 1973; 182 pp. Tr.,
      David McDuff.

740   _____. Le Bruit des Temps. Paris: Age d'Homme, 1972;
      144 pp.

741   _____. Entretiens sur Dante. Paris: Age d'Homme, 1977,
      Republished in USSR after samizdat circulation.

742   _____. Tristia et autres poèmes. Paris: Gallimard,
      1975; 344 pp. Biling. ed.

743   _____. "Chetvertaia proza," "Pis'ma." GRANI (Frank-
      furt): No. 63, March 1967; pp. 16-30. (From Feniks 1966,
      #337).

      _____. "Tiuremshchiki liubiat chitat' romany. . . ."
      POSEV (Frankfurt): No. 22 (1097), June 2, 1967; p. 3.

      _____. "Fourth Prose." RUS. LIT. TRIQUARTERLY (Ann
      Arbor, Mich.): No. 11, Winter 1975; pp. 51-61. Tr., Jane
      Gary Harris.
         Written 1929-31, a short feuilleton against "authorized"
      literature and literary hacks, partly in response to so-
      called "Eulenspiegel" affair, when Mandel'shtam was at-
      tacked for plagiarism. Eng. tr. also in SCAMMELL (#1005),
      HARRIS and LINK (#735).
         The letters date from 1935-37, and were written to
      Chukovskii appealing for help. Eng. tr. in HARRIS and
      LINK (#735).

744   _____. "Dva neizdannykh stikhotvoreniia O. Mandel'-
      shtama"; "Ia pishu stsenarii." ["Two Unpublished Poems
      by O. Mandel'shtam"; "I Write a Scenario"] VESTNIK RSKhD
      (Paris): No. 98, IV-1970; pp. 66-70.
         Poems plus humorous sketch, dating from late 1920s or
      early 1930s, on the problems involved in creating a
      scenario: Mandel'shtam in search of a "plot." Eng. tr.
      of latter in HARRIS and LINK (#735).

745   _____. "Dvadtsat' dva neizdannykh stikhotvoreniia: 'Ty
      ulybaesh'sia komu. . .'; 'V prostorakh sumerechnoi zaly
      . . .'; 'V kholodnykh perelivakh lir. . .'; 'Besshumnoe
      vereteno. . .'," etc. VESTNIK RSKhD (Paris): No. 97,
      III-1970; pp. 107-17. Poems.

746   MANDEL'SHTAM, OSIP. "Iz literaturnogo naslediia Osipa Mandel'-
       shtama: 'Pushkin i Skriabin.'" VESTNIK RSKhD (Paris):
       No. 72-73, I-II-1964; pp. 61-67.
           Essay begun in 1915, date of completion uncertain.
       Mandel'shtam sees Scriabin as the next stage, after Push-
       kin, of "Russian Hellenism." Fragmentary analysis of
       Christianity and its "free" relationship to art, Scriabin
       as a non-Christian artist. Eng. tr. in HARRIS and LINK
       (#735).

747   _____. "K 700-letiiu so dnia rozhdeniia Dante." VEST-
       NIK RSKhD (Paris): No. 79, IV-1965; pp. 22-27.
           Excerpt from "Razgovor o Dante"; full Russian text in
       Sob. soch. (#732), full Eng. text in HARRIS and Link (#735).

748   _____. "Materialy k biografii Osipa Mandel'shtama."
       VESTNIK RKhD (Paris): No. 120, I-1977; pp. 236-62.
           Includes five previously unpub. letters to his wife,
       dating from 1925 and '26, and six letters dealing with
       translation and plagiarism charges, apartment problems.
       Eng. tr. in HARRIS and LINK (#735).

749   _____. "Neapolitanskie pesenki." VESTNIK RKhD (Paris):
       No. 115, I-1975; pp. 183-87. Poems.

750   _____. "Neizdannye stikhi: 'Muzyka tvoikh shagov. . .';
       'V neprinuzhdennosti tvoriashchego obmena'; 'Dovol'no
       lukavit'. . .'; 'Piligrim'; 'Skvoz' voskovuiu zanaves'
       . . .'; '. . . korobki. . .'; 'List'ev sochustvennyi shoro-
       khi'; 'V izgolov'i chernoe raspiatie. . .'; 'Strekozy
       bystrymi krugami. . .'; 'Medlenno urna pustaia'; 'Ia znaiu,
       chto obman. . .'; 'Kogda podymaiu. . .'; 'Dushu ot vnesh-
       nikh uslovii. . .'; 'Dozhdik laskovyi. . .'; 'Ne sprashi-
       vai: ty znaesh'. . . ." VESTNIK RSKhD (Paris): No. 111,
       I-1974; pp. 172-81.
           Early poems, c. 1909-11.

       _____. "Neizdannye stikhi Osipa Mandel'shtama: 'Dovol'-
       no lukavit': ia znaiu. . .'; 'V izgolov'i chernoe ras-
       piatie. . .'; 'Ia znaiu, chto obman v videnii nemyslim. . .';
       'Dusha ot vneshnikh uslovii. . .'; 'Dozhdik laskovyi,
       tikhii i tonkii. . .'; 'Ne sprashivai: ty znaesh'. . . ."
       NOV. RUS. SLOVO (New York): Sept. 29, 1974; p. 5. Poems.

751   _____. "Piat' neizdannykh stikhotvorenii O. E. Mandel'-
       shtama." VESTNIK RSKhD (Paris): No. 64, I-1962; pp. 48-
       50. Poems written 1935-37.

MANDEL'SHTAM

752   MANDEL'SHTAM, OSIP. "Dva neizdannykh stikhotvoreniia: 'Zhe-
       lezo,' 'Tianuli zhily. . .'; 'O p'ese A. Chekhova Diadia
       Vania'; 'Otryvok iz stati o perevodakh'." VESTNIK RKhD
       (Paris): No. 118, II-1976; pp. 228-31.
           Two poems plus short essay on translation; the latter
       in Eng. tr. in HARRIS and LINK (#735).

753   _____. "Stikhi o neizvestnom soldate." VESTNIK RSKhD
       (Paris): No. 75-76, IV-1964; pp. 98-101.
           Poem written in 1937.
           Ardis Press (Ann Arbor, Mich.) has also printed facsimi-
       les of the first editions of Kamen' (first book of verse,
       printed in 1913, rep. in 1923), Tristia (first printed in
       1922 in Berlin, rep. in Moscow in 1923) and Ègipetskaia
       marka (first printed 1928).

754   [_____.] "Vecher pamiati Mandel'shtama v MGU: pod predse-
       datel'stvom I. Èrenburga." ["An Evening in Memory of
       Mandel'shtam at MGU, under the Chairmanship of Erenburg"]
       GRANI (Frankfurt): No. 77, Oct. 1970; pp. 82-88.
           Transcript of remarks by Erenburg, Stepanov, Tarkovskii,
       Shalamov at memorial evening May 13, 1965.

755   MAR, SUSANNA. [d. 1965] "Korni"; "Pokhorony poèta." NOVYI
       ZHURNAL (New York): No. 113, Dec. 1973; p. 127. (Poet's
       real name was Susanna Grigor'evna Chelkhushian.)
           Poems.

756   _____. "Lirika"; "V neoplatnom dolgu." NOVYI ZHURNAL
       (New York): No. 112, Sept. 1973; pp. 71-72. Poems.

757   MARAMZIN, VLADIMIR. [b. 1934, em. 1975] Blondin obeego
       tsveta. [A Blonde of Both Colors] Ann Arbor, Mich.:
       Ardis, 1975; 39 pp.
           Novella portraying disintegration of consciousness of
       Russian intelligentsia, mostly via language, in form of
       notes of the "Blonde," a conformist artist who is homo-
       sexual.

758   _____. "Chelovek, kotoryi veril v svoe osoboe naz-
       nachenie." ["The Man Who Believed in His Own Special
       Position"] VREMIA I MY (New York/Paris/Jerusalem): No.
       15, March 1977; pp. 3-65. Story.

759   _____. "Istoriia zhenit'by Ivana Petrovicha." ["The
       History of the Marriage of Ivan Petrovich"] KONTINENT:
       No. 2, 1974; pp. 5-82.
           Novella dated 1964, about a working-class girl who,
       financially strapped, turns prostitute, brings her

customer into the workers' dormitory and makes love with
him in presence of her roommates and finally marries him.

760 MARAMZIN, VLADIMIR. "Sekrety: tsikl rasskazov." ["Secrets:
a Cycle of Stories"] RUS. MYSL' (Paris): Dec. 25, 1975;
p. 9. Stories from mid-1960s.

761 _____. Tianitolkai. Ann Arbor, Mich.: Ardis, 1981.

_____. "Tianitolkai. Rasskaz s avtorskim prodolzheniem."
KONTINENT: No. 8, 1976; pp. 13-47.
Novella from mid-1960s describing author's "invitation"
by KGB for a chat to discuss the state and fate of Russian
literature. (Eerily foreshadows actual interrogation and
trial of Maramzin in 1974; see Khr. zashch. prav No. 12 (#579).

762 MARCHENKO, ANATOLII. [b. 1938] Moi pokazaniia. Frankfurt:
Posev, 1969; 420 pp.; Paris: La Presse Libre, 1969; 369
pp.; New York: Dutton, 1969; 144 pp.

_____. My Testimony. London: Pall Mall and New York:
Dutton, 1969; 415 pp. Tr., Michael Scammell.

_____. (MARTCHENKO) Mon témoignage: Les camps en URSS
après Staline. Paris: Seuil, 1970; 333 pp. Tr., Francois
Olivier.

_____. (MARTSCHENKO) Meine Aussagen. Frankfurt:
Fischer, 1969; 401 pp. Tr., Elisabeth Mahler.
Memoir describing conditions in Soviet camps and prisons
in 1960s by now-prominent dissident who was first arrested
in 1958 for participating in fight in workers' dormitory
(though he didn't) and sent to camp, from which he escaped
and tried to cross Iranian border. Rearrested, he was
charged with treason and sent to Mordovian camp. Having
attempted again to escape, he was sent to Vladimir prison,
where he nearly died of meningitis and permanently lost his
hearing. His book, one of the most important on the subject, describes in great detail the conditions of prisoners' lives, including such acts of "protest" as prisoners'
tattooing themselves with slogans like "Lenin--Hangman";
in hospital the skin is then removed without anesthesia.

763 _____. Ot Tarusy do Chuny s prilozheniem dokumentov o
sude nad Marchenko. [From Taruso to Chuna, plus Documents
on Marchenko's Trial] New York: Khronika, 1976; 123 pp.

_____. (MARTCHENKO) Une Grève de la faim. Paris:
Seuil, 1977; 158 pp.

MARCHENKO

    MARCHENKO, ANATOLII. From Tarusa to Siberia. Royal Oak,
      Mich.: Strathcona, 1980; 139 pp.

    _____. "Rech' Anatoliia Marchenko na sude v gorode
      Kaluge 31 marta 1975 goda." RUS. MYSL' (Paris): May 15,
      1975; p. 5.

    _____. "Rech' A. Marchenko na sude v Kaluge 31 marta
      1975 goda." NOV. RUS. SLOVO (New York): May 21, 1975;
      p. 4.
      Account of his most recent arrest and exile in Siberia,
    his two-month hunger strike, the logic of his struggle
    with the regime.

    MARCHENKO, ANATOLII: See also BRUMBERG (#178), Khr. tek. sob.
      Nos. 3, 8, 10, 35 (#529, #546), Khr. zashch. prav No. 43 (#608).

764 MARCHENKO, ANATOLII and TARUSEVICH, M. (Pseud.) "Tercium
      datur: tret'e dano." KONTINENT: No. 9, 1976; pp. 81-122.
      Criticism of Western governments' approach to Soviet
    Union and discussion of East-West relations generally.

765 MARCHENKO, VALERII. "Moia prekrasnaia ledi." ["My Beautiful
      Lady"] NOV. RUS. SLOVO (New York): March 28, 1976; p. 2.

    _____. (VASILII [sic]) "Moia prekrasnaia ledi." RUS.
    MYSL' (Paris): May 13, 1976; p. 5. Story.

766 MARRAN. (Pseud.) "Mirazhi 'Tiazhelogo peska'." ["The Mi-
      rages of Heavy Sand"] VREMIA I MY (New York/Paris/Jerusa-
      lem): No. 41, May 1979; pp. 119-29.
      Critical analysis of Rybakov's novel which, officially
    published, describes the destruction of a Jewish community
    on the Ukrainian/Belorussian border during the second World
    War.

767 MARTIN, ANDRÉ. Ed. Les Croyants en URSS. Paris: Fayard,
      1970.
      Collection of Orthodox and Baptist documents, 1965-69.

768 MASLOV, S. "So-chustvie: Dialogi Pravoslavnogo i liberala."
      VREMIA I MY (New York/Paris/Jerusalem): No. 42, June 1979;
      pp. 104-32.
      Taking Iz-pod glyb as his starting point, author tries
    to find commonality between liberals and Russian Orthodox
    believers.

769 MEDVEDEV, ROI. [b. 1925] A Discussion with Roy Medvedev:
      Detente and Socialist Democracy. London: Bertrand Russell

Peace Found., 1975 and New York: Monad, 1976; 163 pp.
Tr., Tamara Deutscher.

Includes "Problems of Democratization and Detente" and
"Problems of General Concern." All the other articles are
by socialists, both Western and Eastern.

770   MEDVEDEV, ROI and LERT, RAISA, eds. Dvadtsatyi vek:
obshchestvenno-politicheskii i literaturnyi al'manakh.
I. London: T. C. D. Pubs., 1976; 237 pp.

_____, (MEDWEDJEW) Aufzeichnungen aus dem sowjetischen
Untergrund. Texte aus der Moskauer Samisdat-Zeitschrift
Das XX. Jahrhundert. Hamburg: Hoffmann and Campe, 1977;
311 pp. Tr., Edda Werfel.

Conceived as a continuation of Politicheskii dnevnik,
which appeared in some 75 issues between 1964 and 1970
(see #784). In its first year of publication, 1975, Dvadtsatyi vek came out in 6 issues, in 1976 in 4. The volumes
cited below contain selections from various issues, chosen
by Zhores Medvedev on basis of interest to Western readers
and excluding works which were or will be published
separately.

Issue No. I contains:

MEDVEDEV, ROI: "Voprosy, kotorye volnuiut kazhdogo," on
Soviet dissent, East-West relations, the possibility of
change in Soviet Union, the emigration, Solzhenitsyn,
Kontinent.
LERT, RAISA: '. . . I na kotorye net odnoznachnykh otve-
tov," agreeing and taking issue with Medvedev on the topics
he discusses.
VLAGIN, SERGEI: "Raskaianie: Teoriia, istoriia i retsept
dnia," challenging Solzhenitsyn's views as presented in
Iz-pod glyb, especially the notion that internal freedom
is possible in unfree circumstances and Solzhenitsyn's in-
terpretation of Russian history as providing authoritarian,
but still tolerable and responsible leaders. Eng. tr. in
Samizdat Register 1 (#772), with Vlagin's name given as
Elagin.
IAMPOL'SKII, BORIS: "Iz vospominanii," reminiscences of
Vasilii Grossman and Iurii Olesha; author died in 1973.
VITKOVSKII, DMITRII: "Polzhizni," memoirs beginning with
his arrest in 1926, transport to Siberia, rearrest in 1931,
work on Belomor Canal, and then in Tuloma, north of the
Arctic Circle, rearrest in 1938 after about two years'
freedom but released after sitting in prison about two
years, exile in Ukraine and eventual rehabilitation.

MEDVEDEV

771   MEDVEDEV, ROI, ed. Dvadtsatyi vek, II. London: T.C.D. Pubs.,
      1977, 256 pp.

      Issue No. II contains:

      MEDVEDEV, ROI: "Stalin. Nekotorye stranitsy iz politi-
      cheskoi biografii," additional materials not included in
      K sudu istorii, on Stalin's relationships with various
      Party officials, growth of bureaucratic and party apparat,
      the collectivization and purge of kulaks, great purges, the
      continuation of repression during the war, Stalin and Mao.
      Eng. tr. in Robert Tucker, ed., Stalinism: Essays in
      Historical Interpretation (New York: W. W. Norton, 1977).
      BOGIN, M.: "Komponenty sotsializma," attempt at defining
      socialism and its various components and relationships--
      socialism and power, socialism and ownership.
      KRASIKOV, A.: "Tovar nomer odin," on the economics of
      alcoholism. Eng. tr. in Samizdat Register I & II (#772 & #773).
      LAKSHIN, VLADIMIR: "Solzhenitsyn, Tvardovskii i 'Novyi
      mir'," part of his book of same name (see #654).
      LEBEDENKO, ALEKSANDR: "Budni bez vykhodnykh," memoir of
      pre-war and war-time camp.

772   _____. Samizdat Register. I: Voices of the Socialist
      Opposition in the Soviet Union. London: Merlin Press,
      1977; 316 pp. and New York: W. W. Norton.
          Includes the following essays, all taken from the first
      three issues of Dvadtsatyi vek:

      MEDVEDEV, ROI: "The October Revolution and the Problem of
      History as a Law-Governed Process," tr. by Brian Pearce;
      on the inevitability of the revolution, its timing (whether
      it was premature) and its historical circumstances.
      MIRONOV, FILIP: "Mironov's Last Letter," tr. by Brian
      Pearce, later included in MEDVEDEV and STARIKOV (#795);
      Mironov, Cossack leader who fought with Bolsheviks during
      Civil war, was imprisoned in March 1921 and shot April 2,
      1921; his letter justifies the actions for which he was
      arrested.
      KRASIKOV, A. (BAITALSKII, MIKHAIL): "Commodity Number
      One." See #771. Tr., Brian Pearce.
      ZIMIN, A.: "On the Question of the Place in History of
      the Social Structure of the Soviet Union," tr. by Brian
      Pearce; comparing the "asiatic mode of production" with
      "complete socialism," which he sees as a stagnant society
      that cannot move forward and still preserve itself.
      IAKUBOVICH, M. P. (YAKUBOVICH): "From the History of
      Ideas," tr. by Tamara Deutscher; survivor of 20 years in
      labor camps analyzes the events of 1917.

KOPELEV, LEV: "A Lie is Conquered Only by Truth," tr. by Ellen Wood; response to Solzhenitsyn's "Letter to Soviet Leaders," taking issue with Solzhenitsyn's interpretation of history, his anti-Westernism, his reading of the Chinese threat, his attack on ideology as responsible for all the evils of Russia.
ELAGIN, SERGEI [sic]: "Repentance: Its Theory, History and Prescription for Today," tr. by Vera Magyar. See above, listed under Vlagin.
ANDREEV, GERMAN: "The Christianity of L. N. Tolstoy and of the Contributors to 'From Under the Rubble,'" tr. by Vera Magyar, exploring Tolstoi's interpretation of Christianity, its incompatibility with Russian Orthodoxy, and criticizing contributors to Iz-pod glyb for their support of "autocracy, orthodoxy and nationalism."

773   MEDVEDEV, ROI. Samizdat Register. II: New York: Norton, 1981; 323 pp. Includes:

MEDVEDEV, ROY: "Stalinism after the Twentieth Congress of the CPSU as the Reflection of Internal and International Problems of the USSR," discussion of de-Stalinization and partial rehabilitation of Stalinism; "Problems of Democracy East and West," on censorship, nationalities issue, the intelligentsia; "On A. D. Sakharov's Book 'My Country and the World'"; tr., M. Colenso; evaluation of and polemic with Sakharov's views; "Solzhenitsyn: Truth and Politics," tr., George Saunders; a discussion of Volume III of Gulag.
YAKUBOVICH, M. P.: "L. B. Kamenev," tr., Tamara Deutscher; on Kamenev's personality and role in Russian history; "G. Zinoviev," on Lenin and Zinoviev's relationship and Zinoviev's views on and role in the revolution.
BOGIN, M.: "Components of Socialism," see above.
PESTOV, N.: "Communism and the Soviet Union at the end of the Twentieth Century," on the possibilities, finally, of moving toward genuine communism.
BECHMETYEV, A.: "From a Philosophical Diary," reflections on ethics and philosophy in Marxism.
KRASIKOV, A.: "Commodity Number One," tr., Brian Pearce; see #771.
DAVYDOV, M. B.: "Comparative Mechanisation of Agriculture in the USSR and Other Countries"; summary of unpublished article.
MAKSUDOV, M. (BABENYSHEV, A.): "Losses Suffered by the Population of the USSR 1918-1958," tr., Naurika Lenner; assessment of minimum number of losses, calculated by using official Soviet data, due to war caualties, migrations, poor hygiene, famine, camp exterminations et al.

MEDVEDEV

774   MEDVEDEV, ROI. <u>Faut-il</u> <u>rehabiliter</u> <u>Staline</u>? Paris: Seuil,
1969: 96 pp. Tr., Francois Olivier.
Collection of articles.

775   _____. "Jews in the USSR." SURVEY (London): Vol. 17,
No. 2 (79), Spring 1971; pp. 184-200.
Brief history of Stalin's anti-Semitic policies and cur-
rent discrimination; divides Soviet Jews into assimila-
tionists, non-assimilationists and would-be emigres to
Israel, and comments on their various needs and rights.

776   _____. <u>K</u> <u>sudu</u> <u>istorii</u>: <u>Genezis</u> <u>i</u> <u>posledstviia</u> <u>staliniz</u>-
<u>ma</u>. New York: Knopf, 1971; 1974; 1136 pp. 1974 ed. re-
vised and supplemented.

_____. <u>Let</u> <u>History</u> <u>Judge</u>. New York: Knopf and London:
Macmillan, 1971; 566 pp. Tr., Colleen Taylor.

_____. <u>Le</u> <u>Stalinisme</u>. <u>Origines</u>, <u>histoire</u>, <u>conséquences</u>.
Paris: Seuil, 1972; 640 pp. Tr. from English.

_____. (MEDWEDJEW) <u>Die</u> <u>Wahrheit</u> <u>ist</u> <u>unsere</u> <u>Stärke</u>:
<u>Geschichte</u> <u>und</u> <u>Folgen</u> <u>des</u> <u>Stalinismus</u>. Frankfurt: Fischer,
1973; 673 pp. Tr., Gunter Danehl.
Scholarly history of Stalin era written from pro-
Leninist, anti-Stalinist perspective, using "Stalinism" to
mean "personal despotism sustained by mass terror and by
worship of the despot" (from ed.'s introduction), a de-
formation of essentially healthy system.

777   _____. <u>Kniga</u> <u>o</u> <u>sotsialisticheskoi</u> <u>demokratii</u>. Amsterdam: Herzen, 1972; 402 pp.

_____. <u>On</u> <u>Socialist</u> <u>Democracy</u>. New York: Knopf, 1975;
405 pp. Tr., Ellen de Kadt.

_____. <u>De</u> <u>la</u> <u>démocratie</u> <u>socialiste</u>. Paris: Grasset &
Fasquelle, 1972; 386 pp. Tr., Sybil Geoffroy.

_____. (MEDWEDJEW) <u>Sowjet</u> <u>Bürger</u> <u>in</u> <u>Opposition</u>: <u>Plä</u>-
<u>doyer</u> <u>für</u> <u>eine</u> <u>sozialistische</u> <u>Demokratie</u>. Hamburg, Düssel-
dorf: Clausen, 1973; 368 pp. Tr., Wilhelm Thaler.
Analysis of different political forces at work in the
USSR, the possibility of democracy under socialism, different types of opposition; written from liberal Marxist
perspective which holds that genuine socialism is impossible without democracy. Shows how the bureaucratic structure of the Soviet Union has become an obstacle to every
kind of progress, and feels change has to come from the top.

778   MEDVEDEV, ROI. "A Lesson for Both Sides." NEW YORK TIMES:
       Jan. 24, 1975.
       On East-West Relations.

779   _____. "O knige Solzhenitsyna 'Arkhipelag GULag'."
       RUS. MYSL' (Paris): Feb. 28, 1974; p. 5; March 7, 1974;
       p. 5.

       _____. "O knige Solzhenitsyna 'Arkhipelag GULag'."
       NOVYI ZHURNAL (New York): No. 115, June 1974; pp. 211-27.

       _____. "On Gulag Archipelago." NEW LEFT REVIEW: No. 85,
       May-June 1974; pp. 25-36. Tr., Tamara Deutscher.
       Analysis of first volume of <u>Gulag</u>, praising it but dis-
       agreeing with some of Solzhenitsyn's judgments, such as
       the inevitability of Stalinism and the relative unimport-
       ance of Stalin himself. Also challenges view of Lenin in
       book. See also MANDEL, E., MEDWEDJEW, R., GRIGORENKO, P.
       <u>Revolutionäre</u> <u>oder</u> <u>bürgerliche</u> <u>Kritik</u> <u>der</u> <u>Sowjetunion</u>.
       <u>Solschenizyn's</u> <u>'Archipel Gulag</u>.' Frankfurt: ISP, 1974,
       44 pp.

780   _____. <u>Nikolai</u> <u>Bukharin</u>: <u>The</u> <u>Last</u> <u>Years</u>. New York and
       London: W. W. Norton, 1980; 176 pp. Tr., A. D. P. Briggs.
       Much new information on last years of Bukharin's life,
       based on information to some extent provided by Soviet in-
       formants (unpublished memoirs, some parts of which were
       circulated in samizdat in <u>Politicheskii</u> <u>dnevnik</u>).

781   _____. <u>The</u> <u>October</u> <u>Revolution</u>. New York: Columbia
       Univ. Press, 1979; 240 pp.

       _____. <u>La</u> <u>Révolution</u> <u>d'Octobre</u>. Paris: Maspero, 1978;
       246 pp.

       _____. (MEDWEDJEW) <u>Oktober</u> <u>1917</u>. Hamburg: Hoffmann
       and Campe, 1979; 238 pp. Tr., Helga Jaspers.
       Series of essays dealing with 1917-1918 Civil War (Bol-
       shevik Policy), presenting the February revolution as
       spontaneous and ascribing to Lenin the crucial role in the
       Bolshevik triumph.

782   _____. <u>On</u> <u>Stalin</u> <u>and</u> <u>Stalinism</u>. Oxford: Oxford Univ.
       Press, 1979; 205 pp. Tr., Ellen de Kadt.
       Madvedev's reflections on the struggle between Stalin
       and Trotskii and his evaluation of the Stalin era as
       tempered (after <u>K</u> <u>sudu</u> <u>istorii</u>) by much new information he
       received from many informants; he is far more critical of
       Lenin and Lenin's role in planting seeds which grew into
       Stalinism.

MEDVEDEV

783 MEDVEDEV, ROI. <u>Political</u> <u>Essays</u>. Nottingham: Spokesman
     Books, 1976; 151 pp. Tr., Tamara Deutscher, Brian Pearce,
     Marilyn Vogt and Reuben Ainsztein.
         Includes "Democracy and Detente," "Dissent and Free
     Discussion," "Watergate: A View from the Soviet Union,"
     "Trade and Democratisation," and several essays constitut-
     ing a discussion with Solzhenitsyn (on <u>Gulag</u>, on Solzhe-
     nitsyn and Tvardovskii, etc.). Several essays appeared
     in <u>New</u> <u>Left</u> <u>Review</u>, one in <u>Intercontinental</u> <u>Press</u> and part
     of one in <u>The</u> <u>Sunday</u> <u>Times</u> (London).

784 _____. Ed., <u>Politicheskii</u> <u>dnevnik</u>. Vol. 1, 1964-70.
     Amsterdam: Herzen, 1972; 838 pp.

     _____. "Political Diary." SURVEY (London): Vol. 18,
     No. 3 (84), Summer 1972; pp. 209-22.
         Medvedev's editorship is not indicated in Volume 1; it
     is published anonymously. But in Volume 2 he is identi-
     fied as editor of both volumes.
         Volume 1 includes items from issues 3, 9, 25, 30, 33,
     43, 46, 55, 63, 67, 72: comments on current affairs, de-
     nunciations of official press's lies and falsifications,
     verbatim reports from conference where ideological tutor
     instructs writers and journalists; reports of sessions
     where dissidents are judged by colleagues for "subversive"
     views; reminiscences from camps; excerpts from banned
     documents; memoirs by eyewitnesses of the 1917 revolution.
     <u>Survey</u> excerpts from issues 9, 30, 33, 55 and 64.

785 _____. Ed., <u>Politicheskii</u> <u>dnevnik</u>, Vol. 2. Amsterdam:
     Herzen, 1975; 864 pp.

     _____. Ed. <u>An</u> <u>End</u> <u>to</u> <u>Silence</u>. New York and London:
     Norton, 1982; 373 pp. Tr., G. Saunders.
         Vol. 2 includes more reminiscences, historical docu-
     ments, etc.

786 _____. "Pravda o sovremennosti." ["The Truth About To-
     day"] POSEV (Frankfurt): No. 1, Jan. 1970; pp. 39-45.
         Marxist critique of Soviet Marxism, disavowed by Med-
     vedev: see POSEV No. 5, May 1970; pp. 27-28.

787 _____. "Problema demokratizatsii i problema razriadki."
     RUS. MYSL' (Paris): Dec. 6, 1973; pp. 4-5.

     _____. "Roi Medvedev o demokratizatsii i o razriadke."
     NOV. RUS. SLOVO (New York): May 15, 1974; p. 2; May 16,
     1974; p. 2; May 17, 1974; pp. 2-3.

MEDVEDEV, ROI. "Problems of Democratization and Detente."
NEW LEFT REVIEW (London): No. 83, Jan.-Feb. 1973; pp.
27-40.
Reply to appeals to West by other dissidents, the ex-
tremism and parochialism of which he attributes largely to
repressive measures employed against them by state; hope
for democracy only in coalition between forces "from above"
and "from below"; also analyzes role of external pressures
like trade sanctions. In Political Essays (#783).

788   . Problems in the Literary Biography of Mikhail
Sholokhov. Cambridge: Cambridge Univ. Press and New York:
Columbia Univ. Press, 1977; 227 pp. Tr., A. D. P. Briggs.

          . Qui a écrit le Don paisible? Paris: Bourgois,
1975; 288 pp.
From Dvadtsatyi vek; on the charges of plagiarism
leveled against Sholokhov. Medvedev concludes that Sholokhov created only part of the novel, and that those parts
are weaker than the rest, which was probably the work of
F. D. Kriukov (1870-1920).

789   . (MEDWEDJEW) Solschenizyn und die sowjetische
Linke. Eine Auseinandersetzung mit dem Archipel Gulag und
weitere Schriften. Berlin: Olle and Wolter, 1977; 100 pp.
Tr., Hans Schröder. Collection of articles.

790   . "What Lies Ahead for Us?" NEW LEFT REVIEW:
No. 87-88, Sept.-Dec. 1974; pp. 61-74. Tr., Brian Pearce.
Response to Solzhenitsyn's Letter to Soviet Leaders;
touches on nationalities, role of church, nature of Marxism, and expresses hope for reforms coming from above.
Inc. in Political Essays (#783) and in MEERSON-AKSENOV
and SHRAGIN (#801).

791 MEDVEDEV, ROI and MEDVEDEV, ZHORES. Kto sumasshedshii?
London: Macmillan, 1971; 163 pp.

          . A Question of Madness. New York: Knopf and
London: Macmillan, 1971; 223 pp. Tr., Ellen de Kadt.

          . Un cas de folie! Paris: Julliard, 1972; 250 pp.
Tr., Jean Bloch Michel.

          . (MEDWEDJEW) Sie sind ein psychiatrischer Fall,
Genosse. Munich: Praeger, 1972; 217 pp. Tr., Leopold
Voeker.
Record of Zhores Medvedev's involuntary confinement in
a psychiatric hospital in June 1970. Some excerpts con-
tained in "Soviet Mental Prisons" (#1130).

MEDVEDEV

792 MEDVEDEV, ROI and MEDVEDEV, ZHORES. N. S. Khrushchev. Gody
     u vlasti. Ann Arbor, Mich.: Xerox Univ. Microfilm #5.

     _____. Khrushchev: The Years in Power. New York:
     Columbia Univ. Press, 1976 and London: Oxford Univ. Press,
     1977; 198 pp. Tr., Andrew Durkin.

     _____. Krouchtchev: Les Annees de Pouvoir. Paris:
     Maspero, 1977; 220 pp. Tr., M. Kahn.
     Portrays Khrushchev as eager to destroy Stalinism,
     solve agricultural problems, etc.

793 _____. "N. Khrushchev na pensii." NOVYI ZHURNAL (New
     York): No. 133, Dec. 1978; pp. 258-76.

     _____. "Khrushchev in Retirement." INDEX ON CENSORSHIP
     (London): Vol. 8, No. 3, May-June 1979; pp. 3-11. Tr.,
     Marjorie Farquharson.
     Additional chapter (by Roi) which arrived in West too
     late for inclusion in book. Deals with Presidium and Ple-
     num meeting where Khrushchev was deprived of power; also
     with the period up to his death.

794 MEDVFDEV, ROI and PLIUCHTCH (PLIUSHCH), LEONIDE. Demain
     l'U.R.S.S. Paris: Syros, 1976; 174 pp.

795 MEDVEDEV, ROI and STARIKOV, SERGEI. Philip Mironov and the
     Russian Civil War. New York: Knopf, 1978; 267 pp.
     Analysis of career of Cossack leader who fought with the
     Bolsheviks but was arrested and charged with treason for
     having disobeyed orders. Includes his letter justifying
     his actions. He was shot in 1921.

     _____. La révolution d'Octobre était-elle inéluctable?
     Paris: Albin Michel, 1976; 192 pp.

     MEDVEDEV, ROI: See also SAKHAROV, TURCHIN and MEDVEDEV
     (#988), Samizdat I (#989), MEERSON-AKSENOV and SHRAGIN
     (#801), SAUNDERS (#1001).

796 MEDVEDEV, ZHORES. [b. 1925, em. 1973] Desiat' let posle
     "Odnogo dnia Ivana Denisovicha." London: Macmillan, 1973;
     223 pp.

     _____. Ten Years After Ivan Denisovich. New York:
     Knopf, 1973; 202 pp. Tr., Hilary Sternberg.

     _____. Dix ans dans la vie de Soljénitsyne. Paris:
     Grasset & Fasquelle, 1974; 304 pp. Tr., P. Le Gall.

MEDVEDEV, ZHORES. (MEDWEDJEW) Zehn Jahre im Leben des Alexander Solschenizyn: eine politische Biographie. Darmstadt, Neuwied: Luchterhand, 1974; 214 pp. Tr., Wolfgang
Kasack.
Account of Solzhenitsyn's fall from favor after the
publication of Ivan Denisovich, and the concomitant fate
of Tvardovskii and Novyi mir.

797 _____. Mezhdunarodnoe sotrudnichestvo uchennykh i
natsional'nye granitsy; taina perepiski okhraniaetsia zako-
nom. London: Macmillan and New York: St. Martin's Press,
1970; 597 pp.

_____. The Medvedev Papers: The Plight of Soviet Sci-
ence Today. London: Macmillan, 1971; 471 pp. Tr., Vera
Rich.

_____. Savants soviétiques et relations internationales.
Paris: Julliard, 1973; 364 pp. Tr. from Eng., M. J.
Milcent.

_____. Le Secret de la correspondance est garanti par
la loi. Paris: Julliard, 1972; 288 pp.
Part one examines Soviet practices in controlling and
restricting international contacts of Soviet scholars and
other citizens, including the procedures by which Soviets
receive passports, arrange trips abroad, etc. Part two
deals with postal censorship (of non-political mail, such
as scientific correspondence), techniques and consequences.

798 _____. "Rasskaz o roditeliakh." NOVYI ZHURNAL (New
York): No. 112, Sept. 1973; pp. 190-207.
Autobiographical sketch of the arrest of Medvedev's
father and the consequences of both arrest and his subsequent rehabilitation for the family.

799 _____. The Rise and Fall of T. D. Lysenko. New York:
Columbia Univ. Press, 1969; 284 pp. Tr., Michael Lerner.

_____. Grandeur et chute de Lyssenko. Paris: Galli-
mard, 1971; 320 pp. Tr. from Eng., Pierre Martory.

_____. (MEDWEDJEW) Der Fall Lyssenko: eine Wissen-
schaft kapituliert. Hamburg: Hoffmann and Campe, 1971;
303 pp. Tr., Peter Weidner.

_____. "Biologicheskaia nauka i kul't lichnosti: Ocher-
ki po istorii tridtsatiletnei biologo-agronomicheskoi

MEERSON-AKSENOV

diskussii." GRANI (Frankfurt): No. 70, Feb. 1969; pp.
127-66; No. 71, May 1969; pp. 78-161.

Discussion of Lysenko, Soviet geneticist who attacked
Mendelian theories of inheritance (and their leading Soviet
proponent, Nikolai Vavilov), and instead, together with
I. V. Michurin, espoused Lamarckianism (changing environment to change inherited characteristics). This became for
30 years the sole acceptable theory in Soviet genetics and
agrobiology. Medvedev discusses both the history of the
affair, and the final years of Lysenko's tenure as director
of the Academy of Science's Genetics Institute (in 1965),
and more generally the relationship between politics and
science, including the Brezhnev era, in the Soviet Union.
This book was cause of Medvedev's incarceration in psychiatric hospital (see Kto sumasshedshii?, #791).

800   MEERSON-AKSENOV, MIKHAIL. [b. 1944, em. 1973] "Narod Bozhii
i pastyri." ["God's People and Pastors"] VESTNIK RSKhD
(Paris): No. 104-105, II-III-1972; pp. 101-26.

Response to Solzhenitsyn's letter to Pimen, examining
contemporary Russian Orthodoxy in historical perspective.
The church and its hierarchy need not be--are not, in prin-
ciple--the same thing; hierarchical isolation has made
Orthodoxy defenseless in the face of state interference;
the church has secularized itself and compromised with the
state. Calls for creation of truly ecumenical church, independent of the state and rid of narrow-minded nationalism. Eng. in MEERSON-AKSENOV and SHRAGIN (#801).

801   MEERSON-AKSENOV, MIKHAIL and SHRAGIN, BORIS. The Political,
Social and Religious Thought of Russian "Samizdat"--An
Anthology. Belmont, Mass.: 1977; 624 pp. Tr., N. Lupinin.
Includes:
GRIGORENKO, PETR: "To the Participants of the Budapest
Conference," appeal to Conference of Communist Parties
(1968).
MEDVEDEV, ROI: "What Awaits Us in the Future?" see "What
Lies Ahead For Us?" (#790).
POMERANTS, GRIGORII: "The Moral Aspect of Personality,"
see POMERANTS, "O roli nravstvennogo oblika lichnosti. . . ."
(#950).
ALTAEV, O.: "The Dual Consciousness of the Intelligentsia
and Pseudo-Culture," see ALTAEV (#51).
VENTSOV, LEV: "To Think!" see SHRAGIN (#1059).
AMAL'RIK, A.: "An Open Letter to A. Kuznetsov," see
AMAL'RIK (#57).
ESENIN-VOL'PIN, ALEKSANDR: "A Fountain Pen for Peter
Grigor'evich Grigorenko!" (see ESENIN-VOL'PIN (#316); also
in ARTEMOVA et al. (#79).

CHALIDZE, VALERII: "Important Aspects of Human Rights in the Soviet Union," report written for Human Rights Committee Dec. 10, 1970 and pub. in samizdat journal Social Problems, No. 8. Deals with legal rights in USSR, and proposes framework for system for defense of human rights from judicial point of view.
ZHITNIKOV, K.: "The Decline of the Democratic Movement," see ZHITNIKOV (#1298).
NELIDOV, DMITRII: "Ideocratic Consciousness and Personality," see NELIDOV (#844).
SAKHAROV, ANDREI: "On Aleksandr Solzhenitsyn's 'Letter to the Soviet Leaders'," see SAKHAROV (#981).
KOPELEV, LEV: "The Lie Can be Defeated Only by Truth," see MEDVEDEV (#772).
GORSKII, V.: "Russian Messianism and the New National Consciousness," see GORSKII (#429).
OSIPOV, VLADIMIR: "Three Attitudes Toward the Homeland," see OSIPOV (#888).
SKURATOV, ANATOLII: "At the Sources of Russian National Consciousness"; pseud. of ANATOLII IVANOV; from Veche No. 1. On Aksakov and the Slavophiles.
AGURSKII, MIKHAIL: "The Intensification of Neo-Nazi Dangers in the Soviet Union," see AGURSKII (#9).
"Entrance Into Politics: Necessary Explanations," (Anon.) from Seiatel', on the organization of political activity directed toward comprehensive democratization; see Kh. tek. sob. No. 26 (#540).
TOPOLEV, S.: "From Samizdat to Kolizdat," discussing samizdat characteristics, mostly its limitations, and the advantages of collective publications. See Vol'noe slovo No. 7 (#1232) (from sam. journal Svobodnaia mysl')
MEERSON-AKSENOV, M.: "The People of God and the Pastors," see MEERSON-AKSENOV (#800).
KOLESOV, A.: "Gift and Responsibility," see KOLESOV (#614).
BARABANOV, EVGENII: "The Moral Prerequisite of Christian Unity," see BARABANOV (#92).
IAKUNIN, GLEB and REGEL'SON, LEV: "To the Delegates to the Fifth Assembly of the World Council of Churches," plea for genuine spirit of ecumenicism in support of all persecuted Christians and non-Christians. Also appeared in Religion in Communist Dominated Areas (New York): 15/30, June 1966). "The Jewish Question in the USSR" (Anon.), see "Evreiskii vopros v SSSR" (#329).

MEERSON-AKSENOV, MIKHAIL: See also LITVINOV et al. (#702).

802   DE MEEUS, ANTHONY, ed. Livre Blanc sur l'internement psy-chiatrique de dissidents sains d'esprit en URSS. Brussels:

MEIMAN

Comité International pour la Défense des Droits de l'homme en URSS, 1974.
Collection of documents pertaining to abuses of psychiatry in treatment of dissidents.

803 MEIMAN, NAUM. [b. 1912] "Monument u Bab'ego Iara." ["Monument at Babii Iar"] KONTINENT: No. 15, 1977; pp. 179-84.
On the absence of a monument, and the absence of reference to Jews on the monument erected in Kiev (i.e., not at the site of massacre).

804 [MELCHUK, IGOR.] "The Case of Igor Melchuk: Trial at the Academy 25-3-76." SURVEY (London): 2 (103), Spring 1977-78; pp. 126-40.
Minutes of meeting at which Melchuk, a linguist, was refused reelection to his institute because of a letter he sent to the New York Times defending Sakharov.

805 MEL'NIKOV, S. V. "Teksty i kod kommunizma: zametki o bol'-shevistskoi mental'nosti." ["Texts and Code of Communism"] VREMIA I MY (New York/Paris/Jerusalem): No. 47, Nov. 1979; pp. 62-87 and No. 48, Dec. 1979; pp. 101-20.
Analysis of October revolution and Leninist party, today's children and grandchildren of the Central Committee, the party vs. the government, the mystique of the party.

806 MEN', ALEKSANDR. "Evrei i khristianstvo." ["Jews and Christianity"] VESTNIK RKhD (Paris): No. 117, I-1976; pp. 112-17. Relationship between the two.

MEN', ALEKSANDR: See also Nadezhda (#827).

807 MERTSALOV, L. "Novosely"; "Moi cheren'koi. . ."; "Napervo im postavili bozhka. . ."; "Otechestvo." GRANI (Frankfurt): No. 84, July 1972; pp. 31-33.
Poems from Literaturnyi al'manakh "N," Moscow samizdat journal from 1967.

808 Metropol'. Ann Arbor, Mich.: Ardis, 1979.
Almanac put together by various well-known Soviet authors in hopes of publishing it. Publication was refused; various measures, of differing degrees of severity, were taken against individual contributors. The facsimile edition includes:

AKHMADULINA, BELLA: "Mnogo sobak i sobaka." ["Many Dogs and the Dog"]. Story.
VYSOTSKII, VLADIMIR: "Lech' na dno," "Stikhi i pesni: 'Rebiata, napishite mne pis'mo'; 'tot vecher. . .';

A Critical Guide

'Ryzhaia shalava'; 'Na bol'shom karetnom'; 'Esli ia bogat,
kak tsar' morskoi. . .'; 'Na neitral'noi polose'; 'Parodiia
na plokhoi detektiv'; 'O sentimental'nom boksere'; 'O dikom
vepre'; 'Pro nechist';' 'Golodets'; 'Lukomor'ia bol'she
net'; 'Na smert' Shukshina'; 'Okhota na volkov'; 'Ban'ka
po-belomu'; 'Gorizont'; 'On byl khirurgom. . .'; 'Dialog'."
Poems/songs.
SAPGIR, GENRIKH: "Polifonion"; "Iz knigi Golosa: 'Golos';
'Radiobred'; 'Obez'ian'"; "Iz knigi Sonety na rubashkakh:
'Sonet 3'; 'Rukopis';' Podmoskovnyi peizazh s kukloi';
'Diagramma zhizn';' 'Liubov';' 'Raznoe'." Poems.
REIN, EVGENII: "Troeglavaia gidra semeistva. . ."; "Stikhi:
'Vologda'; 'Monastyr';' 'Kliuchik'; 'Kholodnym letnim dnem';
'Tridtsatoe sentiabria'; '15 let nazad'; 'Net vyleta.
Zima. . .'; 'Podpis' k razorvannomu portretu'; 'Grai voroni
nad bul'varom. . .'; 'Fontan'; 'U lukomor'ia'; 'Krestov-
skii'; 'Chetyre'; 'Balkon'; 'Iaponskoe more'; '599/600';
'31 dekabria'; 'Karantin'; 'Melencolia'; 'Za desiat' let
dva raza. . .'; 'Nikodim'." Poems.
LISNIANSKAIA, INNA: "U nishchikh proshu podaian'ia. . .";
"V den' Vladimira, pod voskresen'e. . ."; "Pro ogon' i
derevo"; "Ia i vremia. . ."; "Nad sanatornym otdelen'em
. . ."; "V checharde"; "Slepoi." Poems.
LIPKIN, SEMEN: "Put' k khramu"; "Fantastika"; "Khaim";
"V pustyne"; "Krik chaek"; "Kogda v slova ia bukvy sklady-
val. . . ." Poems.
KARABCHIEVSKII, IURII: "Mizantropiia. . ."; "Oseniaia
khronika"; "Elegiia." Poems.
KUBLANOVSKII, IURII: "Vozvrashchenie"; "Vos'mistishiia";
"31 ianvaria"; "Portret"; "Sonet"; "Skhizma nashei liub-
vi. . ."; ". . . Ne Novgorod-kupets." Poems.
VOZNESENSKII, ANDREI: "Nad temnoi molchalivoiu derzha-
voi. . ."; "Shchipovskii pereulok"; "Dozhd' proshel";
"Gekzametr"; "Esenin"; "Derzhavin"; "Posle." Poems.
KOZHEVNIKOV, PETR: "Melodii nashikh dnevnikov." ["The
Melodies of our Diaries"] Story in form of alternating
diary entries of teen-aged boy and girl.
POPOV, EVGENII: "Chertova diuzhina rasskazov." ["A
Baker's Dozen of Stories"] Story.
GORENSHTEIN, F.: "Stupeni." ["Rungs"] Novella.
BITOV, ANDREI: "Proshchal'nye den'ki," ["Farewell Days"],
from Vospominaniia o real'nosti. Story.
ALESHKOVSKII, IUZ: "Tri pesni: 'Lesbiiskaia'; 'Okuro-
chek'; 'Lichnoe svidanie'." Poems.
ISKANDER, FAZIL: "Malen'kii gigant bol'shogo seksa."
["The Little Giant with the Big Organ"] Story.
VAKHTIN, BORIS: "Dublenka." ["The Vest"] Story.
ARKANOV, ARKADII: "I vse ran'she i ran'she opuskaiutsia
sinie sumerki." ["And Navy Twilights Descend Earlier and
Earlier"] Story.

Metropol'

> EROFEEV, VIKTOR: "Rasskazy"; "Trekhglavoe detishche."
> ["Stories"; "Trichaptered Creation"] Stories.
> AKSENOV, VASILII: "Chetyre temperamenta." ["Four Tempera-
> ments"] Play.
> ROZOVSKII, MARK: "Teatral'nye kolechki, slozhennye v
> spiral'." ["Theater Circles, Gathered in a Notebook"]
> Essay.
> RAKITIN, VASILII: "Cherez." ["Through"] On the artistic
> avant-garde.
> TROSTNIKOV, VIKTOR: "Stranitsy iz dnevnika." ["Pages
> from a Diary"] Philosophic essay.

809   MIKHAILOV, ARKADII. "Iul'. Ploty"; "Pesnia"; "Kartoshka."
       GRANI (Frankfurt): No. 70, Feb. 1969; pp. 108-10. Poems.

810   _____. "Tri stikhotvoreniia: 'Akvarel',' 'Detskoe',
       'Les,'"; "Smert' studenta." GRANI (Frankfurt): No. 61,
       Oct. 1966; pp. 55-61. Poems.

     MIKHAILOV, ARKADII: See also BOSLEY (#147).

     MIKHAILOV, ARTEMY: See Sfinksy (#1011); BOSLEY (#147).

     MIRONOV, ALEKSANDR: See Sfinksy (#1011).

811   "Mirovomu gegemonu." (Anon.) ["Toward World Hegemony"]
       RUS. MYSL' (Paris): Jan. 2, 1975; p. 7.
       Satiric sketch.

812   "Molitva." (Anon.) RUS. MYSL' (Paris): Dec. 21, 1967; p. 4.
       Poem.

813   MOROZ, VALENTIN. [b. 1936] "Khronika soprotivleniia."
       ["Chronicle of Opposition"] KONTINENT: No. 3, 1975;
       pp. 161-86.
       Personal account of the formation of the Ukrainian dis-
       sident movement and its historical roots: self-preserva-
       tion as the main basis of opposition.

814   _____. "Pervyi den'." RUS. MYSL' (Paris): April 6,
       1972; p. 8. Poem.

815   _____. Report from the Beria Reserve. Toronto: Peter
       Martin Assoc., 1974; 63 pp. Tr., John Kolasky.

       _____. "Reportazh iz zapovednika imeni Beriia." NOVYI
       ZHURNAL (New York): No. 93, Dec. 1968; pp. 172-203.
       Examination of Ukrainian dissent, Russian policy toward
       Ukraine and the russification thereof, information on

interrogation, treatment of prisoners in camps and descriptions of KGB men, all drawn from his personal experience as Ukrainian dissident. Eng. tr. also in BROWNE (#175).

816   MOROZ, VALENTIN. "Valentin Moroz' Defense Speech." SURVEY (London): Vol. 18, No. 1 (82); pp. 219-22.
Re the inevitable growth of Ukrainian nationalism.

MOROZ, VALENTIN: See also BROWNE (#175), CHORNOVIL and MOROZ (#236).

MOROZOV, SERGEI: See Feniks 1966 (#337); SMOG (#1080); Sfinksy (#1011).

MOSKOVIT: See EFIMOV, IGOR'.

817   Moskovskoe vremia. KONTINENT: No. 28, 1981; pp. 7-18.
Samizdat journal, to be published by YMCA. Kontinent excerpts from it the following poetry: T. Poletaeva's "I ia vkhozhu, kak vkhodiat za porog. . ."; "Kogda zatianutost' vidna. . . ." and "Vsekh oplakav--. . ."; A. Soprovskii's "Zemli osennei chernye plasty. . ."; "Ty pomnish'--most, . . ."; "Nastanet den'. . . ." and "Sogreet leto zvezdy nad zemlei"; V. Dmitriev's "Poka idu na povodu. . . ." and "I s uma ne soidu"; S. Gandlevskii's "Daleko ot solenykh stepei saranchi. . . ." and "Podstupal vesennii vecher. . . ."

818   "Motsart i Sal'eri: nebol'shaia tragediia." (Anon.) ["Mozart and Salieri: A Minor Tragedy"] RUS. MYSL' (Paris): Sept. 18, 1975; p. 12.
Satiric poem listed under Bokov, Nikolai in Table of Contents; he edited Kacheli sud'by, the samizdat collection from which it comes.

819   MURAVINA, NINA. "V. Voinovich: 'Ivan Chonkin'." VESTNIK RKhD (Paris): No. 115, I-1975; pp. 188-200.
Essay on Voinovich's satiric novel, The Life and Extraordinary Adventures of Private Ivan Chonkin (#1223).

820   "My shli ètapom. I ne raz. . . ." (Anon.) GRANI (Frankfurt): No. 57, Jan. 1965; pp. 3-4.
Poem. By same author as "On byl v takoi glubokoi t'me" (#877). Eng. tr. in LANGLAND et al. (#656). NB: Author later identified as MANDEL (#717).

821   "Mysli-prozhektory." (Anon.) ["Thoughts-Searchlights"] POSEV (Frankfurt): No. 11, Nov. 1971; pp. 12-13.
Collection of reflections on the ideas and "personality" of Veche; from Veche No. 2.

N

822   N.   "Starinnyi skit."   RUS. MYSL' (Paris):   Sept. 10, 1970;
       p. 8.   Poem.

823   _____ .   "Osen'."   RUS. MYSL' (Paris):   Oct. 1, 1970;
       p. 8.   Poem.

824   N., ALEKSANDR.   "Mal'chik iz durdoma."   ["The Boy From the
       Idiot-House"]   VREMIA I MY (New York/Paris/Jerusalem):
       No. 43, July 1979; pp. 5-70 and No. 44, Aug. 1979; pp. 5-98.
       A normal, nowise dissident boy accidentally ends up in
       a psychiatric hospital for political prisoners and can't
       get out; how it changes him.

825   N. Iu. M.   "Ostanovis'!"   RUS. MYSL' (Paris):   Jan. 28, 1971;
       p. 3.   Poem.

826   NABOKOVA, E.S.   "Neravnyi boi."   RUS. MYSL' (Paris):   Jan. 29,
       1976; p. 6.   Poem.

827   Nadezhda, Nos. 1-5. [Hope]   Frankfurt: Posev, 1981; 408 pp.
          Samizdat Christian journal.   Contains several prayers,
       sermon-like pieces by various church fathers, letters by
       19th century churchman Ignatii (Brianchaninov), sermons
       and texts "found in samizdat" by Father Valentin Sven-
       tsitskii and Aleksandr Men', reminiscences of Father Ioann
       Kronshtadtskii by Bishop Arsenii (Zhadanovskii) which are
       excerpted from his samizdat manuscript, Vospominaniia o
       zamechatel'nykh moskovskikh protoiereiakh.   Also: Bishop
       German's (Riashchentsev) letters written in exile in 1923,
       1936-37, when he disappeared; E. Troianovskaia's "Dobro i
       zlo," chapters from samizdat manuscript of materials "for
       conversations with children about God"; excerpt from A.
       Volkov's memoirs on the Moscow Spiritual Academy; an anony-
       mous essay, "Gotovo serdtse moe: svidetel'stva ob obra-
       shchenii ko Khristu" ["My Heart is Ready"], from samizdat
       journal Prizyv Nos. 11-13 (1977), personal history of
       author's road to Christian faith; V. Aleksandrova's "Dozhd'
       na svetloi nedele," ["Rain during Holy Week"], a spiritual
       diary including a number of poems; poems by A. A. Solodov-
       nikov (d. 1975) from his samizdat manuscript Slava Bogu za
       Vse (1969) [Praise God for All Things]: "Tiur'ma"; "Riza
       Gospodnia"; "V uspenskom sobore"; "Moskovskoe predanie";
       "Letnii zakat" and "Mai--v leshkove."   Also, part of anony-
       mous samizdat manuscript Nepridumannye rasskazy [Uninvented
       Stories].

828   NADEZHDINA, ALEKSANDRA.   "Oda 'Bog'"; "Pole Iezekiilia";
       "Pokaianie"; "Paskha."   VESTNIK RSKhD (Paris):   No. 91-92,
       I-II-1969; pp. 81-84.   Poems.

829   NADEZHDINA, ALEKSANDRA. "Optina"; "Iz tsikla 'Nashi deti'."
      VESTNIK RSKhD (Paris): No. 78, III-1965; pp. 37-45.
         Poems, listed under "Golos iz Rossii" in Table of
      Contents.

830   _____. "Pechory"; "Spor"; "Angel khrama"; "Sobor";
      "Lazar'" "Kto ty?"; "Voskresen'e"; "Smert'"; "Svet";
      "Rozhdestvo." VESTNIK RSKhD (Paris): No. 85, III-1967;
      pp. 50-56. Poems.

831   "Nakhodka v taige." (Anon.) ["Discovery in the Taiga"]
      NOVYI ZHURNAL (New York): No. 84, Sept. 1966; pp. 134-42.
         Reminiscence by former camp inmate of his discovery, in
      1943 in the taiga, of all that was left of a man--the text
      of his death sentence.

832   NARITSA, M. A. [b. 1909] "Moe zaveshchanie." ["My Testa-
      ment"] RUS. MYSL' (Paris): April 18, 1974; p. 5.

      _____. "Moe zaveshchanie." POSEV (Frankfurt): No. 5,
      May 1974; pp. 4-5.
         Brief statement to the effect that author doesn't con-
      sider himself a Soviet citizen, and asking that his work
      be made available to readers.

833   _____. Nespetaia pesnia. [The Unsung Song] Frankfurt:
      Posev, 1964; 127 pp.

      _____. (NARIZA, MICHAEL) Das ungesungene Lied. Stutt-
      gart: Deutsche Verlags-Anstalt, 1962; 197 pp. Tr., Renate
      Neumann.

      _____. (NARYMOV) "Nespetaia pesnia." GRANI (Frank-
      furt): No. 48, Oct.-Dec. 1960, pp. 5-113.
         Autobiographical novel by artist arrested in 1935
      (freed 1940), in 1949 (rehabilitated in 1957) and in 1961.
      Describes the shattering of ideals of a once-loyal Com-
      munist, the fate of his family.

834   _____. "Prestuplenie i nakazanie." ["Crime and Punish-
      ment"] POSEV (Frankfurt): No. 8, Aug. 1971; pp. 35-42.
         Story of his arrest after sending Nespetaia pesnia
      abroad, his incarceration in psychiatric hospital; about
      the liberty and intransigence of the human spirit. Ex-
      cerpt in ARTEMOVA et al. (#79).

835   Natsional'nyi vopros v SSSR. Sbornik dokumentov. [The
      Nationality Question in the USSR] Ed., Roman Kupchinskii.
      Munich: Suchasnist, 1975; 440 pp.

NECHAEV

Collection of documents pertaining to non-Russian nationalities.

836 NECHAEV, VADIM. [em. 1978] "Odinokim sdaetsia ugol." ["Roommate Wanted"] GRANI (Frankfurt): No. 108, April-June 1978; pp. 3-30. Story.

837 NEKIPELOV, VIKTOR. [b. 1928] Institute of Fools: Notes from the Serbsky Institute. New York: Farrar, Straus, Giroux, 1979. Tr., Marco Carynnyk and Marta Horban.

_____. "Institut durakov." VREMIA I MY (New York/Paris/ Jerusalem): No. 23, 1977; pp. 175-205 and No. 24, 1977; pp. 175-206.
Memoir by member of Moscow Helsinki Watch Group of his two-month detention in Serbskii Institute in 1974 (after which he was transferred to camp for two years).

838 _____. "Stalin na vetrovom stekle"; "Kladbishche pobezh-dennykh." ["Stalin on the Windshield," "Cemetery of the Conquered"] KONTINENT: No. 19, 1979; pp. 238-46.
The first describes popular rebirth of Stalin cult (his picture in buses, etc.); the second describes the vandalism of a cemetery where German soldiers are buried.

839 _____. "Chufut-kale"; "Pamiati Iana Palakha"; "Kamesh-kovskie sosny"; "Ballada o pervom obyske"; "Oprichnik"; "Pogost pod sosnami." NOV. RUS. SLOVO (New York): March 24, 1974; p. 5. Poems.

840 _____. "Televizor"; "Tsvetnye sny"; "Derev'ia." GRANI (Frankfurt): No. 107, Jan.-March 1978; pp. 97-101. Poems.

841 _____. "Trakt poèzii russkoi. . ."; "Diuny"; "Kolybel'-naia"; "Ballada o pervom obyske"; KONTINENT: No. 12, 1977; pp. 156-62. Poems.

842 NEKRASOV, VIKTOR. [b. 1911, em. 1974] "O vulkanakh, otshel'-nikakh i prochem." ["On Volcanoes, Hermits and the Like"] GRANI (Frankfurt): No. 74, Jan. 1970; pp. 25-86.
Stories, some published only in samizdat, some published in censored form as "Za dvenadtsat' tysiach kilometrov" in Novyi mir, No. 12, 1965; one, "V mire tainstvennogo," in Novyi mir, No. 1, 1965.

NEKRASOV, VIKTOR: See also Sintaksis (#1072).

843 NEKRICH, ALEKSANDR. [b. 1920, em. 1976] "Voennye istoriki osuzhdaiut Stalina: zasedanie otdela velik. otechestvennoi

voiny (VOV) Instituta Marksizma-Leninizma (IML) pri TsK
KPSS 16 fevralia 1966 goda." ["Military Historians Judge
Stalin"] POSEV (Frankfurt): No. 2 (1077), Jan. 13, 1967;
pp. 3-5.
Transcript of meeting of historians evaluating Stalin's
culpability in Russia's unpreparedness for German invasion
in World War II.

844 NELIDOV, DMITRII. (Pseud.) "Ideokraticheskoe soznanie i
lichnost'." ["Ideocratic Consciousness and Personality"]
VESTNIK RSKhD (Paris): No. 111, I-1974; pp. 185-214.
Analysis of human psychology in totalitarian regime--
alienated consciousness, social adaptation, doublethink,
etc. Argues with ZHITNIKOV (see #1298). Eng. tr. in
MEERSON-AKSENOV and SHRAGIN (#801); also contained in
LITVINOV et al. (#702).

845 NESTEROVSKII, VLADIMIR. "Stikhi: 'Panegirik Sharlotte
Korde'." NOVYI ZHURNAL (New York): No. 128, Sept. 1977;
p. 45. Poem.

846 "Nevezhestvo na sluzhbe proizvola." (Anon.) VESTNIK RSKhD
(Paris): No. 101-102, III-IV-1971; pp. 153-75; No. 103,
I-1972; pp. 223-36; No. 104-105, II-III-1972; pp. 172-77.

_____. "Ignorance in the Service of Arbitrariness."
SURVEY (London): Vol. 19, No. 4 (89), Autumn 1973;
pp. 45-65.

_____. "L'ignorance au service de l'arbitrarie: de la
situation de la psychiatrie contemporaine en URSS." SAMIZ-
DAT MOUSCOU (Paris): 1971-72; 44 pp.
Practicing Soviet psychiatrist discusses the "liquida-
tion" of science of psychiatry in Russia, beginning with
Bleuler's theories of schizophrenia and its history through
Snezhnevskii, creator of Serbskii Institute and his
"scientific" theories.

847 News Bulletin on Soviet Jewry. Tel Aviv. Bimonthly containing documents and information frequently drawn from
samizdat.

848 NIKITIN, V. "Chekhoslovatskaia tragediia." ["The Czech
Tragedy"] POSEV (Frankfurt): No. 8, Aug. 1971; pp. 26-34.
Compares Czech and Hungarian invasions, analyzing
average Soviet citizen's reactions to both and the reasons
for the Soviet incursions.

NIKITIN

849   NIKITIN, V. "Pamiati Tat'iany Vasil'evny Rozanovoi." RUS.
       MYSL' (Paris): Aug. 21, 1975; p. 14. Poem.

850   NIKON et al. "Poslednie dni Optinoi Pustyni." ["The Last
       Days of Optina Pustinia"] VESTNIK RKhD (Paris): No. 117,
       I-1976; pp. 43-57.
       Written in 1920s, describing Russian Orthodox sanctuary.

851   NILOV, G. "Iz-pod glyb--v nebesa." ["From Under the Rubble--
       To the Skies"] VREMIA I MY (New York/Paris/Jerusalem):
       No. 35, Nov. 1978; pp. 94-125.
       Critical evaluation of Iz-pod glyb, because of its
       blanket blame of socialism for all of Russia's ills, its
       dependence on spiritual and not practical avenues for
       change. See AGURSKII et al. (#11).

852   _____. "Paralozh' sovetskoi sistemy." ["The Supra-lie
       of the Soviet System"] VREMIA I MY (New York/Paris/
       Jerusalem): No. 59, March-April 1981; pp. 113-47.
       About the special variety of lying, Soviet-style, be-
       yond "deceivers" and "deceived" as separate categories to
       the total lie of the system--of one-party elections, occu-
       pying Czechoslovakia "at her request," etc.

853   "Noch' pod zvezdami." (Anon.) RUS. MYSL' (Paris): Jan. 8,
       1970; p. 7. Poem.

854   Nonconformity and Dissent in the Ukrainian SSR 1955-75. Ed.,
       George Liber and Anna Mostovych. Cambridge, Mass.: Har-
       vard Ukrainian Research Institute, 1978; 245 pp.
       Bibliography.

       NOR, N.: See Feniks 1 (#336) and BOSLEY (#147).

855   NORD, VIKTOR. "Dorogoi mister Dikkens. . . ." ["Dear Mister
       Dickens"] NOV. RUS. SLOVO (New York): Jan. 20, 1974;
       p. 6. Story.

856   NOVODVORSKAIA, V. [b. 1951] ". . . I za boev griadushchikh
       vystrely spasibo, partiia, tebe." POSEV (Frankfurt):
       No. 6, June 1970; p. 14.

       _____. "Spasibo, partiia, tebe." RUS. MYSL' (Paris):
       July 9, 1970; p. 5.
       Poem (thanking party for "our hatred," for the lies
       and informers, etc. Circulated on Constitution Day 1969).

857   NOVOGUDNII. (IVANOV, A.) "Net, ne veriu, chto smert' bliz-
       ka!"; "Voskovaia svechka dogorela. . ."; "To chto

priobreteno uporstvom. . ."; "Poètu"; "Tiazhelye gromady
oblakov. . ."; "Glukhaia noch'. . ."; "Posle poseshcheniia
petropavlovskoi kreposti"; "Zabor shatalo. . ."; "V lagere";
"Poka uprugi volnyi la. . ."; "Vot ia i ostalsia odinokim. . ."; "Prorok." GRANI (Frankfurt): No. 32, Oct.-
Dec. 1956; pp. 7-18. Poems.

858 NOVOSELOV, MIKHAIL. "Pis'mo k druz'iam." ["Letter to Friends"]
VESTNIK RKhD (Paris): No. 115, I-1975; pp. 17-24.
Written in 1925, letter on religious faith.

859 NOZHKIN, M. "A Volga vpadaet v Kaspiiskoe more, a loshadi
liubiat oves." RUS. MYSL' (Paris): Oct. 21, 1971; p. 5.
Poem.

860 _____. "Soldaty." RUS. MYSL' (Paris): Dec. 16, 1971;
p. 5. Poem.

861 _____. "Strakh"; "Tetia Niusha." RUS. MYSL' (Paris):
Sept. 9, 1971; p. 5. Poem.

NOZHKIN, M.: See also Pesni russkikh bardov (#917).

O

862   "O polozhenii zakliuchennykh v lageriakh SSSR." ["On the
       Situation of Prisoners in the Camps of the USSR"] KONTI-
       NENT: No. 20, 1979; pp. 165-98.
           Compiled by Helsinki Watch Committee (Document #87,
       April 25, 1979); information on prisoners' labor, relations
       between camp administrators and political prisoners, medi-
       cal care.

863   O pytkakh v Gruzii. [On Torture in Georgia] (Anon.) New
       York: Khronika, 1976; 51 pp.
           Collection of documents, letters, etc. See also Vol'noe
       slovo No. 19 (#1241).

864   "Obsuzhdenie maketa 3-go toma istorii KPSS v Institute
       marksizma-leninizma pri TsK KPSS s uchastiem starykh bol'-
       shevikov." GRANI (Frankfurt): No. 65, Sept. 1967;
       pp. 129-56.

       _____. "Discussion of the Draft Third Volume of the
       History of the CPSU." SURVEY (London): No. 63, April
       1967; pp. 159-69.
           Stenographic record of discussion dealing with inter-
       pretation of Stalin; openly critical both of Stalin and
       cult of personality, and of earlier official "history."

       OGURTSOV: See Vol'noe slovo No. 22 (#1244), VSKhSON (#1273).

865   OKHAPKIN, OLEG. "Vtoroi orficheskii gimn fevraliu"; "Kvad-
       riga"; "Letuchii gollandets"; "Borisu Kiprianovu." GRANI
       (Frankfurt): No. 103, Jan.-March 1977; pp. 108-14. Poems.

866   "Okololiteraturnyi mal'chik." ["The Paraliterary Boy"]
       (Anon.) POSEV (Frankfurt): No. 25 (1100), June 23, 1967;
       p. 5. Satiric sketch.

867   OKUDZHAVA, BULAT. [b. 1924] Ausgewählte Gedichte. Frank-
       furt: Posev, 1965; 124 pp. Tr., Mary von Holbeck. Poems.

868   _____. Dva romana (Bednyi Avrosimov; Fotograf Zhora).
       Frankfurt: Posev, 1970; 430 pp.

       _____. "Fotograf Zhora." GRANI (Frankfurt): No. 73,
       Oct. 1969; pp. 99-170.
           The first novel, Poor Avrosimov, was published in the
       Soviet Union; the second, The Photographer Zhora, circu-
       lated only in samizdat. (About the misfortunes of a
       cinematographer.)

869 OKUDZHAVA, BULAT. (OKUDSHAWA) Gedichte und Chansons. Munich:
     Kindler, 1969; 112 pp. Tr., Alexander Kaempfe and Gerhard
     Schindele. Poems.

870 _____. "Gruzinskaia pesnia." NOV. RUS. SLOVO (New York):
     Dec. 10, 1976; p. 3. Poem.

871 _____. "Iz neopublikovannogo: "Beregite nas poètov,
     beregite nas"; "O voine"; "Chernyi kot"; "Èkh ty, sharik
     goluboi"; "Vsia zemlia, vsia planeta"; "Vsiu noch' kricholi
     petukhi"; "Pesenka o durakakh"; "Pesnia o barabanshchike."
     GRANI (Frankfurt): No. 56, Oct. 1964; pp. 185-87.
     Poems, listed under "Stikhi Leningradskikh poètov."

872 _____. "Iz neopublikovannogo." POSEV (Frankfurt):
     No. 4 (975), Jan. 22, 1965; p. 7. Poem.

873 _____. "Master Grisha." GRANI (Frankfurt): No. 65,
     Sept. 1967; p. 18. Poem.

874 _____. Proza i poeziia. Frankfurt: Posev, 1968 and
     1976; 320 pp. Poems plus stories/novellas.

875 _____. "Puteshestvie v drozhkakh po nochnoi Varshave."
     POSEV (Frankfurt): No. 11, Nov. 1974; p. 53. Poem.

     OKUDZHAVA, BULAT: See also Sintaksis No. 2 (#1072); BOSLEY
     (#147); BRUMBERG (#178); LANGLAND et al. (#656); Pesni
     russkikh bardov (#917).

876 OLITSKAIA, EKATERINA. [b. 1898, d. 1974] Moi vospominaniia.
     [My Memoirs] Frankfurt: Posev, 1971; 2 vols.

     _____. "Na ètape." POSEV (Frankfurt): No. 4, April
     1970; pp. 58-61.

     _____. "Solovki: otryvki iz knigi." GRANI (Frankfurt):
     No. 77, Oct. 1970; pp. 89-101.
     Memoirs by former Left Socialist-Revolutionary who was
     first arrested in 1924 and spent virtually all the years
     until Stalin's death in prisons, camps and exile. She
     describes, among many other things, the shooting of social-
     ists in 1923, the trials of the SRs in 1922, the purges of
     the 1920s, SR hunger strikes and the destruction of that
     entire party.

877 "On byl v takoi glubokoi t'me." (Anon.) GRANI (Frankfurt):
     No. 71, May 1969; pp. 13-14.

ONEZHSKAIA

> Poem, by same author as "My shli ètapom. I ne raz. . . ."
> (#820). NB: Author later identified as MANDEL (#717).

ONEZHSKAIA, A.: See Feniks 1 (#336), BOSLEY (#147).

878 "Opisanie sobytii v Pochaevskoi lavre v nashi dni." ["Description of Events in the Pochaev Cave in Our Time"] (Anon.) VESTNIK RSKhD (Paris): No. 84, II-1967; pp. 39-69. On centuries-old religious catacombs.

879 [ORLOV, IURII]. Delo Orlova. New York: Khronika, 1980. Ed., L. Alekseeva. Documents on Orlov's career, arrest and trial.

> ORLOV: See also LITVINOV et al. (#702).

880 ORLOV, IURII et al. "On Prisoners in Soviet Camps." SURVEY (London): Vol. 24, No. 2 (107), Spring 1979; pp. 67-85. Factual account and analysis of life in prison camps by four prisoners: their work, medical services, flow of information, relations with administrators.

881 ORLOVA, RAISA. [em. 1980] Vospominaniia o neproshedshem vremeni. [Memoirs of Time Not Past] Ann Arbor, Mich.: Ardis.

> _____. "My ne khuzhe Goratsiia." VREMIA I MY (New York/Paris/Jerusalem): No. 51, March 1980; pp. 5-26. Excerpt on Galich.

> _____. "V kontse krutogo marshruta." VREMIA I MY (New York/Paris/Jerusalem): No. 49, Jan. 1980; pp. 36-51. Excerpt on Evgeniia Ginzburg. (Written in alternating segments by Orlova and Lev Kopelev.)
> Reminiscences by editor and translator (of, inter alia, Lillian Hellman), of two decades of Moscow intellectual life.

882 OSADCHY, MYKHAYLO. Cataract. New York and London: Harcourt, Brace, Jovanovich, 1976; 240 pp. Tr. from Ukrainian, Marco Carynnyk.

> _____. (OSSADCHY) Cataracte. Paris: Fayard, 1974; 332 pp. Tr., Kalena Uhryn.

> _____. "The Mote (extract)." INDEX ON CENSORSHIP (London): Vol. 1, No. 3/4, Autumn/Winter 1972; pp. 167-74. Tr., Marta Jenkala.
> Memoir dealing with Ukrainian dissent; original, entitled Bil'mo, published by Smoloskyp (Baltimore) in Ukrainian.

883   OSIPOV, VLADIMIR. [b. 1938] "Berdiaevskii kruzhok v Leningrade." ["The Berdiaev Circle in Leningrad"] VESTNIK RSKhD (Paris): No. 104-105, II-III-1972; pp. 153-65.

    _____. "Berdiaevskii kruzhok v Leningrade." POSEV (Frankfurt): No. 11, Nov. 1972; pp. 3-10.
    Describes the organization and program of VSKhSON and the arrests and fates of its members.

884   _____. "K chitateliam Samizdata." ["To the Readers of Samizdat"] GRANI (Frankfurt): No. 85, Oct. 1972; pp. 188-92.
    Additions and corrections to "Ploshchad' Maiakovskogo" (#886).

885   _____. "Piat' vozrazhenii Sakharovu." ["Five Objections to Sakharov"] VESTNIK RKhD (Paris): No. 111, I-1974; pp. 215-20.
    Criticizes Sakharov for his sanguine attitude toward China and technical progress, and for his warnings of the dangers of Slavophilism.

886   _____. "Ploshchad' Maiakovskogo, stat'ia 70-aia." ["Maiakovskii Square, Article 70"] GRANI (Frankfurt): No. 80, Sept. 1971; pp. 107-36.
    Account (by editor of underground 1960 magazine Bumerang and of 1961 Feniks) of emergence of young Moscow opposition and of the unofficial journals, from 1959 to early 1960s. (Contained in Tri otnosheniia. . . . #888.)

887   _____. "Poslednii den' Moskvy." ["Moscow's Last Day"] VESTNIK RSKhD (Paris): No. 111, I-1974; pp. 220-32.
    About the destruction of architectural monuments of old Moscow; from samizdat journal Zemlia (No. 2), which Osipov edited in 1974, before his rearrest and sentencing to 8 years' camp.

888   _____. Tri otnosheniia k rodine. [Three Attitudes to the Homeland] Frankfurt: Posev, 1978.
    Collection of articles, essays and letters (for summary of title piece see below) by editor and writer who edited, in addition to journals mentioned above, Slavophile samizdat journal Veche.

    _____. "Tri otnosheniia k rodine." VESTNIK RSKhD (Paris): No. 103, I-1972; pp. 216-22.
    The three attitudes are hatred, opportunism (by which he means official Soviet nationalism and patriotism as central components of official ideology) and love--of one's race, of one's homeland, etc. Eng. tr. in MEERSON-AKSENOV and SHRAGIN (#801).

OSIPOV

889   OSIPOV, VLADIMIR. "V poiskakh kryshi." ["In Search of a
      Roof"] POSEV (Frankfurt): No. 1, Jan. 1971; pp. 44-50.
      Describes his experiences as a former zek trying to
      find an apartment after his 7-year sentence ended in 1969.

      OSIPOV, VLADIMIR: See also Vol'noe slovo Nos. 9-10 (#1234),
      VSKhSON (#1273), Vol'noe slovo Nos. 17-18 (#1240) and
      Veche (#1198, #1199).

890   "Otklik na leninskii iubilei." (Anon.) RUS. MYSL' (Paris):
      Feb. 3, 1972; p. 5. Poem.

891   "Otkliki na sbornik 'Iz glubiny'." ["Responses to 'From the
      Depths'"] (Anon.) VESTNIK RSKhD (Paris): No. 86, IV-
      1967; pp. 48-53.
      Readers' reactions to the collection of articles which
      appeared in 1918.

892   OZEROV, GEORGII. (SHARAGIN, A.) Tupolevskaia Sharaga. Frank-
      furt: Posev, 1971; 126 pp.

      _____. (CHARAGUINE, A.) En Prison avec Tupolev. Paris:
      Michel, 1973; 159 pp. Tr., N. Krivocheine and M. Gorbov,
      in collab. with Nina Nidermiller. Memoir of camp life.

893   OZHIGANOV, ALEKSANDR: [b. 1950?] "Iz knigi 'Strekoza'";
      'Kolodtsy'; 'Otvet militsioneru'; 'No tol'ko ne rasterian-
      nost'. . .'; 'Dialog'; 'Vospominanie o benderakh'; 'Lenin-
      grad'; 'Rodina'; 'Piat' vospominanii'." ĖKHO (Paris):
      No. 2, 1980; pp. 25-33. Poems.

P

894   P***. "N. A. Berdiaev po lichnym vospominaniiam." ["Personal
       Reminiscence of N. A. Berdiaev"] VESTNIK RKhD (Paris):
       No. 115, I-1975; pp. 142-50.
           From Moskovskii sbornik, samizdat journal.

895   Pamiat'. [Memory] No. 1. New York: Khronika, 1978; 600 pp.
           Historical journal compiled in Moscow. Volume 1 deals
       mostly with Gulag (documents, archival material) and the
       destruction of all political parties and movements in Rus-
       sia; Korolenko's diaries 1917-21.

896   Pamiat'. No. 2. Paris: YMCA, 1979; 598 pp.
           Volume 2 deals with the history of culture, science,
       literature and religion.

           _____. "Dva dokumenta." KONTINENT: No. 15, 1977;
       pp. 283-90.
           First is statement of A.O., who witnessed shootings in
       Kirpichnyi Zavod in Kashketin in 1937; second taken from
       archives of Center of Documentation of Contemporary Jewry
       in Paris, on the relationship between Nazis and Russian
       intellectuals in emigration, dated Jan. 1938 (not original-
       ly samizdat but included in samizdat journal).

           _____. "Dva portreta." VESTNIK RKhD (Paris): No. 124,
       I-1978; pp. 269-98.
           Taken from "Katakomby veka," memoirs of V. Ia. Vasilev-
       skaia,pertaining to "catacomb church," a fragmented dis-
       connected group of churches, often ignorant of one another's
       existence, led by Bishop Afanasii Kovrovskii (Sakharov) from
       1927-45, during which time its members did not accept as
       their head Patriarch Sergii.

897   Pamiat'. No. 3. Paris: YMCA, 1980; 580 pp.
           Includes article on social-democratic movement among the
       youth in 1920s. Two memoirs about K. Chukovskii, reviews
       (e.g., of Marchenko's My Testimony), plus congratulations
       from editors to Chronicle of Current Events.

898   "Pamiati moei babushki"; "Bessmertie." ["In Memory of My
       Grandmother"; "Immortality"] (Anon.) VESTNIK RSKhD
       (Paris): No. 72-73, I-II-1964; pp. 68-70.
           Sketches, listed under "Golos iz Rossii" in Table of
       Contents.

       PANKRATOV, IURII: See Sintaksis 1 (#1072), BOSLEY (#147).

899   PASHKOV, I. "Khorosho stoiat' Vasiliem Blazhennym. . . ."
       GRANI (Frankfurt): No. 85, Oct. 1972; p. 59.

PASKIN

Poem, listed under "Iz kontslagernoi poèzii" in Table of Contents.

900 PASKIN, A. P. "O poème 'Sputnik' R. Rozhdestvenskogo." RUS. MYSL' (Paris): Sept. 11, 1975; p. 6. Satiric poem.

901 PASTERNAK, BORIS. [b. 1890, d. 1960] "B. Pasternak i Soiuz Sovetskikh Pisatelei." NOVYI ZHURNAL (New York): No. 83, June 1966; pp. 185-227.

_____. "Judgment on Pasternak: The All-Moscow Meeting of Writers, 31 October 1958." SURVEY (London): No. 60, July 1966; pp. 134-63.
Stenographic record of attack on Pasternak as alienated from the people, as a decadent aesthete and traitor, ending with request for deprivation of his citizenship. From Feniks 1966.

902 _____. Slepaia krasavitsa. London: Collins, Harvill, 1969; 78 pp.

_____. The Blind Beauty; a play. New York: Harcourt, Brace & World and London: Collins & Harvill, 1969; 128 pp. Tr., Max Hayward and Manya Harari.

_____. La Belle aveugle. Paris: Gallimard, 1969; 120 pp. Tr., H. Chatelain.

_____. Die blinde Schönheit. Frankfurt: Insel; 112 pp. Tr., Margrit Doring. Play. Subsequently published in USSR.

903 _____. Doktor Zhivago. Milan: Feltrinelli, 1957; 567 pp.

_____. Doctor Zhivago. New York: Pantheon and London: Collins, 1958; 559 pp. Tr., Max Hayward and Manya Harari. (Later editions available.)

_____. Le Docteur Jivago. Paris: Gallimard, 1958; 652 pp. (Later editions available.)

_____. Doktor Schiwago. Frankfurt: Fischer, 1958; 647 pp. Tr., Reinhold von Walter. In 1960 edition, poems tr. by Heddy Pross-Weerth. (Later editions available.)

_____. Doktor Schiwago. Frankfurt: Fischer, 1961; 638 pp. Tr., Rolf-Dietrich Keil.

PASTERNAK, BORIS. "Doktor Zhivago." NOVYI ZHURNAL (New York): No. 54, Sept. 1958; pp. 5-58.

_____. "Iz knigi B. Pasternaka 'Doktor Zhivago'; 'Smert' Iu. Zhivago." VESTNIK RSKhD (Paris): No. 57, II-1960; pp. 43-44.

_____. "Stikhi iz Rossii." ["Poems from Russia," published anonymously] GRANI (Frankfurt): No. 34-35, April-Sept. 1957; pp. 3-13.

_____. Gedichte von Jurij Schiwago. Frankfurt: Posev, 1965; 121 pp. Tr., Mary von Holbeck.
Important from both literary and political points of view, the first insofar as Zhivago is the novel Pasternak considered his life-work, a novel which, dealing primarily with the Revolution and Civil War years, portrays the crucible in which Soviet Russia was forged through the eyes of a poet/doctor, whose verses climax the book, the second in that the novel marked a reawakening of Russian literature, and in the virulence and ferocity of the campaign mounted against Pasternak.

904 _____. "Iz pisem k zhene." ["From Letters to His Wife"] VESTNIK RSKhD (Paris): No. 106, IV-1972; pp. 201-28.
Letters ranging from 1931 to 1954 (mostly from 1930s and early 1940s) relating to his creative work and to the literary life of the era.

905 _____. "A Letter by Boris Pasternak." ENCOUNTER (London): Vol. XXIII, No. 4, Oct. 1964; pp. 92-93. Tr., Manya Harari.
Letter of condolence to widow of Iashvili, Georgian poet who committed suicide in 1937.

906 _____. "Neizdannoe stikhotvorenie B. Pasternaka: 'Kul't lichnosti zabrosan graz'iu. . .'." VESTNIK RSKhD (Paris): No. 98, IV-1970; p. 71. Poem.

907 _____. "Neizdannyi èkspromt B. Pasternaka (na shestidesiatiletie A. E. Kruchenykh)." VESTNIK RKhD (Paris): No. 116, II-III-IV-1975; p. 185. Poem.

908 _____. "Pis'ma B. L. Pasternaka O. E. i N. Ia. Mandel'shtam." ["Letters to the Mandel'shtams"] VESTNIK RSKhD (Paris No. 104-105, II-III-1972; pp. 229-48.
Letters dating from 1923-46, touching on various publishing and literary matters; one (from 1937) "envying" Mandel'shtam his poems; several to Nadezhda Mandel'shtam after Mandel'shtam's death.

PASTERNAK

909   PASTERNAK, BORIS. "Pis'mo B. Pasternaka." GRANI (Frankfurt):
       No. 122, Oct.-Dec. 1981; pp. 131-34.
              Letter dated Dec. 15, 1955, to a would-be poet, regard-
       ing his own alienation from the "literary establishment,"
       and commenting on correspondent's poems.

910   _____. "Unpublished letters to Akhmatova"; "Unpublished
       Reviews of Akhmatova." RUS. LIT. TRIQUARTERLY (Ann Arbor):
       No. 9, Spring 1974; pp. 522-33.
              The original letters are in Soviet archives; these are
       printed from not necessarily authoritative samizdat texts.
       The letters, dating from 1926, 1929 and 1940, pertain to
       the literary relationship between the two poets and the
       reviews are of collections of her poetry from the 1940s.

911   PASTERNAK, NADEZHDA. [b. 1950, em. 1979] "Vol'no mne: 'Filo-
       sofiia zimy'; 'Poslednee mamino leto'; 'Est' bol'no mne
       . . .'; 'Kak gonchaia zharu na iazyke. . .'; 'Uzhe mne
       nadoeli katera. . .'; 'Den';' 'Liubov' moia. . .'; 'Roial'
       golubye rebra. . .'; 'Nachalo oseni'; 'Poselednee'."
       VREMIA I MY (New York/Paris/Jerusalem): No. 49, Jan. 1980.
       Pre-emigration poems. (Also two others, dated 1979.)

912   _____. "Zapadnia prikosnovenii: 'Dusha, kak chai goria-
       chii'; 'Tak vzdragivaet poplavok'; 'Vechernii chai i
       ptitsy na zabore. . .'; 'Detstvo'; 'Shipovnik ne byl golo-
       sist'; 'O, kak mne tikho s muzykoi vdvoem. . .'; 'Kogda
       sryvaesh' list il' duesh' na ruki. . .'." VREMIA I MY
       (New York/Paris/Jerusalem): No. 51, March 1980; pp. 94-97.
       Poems, all pre-emigration.

913   PAVLOVA, MUZA. [b. 1907] "Iashchiki." ["Boxes"] GRANI
       (Frankfurt): No. 75, April 1970; pp. 125-46.
              Play (mocking the absurdities of bureaucracy).

914   _____. "Kryl'ia." ["Wings"] GRANI (Frankfurt): No.
       76, July 1970; pp. 92-109. Satiric play.

       PAVLOVA, MUZA: See also Sintaksis No. 1 (#1072), BOSLEY
       (#147), LANGLAND et al. (#656).

915   PENSON, BORIS. [b. 1946] "Gulag segodnia: Iz zhizni Mordov-
       skikh lagerei." ["The Gulag Today"] VESTNIK RKhD (Paris):
       No. 115, I-1975; pp. 234-54.
              Report by prisoner (arrested in 1970) in Mordovian camp,
       plus poems; after release he emigrated (1979).

       PENSON, BORIS: See also CHORNOVIL, V. and PENSON, B. (#237).

916 PESKOV, GEORGII. "My i oni." ["We and They"] ÈKHO (Paris):
     No. 1, 1978; pp. 83-87.
         Excerpt from Razgovor s soboi [Conversation with Myself],
     exposing the "dictatorship of the proletariat" as a myth.

917 Pesni russkikh bardov. Paris: YMCA, 1978. Thirty cassette
     recordings and four books of texts, mostly of songs by
     Galich, Okudzhava and Vysotskii, but also by 19 other
     authors, including Kukin, Almasov, Vizbor, Kim et al.

918 PETROV-AGATOV, ALEKSANDR. [b. 1921] "Arestantskie vstrechi:
     nevydumannaia povest'." ["Prison Meetings: An Uninvented
     Story"] GRANI (Frankfurt): No. 82, Dec. 1971; pp. 99-119;
     No. 83, May 1972; pp. 47-76; No. 84; July 1972; pp. 56-90.

     _____. "Arestantskie vstrechi." VESTNIK RSKhD (Paris):
     No. 103, I-1972; pp. 175-80.
         Author, who spent from 1947 to 1967 in prisons and camps,
     was rearrested in 1968 for "anti-Soviet poetry" and sen-
     tenced to seven years. This work describes his 1968 ar-
     rest, questioning, and meetings with other prisoners. Ex-
     tracts appeared in French in Cahiers du Samizdat No. 3
     (Brussels, 1972).

919 _____. "Rossiia, kotoroi ne znaiut." ["The Russia They
     Don't Know"] POSEV (Frankfurt): No. 3, March 1971; pp.
     20-27.
         About VSKhSON--sees in the struggle of the democratic
     movement the beginning of a spiritual rebirth in Russia.

920 _____. "Rossiia, kotoroi ne znaiut." POSEV (Frankfurt):
     No. 5, May 1971; pp. 54-56; No. 6, June 1971; pp. 54-56.
         Poems written in camp (for which his sentence was
     changed to Vladimir prison till the end of its term).

921 _____. "Iz tsikla 'Snachala Kolyma. Potom Mordoviia'."
     GRANI (Frankfurt): No. 80, Sept. 1971; pp. 103-106. Poems.

922 _____. "Tak prokhodit za godom god. . ."; "Na Mordovskoi
     zemle. . . ." GRANI (Frankfurt): No. 89-90, July-Dec.
     1973; p. 102. Poems.

923 PILNIAK, BORIS. [b. 1894, d. (official infor.) 1941] (Pseud.
     of BORIS VOGAU) "Zashtat." ["The Extra"] NOVYI ZHURNAL
     (New York): No. 134, March 1979; pp. 5-24.
         Purportedly the last story written by Pilniak before his
     arrest.

924 [PIMENOV, REVOL'T IVANOVICH]. [b. 1931] "Protokol doprosa
R. I. Pimenova." VESTNIK RSKhD (Paris): No. 100, II-1971;
pp. 188-201.
Transcript of interrogation and record of search of his
home, with a list of 250 confiscated samizdat items.

PIMENOV, R. I.: See also Vol'noe slovo No. 8 (#1233) and
Pamiat', Nos. 1, 2, 3 (#895-97).

925 "Pis'ma brat'ev-èpiskopov iz ssylki." ["Letters from Exile"]
VESTNIK RSKhD (Paris): No. 107, I-1973; pp. 72-90; No.
108-109-110, II-III-IV 1973; pp. 36-54.
Letters, dated 1935-36, of Bishop German, who died in
exile in the north; they deal with personal as well as
spiritual matters.

926 "Pis'ma Valaamskogo startsa skhiigumena Ioanna." ["Letters
from Elder Ioann"] VESTNIK RKhD (Paris): No. 114, IV-
1974; pp. 5-12; No. 117, I-1976; pp. 29-42.
Letters written between 1939 and 1956.

927 "Pis'mo iz Rossii o sbornike 'Iz glubiny'." ["Letter on the
Collection 'From the Depths'"] (Anon.) RUS. MYSL'
(Paris): Dec. 21, 1967; p. 5.
Comment on 1918 collection.

928 PLATONOV, ANDREI. [b. 1899, d. 1951] "14 Krasnykh Izbushek:
Geroi nashego vremeni." ["14 Little Red Huts: A Hero of
Our Time"] GRANI (Frankfurt): No. 86, Dec. 1972; pp. 8-72.
Play, written in 1937. (Author was barely published
between 1931 and World War II, during which he worked as a
war correspondent and published a number of stories about
the war. Again from 1946 till his death he was unable to
publish.)

929 _____. Chevengur. Paris: YMCA, 1972; 375 pp.

_____. Les herbes folles de Tchevengour. Paris: Stock,
1972; 483 pp. Tr., Cecile Loeb.

_____. Unterwegs nach Tschevengur. Darmstadt, Neuwied:
Luchterhand, 1973; 429 pp. Tr., Swetlana Geier.

_____. "Chevengur." VESTNIK RSKhD (Paris): No. 101-
102, III-IV-1971; pp. 239-46.
Novel written in 1929, banned presumably as satire on
communism, though some critics see his satire, Swiftian in
nature, as directed more generally against forces such as
death and human folly.

930   PLATONOV, ANDREI. "Èrik." KONTINENT: No. 10, 1976; pp.
       339-42.
       Story published in <u>Krasnaia derevnia</u> in Voronezh in
       1921, never since officially, only in samizdat circulation.

931   _____. <u>La Mer de Jouvenil</u>. Paris: Michel, 1976;
       192 pp. Novella.

932   _____. <u>The Foundation Pit</u>. <u>Kotlovan</u>. Ann Arbor: Ardis,
       1973; 284 pp. Tr., Thomas P. Whitney.

       _____. <u>La Fouille</u>. Paris: L'Age d'Homme, 1974; 151 pp.

       _____. <u>Die Baugrube</u>. Frankfurt: Suhrkamp, 1971; 167
       pp. Tr., Aggy Jais.

       _____. "Kotlovan." GRANI (Frankfurt): No. 70, Feb.
       1969; pp. 3-107. Novel written in 1930.

933   PLISETSKII, GERMAN. "Iz tsikla 'Mikhailovskie iamby'." GRANI
       (Frankfurt): No. 68, July 1968; pp. 3-4. Poems.

934   _____. "Truba." GRANI (Frankfurt): No. 65, Sept. 1967;
       pp. 5-7. Poem.

       PLISETSKII, GERMAN: See also BOSLEY (#152).

935   PLISETSKII, GEORGII [sic]. "Poèty--pobochnye deti Rossii. . . ."
       RUS. MYSL' (Paris): Dec. 3, 1970.
       Poem. A variant form appears in RUS. MYSL', No. 12,
       1970, listed under SLUTSKII, B. The Dec. 3 version ap-
       pears in a letter, the writer of which claims it to be
       correct version and that the author is Plisetskii. It was
       read at Pasternak's funeral. There is also a question as
       to whether German Plisetskii is meant, rather than Georgii.

936   "Po svoim!" (Anon.) RUS. MYSL' (Paris): Sept. 5, 1968;
       p. 4. Poem.

       PLIUSHCH, LEONID: See KHODOROVICH, T. (#525); <u>Vol'noe slovo</u>
       No. 11 (#1235).

937   POD'IAPOL'SKII, GRIGORII. [b. 1926, em. 1976] <u>Zolotoi vek</u>.
       [<u>The Golden Age</u>] Frankfurt: Posev, 1974; 147 pp.
       Collection of poems.

938   PODRABINEK, ALEKSANDR. [b. 1953] <u>Karatel'naia meditsina</u>.
       New York: Khronika, 1979.

PODRABINEK

> PODRABINEK, ALEKSANDR. Punitive Medicine. Ann Arbor, Mich.:
> Karoma Pub., 1980; 223 pp. Tr., A. Lehrman.
> Author, young paramedic sentenced in 1978 to five years'
> internal exile, describes treatment of dissidents held in
> special psychiatric hospitals; based on interviews with
> former inmates, samizdat sources, etc. Indicts especially
> Serbskii Institute, and calls for international boycott of
> Soviet psychiatry.

> PODRABINEK, P.: See Poiski No. 2 (#941).

939 Poèziia v lageriakh. Israel: Center for Investigation of
Prisons, Psychiatric Prisons and Concentration Camps of
the USSR, 1978.
> Collection of camp poems.

940 Poiski. No. 1. Long Island City, N.Y.: Detinetz (4330 48th
St., D-1; Long Island City, N.Y. 11104), 1979; 380 pp.
> First issue of Moscow samizdat journal, edited by Petr
> Abovin-Egides, Valerii Abramkin, Vladimir Gershuni, Iurii
> Grimm, Raisa Lert, Gleb Pavlovskii and Viktor Sokirko.
> Includes:

> PRYZHOV, P.: "Tret'ia sila"; on the new constitution, com-
> paring it with those of 1918, 1924 and 1936.
> CHICHIBABIN, B.: "Dva stikhotvoreniia: 'Nam stali govo-
> rit' druz'ia. . .'; 'Nastoi na snakh v pustynnom su-
> dake. . .'." Poems.
> DOMBROVSKII, IURII: "Ruchka, nozhka, ogurechik." ["Pen,
> Knife, Pickle"] Story.
> SEDOV, A.: "Stikhotvoreniia: 'L'vov'; 'Iz tsikla' 'Vre-
> mena goda";' 'Propoved', uslyshannaia vo sne'." Poems.
> LIIATOV, M.: "Kakoi-nibud' Mendosa." ["Some Mendosa or
> Other"] Play.
> VOZNESENSKAIA, IULIIA: "Zapiski iz rukava." ["Notes on a
> Sleeve"] On her arrest, her hunger strike, trial, prison
> doctors and nurses, and including a few of her poems.
> GEFTER, M.: "Est' li vykhod." ["Is There a Way Out"]
> On new constitution.
> Also includes assorted short pieces dealing with samiz-
> dat, unofficial culture; Rudenko's final plea.

941 Poiski. No. 2. Poiski Publications. 1980 includes:

> Abovin-Egides, P. and Podrabinek, P.: "Nekotorye aktual'-
> nye problemy demokraticheskogo dvizheniia v nashei strane"
> ["Some Real Problems of the Democratic Movement in Our
> Country"], on practical problems like the kind of day-to-
> day legal work the Helsinki Group could do, how it can co-
> operate with free unions, etc.

942 "Pokhorony Akhmatovoi." ["Akhmatova's Funeral"] (Anon.)
RUS. MYSL' (Paris): Jan. 30, 1969; p. 8.
Short description by someone who attended.

943 "Polet na lunu." ["Flight to the Moon"] (Anon.) POSEV
(Frankfurt): No. 46 (965), Nov. 20, 1964; p. 6.
Satiric poem.

POLETAEVA, T.: See Moskovskoe vremia (#817).

944 POMAZOV, VITALII. [b. 1946] "Stikhi: Posviashchaetsia
Aleksandru Ginzburgu." KONTINENT: No. 17, 1978; pp. 7-10.
Poem.

945 POMERANTS, GRIGORII. [b. 1918] "Chelovek bez prilagatel'-
nogo." ["Man Without an Adjective"] GRANI (Frankfurt):
No. 77, Oct. 1970; pp. 171-98.

_____. "Chelovek bez prilagatel'nogo." RUS. MYSL'
(Paris): Aug. 27, 1970; p. 4; Sept. 3, 1970; p. 5; Sept.
10, 1970; p. 5; Sept. 17, 1970; p. 5; Sept. 24, 1970; p.
5; Oct. 1, 1970; p. 5.

_____. "Chelovek bez prilagatel'nogo." NOV. RUS. SLOVO
(New York): Oct. 10, 1970; p. 2; Oct. 12, 1970; p. 2;
Oct. 13, 1970; p. 2; Oct. 14, 1970; p. 2; Oct. 15, 1970;
pp. 2-3; Oct. 16, 1970; p. 2; Oct. 17, 1970; p. 2.

_____. "Man Without an Adjective." RUSSIAN REVIEW
(Stanford): Vol. 30, No. 3, July 1971; pp. 219-25. Tr.
and abridged by Alexis Korakov. Also appeared in ETHICS.
   Philosophic essay developing the idea that the "people"
(narod) is the repository of national values and that the
disintegration of village life after collectivization and
enforced atheism caused the moral disintegration of the
country.

946 _____. "'Evklidovskii' i 'neevklidovskii' razum v tvor-
chestve Dostoevskogo." ["Euclidean and Non-Euclidean Reason in Dostoevskii's Work"] KONTINENT: No. 3, 1975; pp.
109-50.
   Analysis of Dostoevskian opus with focus on Notes from
Underground as the crucible for Dostoevskii's ideas.

947 _____. "Kvadril'on." ["Quadrillion"] GRANI (Frankfurt): No. 64, June 1967; pp. 150-66.

_____. "Iz literaturno-filosofskogo pamfleta 'Kvadril'-
on' G. Pomerantsa." POSEV (Frankfurt): No. 4 (1079),
Jan. 27, 1967; p. 2.

POMERANTS

From <u>Feniks</u> 1966 (#337); analysis of the moral qualities
of human beings in terms of types created by 19th century
Russian writers.

948   POMERANTS, GRIGORII. "Malye èsse: Schast'e; Ochen' korot-
kaia filosofiia; K teorii zari; Koan; Bog i nichto; Reabili-
tatsiia cherta." ["Short Essays: Happiness; A Very Short
Philosophy; Toward a Theory of Dawn; Koan; God and Nothing;
Rehabilitation of the Devil"] GRANI (Frankfurt): No. 80,
Sept. 1971; pp. 177-90.
Short pieces on the nature and meaning of happiness,
masculine and feminine principles, etc. Included in
<u>Neopublikovannoe</u> (#949).

949   _____. <u>Neopublikovannoe</u>. [<u>Unpublished</u>] Frankfurt:
Posev, 1969; 335 pp.
Collection of his essays, including "Chelovek niotkuda"
["Man from Nowhere"], on intelligentsia and narod; "Dve
modeli poznaniia" ["Two Models of Cognition"], "Tri urovnia bytiia" ["Three Levels of Existence"], assorted short
pieces (see "Malye èsse," #948), "Nravstvennyi oblik
istoricheskoi lichnosti" (see #950) and others.

950   _____. "O roli nravstvennogo oblika lichnosti v zhizni
istoricheskogo kollektiva." ["On the Role of the Moral
Aspect of Personality in the Life of the Historic Collective"] GRANI (Frankfurt): No. 67, March 1968; pp. 134-43.
From <u>Feniks</u> 1966 (#337); Eng. tr. in BRUMBERG (#178)
and MEERSON-AKSENOV and SHRAGIN (#801). Deals with
whether the progress achieved by Stalin (industrialization,
war-readiness, etc.) was real progress, and analyzes the
means by which it was achieved. Fr. tr. in <u>Samizdat</u> <u>I</u> (#989).
POMERANTS: See also LITVINOV et al. (#702).

951   PONOMAREV, ALEKSANDR. (A. MOREV) [d. 1979] "Listy s pepe-
lishcha: 'Proshchal'noe'; 'Mne kazhetsia, chto ia usnul
davno'; 'Blizhe k nochi raspiali ego. . .'; 'Toska gryzet,
byt' mozhet, ottogo. . .'; 'Malina'; 'Ta--drugaia--ne
pridet ko mne. . .'; 'On prishel s voiny.. . .'." VREMIA I
MY (New York/Paris/Jerusalem): No. 52, April 1980;
pp. 101-107. Poems.

POPOVSKII, MARK: See <u>Vol'noe</u> <u>slovo</u> No. 29 (#1250).

952   POPUGAEV, K. P. Ed. "Obzor pressy za 1984 god." ["Survey of
the Press in 1984"] POSEV (Frankfurt): No. 1, Jan. 1972;
pp. 37-40.
Satiric exercise in "Marxist futurology," in form of
paragraphs from Western and Soviet press, by pseudonymous
author.

Prizyv: See Nadezhda (#827).

953   Programma demokraticheskogo dvizheniia Sovetskogo Soiuza.
      [Program of the Democratic Movement of the Soviet Union]
      Amsterdam: Herzen, 1970; 76 pp.
          First attempt to formulate in one general statement the
      goals of different groups of dissidents and provide a
      vision of the possible political future of the country.
      Acknowledges Declaration of Human Rights as foundation of
      social concept, proposes establishment of new state with
      free elections, constitutional court system, abolition of
      secret police, etc.

PROKOFIEV, O.: See Sintaksis (#1072).

PRYZHOV, P.: See Poiski No. 1 (#940).

954   PUSHLER, NESTOR. "Parodii: 'Ofigenie v glavlite,' 'Iz zk'."
      KONTINENT: No. 19 (1979); pp. 7-20.
          Series of parodic poems, by pseudonymous author.

R

955 RADYGIN, ANATOLII. [b. 1934, em. 1973] "Po obitaemym ostro-
vam Arkhipelaga." ["Through the Inhabited Islands of the
Archipelago"] POSEV (Frankfurt): No. 3, March 1975;
pp. 47-52; No. 4, April 1975; pp. 33-40; No. 5, May 1975;
pp. 41-45; No. 6, June 1975; pp. 34-40; No. 7, July 1975;
pp. 29-35; No. 9, Sept. 1975; pp. 36-56; No. 10, Oct. 1975;
pp. 46-52.
Memoir of his 10 years in the Gulag (1962-72, for at-
tempting to cross the border to Turkey); describes his arrest and investigation, analyzes the "slave mentality" of
the arrested; treatment of medical patients in camps, etc.

956 _____. (RODYGIN [sic]) "Venok sonetov." VESTNIK RSKhD
(Paris): No. 101-102, III-IV-1972; pp. 231-38.

_____. "Venok sonetov." AMI (Jerusalem): No. 3, 1973;
pp. 80-89, (Journal no longer exists). Poems.

957 "Razgovor tekhnologa Petukhova s afrikanskim printsem."
(Anon.) NOV. RUS. SLOVO (New York): Oct. 8, 1976; p. 3.
Satiric poem.

RAZUMNYI, SERGEI: See EVDOKIMOV, BORIS

958 REGEL'SON, LEV. [b. 1942] "Da ne budet u tebia inykh bogov."
["Thou Shalt Have No Other Gods"] VESTNIK RKhD (Paris):
No. 117, I-1976; pp. 94-101.
What God requires of man and what man's response should
be--a heart given to God, demanding nothing, and love
which seeks no object but God.

959 _____. "Ideal sobornosti i chelovecheskaia lichnost'."
["The Ideal of Conciliarism and Human Personality"] VEST-
NIK RKhD (Paris): No. 124, I-1978; pp. 36-74.
Re subordination of individual to spiritual community.

REGEL'SON, LEV: See also BARABANOV, AGURSKII et al. (#95),
BOURDEAUX (#148), MEERSON-AKSENOV and SHRAGIN (#801),
Vol'noe slovo No. 24 (#1246).

960 REIN, EVGENII. [b. 1935] "Dinarii kesaria." KOVCHEG: No. 2,
1978; pp. 49-54. Poem.

REIN, EVGENII: See also Sintaksis No. 3 (#1072), Metropol'
(#808).

961 REMEZOV, ANDREI. (I. IVANOV) Est' li zhizn' na Marse? [Is
There Life on Mars?] Paris: Institute Litteraire, 1961;
100 pp. Satiric play.

A *Critical Guide*

962   Renaissance du bolchévisme en URSS: Mémoires d'un bolchevik-
       Léninist. (Anon.) Paris: Maspero, 1970.
          Memoirs of a Trotskyist, written about 1968, about
       party political struggles in 1920s, then prisons and
       camps. Also includes documents by Iakir, Pliushch et
       al. Portions included in SAUNDERS (#1001); from MED-
       VEDEV (#784).

963   REVEL, J. F., Ed. Litterature Russe Clandestine. Paris:
       Michel, 1971; 368 pp. Tr., C. Lopez.
          Samizdat prose of the 1960s.

964   ROKHLIN, BORIS. "Tan'ka." GRANI (Frankfurt): No. 121, July-
       Sept. 1981; pp. 5-106.
          Play, taken from Leningrad samizdat almanac Chasy No.
       11 (1978).

965   ROSSOV, IAROSLAV. "Gori." NOVYI ZHURNAL (New York): No.
       106, March 1972; p. 49.
          Poem, omitted from Table of Contents.

966   ROZANOVA, TAT'IANA. "Iz vospominanii ob ottse." ["From
       Memoirs About My Father"] VESTNIK RSKhD (Paris): No. 112-
       13, II-III-1974; pp. 147-59.
          Excerpt pertaining to Rozanov's illness and death.

967   RUBIN, IL'IA. [d. 1977] Poeziia. Kritika. Proza. [Poetry,
       Criticism, Prose] Tel Aviv: Moskva-Ierusalim, 1978.
          Collection of works, many of which circulated in samiz-
       dat; author emigrated shortly before his death.

968   RUDNEV, ALEKSEI. "Uslovie dialoga." ["Condition of a Dia-
       logue"] VESTNIK RSKhD (Paris): No. 106, IV-1972; pp. 46 -
       56. On detente.

       RUSLANOV, IVAN: See EVDOKIMOV, BORIS

969   La Russie Contestataire: Documents de l'Opposition Soviéti-
       que. (Anon. ed.) Paris: Fayard, 1971; 330 pp. Tr.,
       S. Obolensky.
          Eclectic collection of documents, including Grigorenko's
       diaries, Fainberg's letter on psychiatry, etc.

970   Russischer Samisdat. Stimmen aus dem "anderen Russland".
       Bern: Kuratorium geistige Freiheit. Beginning in 1972,
       16 issues have appeared: texts and documents.

971   RUSSKII, GENNADII. (Pseud.) "Kleima." ["Brands"] KONTINENT:
       No. 22, 1980; pp. 7-41; No. 26, 1980; pp. 15-59.
          On early saints of Northern Russia.

Russkoe

972   Russkoe slovo. [Russian Word] GRANI (Frankfurt): No. 66,
      Dec. 1967; pp. 5-34.
          Samizdat journal, dated July 1966, reprinted in its en-
      tirety; contains short articles, including statement by
      the Ryleev Club of the journal's editorial purpose, N.
      Èidelman's "Serno," on revolutionary killed in 1866, S.
      Artamonov's "Filosofiia Montesk'e," and poems by V. Vos-
      kresenskii, E. Kushev, I. Golubev, T. Smol'ianinova, N.
      Solntseva, I. Vladimirskaia. Some items included in
      GERSTENMAIER (#375).

973   RZHEVSKII, LEONID. (Pseud.) "A Typology of Cultures Based
      on Attitudes to Death." SURVEY (London): Vol. 22, No. 2,
      Spring 1976; pp. 36-56.
          Divides cultures into those "open to unknown and alien
      and recognizing the value of truth," and those closed to
      the unknown and alien and not recognizing the value of
      truth, Russia belonging to the latter category. This by
      way of exploring Russian fatalism and hopelessness.

974   RYZHOV, LEV. "Pervaia Paskha Iisusa." RUS. MYSL' (Paris):
      May 8, 1975; p. 10. Poem.

      RYZHOV, LEV: See also Feniks 1966 (#337), BOSLEY (under
      RYZHOVA [sic], #147) and "Iz stikhov molodykh poètov pod-
      pol'nogo moskovskogo zhurnala 'Feniks 1966'," in VESTNIK
      RSKhD (Paris): No. 85, III-1967; pp. 57-58.

S

975 SAKHAROV, ANDREI. [b. 1921] "Beseda s pervym Zam. General'-
nogo Prokurora." VESTNIK RSKhD (Paris): No. 108-109-110,
III-III-IV-1973; pp. 238-46.

_____. "Polnyi tekst otcheta A. D. Sakharova o besede s
zam. general'nogo prokurora." RUS. MYSL' (Paris): Oct. 18,
1973; p. 5.

_____. "The Deputy Prosecutor General and I." INDEX ON
CENSORSHIP (London): Vol. 2, No. 4, Winter 1973; pp. 19-23.
Transcript of Sakharov's "chat" with the prosecutor,
Aug. 21, 1973, in which Maliarov warns him of the future
consequences of his behavior. Eng. tr. also in New York
Times, Aug. 29, 1973.

976 _____. "Dvizhenie za prava cheloveka v SSSR i vostochnoi
Evrope--tseli, znachenie, trudnosti." ["Movement for Human
Rights in the USSR and Eastern Europe--Goals, Significance,
Difficulties"] KONTINENT: No. 19, 1979; pp. 171-88.
As title indicates, program and problems of human rights
activists.

977 _____. "Iadernaia ènergetika i svoboda zapada." ["Nuclear Energy and Freedom of the West"] KONTINENT: No. 16,
1978; pp. 189-94.
Points out the differences between nuclear energy and
nuclear weaponry, in terms of safeguards. Dated Nov. 1977.

978 _____. Memorandum. Frankfurt: Posev, 1970; 102 pp.
Collection including articles and interviews.

979 _____. "Mir cherez polveka." ["The World in Half a
Century"] KONTINENT: No. 7, 1976; pp. 241-56.
Warning of various dangers--thermonuclear war, wasting of
resources--and steps that can be taken to avert them, together with a plea for support of human rights. (Written
for Saturday Review in 1973 but did circulate in samizdat.)

980 _____. "Mir, progress, prava cheloveka." ["Peace, Progress, Human Rights"] RUS. MYSL' (Paris): Dec. 25, 1975;
pp. 3, 4.

_____. "Mir, progress, prava cheloveka." POSEV (Frank-
furt): No. 1, Jan. 1976; pp. 25-31.
Sakharov's Nobel acceptance speech, on dangers of nuclear weaponry and of trying to turn back the clock on tech-
nological progress; on the need for an open society, for
detente, and for observance of the Helsinki accords.

SAKHAROV

981　SAKHAROV, ANDREI. "O pis'me Aleksandra Solzhenitsyna 'Vozhdiam Sovetskogo Soiuza'." ["On A. Solzhenitsyn's 'Letter
to Soviet Leaders"] New York: Khronika, 1974; 14 pp.

　　　　　　——. "O pis'me Aleksandra Solzhenitsyna 'Vozhdiam
Sovetskogo Soiuza'." NOV. RUS. SLOVO (New York): April
23, 1974; p. 2.

　　　　　　——. "Tol'ko v global'nom masshtabe. . . ." POSEV
(Frankfurt): No. 5, May 1974; pp. 31-36.

　　　　　　——. "O pis'me A. Solzhenitsyna 'Vozhdiam Sovetskogo
Soiuza'." RUS. MYSL' (Paris): May 23, 1974; p. 5.
　　　Response to Solzhenitsyn's "Letter to the Soviet
Leaders," in which he challenges Solzhenitsyn's assertions
that Russia's problems stem solely from Soviet ideology,
that Marxism is a Western and anti-religious idea which
perverted the healthy development of Russia, and that progress is pernicious. Eng. tr. in MEERSON-AKSENOV and
SHRAGIN (#801) and in The Times (London), April 16, 1974.

982　　　　　——. O strane i mire. New York: Khronika, 1975; 79 pp.

　　　　　　——. O strane i mire: sbornik proizvedenii. New
York: Khronika, 1976; 183 pp. (Contains title essay and
several interviews.)

　　　　　　——. My Country and the World. New York: Knopf,
1975; 109 pp. Tr., Guy Daniels.

　　　　　　——. Mon pays et le monde. Paris: Seuil, 1975; 112
pp. Tr., P. Deyfat.

　　　　　　——. (SACHAROW) Mein Land und die Welt. Vienna,
Munich, Zurich: Molden, 1975; 119 pp. Tr., Hans Müller.

　　　　　　——. "O strane i mire." RUS. MYSL' (Paris): Aug. 7,
1975; p. 3.

　　　　　　——. "O svobode vybora strany prozhivaniia." RUS.
MYSL' (Paris): Sept. 4, 1975; p. 5.

　　　　　　——. "Liberal'naia intelligentsiia na zapade, ee
illiuzii, ee otvetsvennost'." RUS. MYSL' (Paris): Sept.
11, 1975; p. 5.

　　　　　　——. "Problemy razoruzheniia." RUS. MYSL' (Paris):
Sept. 25, 1975; p. 5.

SAKHAROV, ANDREI. "Problemy razoruzheniia." NOVYI ZHURNAL
(New York): No. 121, Dec. 1975; pp. 223-30.
   Discussion of Soviet life and its internal problems;
the freedom to choose one's country of residence; problems
of disarmament; Western failure to understand Soviet society; the illusions and responsibilities of Western intellectuals.

983   _____. "Pamiatnaia zapiska." NOV. RUS. SLOVO (New York):
July 16, 1972; p. 5; "Posleslovie" in NOV. RUS. SLOVO,
July 5, 1972; p. 1.

_____. "Pamiatnaia zapiska." RUS. MYSL' (Paris): Aug.
10, 1972; p. 5. "Posleslovie" in same issue, p. 6, reprinted from July 6 issue (p. 3).

_____. "Memorandum." SURVEY (London): Vol. 18, No. 3
(84), Summer 1972; pp. 223-34; "Afterword" pp. 234-40.
   Sets forth questions to be discussed: amnesty for
political prisoners, freedom of information, arms control.

984   _____. Razmyshleniia o progresse, mirnom sosushchestvo-
vanii i intellektual'noi svobode. Frankfurt: Posev, 1968;
64 pp.

_____. Progress, Coexistence and Intellectual Freedom.
New York: Norton, 1968; 158 pp. (see also N.Y. Times,
July 22, 1968).

_____. Réflexions sur le progrès, la coexistence paci-
fique et la liberté intellectuelle. Beauvais: M. Houde-
ville et fils, 1968; 32 pp.

_____. La liberté intellectuelle en URSS et la coexist-
ence. Paris: Gallimard, 1969; 191 pp. Tr., Serge
Bricianer.

_____. (SACHAROW) Memorandum: Wie ich mir die Zukunft
vorstelle (Gedanken über Fortschritt, friedliche Koexistenz
u. geistige Freiheit). Frankfurt: Posev, 1968; 62 pp.
and Zurich: Diogenes, 1968; 108 pp. Tr., E. Guttenberger.

_____. "Razmyshleniia o progresse, mirnom sosushchestvo-
vanii i intellektual'noi svobode." RUS. MYSL' (Paris):
Aug. 1, 1968; p. 5; Aug. 8, 1968; p. 5; Aug. 15, 1968;
p. 5; Aug. 22, 1968; p. 5; Aug. 29, 1968; p. 5.

_____. "Razmyshleniia o progresse, mirnom sosushchestvo-
vanii i intellektual'noi svobode." NOV. RUS. SLOVO (New

SAKHAROV

York):   July 24, 1968; p. 2; July 25, 1968; p. 2; July 26,
1968; p. 2; July 27, 1968; p. 2; July 29, 1968; p. 2;
July 30, 1968; p. 2; July 31, 1968; p. 2; Aug. 1, 1968;
pp. 2-3; Aug. 2, 1968; p. 2.
   Manifesto includes recommendations for guarantees of intellectual freedom, propositions concerning world health,
avoidance of nuclear war, consequences of famine. Challenges Soviet leadership and "people of good will" to discussion, and suggests, for final victory over Stalinism,
intensification of strategies for peaceful coexistence,
weakening of dogmatic and bureaucratic chains hindering the
economy, unmasking of Stalin, political amnesty, repeal of
unconstitutional laws and freedom of press and information.

985   SAKHAROV, ANDREI. Sakharov o sebe. New York: Khronika,
1974.

_____ . Sakharov Speaks. New York: Knopf and London:
Harvill, 1974; 245 pp. Tr., Guy Daniels.

_____ . Sakharov parle. Paris: Seuil, 1974; 240 pp.
Tr., E. Vincent.

_____ . (SACHAROW) Stellungnahme. Vienna, Munich, Zurich:
Molden, 1974; 223 pp. Tr., Ernst Neumayr.
   Includes "Razmyshleniia," 1971 Memorandum, various interviews; introduction appears in New York Times March 5,
1974.

986   _____ . Trevoga i nadezhda. [Anxiety and Hope] New
York: Khronika, 1978.

_____ . Un An de lutte. Paris: Seuil, 1978.

_____ . (SACHAROW) Furcht und Hoffnung. Vienna, Munich,
Zurich: Molden, 1978; 220 pp.
   Reformulation of his basic position on the ties between
justice and human rights in one part of the world and the
security of all humankind; gives picture of contemporary
Soviet society, calling it the most refined and developed
form of totalitarian-socialist society.

987   _____ . V bor'be za mir. [In the Struggle for Peace]
Frankfurt: Posev, 1973; 303 pp.
   Collection of articles, interviews.

SAKHAROV, ANDREI: See also BRUMBERG (#178). NB: Many of
Sakharov's assorted letters, protests, appeals, etc. appear in various issues of Khronika tekushchikh sobytii and
in Khronika zashchity prav.

988 SAKHAROV, A., TURCHIN, V. and MEDVEDEV, R. "Pis'mo." NOV.
     RUS. SLOVO (New York): April 29, 1970; p. 2; April 30,
     1970; p. 2; May 1, 1970; p. 2; May 2, 1970; p. 2.

     _____. "Obrashchenie sovetskikh uchenykh k partiino-
     pravitel'stvennym rukovoditeliam SSSR." RUS. MYSL' (Paris):
     April 30, 1970; p. II.

     _____. "Neobkhodima postepennaia demokratizatsiia."
     POSEV (Frankfurt): No. 7, July 1970; pp. 36-42.

     _____. "Appeal of Soviet Scientists to the Party and
     Government Leaders of the USSR." SURVEY (London): Vol. 16,
     No. 3 (76), Summer 1970; pp. 160-70.
        Outline for need for democratization, because democrati-
     zation would reenforce Soviet society's order and ideology;
     it could be achieved by cooperation between CPSU and the
     population, and achieved gradually. Eng. tr. also in
     Sakharov Speaks (#985) and SAUNDERS (#1001); included in
     GERSTENMAIER (#375). Originally appeared in Neue Zürcher
     Zeitung, April 22 and 24, 1970.

989 Samizdat I. (Anon. ed.) Paris: Seuil, 1969; 645 pp.
        Trotskyist collection of documents; SAUNDERS (#1001) is
     based largely on this text.

990 The Samizdat Bulletin: Extracts from samizdat in English.
        A publication issued more or less monthly, in publication
     since 1973. POB 6128, San Mateo, California, 94403. In-
     cludes a wide variety of materials from many sources, both
     samizdat and non-samizdat (the latter including interviews
     with émigrés, for instance, or appeals by Solzhenitsyn).

991 "Samizdatovskii iumor khrushchevskoi pory." (Anon.) NOV.
     RUS. SLOVO (New York): May 14, 1976; p. 3. Satiric poem.

     SAMOILOV, DAVID: See Sfinksy (#1011), BOSLEY (#147).

992 SAMOKHIN, ANDREI. (Pseud.) "Idol na ploshchadi." ["Idol on
     the Square"] POSEV (Frankfurt): No. 12, Dec. 1973;
     pp. 31-39.
        Traces the role of religion in several national histo-
     ries, and the replacement of Christianity with Communist
     religion--from Kant, Fourier, and Marx to Lenin.

993 _____. "Razriadka." ["Detente"] POSEV (Frankfurt):
     No. 11, Nov. 1975; pp. 28-33.
        Analysis of detente--its benefits for the Soviet Union,
     disadvantages for the West, and the West's misunderstand-
     ing of Soviet manipulation of detente.

SAMOKHIN

994   SAMOKHIN, ANDREI. "Zachem nuzhna voina s Kitaem?" ["Why is
      War with China Necessary?"] POSEV (Frankfurt): No. 9,
      Sept. 1973; pp. 16-27.
         Brief history of Sino-Soviet relations, as well as
      analysis of future relations. Sees Soviet policy as de-
      liberately provoking war: the government uses the Chinese
      threat as a means of unifying the people, and could use
      war as a means of nullifying all dissent (people who would
      survive would be so grateful for survival that freedoms and
      rights would be matters of complete indifference to them).
      Details both external and internal signs of impending war.

995   SAPGIR, GENRIKH. [b. 1928] "Kogda slonu. . ."; "Sonet";
      "Peizazh prost. . ."; "Khochu pevtsa skhvatit' za golos, . .";
      "Belesoglazyi, belobrovyi. . ."; "Iz konverta. . . ." GRANI
      (Frankfurt): No. 95, Jan.-Mar. 1975; pp. 44-48.
         Poems, listed in Table of Contents under BETAKI.

996   _____. "Proshchanie so staroi Moskvoi"; "Besstrashnaia."
      TRET'IA VOLNA (Paris): No. 5, 1970; pp. 53-54. Poems.

997   _____. Sonety na rubashkakh. [Sonnets on Shirtsleeves]
      Paris: Tret'ia volna, 1978.
         Collection of poems. Some included in TRET'IA VOLNA
      (Paris): No. 2, 1977; pp. 6-10.

998   _____. "Iz knigi 'Sonety na rubashkakh'; 'Diagramma
      zhizni'; 'Sonet vo sne'; 'Nechto-nichto'; 'Maleevka';
      'Sonet-stat'ia'." KONTINENT: No. 16, 1978; pp. 133-36.
         Poems from Sonety na rubashkakh.

999   _____. "Skvoz' bol' i bred: 'Shkatulka med' surguch
      butyl' s kleimom. . .'; 'Ona'; 'Rvanyi sonet'; 'Zemlia'."
      VREMIA I MY (New York/Paris/Jerusalem): No. 32, Aug. 1978;
      pp. 101-103. Poems from Sonety na rubashkakh.

      SAPGIR, GENRICH: See also Sintaksis 1 (#1072), BOSLEY (#147),
      Metropol' (#808).

1000 SARNOV, KIRILL. (Pseud.) "Vechera Pashi Mosina." ["The
      Pasha's Evenings"] KOVCHEG (Paris): No. 1, 1978; pp. 50-
      63. Story.

1001 SAUNDERS, GEORGE, Ed. Samizdat: Voices of the Soviet Oppo-
      sition. New York: Monad Press, 1974; 464 pp.
         Collection of dissident Marxist documents, mostly though
      not exclusively samizdat. Includes "Memoirs of a Bolshevik-
      Leninist" (see Renaissance du bolchévisme en URSS [#962]),
      memoirs by Aleksandra Chumakova, who was associated with

Trotskiists in 1920s; E. M.'s article on Trotskii's murder
and various texts by Grigorenko, Pliushch, Iakhimovich et
al. Based on Samizdat I (#989).

1002   SAVITSKII, P. (VOSTOKOV, P.) "Pamiati èpiskopa Afanasiia."
VESTNIK RSKhD (Paris): No. 81, III-1966; pp. 17-19.
Poem, written between 1948 and 1951.

1003   _____. (VOSTOKOV) "Zvezda"; "Ia ne mechtaiu, ne to-
skuiu. . ."; "Svet i t'ma"; "Zvezdy"; "Svet piat'desiat
chetvertoi paralleli"; "Imia"; "Iabloko"; "Rossiiskii ter-
mos"; "V lesakh"; "Moskva"; "Stoikost' russkaia"; "Serdtse";
"Vosem' strok o liubvi"; "Pechat' ognepal'naia"; "Gost'";
"Vest':; "Bessmertie mysli"; "Put' liubvi"; "Liubov' k
zhizni." GRANI (Frankfurt): No. 39, July-Sept. 1958;
pp. 83-91. Poems.

1004   _____. "Otryvok"; "Lesorubu"; "Pozhelan'e"; "Verui i
boris'!"; "Neissiakaiushchii istochnik"; "Utro"; "Prostoe";
"Starost'"; "Voin"; "Mudrost'"; "Ubezhden'e"; "Vera";
"Golos." GRANI (Frankfurt): No. 43, July-Sept. 1959;
pp. 103-108. Poems listed under "Stikhi is Rossii" in
Table of Contents.

1005   SCAMMELL, MICHAEL, Ed. Russia's Other Writers. London: Long-
man, 1970 and New York: Praeger, 1971; 216 pp.
Collection of prose pieces, all but two of which are
samizdat. Includes: Maksimov's "House in the Clouds,"
Ulianskii's "The Fleecy Jacket," Mandel'shtam's "Fourth
Prose," Goriushkin's "Before Sunrise," Shalamov's "A Good
Hand" and "Caligula," Bukovskii's "Miniature Stories" and
Vel'skii's "My Apologia."

SEDOV, A.: See Poiski No. 1 (#940).

1006   Seiatel'. [The Sower] NOV. RUS. SLOVO (New York): Dec. 11,
1972; p. 2; Dec. 12, 1972; p. 2; Dec. 13, 1972; p. 2.
Samizdat journal (only two issues of which reached the
West) of a social-democratic party. See also Vol'noe
slovo No. 5 (#1230). Eng. tr. of excerpt in MEERSON-
AKSENOV and SHRAGIN (#801), under "Entrance into Politics:
Necessary Explanations."

1007   SELIKHOV, N. (Pseud.) "Svetilo"; "Progulka arestanta";
"Vera bitnika." GRANI (Frankfurt): No. 56, Oct. 1964;
pp. 179-81.
Poems listed under "Stikhi molodykh leningradskikh
poètov" in Table of Contents.

SEMEKA

1008   SEMEKA, ELENA, Ed. <u>Delo</u> <u>Dandarona</u>. Florence: Edizione
        Aurora, 1974; 71 pp.
            Collection of documents pertaining to case of Dandaron,
        scholar of Buddhism.

1009   SEREBROV, FELIKS. "Derzhis', derzhis', ne padai dukhom:
        'Ekaterinskie tiur'my'; 'I svobodnyi razboinichii strug
        . . .'; 'Kameshkovo'; 'Èkspromt'; 'Pila'." KONTINENT:
        No. 18, 1978; pp. 177-81. Poems.

1010   SEVERSKII, IVAN. "'Ishchu cheloveko-bozhestva?'" ["Do I Seek
        a Man-God?"] VESTNIK RKhD (Paris): No. 116, II-III-IV-
        1975; pp. 247-51. Religious essay.

1011   <u>Sfinksy</u>. GRANI (Frankfurt): No. 59, Dec. 1965; pp. 7-77.
            Samizdat journal, dated July 1965, edited by V. Tarsis.
        Contains poetry by V. Aleinikov, V. Batshev, A. Vasiutkov,
        Iu. Vishnevskaia, P. Vladimirov, A. Galich, E. Golovin,
        L. Gubanov, V. Gusev, B. Dubin, V. Kovshin, A. Mironov,
        A. Mikhailov, S. Morozov, D. Samoilov, M. Slavkov, B. Slut-
        skii, Iu. Stefanov, L. Shkol'nik, V. Èrl'; stories by
        Tarsis, A. Usiakin, M. Shelgunov and Mark Èdvin. Certain
        items included in GERSTENMAIER (#375), BOSLEY (#147), LANG-
        LAND et al. (#656).

1012   SHABUTSKII. "Brodiaga." RUS. MYSL' (Paris): Nov. 18, 1971;
        p. 5. Poem.

1013   SHAFAREVICH, IGOR'. [b. 1923] <u>Sotsializm</u> <u>kak</u> <u>iavlenie</u> <u>miro-</u>
        <u>voi</u> <u>istorii</u>. Paris: YMCA, 1975.

        _____. The <u>Socialist</u> <u>Phenomenon</u>. New York: Harper &
        Row, 1981; 317 pp. Tr., W. Tjalsma.

        _____. "Sotsializm i individual'nost'." VESTNIK RKhD
        (Paris): No. 120, I-1977; pp. 117-29. Excerpt dealing
        with equality in Christian and socialist contexts.
            Study of psychological and historical roots of social-
        ism; examines idea of communality from early times through
        the 20th century.

1014   _____. <u>Zakonodatel'stvo</u> <u>o</u> <u>religii</u> <u>v</u> <u>SSSR</u>. [<u>Legislation</u>
        <u>of</u> <u>Religion</u> <u>in</u> <u>the</u> <u>USSR</u>] Paris: YMCA, 1973; 80 pp.

        _____. (CHAFAREVITCH) <u>La</u> <u>législation</u> <u>sur</u> <u>la</u> <u>religion</u>
        <u>en</u> <u>URSS</u>. Paris: Seuil, 1974; 123 pp.
            Reports, by Shafarevich as member of Committee on Human
        Rights, of creation and liquidation of religious societies.

SHAFAREVICH, IGOR': See also AGURSKII et al. (#11), DUDKO (#301, #302).

1015 SHALAMOV, VARLAM. [b. 1907, d. 1982] Kolymskie rasskazy. London: Overseas Pubs. Ltd., 1978; 896 pp.

_____. Kolyma Tales. New York and London: W. W. Norton, 1980; 222 pp. Tr., John Glad.

_____. Graphite. New York and London: W. W. Norton, 1980; 287 pp. Tr., John Glad.

_____. (SCHALAMOW) Artikel 58. Die Aufzeichn. d. Häftlings Schalamow. Cologne: Middelhauve, 1967; 195 pp. Tr., G. Drohla.

_____. (CHALAMOV) Article 58: Memoires du prisonier Chalamov. Paris: Gallimard, 1969; 261 pp. Tr. from German, M. L. Ponty.

_____. (CHALAMOV) Recits de Kolyma. Paris: Les lettres nouvelles, 1969; 255 pp. Tr., Olivia Simon and Katia Kerel.

_____. (SCHALAMOW) Kolyma: Insel im Archipel. Munich: Langen-Müller, 1975; 195 pp. Tr., G. Drohla.
    Collections of stories; contents not identical. All subsequent Shalamov entries are of individual stories published separately. Author was first arrested in 1929, receiving sentence of five years in Solovki, the former monastery turned concentration camp. He was rearrested in 1937, received five years in Kolyma. In 1942 his sentence was extended "till the end of the war"; in 1943 he received an extra 10-year sentence (for having described Bunin as a "classic author of Russian literature"). He spent 17 years in Kolyma. His stories are characterized by flat, dry, documentary-like tone of narrative and offer a detailed picture of life and death in Kolyma.

1016 _____. "Anevrizma aorty"; "Kusok miasa"; "Pripadok"; "Biznesmen"; "Zhenshchina blatnogo mira"; "Sergei Esenin i vorovskoi mir." ["Aortal Aneurism"; "A Piece of Meat"; "The Seizure"; "Businessman"; "Woman of the Criminal World"; "Sergei Esenin and the Thieves' World"] GRANI (Frankfurt): No. 77, Oct. 1970; pp. 15-48.

1017 _____. "Bol'." ["Pain"] NOV. RUS. SLOVO (New York): July 14, 1974; p. 8.

SHALAMOV

1018   SHALAMOV, VARLAM. "Bukinist." ["The Used-Book Dealer"]
NOVYI ZHURNAL (New York): No. 110, March 1973; pp. 5-19.

1019   _____. "Domino." ["Dominoes"] NOVYI ZHURNAL (New York):
No. 118, March 1975; pp. 13-22.

1020   _____. "Dva rasskaza: 'Detskie kartinki'; 'V bane'."
["Children's Pictures"; "In the Bathhouse"] NOVYI ZHURNAL
(New York): No. 120, Sept. 1975; pp. 20-28.

1021   _____. "Dva rasskaza: 'Kaligula'; 'Pocherk'." ["Caligula"; "Handwriting"] POSEV (Frankfurt): No. 1 (1076),
Jan. 7, 1967; pp. 3-4. Eng. tr. of first in SCAMMELL
(#1005).

1022   _____. "Dve vstrechi"; "Bezymiannaia koshka." ["Two
Meetings"; "The Nameless Cat"] NOVYI ZHURNAL (New York):
No. 103, June 1971; pp. 21-30.

1023   _____. "Dve vstrechi"; "Chuzhoi khleb." ["Two Meetings";
"Strange Bread"] VESTNIK RSKhD (Paris): No. 89-90, III-
IV-1968; pp. 90-94.

1024   _____. "Èsperanto"; "Inzhener Kiselev"; "Lagernaia svad'-
ba"; "Tatarskii mulla i chistyi vozdukh"; "Poslednii boi
maiora Pugacheva"; "Po lendlizu"; "Liubov' Kapitana Toli";
"Mendelist"; "Pogonia za parovoznym dymom." ["Esperanto";
"Engineer Kiselev"; "Camp Wedding"; "The Tatar Mullah and
Fresh Air"; "Major Pugachev's Last Battle"; "Captain Toli's
Love"; "In Pursuit of Steam"] GRANI (Frankfurt): No. 76,
July 1970; pp. 16-72.

1025   _____. "Gerkules"; "Iagody." ["Hercules"; "Berries"]
NOVYI ZHURNAL (New York): No. 112, Sept. 1973; pp. 27-32.

1026   _____. "Gorod na gore." ["City on the Hill"] NOVYI
ZHURNAL (New York): No. 107, June 1972; pp. 38-49.

1027   _____. "Grafit"; "Utka." ["Graphite"; "The Duck"]
NOVYI ZHURNAL (New York): No. 101, Dec. 1970; pp. 6-13.

1028   _____. "Kak èto nachalos'." ["How it Began"] NOVYI
ZHURNAL (New York): No. 119, June 1975; pp. 5-15.

1029   _____. "Kolymskie rasskazy: 'Sententsiia'; 'Posylka';
'Kant'; 'Sukhim paikom'." ["Sententiousness"; "The Parcel";
"Kant"; "Dry Rations"] NOVYI ZHURNAL (New York): No. 85,
Dec. 1966; pp. 5-34.

1030   SHALAMOV, VARLAM. "Kolymskie rasskazy: 'Na predstavku';
'Zaklinatel' zmei'." ["On Credit"; "The Snake Charmer"]
NOVYI ZHURNAL (New York): No. 86, March 1967; pp. 5-20.

1031   _____. "Kolymskie rasskazy: 'Krest'; 'Odinochnyi zamer';
'Stlanik'." ["The Cross"; "An Individual Assignment";
"Stlanik"] NOVYI ZHURNAL (New York): No. 89, Dec. 1967;
pp. 7-18.

1032   _____. "Kolymskie rasskazy: 'Sherri-brendi'; 'Sgu-
shchennoe moloko'; 'Plotniki'; 'Khleb'." ["Sherry Brandy";
"Condensed Milk"; "Carpenters"; "Bread"] NOVYI ZHURNAL
(New York): No. 91, June 1968; pp. 5-23.

1033   _____. "Kolymskie rasskazy: 'Nachal'nik politupravle-
niia'; 'Riabokon';' 'Marsel Prust'." ["Chief of Political
Control"; "Sandgrouse"; "Marcel Proust"] NOVYI ZHURNAL
(New York): No. 96, Sept. 1969; pp. 31-43.

1034   _____. "Lend-Lease"; "The Used-Book Dealer." SURVEY
(London): No. 2 (107), Spring 1979; pp. 51-66.

1035   _____. "Nadgrobnoe slovo." ["Eulogy"] NOVYI ZHURNAL
(New York): No. 100, Sept. 1970; pp. 62-75.

1036   _____. "Prichal ada"; "Khrabrye glaza." ["Mooring of
Hell"; "Valiant Eyes"] NOVYI ZHURNAL (New York): No. 108,
Sept. 1972; pp. 15-21.

1037   _____. "Protezy"; "Prokurator Iudei." ["Prosthesis";
"The Procurator of Judea"] NOVYI ZHURNAL (New York): No.
117, Dec. 1974; pp. 47-52.

1038   _____. "Rasskazy: 'Berdy onzhe'; 'Ekzamen'." ["The
Test"] NOVYI ZHURNAL (New York): No. 102, March 1971;
pp. 37-50.

1039   _____. "Raush-narkoz." NOVYI ZHURNAL (New York): No.
125, Dec. 1976; pp. 45-50.

1040   _____. "Smytaia fotografiia." ["The Wiped-Away Photo-
graph"] NOVYI ZHURNAL (New York): No. 111, June 1973;
pp. 5-8.

1041   _____. "Taiga zolotaia." ["Golden Taiga"] NOVYI ZHUR-
NAL (New York): No. 121, Dec. 1975; pp. 6-10.

1042   _____. "Tishina." ["Quiet"] NOVYI ZHURNAL (New York):
No. 113, Dec. 1973; pp. 39-46.

SHALAMOV

1043   SHALAMOV, VARLAM. "V bol'nitsu." ["In the Hospital"] NOVYI
        ZHURNAL (New York): No. 116, Sept. 1974; pp. 78-83.

1044   _____. "Vizit mistera poppa." ["Mister Popp's Visit"]
        NOV. RUS. SLOVO (New York): July 7, 1974; p. 2.

1045   _____. "Vizit mistera Poppa"; "Bol'." ["Mister Popp's
        Visit"; "Pain"] NOVYI ZHURNAL (New York): No. 115, June
        1974; pp. 42-59.

1046   _____. "Za pis'mom"; "Ogon' i voda." ["For the Letter";
        "Fire and Water"] NOVYI ZHURNAL (New York): No. 104,
        Sept. 1971; pp. 29-40.

1047   _____. "Zagovor iuristov." ["Conspiracy of Jurists"]
        NOVYI ZHURNAL (New York): No. 106, March 1972; pp. 31-49.

1048   _____. "Zhitie inzhenera Kipreeva"; "Khleb"; "Liturgia."
        ["The Life of Engineer Kipreev"; "Bread"; "Liturgy"] NOVYI
        ZHURNAL (New York): No. 98, March 1970; pp. 6-23.

        SHALAMOV, VARLAM: See also SCAMMELL (#1005).

1049   SHAVROV, VADIM. [b. 1924] "Vesennie mysli i vospominaniia."
        ["Spring Thoughts and Memories"] GRANI (Frankfurt): No.
        63, March 1967; pp. 97-110.
            Memoir of the son of a Bolshevik revolutionary turned
        religious believer--how and why he became one.

        SHAVROV, VADIM: See also LEVITIN and SHAVROV (#683).

        SHCHUKIN, A.: See Feniks 1 (#336), BOSLEY (#147)

1050   SHEF, GENRIKH (ALEKSANDR [sic]). [b. 1938?] "Figuron-
        chik." ["The Signature"] GLAGOL (Ann Arbor, Mich.):
        No. 2, 1978; pp. 39-64.
            Story, dated 1963, from samizdat collection.

1051   _____. "Mitina ogliadka." ["Mitya's Look Backward"]
        ÈKHO (Paris): No. 2, 1978 (?).
            Story from samizdat collection, dated 1963.

1052   _____. "Moia istoriia s topolem"; "Zhizn' v bespreryvnom
        bege." ["My Story of an Axe"; "Life on the Run"] ÈKHO
        (Paris).
            Stories from samizdat collection, the first from 1963,
        the second 1970.

1053 SHEL'GA. "Suslov M.A." POSEV (Frankfurt): No. 1 (1128),
      Jan. 1968; pp. 12-13.
      From Kolokol; attacks Politburo member for his role in
      the racial policies of Stalin's regime.

SHEL'GUNOV, M.: See Sfinksy (#1011).

SHESTAKOV, V.: See Sintaksis (#1072).

1054 SHIFFERS, EVGENII. [b. 1934] "Skul'ptury i alfavit mastera
      È. Neizvestnogo." ["Sculptures and Alphabet of Master E.
      Neizvestnii"] KONTINENT: No. 8, 1976; pp. 337-47.
      Explores the religious bases of Neizvestnii's art.

1055 SHIMANOV, GENNADII. [b. 1937] "Iz interv'iu sotrudniku samiz-
      datskogo zhurnala 'Evrei v SSSR'." ["From an Interview
      with a Staffmember of the Samizdat Journal 'Jews in the
      USSR'"] VESTNIK RKhD (Paris): No. 121, II-1977; pp. 119-27.
      Shimanov, a nationalist who is often considered an anti-
      Semite, defends here his right to criticize Jews without
      being branded anti-Semitic.

1056 _____. "Zapiski iz krasnogo doma." GRANI (Frankfurt):
      No. 79, April 1971; pp. 101-57.

      _____. Notes from the Red House. Montreal: Monastery
      Press, 1971.

      _____. "Souvenirs de la maison rouge." ESPRIT (Paris):
      No. 416, Sept. 1972.
      About his unlawful confinement in psychiatric hospital
      because of his religious views, his interviews with psy-
      chiatrists and with fellow-inmates.

SHKOL'NIK, L.: See Sfinksy (#1011); BOSLEY (#147).

1057 SHPILLER, VSEVOLOD. "Besedy vo vremia 'passii'." ["Chats
      during the 'Passion'"] VESTNIK RSKhD (Paris): No. 104-
      105, II-III-1972; pp. 5-41. Sermons.

1058 SHRAGIN, BORIS. [b. 1926, em. 1974] (Kh. U.) "Detstvo
      butaforskogo rebenka." ["Childhood of an Illusory Child"]
      VESTNIK RSKhD (Paris): No. 93, III-1969; pp. 68-80.
      Review of Sartre autobiography.

1059 _____. (VENTSOV, LEV) "Dumat'." ["To Think"] VESTNIK
      RSKhD (Paris): No. 98, IV-1970; pp. 93-106.
      Essay on intellectual opposition to dominant tendencies
      inimical to culture, which are embodied in official policy

SHRAGIN

and propaganda as well as in bourgeois consumer mentality. Moral struggle is not enough--he sees a need for a spiritual and cultural struggle. Eng. tr. in MEERSON-AKSENOV and SHRAGIN (#801).

1060 SHRAGIN, BORIS. (Kh.U.) "Opyt zhurnal'noi utopii." ["The Experience of Journalistic Utopia"] VESTNIK RSKhD (Paris): No. 108-109-110, II-III-IV-1973; pp. 6-23.
Letter to Vestnik's editor on his policy of publishing samizdat.

1061 _____. (VENTSOV, LEV) "Poeziia Aleksandra Galicha." ["Galich's Poetry"] VESTNIK RSKhD (Paris): No. 104-105, II-III-1972; pp. 211-28.
Analysis of Galich's oeuvre.

SHRAGIN: See also LITVINOV et al. (#702).

1062 SHVARTS, ELENA. "Kinfiia." GLAGOL (Ann Arbor, Mich.): No. 3, 1981; pp. 117-25. Poem.

1063 _____. "Semeinye predaniia." ["Family Betrayal"] ÈKHO (Paris): No. 3, 1980; pp. 78-99. Story.

1064 SINIAVSKII, ANDREI. [b. 1925, em. 1973] (TERTS) Fantasticheskie povesti. Paris: Institut Littéraire, 1961; 208 pp.

1065 _____. (TERTS) Fantasticheskie povesti. New York: Interlanguage Literary Assoc., 1967; 454 pp.

1066 _____. (TERTS, ABRAM) Fantasticheskii mir Abrama Tertsa. New York: Chekhov, 1966.

_____. (TERTZ) Fantastic Stories. New York: Pantheon, 1963; 213 pp. Tr., Max Hayward and Ronald Hingley.

_____. (TERTZ) Le Verglas. Paris: Feux croisés, 1963; 399 pp. Tr., Sonia Lescaut.

_____. (TERZ) Phantastische Geschichten. Sämtliche Erzählungen. Vienna, Hamburg: Zsolnay, 1967; 350 pp. Tr., Eduard Suslik and Anna Moravec.

_____. (TERTS) On Socialist Realism. New York: Pantheon, 1960; 95 pp. Tr., G. Dennis.

_____. (TERTS) The Trial Begins. New York: Pantheon and London: Harvill, 1960; 128 pp. Tr., Max Hayward.

_____. (TERZ) Der Prozess beginnt und andere Prosa. Frankfurt, Hamburg: Fischer, 1966; 155 pp. Tr., Gisela Drohla and Eduard Suslik.

SINIAVSKII, ANDREI. "The Icicle: A Winter's Tale." EN-
COUNTER (London): Vol. XVIII, No. 2, Feb. 1962; pp. 44-72.
Tr., Max Hayward.

_____. "Pkhentz." ENCOUNTER (London): Vol. XXVI, No. 4,
April 1966; pp. 3-13.

_____. "The Trial Begins." DISSENT (New York): 1959.

_____. "The Trial Begins." ENCOUNTER (London): Vol.
XIV, No. 1, Jan. 1960; pp. 3-37. Tr., Max Hayward.

_____. "You and I." SURVEY (London): No. 41, April
1962; pp. 151-61. Tr., Max Hayward.

_____. (TERTZ) The Makepeace Experiment (Liubimov).
New York: Pantheon, London: Harvill, 1965; 192 pp.
Tr., Manya Harari.

_____. (TERZ) Ljubimow. Hamburg, Vienna: Zsolnay,
1980; 240 pp. Tr., L. Stuart.
Stories, novella and essay; author, together with Iulii
Daniel', was tried Feb. 10-14, 1966 and received a seven-
year camp sentence for publishing his work abroad, for
calling communism a "new religion," for "slandering the
future of human society." The trial itself, far from
frightening into submission the intellectual opposition in
the Soviet Union, served to crystallize it into the Democratic Movement. (GINZBURG, A., #380). The works themselves often apply a surrealist technique, unconventional
language and fantastic grotesquerie in satiric fashion to
various institutions or sacred cows of Soviet society. On
Socialist Realism analyzes Soviet literary dogma in relation to past and present Russian literature; The Trial Begins describes the period of the Doctors' Plot, the last
years of Stalin; it was for these, and Liubimov, that he
was officially charged.

1067   _____. For Freedom of Imagination. New York: Holt,
Rinehart & Winston, 1971; 212 pp. Tr., Laszlo Tikos and
Murray Peppard.

_____. Plaidoyer pour la liberté de l'imagination.
Paris: Hachette, 1973; 256 pp. Tr., Frank Straschitz.
Collection of essays.

1068   _____. "V zashchitu piramidy." GRANI (Frankfurt):
No. 63, March 1967; pp. 114-39.

SINIAVSKII

SINIAVSKII, ANDREI. "V zashchitu piramidy." POSEV (Frankfurt): No. 4 (1079), Jan. 27, 1967; p. 2.

_____. "On Evtushenko." ENCOUNTER (London): Vol. XXVIII, No. 4, April 1967; pp. 33-43.
Critical analysis of Evtushenko's 1965 poem, "Bratsk Station," originally written for Novyi mir but published only in Feniks 1966.

1069   _____. Golos iz khora. London: Stenvalley, 1973 and New York: Octagon, 1974; 338 pp.

_____. Voices of the Chorus. London: Stenvalley, 1974; 339 pp. and New York: Farrar, Straus & Giroux, 1976; 318 pp. Tr., Kyril FitzLyon and Max Hayward.

_____. Une voix dans le choeur. Paris: Seuil, 1974; 304 pp. Tr., A. and M. Aucouturier.

_____. (SINJAWSKIJ) Eine Stimme aus dem Chor. Vienna, Hamburg: Zsolnay, 1974; 366 pp. Tr., Swetlana Geier; Eine Stimme im Chor. Munich: Taschenbuch, 1978.

_____. "Golos iz khora." RUS. MYSL' (Paris): Nov. 15, 1973; p. 5.
Based on letters written to his wife while he was in camp; a sort of diary, mixing musings on literature, art, sex, folklore, etc., with prisoners' conversations.

1070   _____. (TERTS) Mysli vrasplokh. New York: Raus, 1966; 157 pp.

_____. (SINYAVSKY) Unguarded Thoughts. London: Collins & Harvill, 1972; 95 pp. Tr., Manya Harari.

_____. Pensées impromptues. Paris: Bourgois, 1968; 119 pp. Tr., T. Roy.

_____. (TERZ) Gedanken hinter Gittern. Vienna, Hamburg: Zsolnay, 1968; 108 pp. Tr., Hendrik Berinson.

_____. "Thought Unaware." NEW LEADER (New York): July 16, 1965. Tr., Andrew Field and Robert Szulkin.
Collection of aphorisms and thoughts--on art, literature and a variety of other subjects.

1071   _____. (TERTS) Progulki s Pushkinym. London: Collins and Overseas Pub. Interchange, 1975; 178 pp.

SINIAVSKII, ANDREI. (TERTZ) Promenades avec Pouchkine.
Paris: Seuil, 1976; 155 pp. Tr., Louis Martinez.

_____. (SINJAWSKI) Promenaden mit Puschkin. Berlin:
Ullstein, 1977; 186 pp. Tr., S. Geier.
Written in camp (published after emigration); highly
personal and idiosyncratic, impressionistic and intelligent
critique of Pushkin's genius.

SINIAVSKII, ANDREI: See also BRUMBERG (#178), GINZBURG (#380),
Vol'noe slovo No. 14-15 (#1238).

1072   Sintaksis 1-3. GRANI (Frankfurt): No. 58, June 1965;
pp. 95-193.
Moscow-Leningrad samizdat journal, 1959-60. Includes
poems by A. Aronov, V. Burich, N. Glazkov, Vse. Nekrasov,
M. Pavlova, Iu. Pankratov, G. Sapgir, I. Kharabarov, I.
Khomin, S. Chudakov, A. Avrusin, B. Akhmadulina, N. Bialosinskaia, S. Kalashnikov, E. Kotliar, N. Kotrelev, B. Okudzhava, O. Prokofiev, A. Timofeevskii, V. Shestakov, D.
Bobyshev, I. Brodskii, G. Gorbovskii, M. Eremin, S. Kulle,
A. Kushner, E. Rein, N. Slepakova, V. Ufliand and poems
and stories by V. Goliavkin. Edited by Aleksandr Ginzburg.

Sintaksis: see also BOSLEY (#147), LANGLAND et al. (#656).

1073   "Skazka pro Vas'ku nemeshaeva gorodskogo vor." ["Tale of Vas'-
ka the City Thief"] KOVCHEG (Paris): No. 3, 1979; pp. 3-8.
Modern fable.

1074   SKEISHAROV, BORIS. (Pseud.) "O svobode i fashizme." ["On
Freedom and Fascism"] POSEV (Frankfurt): No. 7, July
1974; pp. 20-22.
In defense of Iakir, after the latter's "confession" to
KGB implicating several dissidents. Criticizes those who
attack Iakir rather than Iakir's "torturers," those who
condemn the victim rather than the system.

1075   SLAVINSKY, M., Ed. La Presse Clandestine en URSS, 1960-1970.
Paris: Nouvelles Editions Latines, 1970.
Collection of texts from assorted samizdat sources.

1076   SLAVKOV, MAKAR. "Koshmar." GRANI (Frankfurt): No. 70,
Feb. 1969; pp. 118-19. Poem.

SLAVKOV, MAKAR: See also SMOG (#1080), Sfinksy (#1011).

SLEPAKOVA, N.: See Sintaksis (#1072).

"Slovo natsii"

"Slovo natsii": See "A Word to the Nation." (#1280).

SLUTSKII, B.: See PLISETSKII, GEORGII

1077   SLUTSKII, BORIS. [b. 1919] "Tetrad' stikhov iz Rossii."
        GRANI (Frankfurt): No. 47, July-Sept. 1960; pp. 3-15.
        Poems, subsequently published in Literaturnaia gazeta,
        Nov. 24, 1962.

SLUTSKII, BORIS: See also Sfinksy (#1011).

1078   SMIRNOV, ALEKSEI. "Prevozmogi tosku. . . ." RUS. MYSL'
        (Paris): Nov. 27, 1975; p. 11. Poem.

1079   SMIRNOV, S. S. "Chego zhe ty khokhochesh'?" ["So Why are
        You Laughing?"] POSEV (Frankfurt): No. 6, June 1970;
        pp. 57-59.
        Satiric story from a samizdat anthology of parodies on
        Kochetov's "Chego zhe ty khochesh'?" ["So What Do You
        Want?"]

1080   "SMOG--nezavisimaia literaturnaia organizatsiia molodezhi v
        Rossii obrashchaetsia k svobodnomu miru." ["SMOG-- In-
        dependent Literary Organization of Youth in Russia Appeals
        to the Free World"] POSEV (Frankfurt): No. 7 (1030),
        Feb. 11, 1966; p. 1.

        _____. "S.M.O.G.--nezavisimaia literaturnaia organi-
        zatsiia molodezhi v Rossii obrashchaetsia k svobodnomu
        miru." RUS. MYSL' (Paris): Feb. 17, 1966; p. 5.

        _____. "SMOG--Vozzvanie." GRANI (Frankfurt): No. 61,
        Oct. 1966; pp. 14-15. "Stikhi iz sbornikov SMOGa"; pp.
        18-24.
        Declaration of intent by SMOG, acronym variously given
        as Samoe molodoe obshchestvo geniev (The youngest society
        of geniuses); Smelost', Mysl', Obraz, Glubina (Boldness,
        Thought, Image, Depth); and Szhatyi mig otrazhennoi giper-
        boly (Compressed Instant of Reflected Hyperbole). The
        group generally reacts against Soviet greyness, both social
        and literary, experiments with language. Poetry is by L.
        Gubanov, V. Aleinikov, Iu. Kublanovskii, S. Morozov, Iu.
        Vishnevskaia, M. Slavkov and V. Batchev.

SMOLIANINOVA, T.: See Russkoe slovo (#972).

SMOT: See Vol'noe slovo No. 34 (#1254).

A Critical Guide

SOLNTSEVA, N.: See Russkoe slovo (#972).

SOLODOVNIKOV, A.: See Nadezhda (#827).

1081 SOLOV'EV, OLEG. "Dushevnobol'noi?--Net, sotsial'no opasnyi."
["Mentally Ill?--No, Socially Dangerous"] KONTINENT:
No. 18, 1978; pp. 243-60.
Personal memoir of his life leading up to his arrest in
1969 (for distributing "antigovernment" pamphlets in several cities) and his three-year stay in psychiatric hospitals.

SOLZHENITSYN, ALEKSANDR. [b. 1918, em. 1974]
The following are bibliographies of Solzhenitsyn's
writings:

1082 Donald M. Fiene, Comp. A. Solzhenitsyn: An International
Bibliography of Writings By and About Him. Ann Arbor,
Mich.; Ardis, 1973. Includes works from 1962-1973.

1083 M. Nicholson: "Solzhenitsyn in 1976: A Bibliographical
Reorientation." RUS. LIT. TRIQUARTERLY (Ann Arbor, Mich.):
No. 14, Winter 1976; pp. 464-82.

1084 A. Artemova. "Bibliografiia proizvedenii A. Solzhenitsyna,"
contained in A. Solzhenitsyn, Sobranie sochinenii. Frankfurt: Posev, 1970; Vol. VI, pp. 367-85. Updated in 1973
edition of volume 6.

1085 Francois D'Argent. "Essai de bibliographie d'Alexandre
Soljenitsyne," contained in Nivat and Aucouturier, eds.,
Soljenitsyne. Paris: L'Herne, 1971; pp. 493-511.

1086 J. M. and C. L. Senner. "A. Solzhenitsyn: A Bibliography
of Works by and About Him in German, 1973-1975." RUS. LIT.
TRIQUARTERLY (Ann Arbor, Mich.): No. 14, Winter 1976;
pp. 483-505.

The following list begins with collections of Solzhenitsyn's works and gives content annotation only on subsequent individual listings.

1087 _____. Sobranie sochinenii v shesti tomakh. Frankfurt:
Posev, 1969-1973.

1088 _____. Sochineniia. Frankfurt: Posev, 1968; 316 pp.

1089 _____. Rasskazy. Frankfurt: Posev, 1976; 372 pp.

SOLZHENITSYN

NB. A new multivolume Russian-language collection of Solzhenitsyn's works is currently being published by YMCA; as of Jan. 1982, 9 volumes have appeared.

1090   SOLZHENITSYN, ALEKSANDR. (SOLSCHENIZYN) Die grossen Erzählungen. Munich, Berlin: Herbig, 1974; 448 pp. Tr., W. Loser et al.

1091   _____. (SOLSCHENIZYN) Im Interesse der Sache. Gesammelte Erzählungen. Darmstadt: Luchterhand, 1974; 456 pp. Tr., M. von Holbeck, L. Labas, E. Marin, C. Meng.

1092   _____. (SOLSCHENIZYN) Meistererzählungen. Stuttgart: Europ. Bildungsgemeinschaft; Gütersloh: Bertelsmann; Vienna: Buchgemeinschaft Donauland; Berlin: Dt. Buchgemeinschaft, 1974; 451 pp. Tr., M. von Holbeck et al.

1093   _____. Stories and Prose Poems. London: Bodley Head; 242 pp. and New York: Farrar, Straus & Giroux, 1971; 267 pp. Tr., M. Glenny. Samizdat works included are "Right Hand," "Easter Procession" and 16 "prose poems."

1094   _____. Arkhipelag Gulag, 1918-1956. (Opyt khodozhestvennogo issledovaniia). Paris: YMCA. Parts I-II: 1973; 606 pp. Parts III-IV: 1974; 657 pp. Parts V-VI-VII: 1975; 583 pp.

_____. The Gulag Archipelago. New York and London: Harper & Row. Parts I-II: 1974; 660 pp. Parts III-IV: 1975; 712 pp. Parts V-VI-VII: 1976. Tr., Thomas P. Whitney.

_____. (SOLJENITSINE) L'Archipel du Goulag, 1918-1956. Paris: Seuil. Vol. 1: 1974; 446 pp. Tr., J. Lafond, J. Johannet, R. Marichal, S. Oswald and N. Struve. Vol. 2: 1974; 512 pp. Vol. 3: 1976; 480 pp. Tr., G. and J. Johannet and N. Struve.

_____. (SOLSCHENIZYN) Der Archipel Gulag. Frankfurt: Büchergilde Gutenberg. Vol. 1: 1972; 761 pp. Tr., Anna Peturnig. Vol. 2: Frankfurt: Scherz, 1974; 700 pp. Tr., A. Peturnig. Vol. 3: Frankfurt: Scherz, 1976; 670 pp. Tr., A. Peturnig and E. Walter. Three-volume edition also printed by Rowohlt, 1978.

_____. "Arkhipelag Gulag." NOV. RUS. SLOVO (New York): Jan. 8, 1974; p. 2; Jan. 9, 1974; p. 3; Jan. 10, 1974; p. 3; Jan. 13, 1974; pp. 2, 7.

SOLZHENITSYN, ALEKSANDR. "Arkhipelag Gulag." RUS. MYSL'
(Paris): Jan. 10, 1974; p. 3; Jan. 24, 1974; p. 4; Jan.
31, 1974; p. 5; Feb. 7, 1974; p. 4; Feb. 14, 1974; p. 5;
Feb. 21, 1974; pp. 4, 5; Sept. 12, 1974; p. 5; Sept. 19,
1974; pp. 4, 5; Sept. 26, 1974; pp. 6-7; Oct. 3, 1974;
pp. 4-5.

_____. "Burevestnik na Solovkakh." NOV. RUS. SLOVO
(New York): June 20, 1974; p. 3; June 21, 1974; p. 3.
   Basically, a history of the sufferings of the millions
of inmates in Stalin's camps and prisons, with hundreds of
individual "case histories," many of them (and much of his
information overall) given him by survivors of the Gulag.
Particularly controversial is his interpretation of the
Vlasovites.

1095   _____. Avgust chetyrnadtsatogo. Paris: YMCA, 1971;
573 pp.

_____. August 1914. New York: Farrar, Straus & Giroux,
1972; 622 pp. Tr., Michael Glenny.

_____. (SOLJENITSINE) Août quatorze. Paris: Seuil,
1972; 512 pp. Tr., Michel Aucouturier, Georges Nivat,
Jean-Paul Sémon. Also a two-volume edition put out by
Gallimard (Paris), 1974.

_____. (SOLSCHENIZYN) August neunzehnhundertvierzehn.
Munich: Langen-Müller, 1971; 765 pp. Tr., Alexander
Kaempfe. Also Darmstadt, Neuwied: Luchterhand, 1972; 780
pp. and Stuttgart: Dt. Bücherbund, 1974; 640 pp., both
tr. by Swetlana Geier.

_____. Avgust chetyrnadtsatogo." NOV. RUS. SLOVO (New
York): Aug. 9, 1971; p. 4; Aug. 19, 1971; p. 4.

_____. "Posleslovie Solzhenitsyna k russkomu zarubezh-
nomu izdaniiu 1971 romana 'Avgust chetyrnadtsatogo'."
RUS. MYSL' (Paris): June 24, 1971; p. 2.

_____. "Ètiud o monarkhe." VESTNIK RKhD (Paris): No.
124, I-1978; pp. 153-250. (Previously unpublished
chapter [#67].)
   Historical novel dealing with Russian society on the
eve of World War I and the Russian Army's East Prussian
campaign of Aug. 1914 as seen through the eyes of both
soldiers and commanders.

SOLZHENITSYN

(See also <u>Avgust</u> <u>chetyrnadtsatogo</u> <u>chitaiut</u> <u>na</u> <u>rodine</u>:
<u>sbornik</u> <u>statei</u> <u>i</u> <u>otzyvov</u> [#83].)

1096   SOLZHENITSYN, ALEKSANDR. <u>Bodalsia</u> <u>telenok</u> <u>s</u> <u>dubom</u>. Paris:
YMCA, 1975; 629 pp.

_____. <u>The</u> <u>Calf</u> <u>and</u> <u>the</u> <u>Oak</u>. New York: Harper & Row,
1979; 568 pp. Tr., Harry Willetts.

_____. (SOLJENITSYNE) <u>Le</u> <u>Chêne</u> <u>et</u> <u>le</u> <u>veau</u>: <u>Mémoires</u>
1953-74. Paris: Seuil, 1975; 544 pp. Tr., R. Marichael.

_____. (SOLSCHENIZYN) <u>Die</u> <u>Eiche</u> <u>und</u> <u>das</u> <u>Kalb</u>. <u>Memoiren</u>
1953-74. Darmstadt, Neuwied: Luchterhand, 1976; 711 pp.

_____. "Telenok s dubom." NOV. RUS. SLOVO (New York):
Feb. 20, 1975; p. 2; Feb. 27, 1975; p. 2.
Memoir of his relationship with the literary establish-
ment, especially with <u>Novyi</u> <u>mir</u> and its editor, Aleksandr
Tvardovskii, as well as his battles with the KGB. Portions
appeared in English in <u>Life</u>, <u>Kenyon</u> <u>Review</u> and <u>New</u> <u>York</u>
<u>Times</u> <u>Book</u> <u>Review</u>.

1097   _____. "Dva lagernykh stikhotvoreniia: 'Na sovetskoi
granitse'; 'Rossiia?'" VESTNIK RKhD (Paris): No. 117,
I-1976; pp. 148-57.
Two poems, written in 1951 and 1952.

1098   [_____]. "How People Read 'Ivan Denisovich'." SURVEY
(London): No. 74/75, Winter-Spring 1970; pp. 207-20.
Excerpted reactions from Soviet readers, some of them
grateful ex-zeks, some of them highly critical.

1099   _____. "Ia odin, a klevetnikov sotni: zapis' zasedaniia
sekretariata Soiuza pisatelei s A. Solzhenitsynym." POSEV
(Frankfurt): No. 8 (1135), Aug. 1968; pp. 8-13.
Transcript of the Writers' Union meeting at which Solzhenitsyn was expelled. Eng. tr. included in <u>Solzhenitsyn</u>
(ed., Labedz, #1119).

_____. <u>Iz-pod</u> <u>glyb</u>. See AGURSKII, MIKHAIL et al. (#11).

1100   _____. (SOLJENITSYNE) <u>Krokhotnye</u> <u>rasskazy</u>. Paris:
Cinq Continents, 1970; 32 pp.

_____. <u>Six</u> <u>Etudes</u>. Northfield, Minn.: College City
Press, 1971; 20 pp. Tr., James Walker.

SOLZHENITSYN, ALEKSANDR. Zacharie l'escarcelle. Ètudes et miniatures. La Main Droite. Paris: Julliard, 1971; 144 pp.

_____. (SOLSCHENIZYN) . . . den Oka-Fluss entlang. 15 Kurzgeschichten u. eine Erzählung. Frankfurt: Posev, 1965; 76 pp. Tr., Mary von Holbeck et al.

_____. "Rukopis' iz Rossii: Ètiudy i krokhotnye rass-kazy." GRANI (Frankfurt): No. 56, Oct. 1964; pp. I-XI and No. 80, Sept. 1971; pp. 8-9. The first group published anonymously.

_____. "Ètiudy i krokhotnye rasskazy." POSEV (Frank-furt): No. 4 (975), Jan. 22, 1965; pp. 6-7.

_____. "Puteshestviia vdol' Oki." VESTNIK RSKhD (Paris): No. 75-76, IV-1964; p. 85.

_____. "Breathing." ENCOUNTER (London): Vol. XXIV, No. 3, March 1965; pp. 3-9, Tr., Harry Willetts.

_____. "Means of Motion." RUS. LIT. TRIQUARTERLY (Ann Arbor, Mich.): No. 11, Winter 1975; p. 490.
Short sketches and stories.

1101 _____. Mir i nasilie. Frankfurt: Posev, 1974; 102 pp.

_____. "Mir i nasilie." POSEV (Frankfurt): No. 12, Dec. 1973; pp. 17-20.

_____. "Mir i nasilie." RUS. MYSL' (Paris): Oct. 25, 1973; p. 1.

_____. "Mir i nasilie." NOV. RUS. SLOVO (New York): Oct. 9, 1973; p. 3.

_____. "Mir i nasilie." VESTNIK RSKhD (Paris): No. 108-109-110, II-III-IV-1973; pp. 216-24.

_____. "Peace and Violence." INDEX ON CENSORSHIP (Lon-don): Vol. 2, No. 4, Winter 1973; pp. 47-51. Tr., B. Thornberry and M. Scammell.
Commissioned for Le Monde, which refused originally to print it; it was first published in Aftenposten (Oslo), but circulated immediately in samizdat. Criticizes posi-tion of "advocates of peace," saying that the "peace/war" opposition is false. Rather, the genuine moral opposites are peace and violence. Discusses various forms of

SOLZHENITSYN

    violence, including organized state violence; nominates
Sakharov for Nobel Peace Prize.

1102   SOLZHENITSYN, ALEKSANDR. "Molitva." ["Prayer"] RUS. MYSL'
    (Paris): Sept. 24, 1970; p. 1.

    _____. "Neizdannoe proizvedenie A. Solzhenitsyna--
Molitva." VESTNIK RSKhD (Paris): No. 81, III-1976; p. 22.
Prayer.

1103   _____. Nobelevskaia lektsiia 1970 goda po literature.
Paris: YMCA, 1972; 30 pp.

    _____. The Nobel Lecture in Literature. New York:
Harper & Row, 1972; 38 pp. Tr., Thomas Whitney. London:
Bodley Head, 1972; 27 pp. Tr., BBC Rus. Service. New
York: Farrar, Straus & Giroux, 1972; 69 pp. Tr., F. D.
Reeve. London: Stenvalley, 1973; 55 pp. Tr., N. Bethel.

    _____. (SOLJENITSINE) Les Droits de l'écrivain. Dis-
cours de Stockholm. Paris: Seuil, 1972; 128 pp. Tr.,
M. de La Vega.

    _____. "Nobelevskaia lektsiia 1970 goda po literature."
In Les Prix Nobels en 1971. Stockholm: Imprimerie Royale
P.A. Norstedt & Soner, 1972.

    _____. "Nobelevskaia lektsiia 1970 goda po literature."
GRANI (Frankfurt): No. 85, Oct. 1972; pp. 156-75.

    _____. "Nobelevskaia lektsiia po literature 1970 goda."
RUS. MYSL' (Paris): Sept. 7, 1972; pp. 3-4.

    _____. "Nobelevskaia rech' Solzhenitsyna." NOV. RUS.
SLOVO (New York): Aug. 30, 1972; p. 2; Aug. 31, 1972;
p. 2; Sept. 1, 1972; pp. 2-3.

    _____. "The Nobel Lecture in Literature." The NEW YORK
TIMES: Sept. 30, 1972 and Oct. 7, 1972. Tr., Thomas P.
Whitney.

    _____. "Nobel Prize Speech." INDEX ON CENSORSHIP (Lon-
don): No. 3/4, Autumn/Winter 1972; pp. 11-24. Tr., M.
Scammell.
    Discussion of the role and responsibility of art in
today's world.

1104   _____. "Olen' i shalashovka." GRANI (Frankfurt):
No. 73, Oct. 1969; pp. 3-95.

SOLZHENITSYN, ALEKSANDR. The Love-Girl and the Innocent.
New York: Farrar, Straus & Giroux and London: Bodley
Head, 1969; 131 pp. Tr., Nicholas Bethell and David Burg.

_____. (SOLJENITSINE) La fille d'amour et l'innocent.
Paris: Laffont, 1971; 288 pp. Tr., Alain Prechac. Paris:
L.G.F., 1977; 314 pp.

_____. (SOLSCHENIZYN) Nemow und das Flittchen. Neu-
wied, Berlin: Luchterhand, 1971; 136 pp. Tr., Gisela
Drohla. Play.

1105 _____. "Paskhal'nyĭ krestnyi khod." ["Easter Procession"] VESTNIK RSKhD (Paris): No. 91-92, I-II-1969;
pp. 71-74.

_____. "Paskhal'nyi krestnyi khod." GRANI (Frankfurt):
No. 71, May 1969; pp. 3-6.

_____. "Paskhal'nyi krestnyi khod." RUS. MYSL' (Paris):
March 20, 1969; p. I.
    Sketch/story. Eng. tr. in Stories and Prose Poems
(#1093).

1106 _____. "Pis'mo IV vsesoiuznomu s"ezdu sovetskikh pisatelei." POSEV (Frankfurt): No. 24 (1099), June 16, 1967;
pp. 3-4.

_____. "Pis'mo A. I. Solzhenitsyna." NOV. RUS. SLOVO
(New York): June 18, 1967; p. 8.

_____. "Vmesto vystupleniia: pis'mo IV vsesoiuznomu
s"ezdu sovetsikh pisatelei. V prezidium s"ezdu i delega-
tam. Chlenam SSP. Redaktsiiam literaturnykh gazet i
zhurnalov." RUS. MYSL' (Paris): June 22, 1967; p. 3.

_____. "Pis'mo IV-mu Vsesoiuznomu S"ezdu Sovetskikh
Pisatelei." VESTNIK RSKhD (Paris): No. 84, II-1967;
pp. 5-9.

_____. "Pis'mo A. Solzhenitsyna vsesoiuznomu s"ezdu
sovetskikh pisatelei." GRANI (Frankfurt): No. 66, Dec.
1967; pp. 162-67.

_____. "An Open Letter . . . to the 4th Congress of
Soviet Writers." SURVEY (London): No. 64, July 1967;
pp. 177-81.
    Protest against censorship; asks Union to condemn and
try to abolish it.

SOLZHENITSYN

1107   SOLZHENITSYN, ALEKSANDR. Pis'mo vozhdiam Sovetskogo Soiuza.
         Paris: YMCA, 1974; 51 pp.

         _____. Letter to the Soviet Leaders. London: Collins
         & Harvill and New York: Harper & Row, 1974; 59 pp. Tr.,
         Hilary Sternberg.

         _____. (SOLJENITSINE) Lettre aux dirigeants de l'Union
         soviétique et autres textes. Paris: Seuil, 1974; 135 pp.

         _____. (SOLSCHENIZYN) Offener Brief an die sowjetische
         Führung: Lebt nicht der Lüge. Darmstadt, Neuwied: Luch-
         terhand, 1974; 64 pp. Tr., Wolfgang Kasack.

         _____. "Pis'mo vozhdiam Sovetskogo Soiuza." NOV. RUS.
         SLOVO (New York): March 10, 1974; p. 2.

         _____. "Pis'mo vozhdiam Sovetskogo Soiuza." RUS. MYSL'
         (Paris): March 14, 1974; p. 4; May 23, 1974; p. 5.
         Analysis of the threat of war with China, of the unde-
         sirability of progress (in the sense of industrial growth),
         of the failure of collectivization, of prospects for de-
         velopment of the Northeast of the Soviet Union, and of the
         lies of ideology.

1108   _____. "Pis'mo Vserossisskomu Patriarkhu Pimenu." VEST-
         NIK RSKhD (Paris): No. 103, I-1972; pp. 145-49. Also con-
         tains Sergei Zheludkov's response (pp. 156-58), in which
         he criticizes Solzhenitsyn for attacking a man who is de-
         prived of the opportunity to respond, and for telling only
         part of the truth--that is, for ignoring the severely
         limited sphere of activity of the church and for expecting
         it to be "an island of freedom" in unfree Soviety society.

         _____. A Lenten Letter to Pimen, Patriarch of All Rus-
         sia. Minneapolis: Burgess, 1972; 12 pp. Tr., Keith
         Armes.

         _____. (SOLSCHENIZYN) Ein Fastenbrief an den Allrussi-
         schen Patriarchen Pimen. Witten, Berlin: Eckart, 1972;
         11 pp. Tr., Robert Stupperich.

         _____. "Vserossisskomu Patriarkhu Pimenu: Velikopostnoe
         pis'mo." RUS. MYSL' (Paris): March 30, 1972; p. 3.
         Explores the role of faith and religious education in
         Russia's future, the possibility of replacing a "truth of
         force" philosophy with a "force of truth"; bemoans the loss
         of an ethical Christian atmosphere, which for a thousand
         years fostered morality, a certain world-view, folklore,

etc., and says that this loss should be the Patriarch's
chief concern. See also KARELIN (#503).

1109   SOLZHENITSYN, ALEKSANDR. (SOLSCHENIZYN) Pravaia kist' i
drugie rasskazy/Die rechte Hand und andere Erzählungen.
[The Right Hand] Munich: Dt. Taschenbuch, 1974; 131 pp.
Bilingual ed. Tr., Helmuth Dehio.

_____. "Pravaia kist'." GRANI (Frankfurt): No. 69,
Nov. 1968; pp. I-X.

_____. "Pravaia kist'." VESTNIK RSKhD (Paris): No. 89-
90, III-IV-1968; pp. 80-89.

_____. "Pravaia kist'." NOVYI ZHURNAL (New York):
No. 93, Dec. 1968; pp. 25-35.
Story, Eng. tr. in Stories and Prose Poems (#1093); Fr.
tr. in Zacharie l'escarcelle. . . . (#1100, item 3).

1110   _____. Prusskie nochi: poèma. Paris: YMCA, 1974;
64 pp.

_____. Prussian Nights: a poem. New York: Farrar,
Straus & Giroux, 1977. Tr., R. Conquest. Poem.

1111   _____. Rakovyi korpus: Povest' v dvukh chastiakh.
Paris: YMCA, 1968; 446 pp.

_____. Cancer Ward. New York: Dial, 1968; 616 pp.
Tr., Rebecca Frank. London: Bodley Head; Part I-1968,
Part II-1969; New York: Farrar, Straus & Giroux and Lon-
don, New York: Grosset & Dunlap, 1969; 560 pp. Tr.,
Nicholas Bethell and David Burg.

_____. (SOLJENITSYNE) Le pavillon des cancereux.
Paris: Julliard, 1968; 800 pp. Tr., A. & M. Aucouturier,
L. & G. Nivat, Jean-Paul Sémon.

_____. (SOLSCHENIZYN) Krebsstation. Neuwied, Berlin:
Luchterhand, 1968. Tr., Christina Auras, Agathe Jais and
Ingrid Tinzmann.

_____. "Rakovyi korpus." POSEV (Frankfurt): No. 29
(1104), July 21, 1967; pp. 3-5. (Translated from Slovak)

_____. "Rakovyi korpus. Otryvok iz neopublikovannogo
romana A. Solzhenitsyna. Pravo na lechenie." RUS. MYSL'
(Paris): July 27, 1967; p. 6; Aug. 3, 1967; p. 7. (Translated from Slovak)

SOLZHENITSYN

SOLZHENITSYN, ALEKSANDR. "Rakovyi korpus." NOV. RUS. SLOVO (New York): Aug. 19, 1967; p. 2; August 21, 1967; p. 2.

_____. "Rakovyi korpus." GRANI (Frankfurt): No. 67, March 1968; pp. 5-39.

_____. "Razgovor Shulubina s Kostoglotovym: otryvok iz vtoroi chasti povesti 'Rakovyi korpus'." POSEV (Frankfurt): No. 10 (1137), Oct. 1968; pp. 40-45.
Novel which was the center of a political/literary tornado in 1968; Solzhenitsyn submitted the ms. to Novyi mir, Zvezda and Prostor; it was rejected. Set in 1955, its hero has survived war, prison, camp, exile and recurrent cancer; Solzhenitsyn uses the cancer ward and its range of patients as a microcosm of Soviet society and his hero as an explorer into the meaning of happiness and the value of life.

1112 _____. Svecha na vetru: svet, kotoryi v tebe. Series Student: Flegon Press (London): 11/12, 1968; 80 pp.

_____. "Svecha na vetru: svet, kotoryi v tebe." GRANI (Frankfurt): No. 71, May 1969; pp. 15-77.

_____. Candle in the Wind. Minneapolis: Univ. of Minnesota Press, 1973; 141 pp. Tr., Keith Armes in assoc. with Arthur Hudgins.

_____. (SOLJENITSINE) Flamme au vent. La lumière qui est en toi. Paris: Seuil, 1977; 159 pp.

_____. (SOLSCHENIZYN) Die Republik der Arbeit. Kerze im Wind. Zwei Theaterstücke. Darmstadt, Neuwied: Luchterhand, 1977. Play.

1113 _____. V kruge pervom. New York: Harper & Row, 1968; 515 pp.

_____. V pervom krugu [sic]. Frankfurt: Fischer, 1968; 551 pp.

_____. The First Circle. New York: Harper & Row, 1968; 580 pp. Tr., Thomas P. Whitney. London: Collins & Harvill, 1968; 581 pp. Tr., M. Guybon.

_____. (SOLJENITSINE) Le premier cercle. Paris: Laffont, 1968; 576 pp. Tr., Henri Kybarthi.

SOLZHENITSYN, ALEKSANDR. (SOLSCHENIZYN) <u>Der</u> <u>erste</u> <u>Kreis</u> <u>der</u>
<u>Hölle</u>. Frankfurt: Fischer, 1968; 669 pp. Tr., Elisabeth
Mahler and Nonna Nielsen-Stokkeby.

_____. "Iubiliar: glava iz romana 'V kruge pervom'."
POSEV (Frankfurt): No. 11 (1138), Nov. 1968; pp. 45-48.

_____. "Dialekticheskii materializm--peredovoe mirovoz-
renie: iz polnogo varianta romana 'V kruge pervom'."
KONTINENT: No. 1, 1974; pp. 125-42.

_____. "Na prostore (#44)." VESTNIK RSKhD (Paris):
No. 111, I-1974; pp. 70-89. (Previously unpublished
chapter)

_____. "Tverskoi diadiushka (#61)." VESTNIK RKhD
(Paris): No. 112-113, II-III-1974; pp. 160-73. (Previously unpublished chapter)

_____. "Slovo razrushit beton (#90)." VESTNIK RKhD
(Paris): No. 114, IV-1974; pp. 193-203. (Previously unpublished chapter)
    Novel dealing with prisoners in a special camp (sharash-
ka) who can at any time be sent from this privileged first
circle of hell to its lower depths.

1114   [_____]. Zhit' ne po lzhi. Paris: YMCA, 1975; 208 pp.
    Collection (which circulated in samizdat in 1974) deal-
ing with facets of <u>Gulag</u>: its publication, slander of
Solzhenitsyn; his deportation; letters and statements defending Solzhenitsyn; excerpts from Soviet press.

1115   _____. "Zhit' ne po lzhi!" ["Don't Live By the Lie!"]
VESTNIK RSKhD (Paris): No. 108-109-110, II-III-IV-1973;
pp. vii-3.

_____. "Zhit' ne po lzhi!" NOV. RUS. SLOVO (New York):
March 16, 1974; p. 3.

_____. "Zhit' ne po lzhi!" RUS. MYSL' (Paris): March
21, 1974; p. 3.

_____. "Zhit' ne po lzhi." POSEV (Frankfurt): March
1974; pp. 8-10.
    "Let us at least refuse to say what we do not think"--
not to participate in lies or consciously support them.

SOLZHENITSYN

Below are entries pertaining to the "Solzhenitsyn Affair":

1116 SOLZHENITSYN, ALEKSANDR et al. "Delo Solzhenitsyna." ["The Solzhenitsyn Affair"] NOVYI ZHURNAL (New York): No. 93, Dec. 1968; pp. 220-68; No. 94, March 1969; pp. 145-60.

1117 _____. "Dokumenty po delu Aleksandra Solzhenitsyna." ["Documents on the Solzhenitsyn Affair"] POSEV (Frankfurt): No. 3 (1130), March 1968; pp. 18-20.

1118 _____. "Ia odin, a klevetnikov sotni: zapis' zasedaniia sekretariata Soiuza pisatelei s A. Solzhenitsynym." ["I am one, the Slanderers Hundreds: Transcript of the Meeting Between the Writers' Union and A. Solzhenitsyn"] POSEV (Frankfurt): No. 8 (1135), Aug. 1968; pp. 8-13.

1119 _____. Solzhenitsyn: A Documentary Record. Leopold Labedz. New York: Harper & Row, 1971; 229 pp.; London: Penguin, 1972; 387 pp.; Bloomington, Ind.: Indiana Univ. Press, 1973.

1120 _____. Les Droits de l'écrivain: Alexandre Soljenitsyne. Paris: Seuil, 1969.

1121 _____. Bestraft mit Weltruhm: Dokumente zu dem Fall Alexander Solzhenizyn. Ed., Elena Guttenberger. Frankfurt: Posev, 1970.

1122 _____. Über Solschenizyn. Aufsätze, Berichte, Materialien. Neuwied, Darmstadt: Luchterhand, 1973.

1123 _____. Soljenitsyne. Paris: L'Herne, 1971. Ed., Georges Nivat and Michel Aucouturier.
Basically, these documents pertain to the campaign against Solzhenitsyn mounted by the regime, samizdat statements in his defense, the controversies surrounding honors accorded him (such as the Nobel Prize), the debate between "liberals" and "conservatives" over the implications of Solzhenitsyn's statements and fictions, etc. Many individual items are also contained in BRUMBERG (#178), and additional material is to be found in "Svidetel'stva iz SSSR" (#1143).

SOLZHENITSYN, ALEKSANDR: See also AGURSKII et al. (#11), KAVERIN (#508), KARELIN (#503) and INDEX: SOLZHENITSYN.

1124 SOLSCHENIZYN, SCHELUDKOW, KARELIN u.a. Kirche und Politik in der Sowjetunion heute. Zurich: Die Arche, 1973; 112 pp. Tr., Felix Ingold.

Collection of essays, letters, etc. on the church, including the argument among the three listed authors on
Solzhenitsyn's "Letter to Pimen" (#1108).

1125 SOMOV, GEORGII. "Blue Devils." NOVYI ZHURNAL (New York):
      No. 138, June 1980; pp. 5-20. (Title in English)
      Chapter of novel entitled Pushkin.

1126 _____. "Pushkin: Pokhishchenie Ganimeda." ["The Abduc-
      tion of Ganymede"] NOVYI ZHURNAL (New York): No. 140,
      Sept. 1980; pp. 73-89. First chapter of novel.

1127 _____. "Pushkin: Sgovor." ["The Deal"] NOVYI ZHURNAL
      (New York): No. 141, Dec. 1980; pp. 5-57.
      Chapter of novel.

      SOPROVSKII, A.: See Moskovskoe vremia (#817).

1128 SOROKIN, VIACHESIAV. "K probleme dvizheniia." ["On the Prob-
      lem of Movement"] GRANI (Frankfurt): No. 61, Oct. 1966;
      pp. 203-33.
      Analysis of Hegelian philosophy.

1129 "Sovetskaia paskhal'naia." (Anon.) RUS. MYSL' (Paris):
      April 20, 1968; p. 6. Poem.

1130 "Soviet Mental Prisons." SURVEY (London): No. 77, Autumn
      1970; pp. 175-87; No. 4 (81), Autumn 1971; pp. 111-64.
      Samizdat material from various sources on psychiatric
      treatment of dissidents; includes items on Bukovskii,
      Zhores Medvedev, Ol'ga Iofe and Petr Grigorenko.

      STEFANOV, IURII: See Feniks 1 (#336), Sfinksy 1 (#1011),
      Feniks 1966 (#337), BOSLEY (#147).

1131 STEPLOV, ALEKSEI. "Obraztsovoe uchrezhdenie." ["Model In-
      stitution"] RUS. MYSL' (Paris): Sept. 4, 1975; p. 8.
      Story.

1132 "Stikhi: 'Akademik'; 'Vybor'; 'Vyzov'; 'Arlekinada'; 'Pesnia
      o liudiakh'; 'Ubiitsy'; 'Sotsrealizm'; 'Veter s voli'."
      (Anon.) NOVYI ZHURNAL (New York): No. 71, March 1963;
      pp. 128-32. Poems.

1133 "Stikhi iz Rossii: 'Vesenee'; 'V al'bom Èlize'; 'Nakhodka na
      tolkuchem ryn'ke'." GRANI (Frankfurt): No. 49, Jan.-
      July 1961; pp. 12-13. Poems.

"Stikhi

1134   "Stikhi iz Rossii." (Anon.) VREMIA I MY (Tel Aviv): No. 4,
        Feb. 1976; pp. 83-87. Poems.

1135   "Stikhi o Kamchatke." (Anon.) NOVYI ZHURNAL (New York):
        No. 76, June 1964; pp. 55-75. Poems.

1136   "Stikhi o tsare Nikite." (Anon.) NOVYI ZHURNAL (New York):
        No. 81, Dec. 1965; pp. 200-208. Poems.

1137   STRATANOVSKII, SERGEI. "Stikhi." ÈKHO (Paris): No. 4,
        1978. Poems.

1138   STRUGATSKIE, ARKADY and BORIS. [b. 1925 and 1933] Gadkie
        lebedi. [Ugly Swans] Frankfurt: Posev, 1972; 267 pp.

        _____. "Gadkie lebedi: Otryvok iz povesti." GRANI
        (Frankfurt): No. 84, July 1972; pp. 3-19.
        Antiutopian science fiction, giving bleak picture of
        the blind alley into which contemporary society is heading.
        The heroes of the novel are the outcasts, who live in a
        leprosorium behind barbed wire, living on spiritual food
        (one, deprived of books for several days, dies of hunger)
        and the questing children of the city, who eventually join
        with the outcasts to throw out the city elders and build a
        new life.

1139   _____. Ulitka na sklone; Skazka o troike. [Snail on the
        Slope; Tale of the Troika] Frankfurt: Posev, 1972.

        _____. "Skazka o troike." GRANI (Frankfurt): No. 78,
        1970; pp. 38-165.

        _____. (STRUGATZKI) Die Schnecke am Abhang. Frankfurt:
        Suhrkamp, 1978. Tr., A Földcak.
        Both works were officially published in provincial
        journals (the first in Baikal, Nos. 1-2, 1968; the second
        in Angara, Nos. 4-5, 1968) but the journals were immediate-
        ly removed from circulation, the editor (of Baikal, at
        least) fired. Both are stories of the grotesque; the sec-
        ond is the more straightforwardly satiric, describing a
        group who take power at the Institute NOOTHIING and organ-
        ize a Troika on the Rationalization and Utilization of Un-
        explained Phenomena. They circulated in samizdat after
        their official de-publication.

1140   "Sud'ba russkoi stolitsy." ["The Fate of the Russian Capi-
        tal"] (Anon.) GRANI (Frankfurt): No. 84, July 1972;
        pp. 120-67.

Svobodnaia

From samizdat journal <u>Veche</u> No. 1; author wants conser-
vation and restoration of all that remains of ancient Moscow, giving examples of some successful preservation and
historical statistics; undertone of anti-Masonic and anti-
Semitic hysteria.

1141 [SUPERFIN, G.] [b. 1944] "Sud nad G. Superfinom." VESTNIK
RKhD (Paris): No. 114, IV-1974; pp. 271-84.
Excerpts from trial transcript of May 1974, which resulted in Superfin's receiving sentence of five years'
strict regime and two years' exile; he was one of the editors of <u>Khronika tekushchikh sobytii</u>. See also <u>Kh</u>. <u>Tek</u>.
<u>sob</u>. Nos. 30, 32 (#541, #542).

1142 "Svet vo t'me. (Poètika drevneslavianskikh tekstov. Pechat'
ognepal'naia. Zhizn' sokrovennaia. Gost'. Neistoshchi-
maia nit'. Zvezda. Troechastie.)" VESTNIK RSKhD (Paris):
No. 50, III-1958; pp. 48-51.
Anonymous poems written between 1945 and 1954.

1143 "Svidetel'stva iz SSSR." VESTNIK RKhD (Paris): No. 111, I-
1974; pp. 111-35.
Collection of short letters and statements defending
Solzhenitsyn, by, among others, Barabanov, Regel'son,
Kopelev.

1144 SVIRSKII, GRIGORII. [b. 1921, em. 1972] "Why?" SURVEY
(London): No. 2 (83, Spring 1972; pp. 160-67.
Open letter to friends explaining his reasons for emi-
grating to Israel; the author, regularly published in official press before 1965, in 1965 protested at a Writers'
Union meeting against anti-Semitism; in 1968, after defense of Solzhenitsyn and protests against censorship, was
kicked out of party, in 1971 out of the Writers' Union.

1145 _____. <u>Zalozhniki</u>. Paris: Reunis, 1974.

_____. <u>Hostages</u>. New York: Knopf, 1976; 305 pp.
Novel-documentary; exposé of official anti-Semitism
based on experiences of his family and himself from war
years through 1960s.

<u>Svobodnaia mysl'</u>: See <u>Vol'noe slovo</u> No. 7 (#1232).

T

1146   TABACHNIK, B. "Vsego-Diche." NOVYI ZHURNAL (New York): No.
        114, March 1974; pp. 74-94. (Title is name of village)
        Story.

1147   TAGER, ELENA. [b. 1895, d. 1964] "Dnevnik chitatelia. Dva
        stikhotvoreniia iz Rossii." RUS. MYSL' (Paris): Nov. 29,
        1966; p. 4. Poems.

1148   _____. "O Mandel'shtame." ["About Mandel'shtam"] NOVYI
        ZHURNAL (New York): No. 81, Dec. 1965; pp. 172-99.
            Poet, arrested in 1920, again in 1939, and who spent 10
        years in Kolyma and 6 years in exile, remembers her first
        readings of and meetings with Mandel'shtam before the re-
        volution, in 1920, and in 1933, when she attended the in-
        famous reading in the Leningrad Dom pechati, where Mandel'-
        shtam was asked publicly to comment on Soviet poetry, a
        provocation meant to humiliate (and perhaps legally en-
        trap) the poet. Excerpts of her memoirs appear in the
        first volume of MANDEL'SHTAM, Sobranie sochienii v trekh
        tomakh (#732), some anonymously.

1149   TALANTOV, BORIS. [b. 1903, d. 1971] "Bedstvennoe polozhenie
        Pravoslavnoi Tserkvi v Kirovskoi oblasti i rol' Moskovskoi
        Patriarkhii." ["The Calamitous Situation of the Orthodox
        Church . . . and the Role of the Moscow Patriarch"] VEST-
        NIK RSKhD (Paris): No. 83, I-1967; pp. 29-64.
            Describes the closings and destruction of churches in
        the Kirov region during anti-religious campaign of 1959-
        64, and puts part of the blame on the Moscow Patriarch.

1150   _____. "Zhaloba General'nomu Prokuroru SSSR ot B. V.
        Talantova." ["Complaint to the General Prosecutor of the
        USSR"] VESTNIK RSKhD (Paris): No. 89-90, III-IV-1968;
        pp. 49-68.

        _____. "Zhaloba." POSEV (Frankfurt): No. 11 (1138),
        Nov. 1968; pp. 53-60.
            Reveals continuing repressions against believers and
        growing self-consciousness and self-confidence of believ-
        ers; describes his own experiences with KGB because of
        signing letter re religious repressions and general activi-
        ties on behalf of believers.

1151   TALANTOV, BORIS et al. "Ego Sviateishestvu, Sviateishemu
        Patriarkhu Moskovskomu i vseia Rusi, Alekseiiu." ["To His
        Holiness Aleksii, Patriarch of Moscow and all Russia"]
        VESTNIK RSKhD (Paris); No. 82, IV-1966; pp. 3-20.
            Protesting religious repressions and holding the Patri-
        arch partly responsible.

1152   TARSIS, VALERII. [b. 1906, em. 1966] "Iskateli zhemchuga."
GRANI (Frankfurt): No. 64, June 1967; pp. 79-80.
Poem, from <u>Noch'</u> <u>razvoditsia</u> <u>s</u> <u>dnem</u>.

1153   _____. "Nichego dostovernogo"; "Ivan Suma--razrushitel'
mira." ["Inauthentic"; "Ivan Suma--Destroyer of the
World"] GRANI (Frankfurt): No. 61, Oct. 1966; pp. 25-54.
Stories.

1154   _____. <u>Palata</u> No. 7. Frankfurt: Posev, 1966; 148 pp.

_____. <u>Ward 7</u>. New York: Dutton and London: Collins
& Harvill, 1965; 159 pp. Tr., Katya Brown.

_____. <u>Salle 7</u>. <u>La perspective des fous</u>. Paris: Plon,
1966; 191 pp. Tr., Serge Tuli.

_____. <u>Botschaft aus dem Irrenhaus</u>. Frankfurt: Posev,
1965; 180 pp. Tr., Elimar Schubbe.

_____. "Palata No. 7." GRANI (Frankfurt): No. 57,
Jan. 1965; pp. 9-110.

_____. "Golgofa." POSEV (Frankfurt): No. 15 (986),
April 9, 1965; pp. 4-8.
Novel depicting author's involuntary confinement in
psychiatric ward (in 1962-63).

1155   _____. <u>Skazanie o sinei mukhe</u>. <u>Krasnoe i chernoe</u>.
[<u>Tale of the Blue Fly</u>. <u>The Red and the Black</u>] Frankfurt:
Posev, 1963; 168 pp.

_____. <u>Die blaue Fliege--Rot und Schwarz</u>. Munich:
Hanser, 1965. Tr., Josef Hahn.

_____. "Skazanie o sinei mukhe." GRANI (Frankfurt):
No. 52, Dec. 1962; pp. 5-85. (Published anonymously)
Satire on Soviet elite, set in philosophic/scientific
institute; its hero, Ivan Sinemukhov (Bluefly) writes a
seditious piece and comes into conflict with his colleagues and the authorities.

1156   _____. "Veselen'kaia zhizn'." GRANI (Frankfurt): No.
54, Nov. 1963; pp. 3-62; No. 55, June 1964; pp. 3-83.

_____. The Pleasure Factory. London: Collins & Mar-
vill, 1967; 224 pp. Tr., Michael Glenny.

TARSIS

TARSIS, VALERII. "Iz romana 'Veselen'kaia zhizn'." POSEV
(Frankfurt): No. 4 (923), Jan. 24, 1964; pp. 6-7. Novel.

TARSIS, VALERII: See also Sfinksy, which he edited and which
contains one story by him (#1011).

1157 Tashkentsii protsess. [Tashkent Trial] Amsterdam: Herzen,
1976. Texts and documents pertaining to Crimean Tatars.

1158 TENIN, VLAD. Moscow Nights. New York: Olympia, 1971; 288
pp. Tr., Michel le Lasque.
Pornographic novel, very questionable samizdat as place
and date of writing are unknown.

1159 TERNOVSKII, EVGENII. [b. 1941, em. 1974] "Byvaet tak. . . ."
RUS. MYSL' (Paris): March 13, 1975; p. 8. Poem.

1160 _____. "Gody bezvremenshchiny." ["Years of Timeless-
ness"] VESTNIK RSKhD (Paris): No. 108-109-110, II-III-IV-
1973; pp. 174-86.
Analysis of monologic vs. dialogic structure of Maksimov's Seven Days of Creation.

TIMOFEEVSKII, A.: See Sintaksis (#1072).

TOPOLEV, S.: See MEERSON-AKSENOV and SHRAGIN (#801) and
Vol'noe slovo No. 7 (#1232).

1161 "Traktat o prelestiakh knuta." ["Tract on the Charms of the
Knout"] (Anon.) NOVYI KOLOKOL (London): 1972; pp. 55-74.
Sardonic response to Molodaia gvardiia article ("O
tsennostiakh otnositel'nykh i vechnykh," by S. Semanov;
No. 8, 1970) marking 1937 as the year "equality before the
law" was achieved by Soviet citizens.

1162 37. VESTNIK RKhD (Paris): No. 123, IV-1977. Items from
Leningrad samizdat journal which contains translations,
poems, articles, historical texts and letters, etc., edited
by Viktor Krivulin, Tat'iana Goricheva, Lev Rudkevich. Reprinted in Vestnik are the following items:

T. GORICHEVA: "Anonimnoe khristianstvo v filosofii";
["Anonymous Christianity in Philosophy"] pp. 70-85, on
the love of truth and the love of Christ.
T. FEDOROV: "Khristianin i sotsial'naia zhizn'"; ["The
Christian and Social Life"] pp. 86-88, on Christian con-
servatism vs. political conservatism.

B. GROIS: "Dostoevskii i Kirkegor"; pp. 89-110, on the re-
lationship between Dostoevskii's thought and Kierkegaard's.
I. BURIKHIN: "Piat' stikhotvoreniia: 'V tserkvi';"
pp. 111-14, poems.
V. KRIVULIN: "Shest' stikhotvorenii v pamiat' Tat'iane
Grigorevne Gnedich"; pp. 115-19; poems--'Na puti v Push-
kin'; 'Fleita vremeni'; 'Klio'; 'Kotoryi chelovek. . .';"
"Odin den' v Pechorak," on religious meetings (pp. 120-26).
D.S.: "Pushkin i Brodskii"; pp. 127-39, on parallels in
language and use of myth in Pushkin and Brodskii's poetry.
A. KALOMIROV: "Problema sovremennoi russkoi poèzii: I.
Brodskii"; ["Problems of Contemporary Russian Poetry: I.
Brodskii"] pp. 140-51, an analysis of Brodskii's poetic
development.
V. AZARIAN: "Taina russkoi dushi skvoz' belyi èkran";
["The Secret of the Russian Soul on the Blank Screen"]
pp. 152-68, on Tarkovskii's film "Andrei Rublev" and Chris-
tianity.

Vestnik also printed from 37: S. Stratanovskii's "Skomo-
rosh'i stikhi," "Obvodnyi kanal" and "Kolybel'nye stikhi,"
No. 121, II-1977; pp. 303-305, poems, and V. Aleinikov's
"Fontan u okna," in No. 118, II-1976.

37: See also BURIAKOVSKAIA, G. (#212), SHVARTS, E. (#1062).

1163 TRIFONOV, GENNADII. [b. 1949] "Kogda v druz'iakh--lish'
kamni: 'Pis'mo iz tiur'my'; 'O, net, ne plachu ia, ne
plachu. . .'; 'Byt' vechno v mal'chikakh, kogda. . .';
'Perevedi mne nenavist' tvoiu. . .'; 'O, tol'ko by ne
poteriat' tebia. . .'; 'Pered knigoi'; 'Tri mimoletnykh
dnia. . .'; 'Proshchai, govoriu, i prosti'; 'Tseluiu tebia!
Govoriu: . .'; 'Komu-to tvoi znachok v nochi. . .'."
VREMIA I MY (New York/Paris/Jerusalem): No. 48, Dec. 1979;
pp. 88-94. Poems.

TROIANOVSKAIA, E.: See Nadezhda (#827).

1164 "Truba." (Anon.) RUS. MYSL' (Paris): May 18, 1972; p. 4.
Poem.

TSEST, ARKADII: See BOKOV, NIKOLAI

1165 TSETLIN, M. "Favn." RUS. MYSL' (Paris): April 2, 1970;
p. 4. Poem.

1166 TSVETAEVA, MARINA. [b. 1892, em. 1922, returned 1939, d.
1941] "Iz 'Povesti o Sonechke'." ["Story about Sonia"]
VESTNIK RKhD (Paris): No. 116, IV-1975; pp. 166-78.

TSVETAEVA

Story, written in 1937. Vestnik's editors do not give
source, which may be personal archive, for this or subsequent entries.

1167 TSVETAEVA, MARINA. "Neizdannoe stikhotvorenie: 'Viacheslavu
Ivanovu'." VESTNIK RKhD (Paris): No. 118, II-1976;
p. 232. Poem dated 1920.

1168 _____. "Neizdannye stikhi Mariny Tsvetaevoi." VESTNIK
RSKhD (Paris): No. 100, II-1971; pp. 217-23.
Cycle of Love poems written 1917-1918.

1169 _____. "Piat' neizdannykh stikhotvorenii Mariny Tsvetae-
voi: 'Uzkii, nerusskii stan'; 'Polnolun'e i mekh medvezhii';
'Rvan'; 'Pamiati Beranzhe'; 'S verbochkoi svetlosherstoi'."
VESTNIK RKhD (Paris): No. 114, IV-1974; pp. 204-206.
Poems dating from 1915-1918.

1170 TUMERMAN, ALEKSEI. "Delo V. K. Bukovskogo." NOV. RUS. SLOVO
(New York): March 1, 1972; p. 2; March 2, 1972; p. 2;
March 3, 1972; p. 2; March 4, 1972; p. 2; March 8, 1972;
p. 2; March 9, 1972; p. 2; March 10, 1972; p. 2; March 11,
1972; p. 2; March 13, 1972; p. 2; March 14, 1972; p. 2.
Transcript of Bukovskii's trial on Jan. 5, 1972; he was
charged with systematically circulating "slanderous" anti-
Soviet material on psychiatric repression of dissidents,
and was sentenced to two years' prison, five years' exile.

TURCHIN, VALENTIN. [b. 1931, em. 1977] Inertsiia strakha.
New York: Khronika, 1977.

1171 _____. The Inertia of Fear and the Scientific World-
view. New York: Columbia Univ. Press, 1981; 300 pp.
Tr., Guy Daniels.
Critique of Soviet regime and the totalitarian legacy
of its founders, its moral and intellectual stagnation--
based on his experiences and training as a cyberneticist.

TURCHIN, VALENTIN: See also SAKHAROV, TURCHIN and MEDVEDEV
(#988), LITVINOV et al. (#702).

1172 TVARDOVSKII, ALEKSANDR. [b. 1910, d. 1971] "Pis'mo A. Tvardovskogo K. Fedinu." ["Letter to Fedin"] POSEV (Frankfurt): No. 10 (1137), Oct. 1968; pp. 6-10.

_____. "Letter." (Under "Documents: Soviet Union")
SURVEY (London): No. 69, Oct. 1968; pp. 112-21.
Defends Solzhenitsyn, Cancer Ward; criticizes Fedin for
his actions in the Solzhenitsyn affair.

1173   TVARDOVSKII, ALEKSANDR. "Pis'mo A. T. Tvardovskogo k N. Ia.
        Mandel'shtam." VESTNIK RSKhD (Paris): No. 108-109-110,
        II-III-IV-1973; pp. 187-88.
        His response to the manuscript of her memoirs.

1174   _____. "Po pravu pamiati." POSEV (Frankfurt): No. 10,
        Oct. 1969; pp. 52-53.
        Poem (rejecting his earlier defense of collectivization).

TVARDOVSKII, ALEKSANDR: See also BRUMBERG (#178)

1175   [TVERDOKHLEBOV, ANDREI.] "Two Searches and Four Interroga-
        tions." INDEX ON CENSORSHIP (London): No. 3, Autumn 1975;
        pp. 56-67.
        Repressions against human rights activist and dissident.
        Also in Khr. zashch. prav No. 14 (#581).

TVERDOKHLEBOV, ANDREI: See also CHALIDZE, VALERII, Ed.,
Andrei Tverdokhlebov: V zashchitu prav cheloveka (#221),
ALMANAKH SAMIZDATA, No. 2 (#50).

U

1176   UDELOV, F. I. "Dostoevskii i Optina Pustyn'." ["Dostoevskii
       and Optina Pustyn'"] VESTNIK RSKhD (Paris): No. 99, I-
       1971; pp. 4-16.
          On characters in Brothers Karamazov and members of mon-
       astery on whom they were modeled.

1177   _____. "Monastyr' i mir." ["The Monastery and the
       World"] VESTNIK RKhD (Paris): No. 117, I-1976; pp. 23-28.
       Personal reminiscence of Optina Pustyn'.

1178   UFLIAND, VLADIMIR. "Rifmovannaia okolesitsa." ["Rhythmic
       Rubbish"] ÈKHO (Paris): No. 3, 1980; pp. 90-116. Story.

       UFLIAND, VLADIMIR: See also Sintaksis No. 3 (#1072), BOSLEY
       (#147).

1179   Ukrainskii visnyk/Ukrainian Herald. Issues 7-8. Baltimore.
       Smoloskyp, 1976; 209 pp. Original compiler, Maksym Sahay-
       dak; tr. and ed., Olena Saciuk and Bohdan Yasen.
          Includes demographic statistics on "ethnocide" of
       Ukrainians, plus much information on the specific policies
       of russification, such as destruction of Ukrainian churches,
       monuments, persecution of intelligentsia, etc. Also con-
       tains poems by Maksym Sahaydak, and editors have added
       biographical notes on major figures mentioned in text.
       Smoloskyp has published previous issues, as well as Ukrayin-
       sky Pravozakhysny Rokh, documents of Kiev Ukrainian Hel-
       sinki Group.

1180   UL'IANSKII, ANTON. [d. early 1930s] "Mokhnatyi pidzhachok."
       ["The Fleecy Jacket"] GRANI (Frankfurt): No. 69, Nov.
       1968; pp. 99-106.
          Story. Eng. tr. in SCAMMELL (#1005).

1181   _____. "Krivym putem." ["By a Crooked Path"] GRANI
       (Frankfurt): No. 72, July 1969; pp. 93-149. Story.

1182   URUSOV, ALEKSANDR. "Krik dalekikh murav'ev." ["The Cry of
       Distant Ants"] GRANI (Frankfurt): No. 60, June 1966;
       pp. 3-10. Story, from SMOG, April 1965.

       USIAKIN, A.: See Sfinksy (#1011).

       USTINOVA, N.: See Feniks 1966 (#337).

V

1183 "V chem zhe vinovat otets Pavel Adel'geim?" VESTNIK RSKhD
(Paris): No. 106, IV-1972; pp. 320-38. Essay.

1184 V. M. "N. Gorbanevskoi"; "Vstrecha." RUS. MYSL' (Paris):
Jan. 20, 1972; p. 5. Poems.

1185 V. S. "Lavirovanie ili povorot?" ["Maneuver or Turnaround?"]
POSEV (Frankfurt): No. 1 (1128), Jan. 1968; pp. 11-12.
Warns of dangers of new Stalinism. From samizdat
journal Kolokol.

1186 VADOT. K. "Dolli." NOVYI ZHURNAL (New York): No. 119, June
1975; pp. 18-25.
Remniscence of woman whom the author met in camp and
who was shot.

1187 _____. "V zhenskom rabochem lagere." ["In the Women's
Work-Camp"] NOVYI ZHURNAL (New York): No. 115, June 1974;
pp. 182-99; No. 116, Sept. 1974; pp. 253-64.
Author spent 1948-56 in a camp and describes a New
Year's celebration, the building of a railway, and the
daily life of women prisoners.

1188 VAKHTIN, BORIS. [b. 1932, d. 1981] "Nishchii, golubiu
podai!"; "Ee lichnoe delo"; "Kak slozhilas' zhizn' moia."
TRET'IA VOLNA (Paris): No. 5, 1979; pp. 42-52.
Poem and two stories ("Her Personal Affair"; "How My
Life Got Complicated").

1189 _____. "Odna absoliutno schastlivaia derevnia." ["One
Perfectly Happy Village"] ÈKHO (Paris): No. 2, 1978.
Story.

1190 _____. "Stikhi." ÈKHO (paris): No. 4, 1979. Poems.

1191 _____. "Van'ka-Kain." ["Johnny-Cain"] VREMIA I MY
(New York/Paris/Jerusalem): No. 14, 1976. Story.

1192 VARGA, EVGENII. "Rossiiskii put' perekhoda k sotsializmu i
ego rezul'taty." ["The Russian Path to Socialism and its
Results"] GRANI (Frankfurt): No. 68, July 1968; pp. 138-
56; No. 69, Nov. 1968; pp. 134-53.

_____. (Vargi [sic]) "Vyderzhka. . . ." POSEV (Frank-
furt): No. 4 (1079), Jan. 27, 1967; p. 2.
Analysis of economic development in early years after
the Revolution, what path Lenin foresaw for socialism and
the roles of the proletariat, peasants and bourgeoisie.
From Feniks 1966; according to Feniks editors, authorship
uncertain.

VARLAMOVA

1193   VARLAMOVA, I. "Mnimaia zhizn'." ["Imaginary Life"] VREMIA I
       MY (New York/Paris/Jerusalem): No. 31, July 1978; pp. 5-
       76; No. 32, Aug. 1978; pp. 5-75. Novel.

1194   VASIL'EVA, ELIZAVETA. [b. 1887, d. 1928] "Peterburgu."
       NOVYI ZHURNAL (New York): No. 139, June 1980; p. 47.
       Poem, dated St. Petersburg, 1922.

1195   _____. "Rossii." NOVYI ZHURNAL (New York): No. 141,
       Dec. 1980; pp. 105-107. Poem dated Ekaterinodar, 1922.

       VASILEVSKAIA, V.: See Pamiat' (#896).

1196   VASILII. (Pseud.) "Chudesa khimii." ["The Miracles of
       Chemistry"] RUS. MYSL' (Paris): April 6, 1972; p. 7.
       Play. Author later identified as Bokov.

1197   _____. "Smekh posle polunochi." ["Laughter after Mid-
       night"] GRANI (Frankfurt): No. 85, Oct. 1972; pp. 61-155.
       Series of very brief, almost fragmentary impressions,
       anecdotes etc., most relating to the falseness of Soviet
       life, his religious faith, the invasion of Czechoslovakia
       etc.

       VASIUTKOV, A.: See Sfinksy (#1011).

1198   Veche: "Samizdat--zhurnal 'Veche' No. 2 1971." RUS. MYSL'
       (Paris): Dec. 30, 1971; pp. 4-5.
       Excerpt from second issue of nationalist samizdat
       journal.

1199   _____. "Iz khroniki zhurnala 'Veche'." POSEV (Frank-
       furt): No. 7, July 1974; pp. 19-20.
       Excerpts from issues 6, 7, 8 and 9 pertaining to recon-
       struction of Moscow historical and architectural monuments,
       repressions against individuals involved in Veche, the
       plight of Platonov's family.

       Veche: See also "Mysli-prozhektory" (#821, from Veche No. 2),
       Vol'noe slovo No. 9-10 (#1234, reprint of Veche #5), Vol'-
       noe slovo No. 17-18 (#1240 from Veche issues 7-10), "Sud'ba
       russkoi stolitsy" (#1140) from Veche 1; BORODIN (#146),
       KAPITANCHUK (#495); Skuratov in MEERSON-AKSENOV and
       SHRAGIN (#801); VORONOV (#1268); VOLOSHIN (#1265, #1266).

1200   VEGIN, PETR. "Nad kryshami." GRANI (Frankfurt): No. 75,
       April 1970; pp. 115-24. Poem.

1201   VEKSLER, MARAT. [b. 1934] "Stikhi pod èpigrafami"; "Zemlia"; "Bassein, Moskva." KONTINENT: No. 6, 1976; pp. 109-11. Poems.

1202   VEL'SKII, VIKTOR. (Pseud.) "Otkroveniia Viktora Vel'skogo." GRANI (Frankfurt): No. 75, April 1970; pp. 3-114.

_____. "My Apologia." SURVEY (London): No. 77, Autumn 1970; pp. 146-74. Tr., Daniel Weissbort.
First person account by man who, in 1948, betrayed his friends to the MGB; how and why he did it, what the consequences were, how he planned, in 1960, to defect while in Berlin but returned. A sort of spiritual autobiography. Eng. tr. also in SCAMMELL (#1005).

VENTSOV, LEV: See SHRAGIN, BORIS.

1203   "Veter sryvaet poslednie list'ia"; "Tesniatsia liudi u sviatyni"; "O liubvi"; "Glaza kak nozhi. . ."; "Kak govoritsia"; "Opiat' perekhvatilo gorlo. . ."; "Za vsekh--"; "V èti dni rasstreliannykh"; "Velikaia Ekteniia." (Anon.) VESTNIK RSKhD (Paris): No. 77, II-1965; pp. 29-34.
Poems, listed under "Golos iz Rossii"in Table of Contents, written by anonymous priest between 1946 and 1962.

1204   VINS, GEORGII. Testament from Prison. Elgin, Ill.: David Cook Pub. Co., 1975; 283 pp. Tr., Jane Ellis; ed., Michael Bourdeaux.
Writings by and about Baptist preacher, his family and the Reform Baptist movement.

VINS, GEORGII: See also BOURDEAUX and WIENS (#151).

1205   VISHNEVSKAIA, IULIIA. "I sto gektar. . . ." GRANI (Frankfurt): No. 81, Nov. 1971; p. 42. Poem.

1206   _____. "Tol'ko za noch'. . . ." GRANI (Frankfurt): No. 70, Feb. 1969; pp. 115-16. Poem.

VISHNEVSKAIA, IULIIA: See also Sfinksy No. 1 (#1011), SMOG (#1080).

VITKOVSKII, DMITRII: See MEDVEDEV and LERT (#770).

1207   VLADIMIROVA, ELENA. "Kak peredat' surovost' ètikh mest. . ."; "Don Kikhot." VESTNIK RSKhD (Paris): No. 111, I-1974; pp. 108-10.
Poems listed under "Golos Arkhipelaga" in Table of Contents.

VLADIMIROVA

1208   VLADIMIROVA, LIIA. [b. 1938, em. 1973] "Avgust, oseni pos-
       rednik! . ."; "I daty. . ."; "Kak robok smekh. . ."; "Nu
       chto zh, . ."; "A kukushka kukovala, . ."; "My smotrim iz
       raznykh okon. . ."; "Atybaty. . ."; "Khot' nag i bos. . .";
       "I vdovii ston. . ."; "Obernetsia lebed'--. . ."; "Ni obry-
       vistykh skal. . . ." GRANI (Frankfurt): No. 92/93, April-
       Sept. 1974; pp. 117-22. Poems.

1209   _____. "Ètot svet. . ."; "Ne spitsia. . ."; "A ianvar'
       metet,metet. . ."; "Nad nami pozdniaia listva. . . ."
       GRANI (Frankfurt): No. 100, April-June 1976; pp. 11-12.
       Poems.

1210   _____. "Iz tsikla 'Rogozha': 'Den' Ioanna Bogoslova';
       'Metet, metet. . .'; 'Ne obelit' mne ètikh dnei'." GRANI
       (Frankfurt): No. 89/90, July-Dec. 1973; pp. 96-97. Poems.

       VLADIMIROV, P.: See Sfinksy (#1011).

       VLADIMIRSKAIA, I.: See Russkoe slovo (#972).

1211   Vladimirskaia tiur'ma. Ed., Vl. Bukovskii. New York: Khroni-
       ka, 1977.
              Collection of articles and documents on Vladimir Prison.

1212   VLADIMOV, GEORGII. [b. 1931] "Shestoi soldat." ["The Sixth
       Soldier"] GRANI (Frankfurt): No. 121, July-Sept. 1981;
       pp. 5-106. Play.

1213   _____. Vernyi Ruslan: Istoriia karaul'noi sobaki.
       Frankfurt: Posev, 1975; 173 pp.

       _____. Faithful Ruslan: The Story of a Guard Dog. New
       York: Simon and Schuster, 1978; 220 pp. Tr., Michael
       Glenny.

       _____. Le Fidèle Rouslan: Histoire d'un chien de garde.
       Paris: Seuil, 1978; 176 pp.

       _____. (WLADIMOW) Die Geschichte vom treuen Hund Rus-
       lan. Bern, Munich: Scherz, 1975; 219 pp. Tr., Tatiana
       Frickhinger-Garanin.

       _____. "Vernyi Ruslan: Istoriia karaul'noi sobaki."
       GRANI (Frankfurt): No. 96, April-June 1975; pp. 3-173.
              Novel of a guard dog in a Gulag camp who has to adjust
       to the camps being torn down, the guards dismissed, and
       his role rendered superfluous. An honest, noble, loyal
       and intelligent servant of the state reveals precisely
       what such service involves.

1214 VLADIMOV, GEORGII. "Count Me Out." INDEX ON CENSORSHIP
(London): Vol. 7, No. 2, March-April 1978; pp. 19-22.
Vladimov's letter of resignation from the Moscow
Writers' Union.

VLADIMOV, GEORGII: See also Poiski No. 2 (#941).

VLAGIN, SERGEI: See MEDVEDEV and LERT (#770).

1215 [VLASIUK, MARIIA]. "Delo Marii Vlasiuk." VESTNIK RKhD
(Paris): No. 117, I-1976; pp. 265-84.
Documents pertaining to case of religious dissident.

1216 VOINOVICH, VLADIMIR. [b. 1932, em. 1980] Ivan'kiada ili
Rasskaz o vselenii pisatelia Voinovicha v novuiu kvartiru.
Ann Arbor, Mich.: Ardis, 1976; 112 pp.

_____. The Ivankiad or the Tale of the Writer Voino-
vich's Installation in his New Apartment. New York: Farrar, Straus & Giroux, 1977; 132 pp. Tr., David Lapeza.

_____. (VOINOVITCH) L'Ivankiade. Ou comment l'auteur
emménagea dans son nouvel appartement. Paris: Seuil,
1979; 192 pp.
Satiric novella, based on his actual experience in trying to battle one Ivanko for an apartment the author has
an entirely legitimate right to.

1217 _____. "Otkrytoe pis'mo predsedateliu KGB Andropovu."
["Open Letter to Andropov"] RUS. MYSL' (Paris): June 19,
1975; p. 5.

_____. "Za menia otomstit soldat Chonkin!" POSEV
(Frankfurt): No. 6, June 1975; pp. 7-8.
Describes, in ironic fashion, his encounters with the
KGB after Chonkin circulated in samizdat and went abroad.

1218 _____. "Proisshestvie v 'Metropole'." ["Incident at
the Metropol"] KONTINENT: No. 5, 1975; pp. 51-96.

_____. "Kak razorit' 'Posev'?" POSEV (Frankfurt): No.
11, Nov. 1975; p. 27.
Ironic account of his conversation with KGB questioner
and the attempt on the KGB's part to poison him.

1219 _____. "Putem vzaimnoi perepiski." GRANI (Frankfurt):
No. 87-88, Jan.-April 1973; pp. 122-91.
Novella depicting illusions and reality of ordinary
Russian village life. Eng. tr. in In Plain Russian (New
York: Farrar, Straus & Giroux, 1979).

VOINOVICH

1220   VOINOVICH, VLADIMIR. "VAAP, ili VAPAP." POSEV (Frankfurt):
       No. 11, Nov. 1973; pp. 9-10.

       _____. "Letter to Comrade Pankin." INDEX ON CENSOR-
       SHIP (London): No. 2, Summer 1975; pp. 52-53.
       Satiric discussion of possible forms of activity for
       All-Union Copyright Agency (VAPAP). Eng. tr. also in
       In Plain Russian (see above).

1221   _____. "Sovershenno sekretno!" ["Top Secret!"] NOV.
       RUS. SLOVO (New York): No. 12, 1976; p. 3.

       _____. "Sovershenno sekretno!" RUS. MYSL' (Paris):
       Nov. 4, 1976; p. 2.
       Satiric letter to Minister of Communications on the tap-
       ping and cutting off of his phone. Eng. tr. in In Plain
       Russian (see above).

1222   _____. "Zaiavlenie V. Voinovicha. RUS. MYSL' (Paris):
       March 28, 1974; p. 3.

       _____. "Skol'ko stoit vash patriotizm?" POSEV (Frank-
       furt): No. 5, May 1974; p. 14.

       _____. "Letter to the Writers' Union." INDEX ON CENSOR-
       SHIP (London): No. 2, Summer 1975; p. 55.
       His response to the Writers' Union meeting where he was
       expelled: "your weapon is the lie." Eng. tr. included in
       The Ivankiad (#1216) and In Plain Russian.

1223   _____. Zhizn' i neobychainye prikliucheniia soldata
       Ivana Chonkina: Roman-anekdot v piati chastiakh. Paris:
       YMCA, 1975; 287 pp.

       _____. The Life and Extraordinary Adventures of Private
       Ivan Chonkin. New York: Farrar, Straus & Giroux, 1977;
       316 pp. Tr., Richard Lourie.

       _____. (VOINOVITCH) Les Aventures singulières du sol-
       dat Ivan Tchonkine. Paris: Seuil, 1977; 269 pp.

       _____. (WOINOWITCH) Die denkwürdigen Abenteuer des
       Soldaten Iwan Tschonkin. Darmstadt, Neuwied: Luchter-
       hand, 1975; 329 pp. Tr., Alexander Kaempfe.

       _____. "Zhizn' i neobychainye prikliucheniia soldata
       Ivana Chonkina: Roman-anekdot v piati chastiakh. I."
       GRANI (Frankfurt): No. 72, July 1969; pp. 3-83.

This volume deals with the war-time adventures of a simple man, almost a simpleton, whose decent, instinctively good impulses are continually and humorously thwarted by self-serving, fearful, dogmatic or otherwise flawed "Soviet men." Extremely funny, extremely painful satire, of the "laughter through tears" order.

1224   VOINOVICH, VLADIMIR. Pretendent na prestol--novye prikliu-
        cheniia soldata Ivana Chonkina. Paris: YMCA, 1979;
        350 pp.

        _____. Pretender to the Throne: The Further Adventures
        of Private Ivan Chonkin. New York: Farrar, Straus &
        Giroux, 1981; 358 pp. Tr., Richard Lourie.

        _____. (WOINOWITCH) Die denkwürdigen Abenteuer des
        Soldaten Iwan Tschonkin. Zurich: Diogenes, 1979; 320 pp.
        Tr., A. Kaempfe.
        This second volume focuses more on the secondary charac-
        ters; while Chonkin is in jail, a whole array of Soviet
        bureaucrats, mercilessly mocked by Voinovich, trip over
        themselves trying to save their own necks. Stalin and
        Hitler also make appearances in the book.

        NB: In Plain Russian (New York: Farrar, Straus & Giroux,
        1979) contains the following samizdat pieces, in addition
        to several works published in the Soviet Union: "From an
        Exchange of Letters," "A Circle of Friends" (an unpub-
        lished chapter of Chonkin, describing Stalin and his circle
        the night before the Nazi invasion), and four open letters.

1225   VOLGIN. (Pseud.) "O mnogopartiinoi sisteme." ["On a Multi-
        party System"] POSEV (Frankfurt): No. 4 (1131), April
        1968; pp. 57-58.
        From samizdat journal Kolokol; why bureaucratically-
        governed states share the common characteristic of a one-party
        system and the repressive consequences of one-party rule.

        VOLKOV, A.: See Nadezhda (#827).

        Vol'noe slovo. Samizdat. Izbrannoe. Dokumental'naia seriia.
        Frankfurt: Posev.

1226   No. 1. Khronika tekushchikh sobytii, #21. See Kh. tek.
        sob. 21 (#535).

1227   No. 2. Khronika tekushchikh sobytii, #22. See Kh. tek.
        sob. 22 (#536).

Vol'noe

1228   No. 3. <u>Khronika</u> <u>tekushchikh</u> <u>sobytii</u>, #23. See <u>Kh</u>. <u>tek</u>. <u>sob</u>. 23 (#537).

1229   No. 4. <u>Khronika</u> <u>tekushchikh</u> <u>sobytii</u>, #24 and #25. See <u>Kh</u>. <u>tek</u>. <u>sob</u>. 24 and 25 (#538).

1230   No. 5. <u>Khronika</u> <u>tekushchikh</u> <u>sobytii</u>, #26. See <u>Kh</u>. <u>tek</u>. <u>sob</u>. 26 (#539).

1231   No. 6. <u>Khronika</u> <u>tekushchikh</u> <u>sobytii</u>, #27. See <u>Kh</u>. <u>tek</u>. <u>sob</u>. 27 (#540).

1232   No. 7. Frankfurt: Posev, 1973; 108 pp. Issue No. 1 of <u>Svobodnaia mysl'</u>, a samizdat journal dated Dec. 1971 and produced by the Democratic Movement. It contains an editorial statement of purpose and the following articles: S. TOPOLEV: "Ot samizdata k kolizdatu," a factual analysis of the operation of samizdat and collective self-printing; Eng. tr. in MEERSON–AKSENOV and SHRAGIN (#801). A. BABUSHKIN: "K itogam vypolneniia vos'mogo piatiletnego plana razvitiia narodnogo khoziaistva SSSR, 1966-1970 goda" ["Toward the Results of Fulfilling the 8th Five-Year Plan for Development of the National Economy, 1966-70"], which includes comparative figures for the USSR and the USA; A. KAZAKOV: "K voprosu o sravnenii zhiznennogo urovnia trudiashchikhsia Rossii, SSSR i drugikh kapitalisticheskikh stran," ["Comparing Standards of Living of Workers of Russia, the USSR and Capitalist Countries"]; before the revolution and today, as well as in Western countries; K. GLUKHOV: "Fotografiia kak metod razmozheniia dokumentatsii," ["Photography as a Method for Reproducing Documents"], instructions for would-be photographers for reproducing samizdat.

     This issue also includes three pamphlets by Citizens' Committee, calling for strikes, protesting shortages and price rises and waste.

1233   No. 8. Frankfurt: Posev, 1973; 107 pp. R. I. Pimenov's "Odin politicheskii protsess" ["One Political Trial"], an account of trial for slander of Soviet society.

1234   No. 9-10. Frankfurt: Posev, 1973; 221 pp. <u>Veche</u> No. 5 plus article by F. Karelin, "Po povodu pis'ma o. Sergiia Zheludkova Aleksandru Solzhenitsynu" (on the Zheludkov-Solzhenitsyn correspondence), see #503.

1235   No. 11. Frankfurt: Posev, 1974; 76 pp. Documents pertaining to case of Leonid Pliushch, arrested Jan. 15, 1972.

1236   No. 12. Frankfurt: Posev, 1974; 127 pp. M. Ia. Maka-
renko's "Iz moei zhizni" ["From My Life"], autobiography of
artist arrested, for various reasons, ten times between
1948 and 1969; the last time he was sentenced to eight
years.

1237   No. 13. Frankfurt: Posev, 1974; 103 pp. Various statements on violations of rights before trials.

1238   Nos. 14-15. Frankfurt: Posev, 1974; 173 pp. "Moe poslednee slovo" ["My Final Word"], collection of defendants'
final pleas, 1966-1974.

1239   No. 16. Frankfurt: Posev, 1974. "Re Patria No. 1," collection of information and documents pertaining to Soviet
Germans.

1240   No. 17-18. Frankfurt: Posev, 1975. Excerpts from Veche,
7, 8, 9 and 10.

1241   No. 19. Frankfurt: Posev, 1975; 87 pp. "Pytki zakliuchennykh v tiur'makh Gruzii" ["Torture of Prisoners in
Georgia"], information and documents on Georgian political
prisoners.

1242   No. 20. Frankfurt: Posev, 1975; 100 pp. Excerpts from
samizdat journal Zemlia, #1-#2, edited by Osipov; combina-
tion of nationalism and Christianity, seeking rebirth of
national morality and culture.

1243   No. 21. Frankfurt: Posev, 1976; 80 pp. "Iz-za koliuchei
provoloki," ["From Behind the Barbed Wire"], documents and
letters from prisoners.

1244   No. 22. Frankfurt: Posev, 1976; 111 pp. VSKhSON. Program of and documents pertaining to Vserossiiskii sotsial-
khristianskii soiuz osvobozhdeniia naroda ["All-Russian
Social-Christian Union for the Liberation of the Nation"],
including Ogurtsov's trial notes. The society was a para-
military and political organization preparing for armed
opposition to the regime. See VSKhSON (#1272).

1245   No. 23. Frankfurt: Posev, 1976; 127 pp. Khronika arkhipelaga Gulag, #1-4. Collection of documents from one year
in one political camp, on hunger strikes, conditions, etc.

1246   No. 24. Frankfurt: Posev, 1976; 111 pp. "Soprotivlenie
religioznym presledovaniiam" ["Opposition to Religious
Persecution"], eight documents on the repressions of the

Vol'noe

church and the persecution of believers, most from Iakunin and Regel'son.

1247 Nos. 25-26. Frankfurt: Posev, 1977; 149 pp. "Gruppa sodeistviia vypolneniiu Khel'sinkskikh soglashennii v SSSR" ["Helsinki Watch Group"], statements, appeals, etc., about various infringements of Basket 3 clauses of Helsinki Agreement, of which USSR was signatory.

1248 No. 27. Frankfurt: Posev, 1977; 144 pp. "Kak vesti sebia na obyske i drugie dokumenty" ["How to Behave During a Search and Other Documents"]. The manual, by Vladimir Al'-brekht, ironically instructs the reader on the best course of behavior for an arrest and investigation; other documents are nine statements by individuals re dissent, including one satiric piece by Voinovich.

1249 No. 28. Frankfurt: Posev, 1977; 96 pp. Sixteen documents on religious persecutions.

1250 No. 29. Frankfurt: Posev, 1978; 109 pp. "Iiun'skie novosti: zapiski neakkreditovannogo" ["June News: Notes from an Unaccredited Writer"] by Mark Popovskii. Reprint of the author's monthly news bulletin printed by his "independent press" in Moscow, about his experiences with KGB, OVIR, etc.

1251 No. 30. Frankfurt: Posev, 1978; 112 pp. "Svobodnyi prof-soiuz trudiashchikhsia" ["Free Trade Union"] Documents pertaining to organization of the first free trade union in Soviet history, established Jan. 1978; its program, statements, complaints, etc.

1252 No. 31-32. Frankfurt: Posev, 1978; 175 pp. "Rabochaia komissiia po rassledovaniiu ispol'zovaniia psikhiatrii v politicheskikh tseliakh" ["Committee to Investigate the Use of Psychiatry for Political Goals"]. Information bulletins (#1-5 and 7-9) of committee, intended to provide as much information as possible on such cases.

1253 No. 33. Frankfurt: Posev, 1979; 122 pp. Dmitrii Dudko's "Vrag vnutri" and "V svete preobrazheniia" ["The Enemy Within" and "In the Light of the Transfiguration"], the first a collection of articles about the "enemy" within the church, as well as youth movement, church tasks, etc.; the second is a weekly bulletin Dudko put out.

1254 No. 34. Frankfurt: Posev, 1979; 127 pp. SMOT. (Svobod-noe mezhprofessional'noe ob"edinenie trudiashchikhsia;

Vol'noe

Free Inter-professional Union of Workers): its program
and structure, as well as four information bulletins on
searches, interrogations, and arrests of members.

1255   No. 35-36. Frankfurt: Posev, 1980. Gleb Iakunin's "O
sovremennom polozhenii Russkoi Pravoslavnoi Tserkvi i per-
spektivakh religioznogo vozrozhdeniia Rossii" ["On the
Current Situation of the Russian Orthodox Church and Possibilities of a Religious Rebirth of Russia"].

1256   No. 37. Frankfurt: Posev, 1980; 110 pp. Iurii Belov's
"Razmyshleniia ne tol'ko o sychevke" ["Reflections Not Only
On an Owl"], autobiographical account by a man who spent
years in psychiatric hospitals and finally emigrated
(spent more than 14 years in imprisonment and exile).

1257   No. 38. Frankfurt: Posev, 1980; 77 pp. Zhenshchina i
Rossiia, #1 (dated Dec. 10, 1979) ["Women and Russia"],
Leningrad feminist samizdat journal. Includes Vera Golubeva's "Obratnaia storona medali" ["The Reverse Side of
the Coin"], about single motherhood, the horrors of some
of the personnel who steal the children's food, etc.;
Iuliia Voznesenskaia's "Pis'mo iz Novosibirska" ["Letter
from Novosibirsk"], on the treatment of women prisoners,
including young girls; and Tat'iana Goricheva's "Raduisia,
slez evinykh izbavlenie," a personal interpretation of the
Virgin Mary. The journal also contains information bulletin on the defense of Tat'iana Velikanova. Goricheva's
piece also appears in POSEV (Frankfurt): No. 9, Sept.
1980; pp. 57-60, under title "Paradoksy zhenskoi èmansi-
patsii" ["Paradoxes of Female Emancipation"].

1258   No. 39. Frankfurt: Posev, 1980; 117 pp. "Khristianskii
seminar" ["Christian Seminar"], texts from various religio-
philosophical groups of young people. Contains many short
pieces (by Goricheva, Galina Grigor'eva, Aleksandr Ogorod-
nikov et al.) on current religious matters.

1259   No. 40. Frankfurt: Posev, 1981. I. Ruslanov's "Zhizn' i
aforizmy Kuz'my Prutkova" ["The Life and Aphorisms of
Kuzma Prutkov"]. (Pseud. of B. Evdokimov.)

1260   No. 41-42. Frankfurt: Posev, 1981; 164 pp. "Initsiativ-
naia gruppa zashchity prav invalidov v SSSR" ["The Initiative Group for the Defense of the Rights of the Disabled
in the USSR"]. Documents pertaining to rights of handi-
capped people.

VOLNY

VOLNY: See EVDOKIMOV, BORIS

1261 VOLOSHIN, MAKSIMILIAN. [b. 1878, d. 1932] "Blagoslovenie."
NOVYI ZHURNAL (New York): No. 134, March 1979; p. 25.
Poem, dated Koktebel (now Planerskoe), 1923.

1262 _____. "Doblest' poèta." NOVYI ZHURNAL (New York): No.
132, Sept. 1978; p. 5. Poem.

1263 _____. "Neizdannye stikhi: 'Pustynia'; 'Tanob'; 'Dob-
lest' poèta'; 'Nadpisi na akvareliakh'; 'Chetvert' veka';
'Iuda apostol'; 'Sviatoi Frantsisk'; 'Khvala Bogomateri'."
VESTNIK RSKhD (Paris): No. 107, I-1973; pp. 140-52.
Poems, written between 1918 and 1927.

1264 _____. "Neizdannye stikhi: 'Duby neroslye pod"emliut
oblik kron'; 'Polet ee sobach'ikh glaz'; 'Net v mire prek-
rasnei svobody'; 'Materinstvo'; 'V slepye dni. . .'; 'Blagoslovenie'; 'Angel smerti'; 'Poètu'; 'On byl iz tekh. . .';
'Zaklinanie'." VESTNIK RKhD (Paris): No. 128, II-1979.
Poems written between 1909 and 1929.

1265 _____. "Sviatoi Serafim." NOVYI ZHURNAL (New York):
No. 72, June 1963; pp. 13-50. Poem, dated 1919.

1266 _____. "Skloniaias'. . .'; 'Vladimirskaia Bogomater'."
NOVYI ZHURNAL (New York): No. 133, Dec. 1978; pp. 5-8.
Poems; the second circulated in Veche.

1267 _____. "Vladimirskaia Bogomater'." VESTNIK RSKhD (Paris):
No. 100, II-1971; pp. 227-29.
Poem, written in 1917; circulated in Veche.

1268 VORONEL', NINA. [em. 1974] Prakh i pepel'. [Dust and Ashes]
Tel Aviv: Moskva-Ierusalim, 1977. Collection of plays.

1269 VORONOV, K. "Demograficheskie problemy Rossii." ["Russia's
Demographic Problems"] GRANI (Frankfurt): No. 98, Oct.-
Dec. 1975; pp. 255-76.
From Veche; discussion of decline in Russia's European
population growth and increase in Asiatic, with explana-
tions of some of the reasons.

1270 VOSKRESENSKII, VLADIMIR. [b. 1946, d. 1970] "Dlia druzei:
'Tost vmesto predisloviia'; 'Kholod. . .'; 'Ia rasskazhu
. . .'; 'Reportazh iz utra. . .'; 'Pamiati materi'; 'Vesna';
'Podumaite. . .'; 'Predvaritel'noe pis'mo'." GRANI (Frank-
furt): No. 99, Jan.-March 1976; pp. 40-47. Poems.

VOSKRESENSKII, VLADIMIR: See also Russkoe slovo (#972).

1271 VOZNESENSKAIA, IULIIA. "Galery, flagy, lageria. . ."; "Zdes'
      utro. . ."; "Kogda moi dom, raskrytyi kak tsvetok. . .";
      "Obnishchavshii tuman pereputal rasluki i sroki." VESTNIK
      RKhD (Paris): No. 128, I-II-1979; pp. 145-46. Poems.

VOZNESENSKAIA, IULIIA: See also Poiski No. 1 (#940), Vol'noe
slovo No. 38 (#1257).

1272 VOZNESENSKII, ANDREI. "Styd." POSEV (Frankfurt): No. 35
      (1110). Sept. 1, 1967; p. 2. Poem.

VOZNESENSKII, ANDREI: See also Metropol' (#808).

1273 VSKhSON: Programma. Sud. V tiur'makh i lageriakh. Ed., John
      Dunlop ("Denlop" in Russian). Paris: YMCA, 1975; 214 pp.
      Long excerpts translated in Dunlop, The New Russian Revolu-
      tionaries (Belmont, Mass.: Nordland, 1976; 344 pp.).

      _____. "Vserossiskii sotsial-khristianskii soiuz osvo-
      bozhdeniia naroda." POSEV (Frankfurt): No. 1, Jan. 1971;
      pp. 38-43.
          Collection of all the important sources for this "social-
      Christian" movement, the three basic principles of which
      are the Christianization of politics, of economics and of
      culture.

VSKhSON: See also Vol'noe slovo No. 22 (#1244), PETROV-AGATOV, (#919).

1274 VVEDENSKII, ALEKSANDR. "Elka u Ivanovykh." GRANI (Frankfurt):
      No. 81, Nov. 1971; pp. 84-110.
      Drama written in late 1920s.

1275 VYSOTSKII, VLADIMIR. [b. 1938, d. 1980] "Pesnia ob ugolovnom
      kodekse." NOV. RUS. SLOVO (New York): Dec. 15, 1976; p. 3.
      Eng. tr., by Misha Allen, in "Songs a Hero Sings," Toronto
      Globe Magazine, Feb. 28, 1970. Poem/song.

1276 _____. "Pesnia pro poputchika." POSEV (Frankfurt):
      No. 1, Jan. 1971; p. 60. Poem/song.

1277 _____. "Voskresnyi den'." NOV. RUS. SLOVO (New York):
      Dec. 17, 1968. Poem/song.

1278 _____. "Okhota na volkov"; "Smotriny"; "Moi drug uekhal
      v Magadan. . .." TRET'IA VOLNA (Paris): No. 2, 1977;
      pp. 44-50. Eng. tr. of the last in PROBLEMS OF COMMUNISM
      (Washington, D.C.): Vol. 19, no. 6, Nov.-Dec. 1970, by
      Misha Allen.

VYSOTSKII

1279   VYSOTSKII, VLADIMIR. "Zhizn' bez sna." ["Life Without
       Dreams"] ÈKHO (Paris): No. 2, 1980; pp. 7-24.
           Story. Title given by editors.

       VYSOTSKII, VLADIMIR: See also Metropol' (#808) Pesni rus-
       skikh bardov (#917).

W

1280   "A Word to the Nation." (Signed: "Russian patriots") SURVEY
        (London): Vol. 17, No. 3 (80), Summer 1971; pp. 191-99.
        Excerpted under <u>Slovo</u> <u>natsii</u> in RUS. MYSL' (Paris): Nov.
        25, 1971; p. 4. Full Russian text appeared in VECHE (Ger-
        many), 1981.
            Nationalist and racist look at political, economic and
        social "realities" in Soviet Union; sees democracy as a
        product of social degeneration, and the Russian nation as
        the most underprivileged in the USSR.

1281   <u>White</u> <u>Book</u> <u>of</u> <u>Exodus</u>. (Anon. ed.) New York: National Con-
        ference on Soviet Jewry, 1972.
            Collection of documents, edited in Moscow, illustrating
        major aspects of persecution of Zionists.

X

1282   X.   "Net, ne iz knizhek nashikh skudnykh. . . ." NOVYI ZHUR-
           NAL (New York): No. 107, June 1972; pp. 36–37.
               Poem, listed in Table of Contents under "Stikhi iz SSSR."

Z

1283   ZAMIATIN, EVGENII. [b. 1884, d. 1937] "Afrikanskii gost'."
       ["African Guest"] NOVYI ZHURNAL (New York): No. 73,
       Sept. 1963; pp. 38-95.
       Drama written in 1929-30.

1284   _____. "Mucheniki nauki." ["Martyrs of Science"]
       NOVYI ZHURNAL (New York): No. 67, March 1962; pp. 12-25.
       Essay.

1285   _____. "O iazyke." ["On Language"] NOVYI ZHURNAL (New
       York): No. 77, Sept. 1967; pp. 97-113.
       Essay written 1920-21.

1286   ZARNITSYN, PAVEL. "Otvet S. Teleginu--utopiia i nadezhda."
       ["Answer to Telegin--Utopia and Hope"] VESTNIK RSKhD
       (Paris): No. 107, I-1973; pp. 153-59. Essay.

1287   Zashchita very v SSSR. [Defense of the Faith in the USSR]
       Frankfurt: Posev, 1966; 104 pp. Paris: Ikthus, 1966.
       Ed., Arkièpiskop Ioann San-Frantsisski.

       Kampf des Glaubens. Dokumente aus der Sowjetunion. Bern:
       Schweizerisches Ostinstitut, 1967.
       Includes works by Levitin-Krasnov, attacking persecution
       of monks and monasteries as well as documents related to
       attempts to close Pochaev monastery in the Ukraine. Eng.
       tr. in BOURDEAUX (#148).

       Zemlia: See Vol'noe slovo No. 20 (#1242); OSIPOV (#887).

1288   ZHELUDKOV, SERGII. "Iz 'Liturgicheskikh zametok'." ["From
       'Liturgical Notes'"] VESTNIK RSKhD (Paris): No. 103, I-
       1972; pp. 63-85; No. 104-105, II-III-1972; pp. 61-85; No.
       106, IV-1972; pp. 15-23; No. 107, I-1973; pp. 29-41.
       Develops the idea of a "church of people of good-will";
       holds that the human spirit, strengthened by God, is strong-
       er than all external circumstances; discusses the liturgi-
       cal service as a means of serving God through artistic means.

1289   _____. "K razmyshleniiam ob intellektual'noi svobode."
       ["Thoughts on Intellectual Freedom"] VESTNIK RSKhD (Paris):
       No. 94, IV-1969; pp. 46-57.
       Response to Sakharov's "Razmyshleniia. . . ," arguing
       that intellectual freedom is essentially a religious or
       spiritual concept.

1290   _____. "Khristianstvo dlia vsekh." ["Christianity for
       Everyone"] VESTNIK RKhD (Paris): No. 115, I-1975; pp. 5-
       16. Essay on the universal meaning of Christianity.

ZHELUDKOV

1291   ZHELUDKOV, SERGII. <u>Pochemu i ia--Khristianin</u>. [<u>Why I am a</u>
       <u>Christian</u>]. Frankfurt: Posev, 1973; 324 pp.
       Collection of his writings.

1292   _____. (SCHELUDKOW) <u>Ist Gott in Russland tot?</u> <u>Bericht</u>
       <u>eines in der UdSSR lebenden ehemaligen Priesters</u>. Stutt-
       gart, Berlin: Kreuz. Tr., Eugen Voss.
       Relationship of religion and society, which he feels
       should be close.

       ZHELUDKOV, SERGII: See also BOURDEAUX (#148), KARELIN (#503),
       SOLZHENITSYN (#1108), <u>Vol'noe slovo</u> No. 9/10 (#1234),
       SOLSCHENIZYN et al. (#1124).

       <u>Zhenshchina i Rossiia</u>: See <u>Vol'noe slovo</u> No. 38 (#1257).

1293   ZHIGALOV, ANATOLII. [b. 1941] "Bubentsy palomnika: 'Usnut'";
       "Zveniashchii kolokol'chik Solntsa. . ."; "Begstvo v derev-
       ne"; "Spoi s vetrom pesniu. . ."; "V pompeiskoi speshke
       broshen v seni. . . ." Poems.

1294   _____ "Doroga v nikuda: 'Kak izbyt' kak zabyt' kak izba-
       vit'sia. . .'; 'Kuda tebia zabrosila sud'bina. . .'; 'Pos-
       lanie'." VREMIA I MY (New York/Paris/Jerusalem): No. 37,
       Jan. 1979; pp. 79-84. Poems.

1295   _____. "Iz konkretnoi poèzii." ÈKHO (Paris): No. 1,
       1980; pp. 99-100. Prose poem.

1296   _____. "Stikhi raznykh let." VREMIA I MY (New York/
       Paris/Jerusalem): No. 7, May 1976; pp. 111-14. Poems.

1297   _____. "Zerkal'naia mozaika: 'Peizazh v stile kiriko';
       'Z.M.': 'V poliakh osobaia uslada. . .'; 'Tak voditsia tak
       viditsia. . .'; 'Ne umerlo--kak?--svetloe? . .'; 'Chto za
       narezh' nam prostranstva na lomanyi gros. . .'; 'Plyvu-
       shchim po volnam plot'. . .'; 'Bez smazki zvuk. . .'; 'Opiat'
       razmerennyi i chutkii. . .'." VREMIA I MY (New York/Paris/
       Jerusalem): No. 32, Aug. 1978; pp. 93-100. Poems.

1298   ZHITNIKOV, K. "Zakat demokraticheskogo dvizheniia." ["The
       Decline of the Democratic Movement"] VESTNIK RSKhD (Paris):
       No. 106, IV-1972; pp. 275-93.
       Analysis of reasons for the failures of the democratic
       movement, including Khrushchev's reforms and their connec-
       tion to the Movement's demands; hopes for its continuation,
       in different forms and with different emphases. Eng. tr.
       in MEERSON-AKSENOV and SHRAGIN (#801).

       ZIMIN, A.: See MEDVEDEV and LERT (#770).

1299   ZORIN, S. and ALEKSEEV, N. (Pseuds.) <u>Vremia ne zhdet</u>. [<u>Time Won't Wait</u>] Frankfurt: Posev, 1970.

_____. "Vremia ne zhdet--nasha strana nakhoditsia na povorotnom punkte istorii." RUS. MYSL' (Paris): July 30, 1970; p. 5; Aug. 6, 1970; p. 5.

_____. "Vremia ne zhdet: nasha strana nakhoditsia na povorotnom punkte istorii." NOV. RUS. SLOVO (New York): Aug. 26, 1970; p. 2; Aug. 27, 1970; p. 2, Aug. 28, 1970; p. 2; Aug. 29, 1970; p. 2; Aug. 31, 1970; p. 2; Sept. 1, 1970; p. 2; Sept. 2, 1970; p. 2; Sept. 3, 1970; p. 2.
Leningrad teacher and engineer warn of dangers of impending war, if current course followed by leadership is maintained; feel leaders are alienated from population and unaware of the real state of the nation. Two directions possible--genuine reforms, or continuation of status quo, which would risk everything including possible atomic confrontation.

1300   ZOSHCHENKO, MIKHAIL. [b. 1895, d. 1958] <u>Rasskazy</u>. Frankfurt: Posev, 1971; 193 pp.
Stories, many of them published only in samizdat in the Soviet Union.

Subject Index

SUBJECT HEADINGS

Only nonfiction items are included in the subject index. Entry numbers follow the name of the author or editor of a work, or in cases of periodicals and some collections, its title.

Arrests, Investigations, Interrogations

Christianity and the Russian Orthodox Church

The Democratic Movement and Samizdat

East-West Relations and Soviet Foreign Policy

Economics and Trade Unionism

Human Rights: Law, Trials, Abuses

Ideology and Philosophy

Intelligentsia and Intellectual History

Jews, Zionism and Anti-Semitism

Literary Criticism

Literary History and Culture

National Minorities (excluding Jews and Ukrainians) and Non-Orthodox Christianity

Nonliterary Culture, Historical and Contemporary

Political Prisoners, 1960-1981

Psychiatry

Russian History pre-1917

Russian Nationalism

Social and Political Commentary on Soviet Life, 1956-1981

Solzhenitsyn

Soviet History, 1917-1930

Soviet History, 1930-1956

Stalinism and De-Stalinization

Stalinist camps, prisons and exile

Ukraine

World War II

THE DEMOCRATIC MOVEMENT AND SAMIZDAT

EAST-WEST RELATIONS AND SOVIET FOREIGN POLICY

ECONOMICS AND TRADE UNIONISM

HUMAN RIGHTS: LAW, TRIALS, ABUSES

IDEOLOGY AND PHILOSOPHY

LITERARY CRITICISM

LITERARY HISTORY AND CULTURE

PSYCHIATRY

RUSSIAN HISTORY PRE-1917

RUSSIAN NATIONALISM

SOCIAL AND POLITICAL COMMENTARY ON SOVIET LIFE, 1956-1981

SOLZHENITSYN

Soviet Dissident Literature

SOVIET HISTORY 1917-1930

Chernova, 230
Dobrovol'skaia, 272
Evdokimov, 323
Kopelev, 619
Levitin-Krasnov and Shavrov, 683
Litvinov et al., 702
Mandel'shtam, N., 731
Medvedev, R., 772, 773, 779,
    781, 782, 784, 785
Medvedev and Starikov, 795

Mel'nikov, 805
Olitskaia, 876
Pamiat' No. 1, 895
Pamiat' No. 3, 897
Poiski No. 1, 940
Renaissance. . . , 962
Samizdat I, 989
Saunders, 1001
Shafarevich, 1013
Solzhenitsyn, 1094
Varga, 1192

SOVIET HISTORY 1930-1956

Allilueva, 48
Antonov-Ovseenko, 73
Berggol'ts, 108
Chernaia kniga, 228
Chukovskaia, 245
"Delo krymskikh tatar," 267
"Delo Slutskogo. . . ," 268
Dziuba, 304
Evdokimov, 324
Ginzburg, E., 382, 383
Gusarov, 453
Iakir, 457
Ishutina, 478
Kopelev, 618
Levitin-Krasnov, 681
Levitin-Krasnov and Shavrov, 683
Litvinov et al., 702

Mandel'shtam, N., 730, 731
Medvedev, R., 770, 771, 773, 776,
    778, 780, 782, 784, 785
Medvedev, Zh., 798, 799
Meerson-Aksenov and Shragin, 801
"Nakhodka v taige," 831
Nekrich, 843
Olitskaia, 876
Pamiat' No. 2, 895, 896
Poiski No. 1, 940
Pomerants, 945, 950
Renaissance. . . , 962
Samizdat I, 989
Saunders, 1001
Shafarevich, 1013
Solzhenitsyn, 1094
"Traktat. . . ," 1161

STALINISM AND DE-STALINIZATION

Chukovskaia, 241
Evtushenko, 332
Ginzburg, E., 382, 383
Grigorenko, 436, 438
Gusarov, 453
Iakir, 457, 458
Kopelev, 618, 619
Lewytzkyj, 684
Mandel'shtam, N., 730, 731
Medvedev, R., 771, 773-76, 779,
    780, 782, 784, 785
Medvedev, R. and Zh., 792
Meerson-Aksenov and Shragin, 801
Nekipelov, 838

"Obsuzhdenie. . . ," 864
Olitskaia, 876
Pamiat' No. 1, 895
Pomerants, 945, 950
Sakharov, 984, 985
Shel'ga, 1053
Siniavskii, 1064-1066
Solzhenitsyn, 1094, 1096, 1098
Svirskii, 1145
Turchin, 1171
Tvardovskii, 1172
Ukr. visnyk, 1179
Vol'noe slovo, 1185
Vel'skii, 1202

237

ADDENDA

AL'BREKHT, VL. Kak byt' svidetelem. [How to Be a Witness] France: 1981; 79 pp.
      Reprint of Vol'noe slovo No. 27 (#1248): Practical advice for behavior during KGB interrogations.

BABEL, I. Zabytye proizvedeniia. [Forgotten Works] U.S.A.: 1978; 250 pp.
      Collection of 50 works never published in the Soviet Union.

BORODIN, L. Povest' strannogo vremeni. [Tale of a Strange Time] Germany: 1978; 239 pp.
      Stories by member of VSKhSON.

BUGAEVA, K. N. Vospominaniia o Belom. [Memoirs about Belyi] U.S.A.: 1981; 392 pp. By poet's widow.

BULGAKOV, M. Ranniaia neizvestnaia proza. [Early Unknown Prose] Germany: 1981; 249 pp.
      Feuilletons and stories of the '20s, published then in newspapers and magazines. Also: Ranniaia neizdannaia proza [Early Unpublished Prose] and Ranniaia nesobrannaia proza [Early Uncollected Prose], publishing information unavailable.

BURIKHIN, IGOR'. Prevrashcheniia na vozdushnykh putiakh. [Transformation on Airy Paths] France: 1981; 62 pp. Poems.

DUDKO, DM. Veriu, Gospodi! [I Believe, Lord!] Canada: 1976; 280 pp. Articles and notes, 1957-69.

_____. Voskresnye sobesedovaniia. [Sunday Interviews] Canada: 1977; 112 pp.

_____. Vovremia i ne vovremia. [Timely and Untimely] Belgium: 1978; 326 pp. Collection of Sermons.

FAIBUSOVICH [KHAZANOV, BORIS]. Zapakh zvezd. [The Scent of Stars] Israel: 1977; 297 pp.
      Collection of verse and prose. Author emigrated in 1982.

GUBERMAN, IGOR' [GARIK]. Datszybao. Israel: 1978; 192 pp.
      Comic verse and epigrams.

KANDEL', FELIKS. Koridor. [The Corridor] Israel: 1981; 252 pp.
      "Corridor" of title refers to hallway of communal apartment; novel depicts Soviet daily life through child's eyes.

KOPELEV, LEV. Vera v slovo. [Faith in the Word] U.S.A.: 1977; 64 pp. Protest letters and statements, 1962-76.

MAKSIMOV, VLADIMIR. <u>Sobranie</u> <u>sochinenii</u>. [<u>Collected</u> <u>Works</u>] Germany: 1974-79; 6 vols.
 Includes post-emigration as well as samizdat works.

MEN', ALEKSANDR. <u>Kak</u> <u>chitat'</u> <u>Bibliiu</u>. [<u>How</u> <u>to</u> <u>Read</u> <u>the</u> <u>Bible</u>] Belgium: 1981; 228 pp.
 Reading guide and commentary.

<u>Pamiat'</u> No. 4. Paris: 1981; 538 pp. [<u>Memory</u>].
 Includes memoirs by Shul'gin, Antsiferov, Kochin; letters from soldiers in 1917; various documents.

<u>Poiski</u> No. 3. [<u>Search</u>]. France: 1981; 255 pp.
 Issue dates from 1978; contains V. Ronkin and S. Khakhaev's "The Past, Present and Future of Socialism," Egides' "To Live as an Empire," Kopelev's "Woe from Love" and other articles.

<u>Sakharovskii</u> <u>sbornik</u>. [<u>Sakharov</u> <u>Collection</u>] U.S.A.: 1981; 261 pp.
 Letters, poems and articles collected in commemoration of Sakharov's 60th birthday.

SAMOKHIN, A. <u>Kitaiskii</u> <u>krug</u> <u>Rossii</u>. [<u>Russia's</u> <u>Chinese</u> <u>Circle</u>] Germany: 1981; 198 pp.
 On Sino-Soviet relations, warning of dangers and risks.

<u>Sobrnik</u> <u>dokumentov</u> <u>obshchestvennoi</u> <u>gruppy</u> <u>sodeistviia</u> <u>vypolneniiu</u> <u>Khel'sinkskikh</u> <u>soglashenii</u>.
 Documents of the Helsinki Watch Group in the USSR. At least six issues have been published by Khronika Press (New York).

SOMOV, EVGENII. <u>Gosudarstvennyi</u> <u>kapitalizm</u>. [<u>State</u> <u>Capitalism</u>] Israel: 1980; 79 pp.
 Scholarly investigation of contemporary Soviet economy.

SHTURMAN, DORA. <u>Nash</u> <u>novyi</u> <u>mir</u>. [<u>Our</u> <u>New</u> <u>World</u>] Israel: 1981; 367 pp.
 Why Marxist-Leninist theory has led to such a disastrous reality.

UFLIAND, VL. <u>Teksty</u> <u>1955-77</u>. [<u>Texts</u>] U.S.A.: 1978; 90 pp. Poems.

VARLAMOVA, INNA. <u>Mnimaia</u> <u>zhizn'</u>. [<u>An</u> <u>Imaginary</u> <u>Life</u>] U.S.A.: 1971; 210 pp.
 Novel set in cancer clinic in '30s, '40s and '50s.

ERRATA

p. 58: GARBOVSKII, G. is incorrectly spelled. The correct spelling is GORBOVSKII.

p. 58, #370: GARIK is the pseudonym of IGOR' GUBERMAN (#448).